The Roosevelt Myth

The Roosevelt Myth

50th Anniversary Edition

by John T. Flynn

Fox &
Wilkes

San Francisco

This edition published in 1998 by
Fox & Wilkes
938 Howard Street, Ste. 202
San Francisco, CA 94103

ISBN 0-930073-27-4 (pb)
ISBN 0-930073-28-2 (hc)

Printed in the USA.

Contents

Introduction to the 50th Anniversary Edition

Albert Jay Nock, distinguished man of letters and philosophical anarchist, was an inspiration to thinkers as diverse as Murray Rothbard and Robert Nisbet, Frank Chodorov and Russell Kirk. A personal friend of the father of William F. Buckley, Jr., he was a kind of guru to the young Buckley as well. In April, 1945, Nock wrote a cheery letter to two of his friends, describing the death of Franklin Roosevelt as "the biggest public improvement that America has experienced since the passage of the Bill of Rights," and suggesting a celebration luncheon at Lüchow's.[1]

Today Nock's unabashed glee would be regarded as obscene, a sacrilege against the civic religion of the United States. Republican no less than Democratic leaders revere and invoke the memory of Franklin Roosevelt. His praises are sung from the *Wall Street Journal* to the *New York Times*, and herds of historians (the phrase is Mencken's) regularly announce that FDR was one of our truly "great presidents." Symbolic of his apotheosis was the dedication, in May, 1997, of the vast Franklin Delano Roosevelt Memorial in Washington, D.C. As the *Times* happily reported, it is "a memorial laced with a zest for the power of government." The current executors of that power had eagerly lent their plundered support, Congress voting $42.5 million, with bipartisan enthusiasm. Amid the hosannas that rose up everywhere in politics and the press, the few dissident voices were inaudible. The dominant credo is that, as an editor of the *Wall Street Journal* has informed us, criticism of FDR is conceivable only from enemies "maddened by hatred of him."

Yet it is a fact that throughout his long presidency FDR was hotly opposed, even pilloried, by a host of intelligent, respected, and patriotic men and women. The most consistent of his adversaries formed a loose coalition known today as the Old Right.[2] There is little doubt that the best informed and most tenacious of the Old Right foes of Franklin Roosevelt was John T. Flynn.

When Flynn came to write his major study of the four-term president, he aptly titled it *The Roosevelt Myth*. Myths continue to abound concerning Roosevelt and his reign; one of the most convenient is that the antagonists of his New Deal were all "economic royalists," self-serving beneficiaries and defenders of the status quo. In Flynn's case, such an accusation is laughable. When he became a critic of the New Deal, Flynn enjoyed a well-established reputation as a progressive and a muckraker, with, as Bill Kauffman writes, "a taste for plutocrat blood."[3]

John Thomas Flynn was born in 1882 into a middle class Irish Catholic family in the suburbs of Washington, and educated first in public schools, then in the parochial schools of New York City. The debate that raged around 1900 on U.S. annexation of the Philippines seems to have exercised a formative influence on the young Flynn: all his life he remained an adamant opponent of western, including American, imperialism. He studied law at Georgetown, but found journalism irresistible. After serving as editor on papers in New Haven and New York, he worked as a freelance writer exposing crooked financial dealings on Wall Street. In the early and mid-1930s, Flynn authored a series of books attacking the trusts and what he viewed as the misdeeds of the securities business. His *God's Gold: The Story of Rockefeller and His Times* (1932) became something of a classic.[4]

Flynn was not a strict libertarian, nor was his thinking on economics notably sophisticated. He fully appreciated the productive dynamism of the private-property market economy. But in his progressive phase, he held that government had a crucial role to play in reining in the "excesses" of capitalism, by thwarting monopolies, protecting small investors, and undertaking moderate social reform. Yet he was never a socialist; to his mind, the hopes for a free and prosperous society lay in a truly competitive private enterprise system.[5] Above all, Flynn always distrusted any close tie-in between the state and big business, at home or abroad. In 1934, he acted as chief researcher for the Nye committee of the U.S. Senate, which investigated the role of the New York banks and the munitions industry ("the merchants of death") in leading the United States into the First World War.

Flynn opposed the New Deal practically from the start. Instead of opening up the economy to competitive forces, Roosevelt seemed bent on cartelizing it, principally through the National Recovery Act (NRA), which Flynn regarded as a copy of Mussolini's Corporate State. As one failed New Deal program followed another, Flynn suspected that Roosevelt would try to divert attention to alleged foreign dangers, a recourse facilitated by world events. The sinking by the Japanese of an American gunboat, the *Panay*, which had been patrolling the Yangtze, precipitated an early crisis. Flynn asked why we had gunboats patrolling Chinese rivers in the first place—and found the answer in the fact that the *Panay* had been convoying tankers of the Standard Oil Company.[6] Incidents such as this, Flynn charged, were exploited by the Administration "to churn up as much war spirit as possible." In 1938, he joined with Norman Thomas and others to establish the Keep America Out of War Congress, composed mainly of pacifists and socialists.

In *Country Squire in the White House* (1940), Flynn set forth themes he would develop more fully in *The Roosevelt Myth*. He painted the Hudson Valley patrician as a dilettante with no principles of his own, a mere power-seeker with a genius for winning votes. Roosevelt had reneged on his promises of progressive reform and instead created a federal Leviathan based on the cynical policy of "tax and tax, spend and spend, elect and elect" (the formula which has since become the bedrock of American politics in our two-party system). Characteristically, it was the government's intimate relationship with the armaments industry that came in for Flynn's sharpest censure.

Roosevelt, who always viewed any criticism of himself as a perversion of true democracy, was outraged. The president of the United States wrote a personal letter to a magazine editor declaring that Flynn "should be barred hereafter from the columns of any presentable daily paper, monthly magazine, or national quarterly."[7] Whether or not as a consequence of FDR's spite, the *New Republic* dropped the column by Flynn it had been publishing since 1933, a sign things were changing in the circles of left-liberalism. In the years to come, FDR would use the FBI, the IRS, and other agencies to spy on, harass, and intimidate his critics.[8] This—and his lying, his *constant lying*—more than any putative mental affliction, explains the hatred that so many cherished for Franklin Roosevelt.

As FDR edged closer to war, the need was felt for a mass-based anti-interventionist organization. In August, 1940, Flynn became one of the founders of the America First Committee and chairman of the New York City chapter. At its height, the America First Committee had over 800,000 card-carrying members, among them E. E. Cummings, Sinclair Lewis, Kathleen Norris, Alice Roosevelt

Longworth, and Irene Castle. (The actress Lillian Gish served for a time on the national board, but was forced to resign when this led to her being blackballed—"blacklisted"?—in Hollywood and on Broadway.) Younger members of America First included John F. Kennedy, Sargeant Shriver, Gerald Ford, and Gore Vidal.[9]

America First was tapping into a deep vein: poll after poll showed that 80% of the people were against going to war with Germany. Soon the Committee was subjected to a relentless campaign of defamation and slander. Its most popular speaker, Charles Lindbergh, was labeled the "No. 1 Nazi fellow traveler" in the United States by Harold Ickes, secretary of the interior and Roosevelt's chief hatchet man, while Robert Sherwood, the president's speechwriter, dismissed the heroic aviator as "simply a Nazi."[10] The smear by the philosopher and socialist John Dewey, that the America First Committee was a "transmission belt" for Nazi propaganda, was echoed by scores of interventionist hacks.[11] Self-appointed "anti-fascist" patriots in Hollywood and elsewhere depicted a vast (imaginary) network of Nazi agitators and saboteurs at work throughout the land, and linked these domestic Nazis to the "isolationists," "Hitler's conscious or unconscious allies."[12]

Flynn termed the campaign a "witch-hunt." He and his ideological comrades would remember the establishment's viciousness when the tables were briefly turned, during the episode known as "McCarthyism."

As the battle over intervention intensified, Flynn observed that Roosevelt was wrecking the constitutional balance in foreign affairs as he had domestically. When the president sent troops to occupy Iceland in July, 1941, Flynn assailed the unconstitutional act and the supine Congress that permitted it: Roosevelt "could not do this if the Congress of the United States had not been reduced to the state of a servile shadow" of what the Founders intended.[13] In the "Four Freedoms" declaration issued by Roosevelt and Churchill, in August, 1941, Flynn saw prefigured the globalist program for America: "the task is forever to be ours of policing the world, inflicting our ideologies and our wishes upon the world."[14]

Roosevelt needed the war and wanted the war, and the war came. The America First Committee dissolved itself, but Flynn did not cease his attacks. In 1944, he published *As We Go Marching*, an analysis of the nature of European fascism and the clear parallels to trends in the United States. "As we go marching to the salvation of the world," Flynn warned, government power expanded, our economic and social life was militarized, and we were coming to resemble the very dictatorships we were fighting.[15] With the end of the war and the death of FDR, Flynn was ready for his summation of the career of the four-term president.

It is fairly obvious that the routine judgment of American historians, that Roosevelt was a truly "great president," has nothing objective about it. Historians, like everyone else, have their own personal values and views. Like other academics they tend to be overwhelmingly on the left. Analyzing one recent poll, Robert Higgs notes: "Left-liberal historians worship political power, and idolize those who wield it most lavishly in the service of left-liberal causes."[16] Why should it be surprising, or even noteworthy, that they venerate Roosevelt and try to get a credulous public to do the same?

For a rather different view, the reader can now turn to *The Roosevelt Myth*, once more in print, which was and, after half a century, remains the major debunking of Franklin Roosevelt. "Polemical as only Flynn could be polemical,"[17] the work was turned down by every publisher the author approached. Flynn was desperate: "For the first time in my life I am peddling a book around like a fresh unknown.... I am at my wits' end." Finally, he met Devin Garrity, head of a small house in New York specializing in Irish and revisionist works, and the book appeared in 1948 under the imprint of Devin-Adair. It quickly became number two on the *New York Times* best-seller list.[18]

Taking every phase of his presidency in turn, Flynn is merciless in exposing Roosevelt as a failure, a liar, and a fraud. Two subsidiary myths which he demolishes are of particular interest today, since they are the main supports for FDR's supposed greatness: his roles in the Depression and in the Second World War.

The mantra, "Roosevelt cured the Depression," exasperated Flynn. (Now it is often replaced with the banal and much more cautious: "He gave the people hope.") Didn't anyone care about facts? he demanded. The "first" New Deal came and went, then came the "second" New Deal, in 1935—and still the Depression, unlike every previous downturn, dragged on and on. Flynn pointed out that in 1938 the number of persons unemployed totaled

"11,800,000—*more than were unemployed when Roosevelt was elected in 1932*" (his italics). Flynn deals with the impotence of successive New Deal programs and the fulminations of the "planners" and "spenders" in his chapters on "The Forgotten Depression" and "The Dance of the Philosophers."

Recent scholarship has bolstered Flynn's analysis. In studying why the slump that started in 1929 became "the Great Depression," the longest-lasting in U. S. history, Robert Higgs identifies a critical factor: the exceptionally low rate of private investment. A chief cause of this failure to invest and create productive jobs, Higgs finds, was "regime uncertainty." For the first time in our history, investors were seriously worried over the security of property rights in America. There had been an

> unparalleled outpouring of business-threatening laws, regulations, and court decisions, the oft-stated hostility of President Roosevelt and his lieutenants toward investors as a class, and the character of the antibusiness zealots who composed the strategists and administrators of the New Deal from 1935 to 1941.[19]

The comfortable mythology has it that businessmen hated Roosevelt because he was "a traitor to his class." The truth is that they feared him as a menace to the private property system, and they restricted their investments accordingly.

On FDR's role before and after our entry into World War II Flynn is scathing. When he wrote his book, Thomas A. Bailey, diplomatic historian at Stanford, had already published the defense of Roosevelt's pro-war policy that has now become standard. Casually conceding the whole revisionist indictment by Charles Beard and others, Bailey wrote:

> Franklin Roosevelt repeatedly deceived the American people during the period before Pearl Harbor.... He was like a physician who must tell the patient lies for the patient's own good.... Because the masses are notoriously shortsighted and generally cannot see the danger until it is at their throats our statesmen are forced to deceive them into an awareness of their own long-run interests. This is clearly what Roosevelt had to do, and who shall say that posterity will not thank him for it?[20]

But Flynn asked: "If Roosevelt had the right to do this, to whom is the right denied?" In 1948, Flynn was speaking for the "patients," the lied to, the duped and manipulated masses, those once known as the free and sovereign citizens of the American Republic. Today, the conventional wisdom is all on the side of the lying Roosevelt and against the people he deceived.

On another subject, also, standards have changed. In our own enlightened times, it is considered entirely in the natural order of things that the United States should have emerged triumphant from the costliest and second-bloodiest war in our history and then been instantly plunged into another struggle against a more powerful foe. Yet in 1948, Winston Churchill himself admitted that: "we have still not found Peace or Security, and ... we lie in the grip of even worse perils than those we have surmounted."[21] A half century ago, this suggested, reasonably enough, that something had gone seriously wrong in the political conduct of the war.

In accounting for the sorry state of the post-war world, Flynn focused on Roosevelt's failures: "Our government put into Stalin's hands the means of seizing a great slab of the continent of Europe, then stood aside while he took it and finally acquiesced in his conquests." Forty years later, Robert Nisbet reinforced Flynn's case, laying out in detail FDR's fatuousness in looking on Stalin—*Stalin*—as a friend and a fellow progressive, his main ally in constructing the New World Order.[22] These facts have, however, made little impression on the herds of historians. It seems that there is no degrading inanity, no catastrophic blunder that is not permitted a truly "great president."

Franklin Roosevelt's impact on America was measureless. Flynn's account—composed in his trademark fighting-Irish style—is still the best analysis of why it was so deeply destructive.

In the years that followed, Flynn became the intellectual mainstay of the Old Right, shedding the remnants of his old-line progressivism and growing more clearly constitutionalist and anti-statist. This was the Flynn of *The Road Ahead* (1949), another best-seller, which reached a printing of 4,000,000 in the *Reader's Digest* condensation. The "road" Flynn warned that we were following was the path of Fabian socialism towards omnipotent government.

As the new president, Harry Truman, engaged the United States in yet another crusade, Flynn sided with what remained of the anti-interventionist movement, which looked to Senator Robert Taft as its leader. Opposed to open-ended American commitments everywhere, suspicious of foreign aid programs that entailed underwriting the status quo in a rapidly changing world, these conservatives became, once again, the target of interventionist slanders. According to Truman, Republicans who opposed his foreign policy were "Kremlin assets," the sort of miscreants who would shoot "our soldiers in the back in a hot war."[23] Once again, the establishment press echoed Administration smears.

All of this has been forgotten now, along with the pre-war campaign of defamation of patriotic Americans as "Nazis." All that remains in the popular memory is the perpetually rehashed tale of a time of terror known as the Age of McCarthyism. Flynn was a fervent supporter of Joseph McCarthy, and in several works he examined the influence of Communists and Communist sympathizers on U.S. foreign policy, especially on China.[24] While it is clear that Flynn basically misunderstood the Chinese revolution, on other points he was closer to the truth than McCarthy's enemies, then and now. Owen Lattimore, for instance, was not the mild-mannered, ivory tower scholar of left-liberal mythology, but a dedicated apologist for Stalin, for the purge-trials and the Gulag.[25] With the continuing release of documents from the 1930s and 40s, from U.S. and Russian archives, the received wisdom regarding the "McCarthyite terror" is due for revision.[26]

In the watershed campaign for the Republican presidential nomination in 1952, Flynn was an ardent supporter of Robert Taft. Eisenhower he saw as simply a front-man for the Eastern Republican establishment, centered in Wall Street, that had foisted Willkie and Dewey on the Party; he felt the same way about Eisenhower's running-mate, Senator Richard M. Nixon.

Flynn continued to oppose globalism to the end. He contended against American meddling in the Middle East; and when Senator McCarthy—true to his own internationalist bent—supported the British-French-Israeli attack on Egypt in 1956, Flynn broke with him. Growing American involvement in Indochina under Eisenhower and John Foster Dulles incensed Flynn. He asked pointedly: "I would like to know who in Asia is going to cross the Pacific and attack us." At the time of the French debacle at Dien Bien Phu, Flynn called on Eisenhower to make it clear that "we're not going to get involved in any kind of war in Indo-China, hot or lukewarm, all out or part-way."[27]

A constant target of Flynn's was the "bipartisan foreign policy," a hoax which functioned to deprive Americans of any choice on questions of peace or war. As a central source of this ruse he identified the Council on Foreign Relations, noting that both Dean Acheson and John Foster Dulles—secretaries of state from nominally opposed parties—as well as most of the other makers of U.S. foreign policy were members of the New York organization. Palpably a front for business interests, the Council's aim was a radical transformation of the attitudes of the American people, their conversion to the dogma that our security required that we "police the whole world, fight the battles of the whole world, make every country in the world like the United States."[28]

Flynn's highlighting of the influence of big business on American foreign policy has inevitably led some writers to link his outlook to Marxism. Nothing could be more wrong-headed. Flailing capitalists for using their links to the state to further their own sinister interests, *especially* their overseas interests, has been a cornerstone of classical liberalism from at least the time of Turgot, Adam Smith, and Jeremy Bentham.

In 1956 occurred a small event that, like Flynn's firing from the *New Republic* in 1938, symbolized the passing of an era in American politics. As Flynn had earlier been dismissed because his anti-war views were inconsistent with the new turn on the left, so now he ran into opposition from a nascent "New Right." William F. Buckley, Jr., nurtured on the American anti-statism of Albert Jay Nock and Frank Chodorov, had fallen in with a crowd of ex-Stalinists, ex-Trotskyists, and conservative European emigrés. His position now was that "we have to accept Big Government for the duration—for neither an offensive nor a defensive war can be waged ... except through the instrument of a totalitarian bureaucracy within our shores." The anti-Communist crusade required high taxes for vast armies and navies, even "war production boards and the attendant centralization of power in Washington."[29]

As editor of *National Review*, Buckley commissioned an article from Flynn. Flynn turned in a bitter critique of the hypertrophic growth of the central government under Republican as well as

Democratic administrations, which concluded: "There has been, since Roosevelt's regime, no plan whatever for restoring the American Republic in its constitutional form."[30] This was not something that Buckley, as committed to global meddling and as indifferent to American constitutionalism as any New Dealer, could accept. The manuscript was returned, ending Flynn's connection with what now passed for the conservative movement in America.

Gregory Pavlik, editor of a recent edition of Flynn's essays, summed it up well: "When Flynn died in 1964 he was an outcast from both the then-fashionable varieties of liberalism and conservatism. His life was a testament to his character—he refused to compromise his deepest convictions for the affection of trendy demagogues of any political stripe."[31]

Ralph Raico
Professor of History
Buffalo State College

Endnotes

1. Albert Jay Nock, *Letters from Albert Jay Nock 1924–1945* (Caldwell, Id.: Caxton, 1949), p. 211.

2. See Sheldon Richman, "New Deal Nemesis: The 'Old Right' Jeffersonians," *The Independent Review*, vol. 1, no. 2 (Fall 1996), pp. 201–248; and Justin Raimondo, *Reclaiming the American Right: The Lost Legacy of the Conservative Movement* (Burlingame, Cal.: Center for Libertarian Studies, 1993).

3. Bill Kauffman, *America First! Its History, Culture, and Politics* (Amherst, N.Y.: Prometheus, 1995), p. 58.

4. Michele Flynn Stenehjem, *An American First: John T. Flynn and the America First Committee* (New Rochelle, N.Y.: Arlington House, 1976), pp. 26–29.

5. Ronald Radosh, *Prophets on the Right: Profiles of Conservative Critics of American Globalism* (New York: Simon and Schuster, 1975), pp. 197–201.

6. Ibid., p. 205.

7. Ibid., pp. 204–205.

8. See, for instance, Robert Dallek, *Franklin Roosevelt and American Foreign Policy, 1932–1945* (Oxford: Oxford University Press, 1979), pp. 289–290; and Richard Nor-

ton Smith, *The Colonel: The Life and Legend of Robert R. McCormick* (Boston: Houghton Mifflin, 1997), pp. 405–406, 424–428.

9. Kauffman, *America First!* On Lillian Gish, see Justus D. Doenecke, ed., *In Danger Undaunted: The Anti-Interventionist Movement of 1940–1941 as Revealed in the Papers of the America First Committee* (Stanford, Cal.: Hoover Institution Press, 1990), p. 14.

10. Wayne S. Cole, *Charles A. Lindbergh and the Battle Against American Intervention in World War II* (New York: Harcourt Brace Jovanovich, 1974), pp. 130, 147.

11. Radosh, *Prophets on the Right*, p. 219.

12. John Earl Haynes, *Red Scare or Red Menace? American Communism and Anticommunism in the Cold War Era* (Chicago: Ivan R. Dee, 1996), pp. 17–36. In December, 1942—in the midst of the war—it was Roosevelt himself who shocked the Washington press corps by mockingly presenting John O'Donnell, the anti-interventionist columnist for the New York *Daily News*, with an Iron Cross for his services to the Reich. Graham J. White, *FDR and the Press* (Chicago: University of Chicago Press, 1979), pp. 44–45. The smears continue to this day. Professor Harry Jaffa ("In Defense of Churchill," *Modern Age*, vol. 34, no. 3 [Spring 1992], p. 281) refers to "Charles Lindbergh and Fritz Kuhn [*Führer* of the pro-Nazi German-American Bund] standing together" in warning that participation in the war would "be mainly in the interest of Jews." Jaffa wishes to evoke the picture of Lindbergh next to Kuhn addressing an anti-war rally. Needless to say, it never happened. They "stood together" against the war in the sense that interventionists after June, 1941 "stood together" with Stalin and his mass-killers in agitating for U.S. entry. Lindbergh did not maintain that it was "in the interest of Jews" for the United States to enter the war; on the contrary, he believed it would damage the status of Jews in America (Cole, *Charles A. Lindbergh*, pp. 157–185). The cause of Jaffa's foolish diatribe is clearly his clammy fear that the voice of America First "is once again abroad in the land."

13. Cole, *Roosevelt and the Isolationists*, p. 432.

14. Ibid., p. 495.

15. The militarization of American life since 1933 is dealt with by Michael S. Sherry, *In the Shadow of War: The United States Since the 1930s* (New Haven, Conn.: Yale University Press, 1995).

16. Robert Higgs, "No More 'Great Presidents,' " *The Free Market*, vol. 15, no. 3, p. 2. Higgs says everything that needs to be said on these politically-inspired surveys of historians, concluding: "God save us from great presidents."

17. Justus D. Doenecke, *Not to the Swift: The Old Isolationists in the Cold War Era* (Lewisburg, Pa.: Bucknell University Press, 1979), pp. 97–98.

18. Stenehjem, *An American First*, pp. 172–173.

19. Robert Higgs, "Regime Uncertainty: Why the Great Depression Lasted So Long and Why Prosperity Resumed After the War," *The Independent Review*, vol. 1, no. 4 (Spring 1997), p. 586. See also the chapter on the New Deal in Higgs's indispensable work, *Crisis and Leviathan: Critical Episodes in the Growth of American Government* (New York: Oxford University Press, 1987), pp. 159–195.

20. Thomas A. Bailey, *The Man in the Street: The Impact of American Public Opinion on Foreign Policy* (New York: Macmillan, 1948), p. 13.

21. Winston S. Churchill, *The Gathering Storm* (Boston: Houghton Mifflin, 1948), p. v.

22. Robert Nisbet, *Roosevelt and Stalin: The Failed Courtship* (Washington, D. C.: Regnery, 1988).

23. Doenecke, *Not to the Swift*, p. 216.

24. E. g., *While You Slept: Our Tragedy in Asia and Who Made It* (1951) and *The Lattimore Story* (1953).

25. After a visit to Kolyma, the most notorious of the Gulag camps, Lattimore described the camp administration as "a combination of the Hudson Bay Company and the TVA." See Robert Conquest, *Kolyma: The Arctic Death Camps* (New York: Viking, 1978), pp. 204–205, 208–212.

26. See, for instance, M. Stanton Evans, "McCarthyism: Waging the Cold War in America," *Human Events*, vol. 53, no. 21 (May 30, 1997), pp. S1-S8.

27. Doenecke, *Not to the Swift*, pp. 241, 243; Radosh, *Prophets on the Right*, p. 261.

28. Radosh, *Prophets on the Right*, p. 258.

29. William F. Buckley, Jr., "A Young Republican's View," *Commonweal*, January 25, 1952, as quoted in Murray N. Rothbard, "The Betrayal of the American Right," unpublished manuscript, pp. 166–167.

30. The essay is published for the first time in John T. Flynn, *Forgotten Lessons: Selected Essays*, Gregory P. Pavlik, ed. (Irvington-on-Hudson, N.Y.: Foundation for Economic Education, 1996), pp. 129–134.

31. Ibid., p. 4.

Preface to the Revised Edition

It has seemed advisable to offer a new edition of this volume for a very obvious reason. In the eight years since it first appeared a great mass of testimony has come from various witnesses whose evidence was not available when the book was written. In the main this testimony has completely buttressed and confirmed the facts as they appeared in the original edition. But some of these new revelations have made necessary certain revisions throughout the text. As an example, Chapter II in Book Three originally made no mention of the treasonable activities of Harry Dexter White, Assistant Secretary of the Treasury under Henry Morgenthau. White dominated that Department and was thus able—as an agent of Soviet Russia—to induce Roosevelt to accept a secret Stalin plan for post-war Germany against the wishes of Roosevelt's own cabinet members, Secretaries Hull and Stimson. The fully documented story of this almost unbelievable betrayal of America's interests will now be found in the chapter mentioned.

Other additions to the Roosevelt story have been made in a Postscript, which serves also as a reappraisal of Roosevelt's character and his regime as we look back over the 11 years since his death. It is hoped that this Postscript will add to and enliven the portrait of Roosevelt and the New Deal which this volume contains.

John T. Flynn
Bayside, L. I.
May, 1956

FOREWORD

This book is in no sense a biography of Franklin D. Roosevelt. It is rather a critical account of that episode in American politics known as the New Deal. As to the President, it is an account of an image projected upon the popular mind which came to be known as Franklin D. Roosevelt. It is the author's conviction that this image did not at all correspond to the man himself and that it is now time to correct the lineaments of this synthetic figure created by highly intelligent propaganda, aided by mass illusion and finally enlarged and elaborated out of all reason by the fierce moral and mental disturbances of the war. The purpose of this book, therefore, is to present the Franklin D. Roosevelt of the years 1932 to 1945 in his normal dimensions, reduced in size to agree with reality.

The war played havoc with history-writing after 1940. Not only did a great curtain of secrecy come down upon performers in the drama of the war, but their portraits and their actions were presented to us through the movies, the radio and the press upon a heroic scale as part of the business of selling the warriors and the statesmen and the war to the people. Their blunders and their quarrels were blotted out of the picture. Only the bright features were left. The casual citizen saw them as exalted beings moving in glory across the vast stage of war, uttering eloquent appeals to the nation, challenging the enemy in flaming words, striding like heroes and talking like gods.

The moment has come when the costumes, the grease paint, the falsely colored scenery, the technicolored spotlights and all the other artifices of make-up should be put aside and, in the interest of truth, the solid facts about the play and the players revealed to the people.

A whole 20-foot shelf of books has appeared glorifying the character and career of Franklin D. Roosevelt. In addition a large number of men and women who were associated with his administrations have published their own versions of their several parts in those administrations. And while these contain some incidental criticisms, the chief effect of all these books is to feed the legend of the world conqueror and remodeler. Curiously, only two or three critical works have appeared and these touch only special sectors of the whole story.

It seemed to me there was room for at least one critical book covering the whole period of Roosevelt's terms as President.

There is much to this story with which I have not attempted to deal either because it is not provable or, if provable, is not yet believable or because it belongs to a domain of writing for which I have neither taste nor experience. I have omitted any account of the bitter struggle which attended our entry into the war or any attempt to determine whether or not we should have gone into the war. That is another story which is reserved for a later day. Similarly no account of the military conduct of the war is included. The facts about that are even more obscure than the political facts and must await the release of a mass of documents still under official lock and key. I have, however, sought to clear up from the recently offered testimony of the chief actors, the diplomatic performances in that shocking and pathetic failure during and after the war. And I have included some account of the incredible mismanagement of our economic scene at home during the war.

I have limited myself severely to facts. A critic may disagree with my interpretation of those facts, but he will not be able successfully to contradict them. I have introduced into the text numbered references to my authorities and these appear at the end of the book. The facts are drawn from official records and reports, the testimony given in congressional investigations, the reports of responsible journalists and a large number of books by men who were actors in these scenes. In the last two years a number of persons who collaborated closely with Roosevelt in his administrations have written their autobiographies. These include five cabinet members—Cordell Hull, James A. Farley, Frances Perkins, Henry L. Stimson and Henry Morgenthau, Jr., the latter of whom published in *Collier's* a number of pages from his diaries. Edward J. Flynn, who managed Roosevelt's third-term campaign; James F. Byrnes, who was known as "Assistant President"; Raymond Moley, Roosevelt's first intimate adviser; Charles Michaelson, public relations man for the Democratic Committee; Admiral Ross T. McIntire, Roosevelt's personal physician; Michael Reilly, head of his Secret Service guard, and many others who have either written books of their recollections or magazine articles touching special episodes. The official reports of General Marshall and General Eisenhower have been published, while other military men have produced memoirs or diaries, such as Generals George Patton, Joseph Stilwell, Claire Chennault, Captain Harry Butcher, whose voluminous diary of his three years with Eisenhower is an invaluable contribution to history, and Major-General John R. Deane, who headed our Military Mission in Moscow during the war. Still others, such as Arthur Bliss Lane, former American Ambassador to Poland, Jan Ciechanowski, former Polish Ambassador to the United States, former Polish Premier Mikolajczyk and others have written detailed accounts of special sectors of the events with which they were specially familiar. In addition, a large number of inspired biographies of Roosevelt by undiscriminating and worshipful admirers have appeared, some of them containing valuable material flowing directly from Roosevelt himself or his family. And, of course, the family have been both the authors as well as the subjects of a number of books. From a wide variety of sources—in the reports of American newspapers and magazines—a great volume of authentic material has originated. No one before this has undertaken to assemble this wealth of scattered data into a continuous and integrated account. Each of the men or women who have written their own stories or who have reported special small areas of the whole field of action has brought to light some missing portion of the whole story of these times. Like so many pieces in a jig-saw puzzle they help to complete the full picture. Thus the memoirs of Stimson, Hull, Deane, Byrnes, Farley are interesting in themselves but the events they describe are not truly revealed until the testimony of each is sifted and made into an integrated story. I have examined every scrap of this material in all these works, along with the vast records of the newspapers, magazines and official reports of the time. I have tried to fit together the multitude of small pieces of the truth and thus arrive at a reasonably faithful story of this period.

In addition to all this I may be permitted to observe that during the administrations of Franklin Roosevelt I was an active journalist and as such very close to the events described in this volume. For most of the time I wrote a daily column which appeared in a large number of American newspapers, a weekly column in an American magazine of opinion and I contributed to numerous national magazines literally hundreds of articles dealing with these events. This work brought me close to the stage of affairs and into intimate touch with the leading characters on both sides. No small part of the material which appears in this volume, therefore, is the product of my own researches and observations at the time the events described occurred.

John T. Flynn
Bayside, L. I.
July, 1948

BOOK ONE:
TRIAL—AND ERROR

Chapter 1: The New Dealer Takes the Deck

Saturday morning, March 4, 1933, as the sun struggled lazily into position through gray clouds hurrying before the chill March winds, Washington was like a beleaguered city. All over the place high officials were up early packing their bags, ready to be off as the legions of the Grand Old Party that had occupied the city for so many years prepared to evacuate. All through the night from every region, by automobile, bus, train and plane, the happy hosts of the conquering Democrats poured into the city, hastening to take over after so many hungry years in the wilderness.

In the White House, President Hoover, a weary and worn man, spent with the vigil of long sleepless nights as he struggled to hold back the tide of the onrushing crisis, was at his desk early for the last dreary duties before laying down his intolerable burden and surrendering the capital into the hands of his gay and laughing successor, already astir a mile away in the Mayflower Hotel.

In mid-morning, Franklin D. Roosevelt, with his wife, his mother and numerous other Roosevelts—children, aunts and uncles and cousins to the fourth degree of consanguinity, repaired from their suite in the Mayflower to St. John's Episcopal Church where Dr. Endicott Peabody, Roosevelt's old headmaster at Groton School, would invoke the blessing of the Lord upon "Thy servant Franklin." All of the new cabinet members were there also, to thank the Lord who had answered their own prayers so pleasantly.

The service over, Mr. Roosevelt, his wife and mother and his oldest son, James, in a presidential car, went quickly to the White House. The wet streets were filling with people, marching clubs, detachments of regulars and national guard troops. The great function of the inauguration—the vast powers of government falling out of one pair of hands into another without turmoil or resistance—was moving into its traditional ritual. At the White House the family got out of the car and entered the mansion for their long tenure. Roosevelt remained in the car and President Hoover got in. The automobile, with its silk-hatted occupants, moved through the gates of the White House and, heavily guarded by Secret Service men and mounted troops, moved on to the Capitol.

The streets were blackening, despite the occasional drizzle, with crowds, some huddled against the cables that lined the sidewalks for a front view of the parade later, others hurrying on to the Capitol grounds to see the inaugural ceremony. Half a million were in the streets, a hundred thousand of them crowded around the reviewing stand in front of the Capitol. This was the biggest throng that had ever assembled for an inauguration.

Throughout the country the masses were in a state of bewilderment and, in some places, despair, as the great economic crisis rolled on to its thunderous climax. The tones and colors of drama were everywhere. There was an authentic hero. There was a villain—a whole drove of villains, the bankers and big business men. The incidents of drama were all about too. Only a week before an assassin's bullet had barely missed Roosevelt. It struck Anton Cermak, the Bohemian mayor and boss of Chicago, who with Al Smith had opposed Roosevelt's nomination. It was the hand of God, said some. Cermak had gone to Miami to meet Roosevelt as he arrived from a sea trip aboard Vincent Astor's yacht the *Nourmahal* a week before the inauguration. Miami was crowded with Democratic office seekers and Cermak was there to make his peace with Roosevelt. Instead he got the bullet intended for Roosevelt and died a few days later. Had he been for Roosevelt in the first place, said the pious Democrats who believe that Providence plays Democratic politics, he would not have had to go to Miami and he would be alive now. Later, as Roosevelt's train sped from New York to Washington carrying himself and his family, word came to him that aboard another train carrying the 65-year-old Senator Thomas J. Walsh and his bride of two days, the aged groom dropped dead in his Pullman drawing room. He was speeding to the capital to be sworn in as Attorney-General.

Every hour brought news of new bank closings—from Texas, Arizona, Oregon, Washington, Wisconsin—bringing to 24 the number of states which had closed their banks. During the preceding night word had come that the banks of New York and Chicago could not stand the strain another day. Governor Lehman, in the early morning hours, had issued an order closing the New York banks. In cities all over the country crowds stood outside closed banks looking woefully through their grated windows.

Farmers were in revolt. They had been intimidating judges, dumping wheat out of overturned trucks into ditches. The fires were out in many factory furnaces. Millions of men were idle. All over the land millions of people turned their faces toward Washington to see what the handsome, smiling new President would do to stem the tide of the disaster.

Economic paralysis lay all about. The arch-villain in this catastrophe was discernible to most people. There he sat in the automobile beside the man who was hurrying to the Capitol to supplant him. He had been hissed at railroad stations. Scurrilous books had been written about his life. Curses had been heaped upon his head. And now he was on his way out to the accompaniment of the glee of his enemies and detractors. Most of his aides and subalterns were gone or waiting to surrender to their successors. In their place came the procession of the righteous captains of the New Deal—Frankfurter and Hull and Henry Wallace and Henry Morgenthau, Moley and Tugwell and Sam Rosenman and Berle and Harry Hopkins and Eleanor Roosevelt and scores of others whose names would soon fill the ears of the nation.

Salvation was in the air. Repeal, also, was in the air. Two weeks before the lame-duck Congress had turned a somersault and voted the amendment to the Constitution ending Prohibition. The wets were making merry with applejack, bathtub gin and prohibition hooch. "Beer by Easter," they cried. Forty-one legislatures were in session waiting eagerly for the chance to approve the wet amendment and to slap taxes on beer and liquor to save their empty treasuries. The old drys were around looking dour but still full of fight. "No surrender! No retreat! No repeal!" they muttered. But the sands were running against them. The United States was through with Prohibition. It would soon end "God's law." The barrooms would be back soon—and full of women and children. A more powerful appetite was aroused. The country, the states, the towns needed money—something to tax. And liquor was the richest target. "Revenue," said one commentator, "unlocked the gates for Gambrinus and his foaming steed."

Here and there in the vast crowds were solemn men who muttered the word "revolution." But this was no revolution. The multitude of visitors in Washington did not want revolution. What they wanted was in the hands of Jim Farley to give and he was already there wrinkling his bland brow over the problem. The Democratic legions were rushing to Washington to save the nation with that sense of joyous dedication with which the old-fashioned volunteer firemen rushed to a saloon fire. But poor Jim faced the problem of fitting 1,250,000 loyal party men into 125,000 jobs. All had gotten letters from Jim signed with his already famous green ink signature. But it looked as if only one out of ten of the faithful would get jobs and the other nine just letters.

As Roosevelt rode to the Capitol beside President Hoover, his face was wreathed in smiles. One of his friendly biographers says he was the happiest man in all that immense throng. The family, too, was in the gayest spirits. And, as usual, everywhere the interest was keen in the President's relatives. His immediate family seemed to have cuddled up quickly in the affections of the people. Here was something they liked. Here was a fine old aristocratic family founded upon long tradition of patriotic service, reared in the finest standards of American home life—the beaming and heroic father who had overcome one of the most terrible of physical handicaps, the devoted and religious wife and mother and the fine, robust, upstanding brood of boys to bring grace and dignity to the home of the nation's Chief Executive.

At the Capitol, Hoover, who was still President, went immediately to the President's room off the Republican side of the Senate chamber to sign last-minute bills passed by the Congress that was in session. Roosevelt, still a private citizen, alighted under the archway of the steps of the main entrance to the Capitol, completely out of sight of the crowds. He had to be borne about in a wheel chair, but was never permitted to be seen thus by the public. Two ramps had been built to the entrance along which he was wheeled out of sight to the office of the sergeant-at-arms of the Senate. From there a temporary wooden passageway was built to a short distance from the platform outside the Capitol portico where he would speak. About 35 feet from that point he got out of his chair, his braces were straightened and on the arm of his son James he walked these 35 feet to the spot where he took the oath. He waited, of course, until the ceremony in the Senate, where John N. Garner was being sworn in as Vice-President, was ended. Then with President Hoover, Vice-President

Garner, his full cabinet and the members of the Senate he made his way to the appointed spot before the great multitude of a hundred thousand citizens.

He stood before Chief Justice Hughes, who held out to him a Bible which had been brought to this country by a remote Roosevelt ancestor 300 years before. Roosevelt touched it, and as the Chief Justice asked solemnly if he would swear to support the Constitution of the United States, he answered in a clear voice: "I DO." This was his first solemn official pledge. Then facing the great throng, he delivered his inaugural address.

"This," he said, "is preeminently the time to speak the truth, the whole truth, frankly and boldly. Nor need we shirk from facing honestly conditions in our country today. This great nation will endure as it has endured, will revive and will prosper. So, first of all, let me assert my firm belief that the only thing we have to fear is fear itself."

It was an extraordinary speech. It put Roosevelt at once in the first rank of American orators. The people wanted courage and hope. His first words gave them that. Then he painted a swift, dramatic picture of the crisis. Values have shrunken. Taxes have risen. "The means of exchange are frozen in the streams of trade." The withered leaves of industrial enterprise lie on every side. Farmers find no markets for their products. The savings of many years in thousands of families are gone. "Only foolish optimism," he conceded, "can deny the dark realities of the moment."

Then he lightened the picture. "Yet our distress comes from no failure of substance. We are stricken by no plague of locusts ... Nature still offers her bounty ... plenty is at our doorstep, but a generous use of it languishes in the very sight of the supply."

Then he nailed down the blame. "Primarily this is because the rules of the exchange of mankind's goods have failed through their own stubbornness and their own incompetence ... They know only the rules of a generation of self-seekers. They have no vision, and when there is no vision the people perish ... The money changers have fled from their high seats in the temple of our civilization. We may now restore the temple to the ancient truths."

Then came a succession of promises which everyone wanted to hear. For the workers: "Our greatest primary task is to put people to work." For the farmers: They must "raise the value of agricultural products and with this the power to purchase the output of our cities." For the investors: They "must end speculation with other people's money." For the whole world: There must be a policy of the good neighbor in a world of neighbors.

Then he accepted his high office as one taking over the command of an army—an army organized for attack. He would recommend measures "that a stricken nation in the midst of a stricken world may require." But—ah, but!—if Congress should fail to go along with him—"I–shall–not–evade–the–clear–course–of–duty–that–will –confront–me." There was an ominous accent of the resolute captain on every word. He would ask for the one remaining instrument—a grant from Congress of "broad executive power to wage a war against the emergency, as great as the power that would be given me if we were in fact invaded by a foreign foe."

Then he summoned the people to war—war on the depression. He asked them for discipline. He talked of "old moral values," of the "stern performance of duty by old and young alike."

Action! Action! Action! The restoration of the old moral values! Driving the money changers from the temple! It was war, war, war upon the great blight. War by a disciplined leader, who promised jobs to the jobless, higher prices to the farmers, the restoration of shrunken property values to business, and over all the tone of great moral principles and great commanding issues.

After the address, as the immense parade of the military and marching clubs of the loyal Democrats passed in review under the dark clouds through which the sun peeped only at intervals, one of those rare incidents occurred, surcharged with the spirit of goodwill and unity. As the New York delegation of marchers passed before the victorious Presidential candidate reviewing them from the stands the crowd suddenly saw that it was led by the man who had fought Roosevelt's nomination so bitterly—Al Smith. The stands rose in a great ovation for the Happy Warrior.

After this, Mr. Hoover, now rid of his great burden, shook hands with the new President and left at once for Philadelphia and later for his home in California. Despite the bitter emotions churned up against him, he left without any Secret Service guard, his secretary's request for that having been graciously refused by the government he had headed but a few minutes before. The new President went to his new home, the White House, where a luncheon was served to 500 guests. The members of his cabinet were sworn in before their relatives and friends in the Oval Room by Justice Cardozo. This was the first time this had been done. Roosevelt told Jim Farley that he was breaking a precedent. "It is my intention to inaugurate precedents like this from time to time," he laughed. The streets outside were given over to the crowds which, whipped up by the marching bands, had become quite merry and milled around until late into the night. The inaugural ball was the gayest, the most crowded in many an inauguration as the guests danced and the crowds outside applauded the coming and going of their favorite heroes, while the newsboys were crying extra editions of the papers telling of the closing of more banks all over the country.

It can be truly said that the nation responded to the ringing utterance of the inaugural address. Congress was prepared to go along in an extraordinary effort. Partisanship sank to its smallest dimensions. Everywhere the new President was hailed with unprecedented applause. In spots the acclaim rose to almost hysterical strains. Rabbi Rosenblum said we see in him a God-like messenger, the darling of destiny, the Messiah of America's tomorrow. Next morning the New York *Times* carried only a single front-page story that had no connection with the inauguration. It had to do with another of those Messiahs of tomorrow. The headline read:

VICTORY FOR HITLER
EXPECTED TODAY
Repression of Opponents Makes
Election Triumph Inevitable

CHAPTER 2: THE HUNDRED DAYS

The festival of the inauguration was but the opening scene. The inaugural address was merely a prologue uttered before the curtain rose upon the stirring drama of the Hundred Days.

The President summoned the new Congress in extraordinary session. He issued an order closing all the banks. Most of them were already closed by state action or by the forces of nature. Congress convened March 9. Then began that hectic and tumultuous hurricane of laws and projects and orders in council which came to be known as the Hundred Days.

Washington was now full of Great Minds and Deep Thinkers—youthful pundits from Harvard and Yale and Princeton and especially Columbia, with charts and equations; cornfield philosophers from Kansas and California and, of course, the unconquerable champions of all the money theories, including free silver, paper money and inflation. There were the advocates of the 30-hour week and of every variety of plan for liberating the poor from their poverty and the rich from their riches. A curious arrangement of Fate set the President up in these first hectic moments as the savior of the rich and the protagonists of sound money from their ancient enemies, so that almost the first chants of gratitude went up from the people who least expected these favors. He spiked the 30-hour law and circumnavigated the inflationist printing-press money crowd. Besides, the public beheld the spectacle of a succession of imperious messages from the President to a Congress made dizzy by the swiftness and variety and novelty of the demands. On March 9, the President called on Congress for legislation to control the opening of the banks and confirm all that he had done. The bill was not ready. But the swift-moving processes of legislation could not wait in this new order for a bill to be prepared. A folded newspaper was tossed into the hopper to serve as a bill until the document could be completed.[1] The bill was then sent to Congress by the President. Congress passed it instantly and gave the President full powers over foreign exchange.

Next day he sent a message in curt and imperious words demanding economy. "For three long years," he said, "the federal government has been on the road toward bankruptcy. For the fiscal year 1931 the deficit was $462,000,000 ... For the fiscal year 1932 it was $2,472,000,000 ... For the fiscal year 1933 it will probably exceed $1,200,000,000 ... For the fiscal year 1934 based on appropriation bills passed by the last Congress and estimated revenues, the deficit will probably exceed $1,000,000,000 unless immediate action is taken." Then he warned: "Too often ... liberal governments have been wrecked on the rocks of loose fiscal policy. We must avoid this danger."

Here at last was the man to put an end to the deficits. Roosevelt declared these deficits had contributed to the banking collapse, had deepened the stagnation in our economic life, added to the ranks of the unemployed. He declared "the credit of the national government is imperiled." And then he asserted, *"The first step is to save it. Recovery depends on that."* The first step was a measure to cut government payroll expenditures 25 per cent. The second step, incredible as it may sound, was to authorize a bill providing in effect for the biggest deficit of all—$3,300,000,000.

March 13, he called on Congress to repeal the Volstead Act. And before the month was out Congress authorized 3.2 per cent beer. Soon the old bars would be open again, slightly disguised under a variety of names and awaiting the arrival of the great day when the Eighteenth Amendment would be repealed.

Then came a parade of tremendous measures. On March 16, the President sent a message calling for the passage of the Agricultural Adjustment Act embodying that amazing farm program which put the name of Henry Wallace in lights and sent so many little pigs to their doom. In a week, Roosevelt summoned the Congress to set up his pet project, the Civilian Conservation Corps (CCC) which in his acceptance speech he had declared was his method of ending the depression—to put a million boys in the forests at a dollar a day. Next came the plan for the Federal Emergency Relief Administration which in the fullness of time would become the Works Progress Administration (WPA) and would introduce to the American people Harry Hopkins, who would become Roosevelt's alter ego and, next to Henry Wallace, the most controversial figure of the regime. Then began a consolidation of agencies in the interest of the Goddess Economy; next the Tennessee Valley Authority (TVA) which was the beginning of a great government power program and brought George Norris and Bob LaFollette and all the old Progressives with their plaudits and offerings to the foot of the throne.

Still the reforms, the projects, the adventures in social reconstruction followed "treading on each other's heels, so fast they came"—bills to supervise the traffic in investment securities, to prevent the foreclosure of farm mortgages, with one to save the owners of city homes from the mortgage incubus, bills to regulate the railroads, bills for federal action in the oil industry.

Meantime committees were in session investigating the crimes of the past—the sins of big business, of the bankers, the railroads, of Wall Street and of the power barons. Washington had become a headline-writer's paradise.

Then came the great *chef d'oeuvre* out of the mills of the gods. That was the National Recovery Act—the NRA. It was rushed through Congress with something more of opposition than had yet appeared. Few had even the foggiest idea what it was, save that it was the Great Charter of Free Business and also the Great Charter of Labor. It was the first of many Great Charters that would come piping hot out of Washington. The summer was at hand—the Washington summer plus the New Deal heat. The country was nearly saved. Only a few more touches remained. There was the bill to buy silver to please the silver people, to repeal the gold clause to please the radicals, to issue federal reserve notes to please the inflationists and a safety clause that left all this in suspended animation at the will of the President to please the conservatives.

By June 16, the program was complete. The banks were open. Business was moving back into activity. The President was kept busy signing bills and presenting the pens used to the proud Congressional sponsors—often using half a dozen pens on a single bill to satisfy all its champions. The President announced the appointment of General Hugh Johnson—a new name to most people—as head of the NRA. He allotted $238,000,000 for building war vessels and another $400,000,000 for state roads. He sent a letter to Congress, now exhausted from its great labors, thanking it for its cooperation and wishing it a happy holiday. Congress adjourned, Roosevelt took a train for Boston where he went aboard a small sailing craft, the *Amberjack II*, in which, with two of his sons, he sailed as skipper to his old boyhood summer home at Campobello on June 28.

The country was breathless. The prevailing mood of the nation was one of good humor. The Stock Exchange had been reopened on March 15 and now the market was moving up. A new batch of optimists was talking about the coming Roosevelt boom. Roosevelt was calling everybody by their first names. People were saying: "What a man!" The country began to have some good-natured fun with the

Brain Trust. Some said the Century of the Professors had arrived. Debutantes were going to lectures on the quantitative theory of money. The book stores were displaying books on the business cycle. The White House reporters were grouped several times a week in simple ignorance around the President's desk, his walls covered with charts and tables, while he gave them lectures on economic theory. The whole nation sat several evenings around their radios to hear the golden voice of the Leader explain to them in simple terms the meaning of all the great measures he was driving through Congress. Jim Farley sat in the Post Office Department where the faithful beat a path to his desk and where he juggled the problem of deciding which Democrat would get a job and which nine Democrats would not. But Congress and the President were solving that problem for him by creating bureaus by the dozen and jobs by the scores of thousands. The hotels, the cocktail lounges and the halls of all the public buildings were crowded with exuberant people.

Praise for the President came from every quarter as the country settled down to the happiest summer it had had in some years. There were, of course, a few discordant voices and a few captious critics. Roosevelt had been compared to Moses. But, murmured the critics, "Will it take him 40 years to lead us out of the wilderness?" They said he was sending his young CCC boys "into the forests to get us out of the woods." Others called his new order "government by ballyhoo." William Green denounced the CCC as a plan to put men to work at a dollar a day. The Anti-Saloon League was bitter. It carped that liquor was being brought back merely to tax and that before we were done we would revive narcotics, lotteries and the fast houses to solve the deficits.

But generally the sounds that rose up out of the country were paeans of praise, and from nowhere so ardent as from business. At the United States Chamber of Commerce dinner on May 13, H. I. Harriman, its president, said

> "Never in the history of this nation has any government more courageously and fully attempted to deal with so many and such far-reaching problems."[2]

The diners rose and cheered this statement to the echo. The Republican Philadelphia *Inquirer* said: "The President—yes the President—has indeed assumed the leadership of the world." A leading manufacturers' journal said: "One morning we will wake up and find the depression gone." Several meetings were held to celebrate its departure. The *Literary Digest* said on June 10 that the industrial revival was being hailed. The *Wall Street Journal* said: "No congressional session in history has performed works which so completely defy all efforts to estimate their effects in advance." On June 18, 1933, the New York *Times* said editorially:

> "The President seized upon a wonderful opportunity in a way that was at once sagacious and dynamic. With insistent determination and great boldness he sought to render the very emergency of the nation, the wreck of business and the fears for the future, the means of establishing his authority and leading both Congress and the country into a more hopeful and resolute temper. In a true sense the public disaster was transmuted into an official triumph for him. But that was because he appeared to the American people to be riding the whirlwind and directing the storm. The country was ready and even anxious to accept new leadership. From President Roosevelt it got a rapid succession of courageous speeches and effort and achievement which inclined multitudes of his fellow citizens to acclaim him as the Heaven-sent man of the hour."

With the President and Congress gone out of Washington the country settled down to acquaint itself with and accommodate itself to the new order of things. As for the President, he was at the pastime he loved best—sailing around our northern coast in a small one-sail vessel as its skipper. Congress had gone home and was out of his way. It had put vast powers into his hands and had put a fabulous sum of money—$3,300,000,000—in addition to all the other specific appropriations for government, into his hands to be spent at his sweet will in any way he desired. The great purse—which is the greatest of all the weapons in the hands of a free parliament to oppose the extravagances of a headstrong executive—had been handed over to him. The "spendthrift" Hoover was in California at his Palo Alto home putting his own affairs in order, while the great Economizer who had denounced Hoover's deficits had now produced in 100 days a deficit larger than Hoover had produced in two years.

Presently all the many forces he had set in motion would be at work. We have seen the new President and his program as it appeared to the people of the country at that time. We must now have a nearer view of this New Deal in action.

Chapter 3: The Banking Crisis

We must return now for a brief space to the two months preceding Mr. Roosevelt's inauguration and to the rising crisis hurried along by the events in the banking world. All through January, as the inauguration came into view, the newspapers chronicled daily the banking failures. Depositors were taking their money out of their own banks. Foreign depositors were withdrawing their balances here, which set in motion an increased flow of gold out of the country. Many large investors were turning their security holdings into cash and this into gold to ship abroad. The fears accumulated; the tension mounted. Then came the crash of the two great banking systems of Detroit and Governor Comstock's declaration of a bank holiday closing all the banks in the state. This sent a tremor through the country.

The next day—February 15, 1933—Mr. Roosevelt, who had been enjoying a vacation aboard Vincent Astor's yacht *Nourmahal* arrived at Miami. As he appeared before the crowd in his automobile, the shot was fired at him that struck Mayor Cermak. This miraculous deliverance came like a benediction upon Roosevelt's unscathed head and illuminated his rising fame with a new brilliance. The next day he was in New York. On the night of February 18, the Inner Circle—an organization of New York City political reporters—was staging its annual banquet and show in the grand ballroom of the Astor Hotel. Every prominent politician in New York State attends this famous spectacle at which the political writers stage burlesque skits about New York politicos. After midnight, i.e. the morning of February 19, and while the stage show was still in progress, Roosevelt, then being President-elect, arrived at the dinner with a large party. He took his seat of honor at the center of the head table. Raymond Moley, then his closest adviser, sat opposite him. The newspaper actors on the stage were going through some particularly hilarious farce and the audience was in uproarious good humor. At this moment Roosevelt signaled to Moley and passed a slip of paper to him under the table. Moley read it. To his amazement it was from the President of the United States, Herbert Hoover, and in his own handwriting.[3] Amidst the rising merriment Moley read with dismay:

> "A most critical situation has arisen in the country of which I feel it my duty to advise you confidentially."

Moley looked toward Roosevelt. His head was thrown back in a roar of laughter at the show. Then Moley read on. Hoover pointed out with complete realism the threat to the whole national banking structure, the flight of gold from the country, the rush of cash from the banks into hiding. Fear, he said, had taken possession of the public mind. Hoover believed, rightly, that a new element had entered the situation—the appearance of terror. The air was full of rumors of inflation and of going off the gold standard. This was leading to the withdrawal of gold from the banks. Hoover enumerated the forces that were causing the trouble:

> "The breakdown in balancing the budget by the House; the proposals for inflation of the currency and the widespread discussion of it; the publication of the RFC loans (to banks) and the bank runs, hoarding and bank failures from this cause and various other events and rumors."

These, he said "had now culminated in a state of alarm which is rapidly reaching the proportions of a crisis."

Hoover believed that Roosevelt should now enter the situation. He proposed that Roosevelt issue some sort of statement to "clarify the public mind." After all, though Hoover was still President, his power to do anything effective was gone. He would be out of the White House in two weeks. A hostile House was in session in Washington. A majority of the people had repudiated his leadership. He could do nothing, and nothing he could say would have any effect now. He appealed to Roosevelt: "It is obvious that as you will shortly be in a position to make whatever policies you wish effective, you are the only one who can give these assurances." Mr. Roosevelt was in a position—the only one who was—to calm the public mind, to make some move or gesture that would encourage confidence and check the rising currents of terror.

When he finished reading, Moley realized that "the breaking point had come." He looked again at Roosevelt, who was in full laughter, bantering with those beside him and autographing programs. When the dinner ended, Roosevelt with his entourage went back to his 65th Street town home. There he seemed completely unmoved by the grave picture Hoover had painted for him—"of," as Moley describes it, "the bony hand of death stretched out over every bank in the country."

Roosevelt's answer to this solemn challenge is as singular an incident as appears in his career. One cannot understand it without at least a look at his whole attitude toward the banking problem. It was then and I am sure still is, a widely held view that Mr. Roosevelt had a plan for dealing with this problem, that he arrived for his inauguration with that plan fully matured. He promptly closed the banks and in a few days opened them and gave to the country a soundly reorganized banking system. It is not easy to rid the popular mind of so deeply rooted an assumption. But let us at least have a look behind the scenes at what was happening which the public eye never beheld. The situation on that fateful February 19, when Moley read Hoover's letter amidst the shouts and laughter of the Inner Circle banquet, certainly called for action. Yet, whatever a generous public may think, it is a fact that the men around Mr. Roosevelt believed that he did not take the banking crisis seriously.

It must be remembered that Mr. Roosevelt had been governor of New York for four years, from 1928 to 1932; that the banking crisis was developing in that state during that time; that many of the worst banking scandals blossomed in the state banks under the jurisdiction of the governor. Senator Hastings of New York State wrote him early in his administration urging him to take some action to check stock market speculation and got no answer. After failure of the City Trust Company, Lieutenant-Governor Herbert Lehman, in Roosevelt's absence, appointed Robert Moses to investigate the banking situation. Moses made his inquiry and denounced the practices of some of the banks. In his report he mentioned the practices of the Bank of the United States. About the same time I wrote in my column an appeal to the governor to do something about these shaky banks. Governor Roosevelt named a commission to do this and, to my horror, appointed a director and counsel of the Bank of the

United States on the commission. Norman Thomas denounced him, charging "that he had completely disregarded the Moses report and solemnly concluded everything would be all right if everybody put his money in a sound bank." His action made it quite clear that the governor had not the slightest understanding of the banking situation. It was a good deal like appointing one of Al Capone's mob to make a study of the gangster problem. Very soon thereafter the Bank of the United States failed. But the governor still remained uninterested. Various appeals were made for some sort of action directly to the governor but he did nothing.

What was the explanation of this peculiar lack of alarm in the face of this serious threat? Later, as it grew more menacing, he remained silent. The Democratic platform made only an oblique reference to it. In his speech of acceptance of the nomination he talked about all sorts of problems, including the woes of Puerto Rico, but never mentioned the banks. In his discussion of the Democratic platform in his first radio address he ignored the banking question. He delivered a group of addresses on various specific problems—agriculture, labor, foreign policy—but none on the growing banking issue. He mentioned the subject only casually in one of these addresses.

After his election when the fatalities among the banks became critical, he remained quite unmoved by it. There can be no doubt about this. Ray Moley, who was at his side through these days, has written that between February 18, when he got Hoover's ominous warning, and March 1, *he could not discover how seriously Roosevelt was impressed with the seriousness of the crisis.*

With this in mind, let us return to the alarming letter which Hoover sent to Roosevelt. Hoover wrote that letter on February 17. He sent it by a Secret Service messenger who put it directly in Roosevelt's hands on February 18. It was the morning of February 19 that Roosevelt went over to the Inner Circle dinner. And all that day he never showed it to anyone. He did not hand it to Moley until hours after he got it. *Twelve days later Hoover had not yet received even an acknowledgment of the letter.* Then, on March 1, he got Roosevelt's reply with this curious explanation. Roosevelt said he had written an answer over a week before but through some oversight of his secretary it had not been sent. When he did reply, twelve days later, he indicated there was nothing he could do.

On March 2, Roosevelt arrived in Washington, as Moley described him, in the gayest possible humor, as fresh as a daisy, while Hoover, still President, his aides and Roosevelt's aides, Woodin, Moley and others were in a state of almost complete exhaustion over their long day and night conferences to meet the crisis.

There must be some explanation of this. And the explanation is simple, as we shall see. Hoover was struggling to save as many banks as possible. Every day the crisis was allowed to run meant the closing of more banks, the flight of more gold, the loss of more tens of millions and hundreds of millions in savings, in values, in business losses. But Hoover was powerless to do anything effective without the concurrence of the new President because he lacked powers to act alone and he would have to get the powers from Congress, or at least an assurance that Congress would validate his assumption of powers. Roosevelt had no wish to stem the panic. The onrushing tide of disaster was sweeping the slate clean for him—at the cost of billions to investors and depositors. The greater the catastrophe in which Hoover went out of power the greater would be the acclaim when Roosevelt assumed power. When, therefore, he read Hoover's letter on February 18, he did nothing because the crisis which Hoover described was what he wanted. When he passed the letter under the table to Moley and when Moley, terrified by the import of the letter, was amazed to see Roosevelt in high glee, he explained it as a bit of showmanship by Roosevelt to conceal from the diners any alarm he might feel. But the real reason was that Roosevelt felt no terror at the news. The letter indicated to him that everything was going as he wished it. And from that day forward, as those around him at the time have testified, he showed not the least concern about doing anything to arrest the onset of the panic. What he wanted was a complete crash. He wished for the panic to sweep on to a total banking disaster. He wished for the public to see his predecessor go out in a scene of utter ruin, thus setting the stage for him to step upon it as the savior who would rebuild from the very bottom.

For this drastic decision there could be, of course, but one excuse, namely that Mr. Roosevelt had a definite plan and that such a plan could be better carried out with a full disaster. What, then, was his plan? We shall see presently.[4]

President Hoover was prepared to act. He had a definite plan. But we must remember that the Congress was Democratic and any plan would require the use of extraordinary powers which would call for Congressional approval. He saw that there was before the country the general problem of the depression, which called for a number of techniques and for time. But within this problem was the banking crisis, which was desperate and had to be dealt with instantly. Roosevelt and Hoover might differ on the means of ending the depression, but it ought to be a simpler matter to agree on a means of stemming the banking crisis which was carrying down good banks as well as bad.

At the beginning of February, Hoover proposed to the Federal Reserve Board that every bank in the country should be closed for just one day. Each bank would then submit a statement of its assets and liabilities. It would list its live assets and its dying or dead assets separately. The Federal Reserve would accept the banks' own statement. The next day all solvent banks would be opened and the government would declare them to be solvent and would guarantee that solvency during the crisis. That would stop the runs. As to the banks with large amounts of inactive assets, the live assets would be separated from the inactive ones. The banks would be reopened, each depositor getting a deposit account in proportion to his share of the active assets. The inactive assets would then be taken over to be liquidated in the interest of the depositors. This was an obviously sound and fair solution. Had it been done countless millions in deposits would have been saved and the banking crisis at least would have been removed from the picture. However, the Attorney-General ruled that the President did not possess the power to issue such an order unless he could have the assurance of Congress that it would confirm his action by an appropriate resolution, and that this, as a matter of political necessity, would have to be approved by the new President who would take office in a month. It was some such plan as this which Hoover had in mind when he wrote Roosevelt on February 17. It had one defect from Roosevelt's point of view. It would not do to allow Hoover to be the instrument of stemming the banking crisis before Roosevelt could do it.

However, Hoover took the view that, as the ultimate responsibility would fall upon Roosevelt, although Roosevelt was without power to act being still a private citizen, he, Hoover, would issue any orders Roosevelt would approve, provided he could do so in conscience and Roosevelt could assure approval by Congress.

But Roosevelt did not answer that letter of February 17 and meantime the crisis had assumed a terrifying aspect. To this was added the fear of inflation and of irresponsible and even radical measures by the new President. One of these, of course, was the agitation which went on behind the scenes for the nationalization of the whole banking system. Men close to the President-elect were known to be for this. The printing-press champions of various kinds of fiat currency had been ardent supporters of Roosevelt. Carter Glass had been weighing Roosevelt's offer of the Treasury portfolio and it was understood that he was trying to get some assurance of a sound money policy. On January 21, he refused the appointment because, it was understood, he feared Roosevelt's inflationary tendencies. On January 31, Henry Wallace said: "The smart thing to do would be to go off the gold standard a little farther than England has done." Conservative newspapers attacked this in varying degrees of disapproval. Bernard Baruch three weeks before the inauguration said: "I regard the condition of the country the most serious in its history. The mere talk of inflation retards business. If you start talking about that you would not have a nickel's worth of gold in the Reserve System the day after tomorrow." By February 19, gold withdrawals from banks increased from five to fifteen million dollars a day. In two weeks $114,000,000 of gold was taken from banks for export and another $150,000,000 was withdrawn to go into hiding. The infection of fear was everywhere. Factories were closing. Unemployment was rising rapidly. Bank closings multiplied daily.

At this point Mr. Roosevelt announced the selection of William Woodin to be his Secretary of the Treasury. Ogden Mills, Hoover's Secretary of the Treasury, got in touch with Woodin at once. And then began that succession of conferences in which Hoover tried to arrest the march toward catastrophe and Roosevelt sought to checkmate him.

The public knew little or nothing of what was going on behind the Treasury and White House doors. The whole story has not before been fully told. Hoover sent for Atlee Pomerene, a distinguished Democrat who was then head of the Reconstruction Finance

Corporation. He begged Pomerene to urge Roosevelt to join him in some action. Pomerene felt he had no influence with the President-elect. Next day Ogden Mills appealed to Woodin to issue a statement that would set at rest the fears of inflation and stop the rush of gold from the banks. Woodin refused. Mils reminded him that in a similar though less grave emergency, Grover Cleveland, eight days before he was inaugurated, had issued a reassuring statement.

It was now dawning on Hoover that he and Roosevelt were talking about two different things. Hoover was talking about saving the banks and the people's savings in them. Roosevelt was thinking of the political advantage in a complete banking disaster under Hoover. Actually, on February 25, Hoover received a message from James Rand that Rexford Tugwell had said that the *banks would collapse in a couple of days and that is what they wanted.*

On February 26, Mills was informed that Woodin would be in Washington next day but was instructed to take no part in dealing with the banking crisis, as the new administration intended "to take over at the lowest point possible," to see the tidal wave rush over the body of Hoover and the Republican party no matter what it cost the unfortunate millions whose bank accounts were melting away in the process. It is now easy to see why up to this point—February 28—Hoover had received not even an acknowledgment of the letter he had written Roosevelt. He therefore wrote Roosevelt again, saying that Congress should be called at once and that he and his colleagues stood ready to cooperate in any way to save the situation until Roosevelt should himself be in power. It was then he received from Roosevelt his incredible explanation that he had answered Hoover and that his answer had inadvertently not been sent. That same day Ogden Mills reported to Hoover that he had just learned that the men around Roosevelt believed that the worse the situation got the more evident to the country would be the failure of the Republican party. "In other words," Mills said, "they do not wish to check the panic."

It was now March 2. Roosevelt arrived this day in Washington accompanied by his family and the Brain Trust. He took up quarters at the Mayflower Hotel. Hoover now believed that the banks which had not gone under were sufficiently strong to survive *if the withdrawal of currency and the flight of gold could be stopped.* He instructed

Mills to draw a proclamation stopping both. Mills took the proclamation to Woodin in the morning. But Roosevelt refused to issue a statement approving it and without that Hoover correctly felt he could not act. A repudiation of his action by the new Democratic Congress would have produced endless chaos. Mills told Hoover that Woodin seemed very much broken up. Woodin was in no sense a radical, and his position at that moment must have been extremely trying. Mills told him American history afforded no such instance of a refusal to cooperate in the presence of a great national emergency. Twenty-one states had now closed their banks. Over two hundred million dollars of gold had been taken out of the banks.

The night of March 2, Hoover urged Roosevelt to approve his plan for stopping gold and currency withdrawals. Roosevelt summoned the Democratic congressional leaders. And while Washington hotels were filling with the gay Democratic hosts, the rival conferences in the Mayflower and the White House were in session. After long hours of discussion the Congressional leaders agreed with Roosevelt to do nothing. There is a little disagreement on history here. Moley says they sent word to the White House that Hoover was free to act as he thought best. Hoover says the message was that Roosevelt refused to issue a statement approving his act.

The following day the situation grew worse. New York and Chicago banks were forced to pay out $110,000,000 in gold to foreigners and $20,000,000 to others, while another $20,000,000 was drained away from the interior banks. At this point the panic spread to the Federal Reserve Board officials. Bankers in New York and Chicago had been in practically continuous session. Fatigue had done its work. Panic spread amongst them. Reserve officials demanded a proclamation closing the banks, but Hoover refused unless Roosevelt agreed to back him up. Washington streets were now gay with the arrival of the marching clubs behind their bands. The decorations were going into place. At Farley's hotel the politicians were crowding with little thought of the banking crisis. They were after the jobs. Rumors of all sorts flew around. None knew, of course, what was going on among the sleepless men in the White House, the Treasury, the Reserve board and the Mayflower—Hoover and his aides getting reports from all over the country as they sought for means to hold back the crisis; Roosevelt and his aides equally bent on promoting it by evading action while the black tide rolled over the nation's banks.

Then in the afternoon these two men—Hoover and Roosevelt—were to meet face to face. On the eve of an inauguration, the President-elect, according to tradition, makes a courtesy call on the President. In the afternoon of March 3, Mr. Roosevelt went to the White House. Hoover decided to use the opportunity to make one last appeal to Roosevelt. He renewed his pleas for approval of a proclamation stopping gold and currency withdrawals. Roosevelt replied that the late Thomas Walsh, his Attorney-General designate, had advised it could be done. But Walsh was dead and Homer Cummings, who would be Attorney-General, had not yet reported on it. Roosevelt thought Hoover could act legally, but *he was not sure* and this was as far as he could go. Roosevelt left Hoover at 5 P.M., saying: "I shall be waiting at my hotel, Mr. President, to learn what you decide."

That night Roosevelt's quarters in the Mayflower were filled with callers. At 11:30 the telephone rang. It was Hoover. He told Roosevelt he was still willing, with his consent, to issue the proclamation against hoardings and withdrawals. He asked Roosevelt if he agreed with him there should be no closings. Roosevelt answered: Senator Glass is here. He does not think it is necessary to close the banks—my own opinion is that the governors of the states can take care of closings wherever necessary. I prefer that you issue no proclamation of this nature. There the conversation ended. Roosevelt then told Glass that the Federal Reserve Board had urged Hoover to close the banks, that Hoover had refused saying most of the banks still open were solvent, and that he told Hoover Senator Glass agreed with him. Then Glass asked Roosevelt what he was going to do. To Glass' amazement, he answered: "I am planning to close them, of course." Glass asked him what his authority was and he replied: "The Enemy Trading Act"—the very act Hoover had referred to and on which Roosevelt had said he had no advice from Cummings as to its validity. Glass protested such an act would be unconstitutional and told him so in heated terms. "Nevertheless," replied Roosevelt, "I'm going to issue a proclamation to close the banks."

After this Moley and Woodin went to the Treasury where they found Mills, Ballantine, Awalt and Eugene Meyer hanging over banking figures. They had been calling up governors urging them to declare holidays. They were agreed that when morning came all over the country there would be crowds of frightened depositors in front of their banks. And so it turned out. Thus the negotiations ended. By noon next day the responsibility would be out of Hoover's hands and in Roosevelt's. And he would have what he had been striving for—a total blackout of banking in the United States.

After delivering his inaugural address, Roosevelt issued a proclamation closing all banks. *The next problem was to open them.* It was assumed by everybody who watched these proceedings that Roosevelt had a plan of his own which he was keeping secret. The strangest feature of this whole comedy-drama is now to come. Having closed the banks, *Roosevelt had not the faintest notion how they were to be reopened. He had not the slightest plan of any kind in his mind. He had not even given the matter a thought.* This, I know, is difficult to believe. Yet it is true, as we shall now see.

By March 4, Roosevelt had decided on three things: (1) He would summon Congress in extra session. (2) He would declare an emergency under the Trading with the Enemy Act, having what Hoover did not have—a friendly Congress that would confirm his act. (3) He would summon the leading bankers to Washington. Congress was called to meet on the 9th. And Will Woodin assured Roosevelt he would have legislation dealing with the banking situation in time.

On Sunday, Moley and the new Attorney-General, Homer Cummings, worked on an emergency proclamation. This invoked the powers granted the President under the Trading with the Enemy Act passed in the First World War. It declared the four days from March 6 to March 9 a bank holiday, forbidding all banks to pay out either gold or currency but providing that the President might in that time permit any or all banks to carry on such transactions as they deemed proper. *In preparing this document, the draft already prepared by Mills and Ballantine for President Hoover was used.* It was issued on Monday, March 6. It was a clearly unconstitutional act but justified by the emergency provided Congressional confirmation could be quickly received and for this confirmation Roosevelt asked, though he had refused to tell Hoover he would do so.

Congress was summoned to meet on Thursday, March 9, and meantime a group of bankers was called in to confer on a plan for reopening the closed banks. While Roosevelt, Moley and Cummings worked in the White House over the proclamation, the bankers met with Woodin and later Moley in the Treasury. There were Melvin Traylor of Chicago, G. W. Davison and George Harrison of New York, Eugene Meyer, Miller of Richmond, Berle, Glass, Congressman Steagall, Adolph Miller, and Ogden Mills and Arthur Ballantine, Secretary and Under-Secretary of the Treasury under Hoover who remained over to help.

The problem before them was how to reopen the banks. They argued all day Sunday. But no program was presented either by the bankers or the administration. Moley reported to Roosevelt at night that the talk had been "absolutely desultory." A sub-committee was named to work at night on plans. Both Moley, representing Roosevelt, and Ogden Mills, representing Hoover, agree that there was no plan, so that the statement I have made that Roosevelt when he closed the banks had no idea how to open them is confirmed.

On Monday, the 6th, various plans were brought forward. The problem could be stated simply. Many banks were absolutely sound. Many others—most others, in fact—were sound but they had been subjected to such excited runs that they were without ready currency to do business and might well be subjected to further runs. There were a number of banks which were unsound, did not have assets to cover 100 per cent of their liabilities and could not be safely opened.

Next, as almost all banks had suffered heavy withdrawals of currency, what would they use for money when they reopened? The problem was to get the currency and gold hoarders to return their hoarded dollars. But in the meantime, how would the banks be provided with fresh supplies of currency? Various suggestions were offered. Some urged the issuance of scrip, as had been used in former bank emergencies. Others were for issuing currency against the live assets of banks. There were proposals to convert Federal Reserve banks into banks of deposit, to guarantee the deposits in banks and to nationalize the banks. Ogden Mills reported in great distress to Hoover that the administration had actually come forward with a proposal *to print 20 billion dollars in currency and redeem the outstanding national debt.* But Mills said that no two men at the conference agreed. Moley says that frayed tempers produced angry exchanges between the New Dealers themselves and that Berle hotly declared that no man at the conference made any sense but Ogden Mills.

Meantime Moley and Woodin met alone and agreed on certain fundamental ideas. They decided that the action must be swift and staccato for its dramatic effect; that the plan, whatever it might be, *must be a conservative one, stressing conventional banking methods and that all left-wing Presidential advisers must be blacked out during the crisis;* and finally that the President must make almost at the same time a *tremendous gesture in the direction of economy.* They felt that Hoover had been looked upon as an expensive President and that people must feel they now had a President who was neither radical nor extravagant.

The following day, March 7, the group agreed on a plan. Ogden Mills said he didn't particularly like it but that it was so much better than the things they escaped from that he would go along. Actually in drafting the bill the group had to depend on Hoover's Secretary and Under-Secretary of the Treasury "whose superb technical assistance," says Moley, made the task possible.

The chief point of disagreement had been on the method of creating fresh supplies of currency. On the night of the 6th, the consensus of opinion had been they must use scrip, which would have served well enough. However, the plan finally adopted came from William Woodin—namely to get authority from Congress to issue fresh supplies of Federal Reserve notes instead of scrip. They would look like money. They would actually be money. They would create less suspicion and resistance. The manner in which he came by this idea must not be overlooked.

Woodin told Moley he sat in his room, played on his guitar a little while, then read a little while, then slept a little while, then played on his guitar a little while again, read some more and slept some more and then thought about the scrip thing and then, by gum! he hit on the idea of Federal Reserve notes and wondered why he hadn't thought of it before. Moley and Woodin rushed over to Roosevelt with the plan, told him about it in twenty minutes; Roosevelt was enthusiastic and so it was adopted.

Actually it was not so simple as that. Ogden Mills, who was one of the two or three men at the conference who knew what it was all about, said that as the discussions proceeded the big bankers came more and more into the ascendency and that in the end G. W. Davison, George Harrison, and Leffingwell and Gilbert of Morgan and Company, were chiefly responsible and that it was a bankers' plan.

The new Congress met at noon Thursday. Roosevelt's message was read and the bill introduced. This was the bill that was represented by a newspaper, as there had yet been no time to make copies. No one but the Congressional leaders had seen it and it was passed in an hour. A few hours later the Senate passed it. Briefly, it validated the things Roosevelt had done under the Trading with the Enemy Act, amended that act to give the President new powers over foreign exchange and banking institutions and the foreign and domestic movements of gold and silver, provided for issuance of Federal Reserve notes to banks up to 100 per cent of their holdings of bonds and 90 per cent of their holdings of rediscountable assets, provided for the progressive reopening of the banks by the Treasury and gave power to the Reconstruction Finance Corporation to subscribe to preferred stock of banking associations and make loans secured by preferred stocks.

The next day Roosevelt sent his now famous message to Congress deploring the disastrous extravagance of the Hoover administration, uttering many of those sentences about balancing the budget, the fatalities of government spending, etc., which were to be quoted against him so many times, and calling for powers to reduce salaries and government expenses. As one reads that message now it is difficult to believe that it could ever have been uttered by a man who before he ended his regime would spend not merely more money than President Hoover, but more than all the other 31 Presidents put together—*three times more, in fact, than all the Presidents from George Washington to Herbert Hoover.* This speech was part of the plan Moley and Woodin had devised to sell the banking plan in a single package with the great economy program.

Then on Sunday, March 12, Roosevelt delivered his first fireside chat. He announced he would begin reopening the banks the next day and he made a simple explanation of the steps he had taken. It was a masterpiece of clear, simple, effective exposition. Like the inaugural address, it produced an electric effect upon the people. One feature about that address remains unknown to most people to this day and that is that it was written, not by Roosevelt or any member of his Brain Trust, but by Arthur Ballantine, Under-Secretary of the Treasury under Hoover, who with Ogden Mills, his chief, had remained at the Treasury to help pilot the country through its famous banking crisis.

To the great audience that listened to the fireside chat, the hero of the drama—the man whose genius had led the country safely through the crisis of the banks—was not any of the men who had wrestled with the problem, but the man who went on the radio and told of the plan he did not construct, in a speech he did not write. Thus Fate plays at her age-old game of creating heroes.

The whole episode reveals a side of Mr. Roosevelt's character not fully understood until later. This was the free and easy manner in which he could confront problems about which he knew very little. It would be very unfair to criticize Mr. Roosevelt because he knew so little about banking practice and literally nothing about banking economics. After all, there are many able men of whom this can be said. His experience had not been in this field and it was a subject to which he had given very little attention. This explains his almost total lack of serious interest in the banking situation as it unfolded in New York State while he was governor. But while in fairness we must recognize that his ignorance of banking problems was not a point to be held against him, it is equally clear that he cannot be held up as a great master-mind in finance who took the banking problem into the convolutions of his massive brain and ground out a solution in a few days. His one contribution to the banking negotiations was a purely political one—the decision that it would be better for him politically to let the whole banking situation go to smash than to permit Hoover to check the crisis before he, Roosevelt, could get into the White House. But that was a costly thing for the nation.

When Roosevelt took office there were 19,000 banks in the country, mostly closed, all closed when he issued his decree. By March 16, about 9,883 were reopened fully and 2,678 on a restricted basis. But over 6,000 remained closed, many of which might have been saved in whole or in part if Roosevelt had been willing to open the way for the government to act after the crisis became acute in February.

That vast mercurial animal known as "The People" is indeed unpredictable. But this much we know of them. Once their imagination is captured by a leader he leads a charmed life as long as the spell lasts. In this case Roosevelt was hailed as a magician as he put into effect a plan worked out for him by bankers and announced it over the air in a speech written for him by one of Hoover's own Treasury officials.

In obedience to the program worked out by Woodin and Moley that the banking solution must be followed by a bold assertion of the policy of economy, his first message to Congress called for the passage of the economy act cutting salaries of government employees 25 per cent. Thus at a stroke he put at rest the apprehensions of conservative critics who suspected he might be in the hands of his radical brain-trusters.

CHAPTER 4: THE NEW NEW DEAL

In the beginning, of course, was Roosevelt. And then came the Brain Trust. After that we had the Great Man and the Brain Trust. The casual reader may suppose this is just a catchy collection of syllables. But it is impossible to estimate the power these few words exercised upon the minds of the American people. After all, a crowd of big business boobies, a lot of butter-fingered politicians, two big halls full of shallow and stupid congressmen and senators had made a mess of America. That was the bill of goods sold to the American people. Now amidst the ruins appeared not a mere politician, not a crowd of tradesmen and bankers and congressmen, but a Great Man attended by a Brain Trust to bring understanding first and then order out of chaos.

Actually there are no big men in the sense in which Big Men are sold to the people. There are men who are bigger than others and a few who are wiser and more courageous and farseeing than these. But it is possible with the necessary pageantry and stage tricks to sell a fairly bright fellow to a nation as an authentic BIG Man. Actually this is developing into an art, if not a science. It takes a lot of radio, movie, newspaper and magazine work to do it, but it can be done.

As Roosevelt began to lay out his plans for nomination by the Democratic Convention in 1932, one of his most pliant and faithful henchmen, Sam Rosenman, suggested that he ought to draw upon the universities for his advice rather than upon business men and politicians. Rosenman suggested Raymond Moley, professor of political science at Columbia and Roosevelt thought it an excellent idea. Moley had already served him well while governor and had only recently advised him in the trial of Sheriff Farley, the Tammany chieftain whom Roosevelt removed from office. It was Moley who wrote Roosevelt's opinion in that case with its stirring declaration of a moral standard for public officials. That finely phrased statement of a high, yet perfectly feasible, ethical code caught the fancy of the public and shed upon Roosevelt its reflected glory.

Moley was asked to form a group of experts in various fields of policy. He invited Rexford Tugwell, Lindsay Rogers, Joseph D. McGoldrick, James W. Angell, Adolf Berle and some others. All were Columbia faculty men save Berle. After Roosevelt's nomination some of these had faded away and others were added—General Hugh Johnson, Charles Taussig, who really added himself, and George Peek.

Because at first there were a number of professors in the group that fact was widely exploited. It was supposed to be something quite new, an idea Roosevelt had invented, going to the fountainheads of learning for advice. Of course there was nothing new in it. Every man who runs for President surrounds himself with men who are supposed to be experts in their various fields and often as not they have been professors. Roosevelt did precisely what every candidate does. But newspapermen began to refer to this aggregation of Roosevelt research advisers as the "Brain Trust." The words had in them the clear implication that the group was made up of beings possessing Big Brains. There was in it the suggestion of ponderous cerebral horsepower. Here was a thinking machine into which Roosevelt could throw any problem and watch it pass mercilessly through the cogitative gears to emerge beautifully broken down into all its ultimate components. Here was the Great Brain itself surrounded by all these bulging foreheads handling easily the tough problems that had baffled the feeble intellects of bankers, magnates and politicos. Now in a new sense the real age of reason had come. It was the Age of the Professors.

The term began with an ingredient of sneer in it. Even Louis Howe, Roosevelt's perennial secretary and factotum, would speak to Roosevelt himself contemptuously of "that brain trust of yours." But beyond doubt the term exercised a powerful influence in convincing Americans that men of the highest intellectual caliber were now dealing with the mystery of the farm, of the depression, of labor, of the banks and of the world.

It was this group of men, subjected of course to those inevitable pressures that come from interested elements such as labor, farmers, business and regions, who put together what was called with great effect the New Deal.

Of course the central subject of it all was the great depression. Mr. Roosevelt's own explanation of that was simplicity itself. The depression was due to the Republicans and to Hoover. More specifically they had fostered economic isolation, they had encouraged monopolies, they had throttled competition, they had permitted the manipulation of credit for speculation in securities and commodities and for the swelling of profits at the expense of the common good.

To meet the country's ills, the New Deal made certain pledges, which described how Roosevelt would save the country.

It would relieve the needy—but no doles. The government would prepare a program of useful public works, such as flood control, soil and forest protection and necessary public buildings. But it would immediately put a million men to work in the forests. This alone would provide the necessary employment. Where public works were self-liquidating—that is where they would pay for themselves—they could be financed by bond issues. But where they were not they must be paid for by taxes. Beyond that, the New Deal would seek to shorten the work week and reduce hours of labor to spread employment.

For the farmer the New Deal would encourage cooperatives and enlarge government lending agencies. But the greatest enemy of the farmer was his habit of producing too much. His surplus ruined his prices. The New Deal would contrive means of controlling the surplus and ensuring a profitable price. But it denounced any proposals to have the federal government go into the market to purchase and speculate in farm products in a futile attempt to increase prices or reduce farm surpluses.

As for business the New Deal proposed strict enforcement of the anti-trust laws, full publicity about security offerings, regulation of holding companies which sell securities in interstate commerce, regulation of rates of utility companies operating across state lines and the regulation of the stock and commodity exchanges.

But greatest of all—the New Deal promised economy. The extravagance of the Hoover administration, its yearly deficits—these were at the bottom of all our ills. The New Deal would abolish useless bureaus, reduce salaries, cut federal expenditures 25 per cent. The New Deal would put an end to government borrowing—it would end the deficits. The New Deal would assure a sound currency at all hazards and finally a competitive tariff with a tariff commission free from presidential interference.

There was nothing revolutionary in all this. It was a platform that Woodrow Wilson might have endorsed. It was actually an old-time Democratic platform based upon fairly well-accepted principles of the traditional Democratic party. That party had always denounced the tendency to strong central government, the creation of new bureaus. It had always denounced deficit financing. Its central principle of action was a minimum of government in business. The government might intervene, as in the anti-trust laws, not to manage business or tell business what it should do, but to prevent business from engaging in practices which interfered with the free action of others. It made war upon those who attempted to impose restraints upon commerce. It was always for a competitive tariff, save for the products of the Southern states which needed protection. And it always proclaimed loudly its solicitude for labor and for the "common man." It always attacked Wall Street, the Stock Exchange, the big bankers.

Mr. Roosevelt in his preelection speeches had stressed all these points—observing the rights of the states so far as to urge that relief, old-age pensions and unemployment insurance should be administered by them, that the federal government would merely aid the states with relief funds and serve as collection agent for social insurance. And above all he rang the changes upon the shocking spendings of the Republicans and the mounting public debt. He called Herbert Hoover "the greatest spender in history." He cried out against the Republican party: "It has piled bureau on bureau, commission on commission ... at the expense of the taxpayer." He told the people: "For three long years I have been going up and down this country preaching that government—federal, state and local—costs too much. I shall not stop that preaching." The statement is a curious one, since I can find among his published addresses while he was governor up until the time of his nomination, not one reference to government deficits. And for a good reason, of course, since as governor he took New York State from the hands of Al Smith with a surplus of $15,000,000 and left it with a deficit of $90,000,000. He was against Big Government. "We must eliminate the functions of government ... we must merge, we must consolidate subdivisions of government and, like private citizens, give up luxuries which we can no longer afford."

He repeated this over and over: "I propose to you that government, big and little, be made solvent and that the example be set by the President of the United States and his cabinet." Toward the end of the campaign he cried: "Stop the deficits! Stop the deficits!" Then to impress his listeners with his inflexible purpose to deal with this prodigal monster, he said: "Before any man enters my cabinet he must give me a twofold pledge: Absolute loyalty to the Democratic platform and especially to its economy plank. And complete cooperation with me in looking to economy and reorganization in his department."

This was the New Deal as it was described to the people in the fall of 1932. Practically any Democrat could subscribe to it. The only slightly radical feature was his declaration about government development of water power. But he was merely following the lead of Al Smith and he assured the people that he believed in private ownership and development of water power with the exception of Muscle Shoals and perhaps three others merely to be yardsticks as a means of checking the rates of private companies.

This New Deal was a program for action strictly within the framework of the traditional American system of government, with emphasis on states' rights, opposition to too powerful central government, opposition to BIG government which should be cut down to its proper size, opposition to high taxes, unbalanced budgets, government debts. Where the name New Deal came from I do not know. Stuart Chase had written a book called "A New Deal" some time before in which he outlined a completely different program. Perhaps the name was swiped from this book. But in any case the Roosevelt New Deal was as I have described it. This was what the people voted for in 1932. Now Mr. Roosevelt, in March, 1933, was in the White House. And there he proceeded to set up what he continued to call the New Deal. How much did it resemble the one voted on in November, 1932?

In the first hundred days of his administration, Mr. Roosevelt put into effect a program of very large dimensions. But it was a program built on a wholly different principle from that which was described as the New Deal.

First of all, his central principle—his party's traditional principle of war upon BIG government—was reversed. And he set out to build a government that in size dwarfed the government of Hoover which he denounced.

The idea of a government that was geared to assist the economic system to function freely by policing and preventive interference in its freedom was abandoned for a government which upon an amazing scale undertook to organize every profession, every trade, every craft under its supervision and to deal directly with such details as the volume of production, the prices, the means and methods of distribution of every conceivable product. This was the NRA. It may be that this was a wise experiment but it was certainly the very reverse of the kind of government which Mr. Roosevelt proposed in his New Deal.

Enforcement of the anti-trust act was a long-time pet of his party and it was considered as an essential instrument to prevent cartels and trusts and combinations in restraint of trade which were supposed to be deadly to the system of free enterprise. The New Deal had called loudly for its strict enforcement. Yet almost at once it was suspended—actually put aside during the experiment—in order to cartelize every industry in America on the Italian corporative model.

That deadly thing, the deficit, which, as he had said was at the bottom of all our woes and which stemmed from big government and extravagant government, was not slain as Roosevelt had proposed. Instead it was adopted and fed and fattened until it grew to such proportions that Hoover began to look like a niggard. The theory that relief should be carried on by the states was abandoned. The idea of self-liquidating public works was abandoned and all forms of relief were carried on by public loans, adding to the national debt. The idea of useful public works was abandoned in favor of hurriedly devised "make-work" which was nothing more than a disguised dole.

The "spendthrift" Hoover had increased his expenditures by 50 per cent in four years over the 1927 level. In four years Mr. Roosevelt increased his 300 per cent over the 1927 level and to 100 per cent over Hoover's. Stop the deficits! Stop the deficits! he had cried. Instead of stopping them he ended his first term with a deficit of 15 billion dollars.[5]

I am not here criticizing what Mr. Roosevelt did. I merely want to fix clearly the fact that what he did was the reverse of what he had described as a New Deal.

When the President had declared for a "sound currency at all hazards" he was using a phrase well-known to describe a currency based on gold. Yet one of his earliest acts was to go off the gold standard and to declare later for a managed currency based on the commodity dollar.

Had a candidate opposing Mr. Roosevelt in the campaign declared that he favored that series of policies and projects which Roosevelt launched when he came to power, there is not the slightest doubt that Roosevelt would have covered him with damnation and ridicule. Actually he did denounce Mr. Hoover who, Roosevelt charged, had asked the farmers to plow under every third row of wheat, cotton and corn and he did denounce and ridicule what he described as attempts by the government to go into the market and speculate in commodities in order to raise prices. Yet he not only asked farmers to plow under the crops but he paid them to do so and ended by compelling them to do so in effect, and his agents were in every market place to purchase crops in order to fix prices—not merely in the grain exchanges and cotton exchanges, but in every kind of exchange and market covering every conceivable crop from eggs and poultry to sweet potatoes, peanuts, apples and applesauce.

Why did the President completely reverse his policy after his inauguration? It must be because he felt the things he was urging before election were not adapted to the realities of the case when he came to power. When he was outlining his policies before election he was completely cocksure of his rectitude and wisdom. Yet all those policies and techniques of which he was so absolutely certain he brushed aside as unusable: What became of his announced intention to demand from every cabinet member two pledges: (1) to abide absolutely by the Democratic platform and (2) to cooperate with him in cutting down the expenses of the departments? He began by cutting expenses 25 per cent. But before the ink was dry on that act he had thrown it into the ashcan with a $3,300,000,000 deficit in the NRA act. And no cabinet member expanded the costs of his department more than the President himself expanded the costs of the Presidential budget.

When was Mr. Roosevelt right? When he was making speeches before the election or when he was acting after the election? We need not accuse him of dishonesty either time. We may say in tolerance that he laid down in perfect honesty a policy when he was a candidate and that when he found himself in Hoover's place he found his first New Deal unsuited to the needs of the time. But we cannot say that the thing called the New Deal in 1932 was the same as the thing which he called the New Deal from 1933 to 1936. He pronounced a definite judgment upon the New Deal he presented so gaudily before the election by completely repudiating it when he became President. It was one thing to challenge Hoover and to abuse him. Faced with the demands of power, he had to confess by his course that the policy he had outlined before the election was a mistake. I do not say it was a mistake. Which policy was nearest right is a question yet to be answered.

At the end of the One Hundred Days Mr. Roosevelt was embarked upon a new New Deal. There were happy young men in Washington bureaus who were calling it the Roosevelt Revolution, and soon we would hear that term in wide use. Others began to call it the Second New Deal. And that is precisely what it was—essentially and in detail, save for a few minor matters, a wholly different thing.

Now let us see what became of this Second New Deal of which Mr. Roosevelt was as completely cocksure as he was of the first New Deal which he had now discarded.

Chapter 5: The Rabbits Go Back in the Hat

All that happened in those four years from 1933 to 1936 is now lost behind the fiery curtain of the war. It seems so long ago. Few remember much about it. Out of the blur remains the impression that this Second New Deal must have been quite a success because in 1936 the people turned out en masse to approve it in the greatest electoral victory in our history. Roosevelt carried every state but two—Maine and Vermont—and many commentators said it meant the end of the Republican party.

What actually happened may come as a surprise as it is reviewed. After all, the problem before Mr. Roosevelt was clear. First he had to open the banks and provide some form of relief for the millions who had been so sorely hit by the panic. Next, and of course more important, he had to take measures to set our economic system to work again. This meant setting business in motion, for it is business that provides the jobs. As part of this, there were flaws in our economic system that had to be corrected in the interest first of more efficient production and second in the interest of social justice.

We have seen what happened in reopening the banks and the plans to put men into the forests to relieve unemployment, and to set up a program of public works. But what was done to revive business—for business is merely a name for that vast complexity of farms and mines and factories and stores and power and transportation systems which provide us with our necessities and luxuries while at the same time providing jobs for our people. This economic program included generally the National Recovery Administration and the Agricultural Adjustment Administration—the NRA and the AAA—plus a program of fiscal measures designed to straighten out our enfeebled and disturbed financial mechanisms.

It is, I am sure, difficult to make Americans of the growing generation, to say nothing of their elders, believe the story of that vast hippodrome, that hectic, whirling, dizzy three-ring circus with the NRA in one ring, the AAA in another, the Relief Act in another, with General Johnson, Henry Wallace and Harry Hopkins popping the whips, while all around under the vast tent a whole drove of clowns and dervishes—the Henry Morgenthaus and Huey Longs and Dr. Townsends and Upton Sinclairs and a host of crackpots of every variety—leaped and danced and tumbled about and shouted in a great harlequinade of government, until the tent came tumbling down upon the heads of the cheering audience and the prancing buffoons. I do not exaggerate, I assure you. Let us have a peep at each of the rings and the performers in them.

First, and most important, was the NRA and its dynamic ringmaster, General Hugh Johnson. As I write, of course, Mussolini is an evil memory. But in 1933 he was a towering figure who was supposed to have discovered something worth study and imitation by all world artificers everywhere. Such eminent persons as Dr. Nicholas Murray Butler[6] and Mr. Sol Bloom,[7] head of the Foreign Affairs Committee of the House, assured us he was a great man and had something we might well look into for imitation. What they liked particularly was his corporative system. He organized each trade or industrial group or professional group into a state-supervised trade association. He called it a corporative. These corporatives operated under state supervision and could plan production, quality, prices, distribution, labor standards, etc. The NRA provided that in America each industry should be organized into a federally supervised trade association. It was not called a corporative. It was called a Code Authority. But it was essentially the same thing. These code authorities could regulate production, quantities, qualities, prices, distribution methods, etc., under the supervision of the NRA. This was fascism. The anti-trust laws forbade such organizations. Roosevelt had denounced Hoover for not enforcing these laws sufficiently. Now he suspended them and compelled men to combine.

At its head Roosevelt appointed General Hugh Johnson, a retired Army officer. Johnson, a product of the southwest, was a brilliant, kindly, but explosive and dynamic genius, with a love for writing and a flair for epigram and invective. He was a rough and tumble fighter with an amazing arsenal of profane expletives. He was a lawyer as well as a soldier and had had some business experience with Bernard Baruch. And he was prepared to produce a plan to recreate the farms or the factories or the country or the whole world at the drop of a hat. He went to work with superhuman energy and an almost maniacal zeal to set this new machine going. He summoned the representatives of all the trades to the capital. They came in droves, filling hotels and public buildings and speakeasies. Johnson stalked up and down the corridors of the Commerce Building like a commander-in-chief in the midst of a war.

He began with a blanket code which every business man was summoned to sign—to pay minimum wages and observe the maximum hours of work, to abolish child labor, abjure price increases and put people to work. Every instrument of human exhortation opened fire on business to comply—the press, pulpit, radio, movies. Bands played, men paraded, trucks toured the streets blaring the message through megaphones. Johnson hatched out an amazing bird called the Blue Eagle. Every business concern that signed up got a Blue Eagle, which was the badge of compliance. The President went on the air: "In war in the gloom of night attack," he crooned, "soldiers wear a bright badge to be sure that comrades do not fire on comrades. Those who cooperate in this program must know each other at a glance. That bright badge is the Blue Eagle." "May Almighty God have mercy," cried Johnson, "on anyone who attempts to trifle with that bird." Donald Richberg thanked God that the people understood that the long-awaited revolution was here. The New Dealers sang: "Out of the woods by Christmas!" By August, 35,000 Clevelanders paraded to celebrate the end of the depression. In September a tremendous host paraded in New York City past General Johnson, Mayor O'Brien and Grover Whalen—250,000 in a line which did not end until midnight.

The second phase was to sign up separate industries into the corporative code authorities. Over 700 codes were created. Business men were told to come to Washington and "write their own tickets," as Roosevelt said. They could scarcely believe their ears. Again the conservatives applauded. The Cleveland *Plain Dealer* said: "The blamed thing works." *Dun & Bradstreet* said: "Critical opposition of certain industrialists to NRA procedure is gradually being turned to wholehearted support."

But little by little the spell began to fade. In spite of all the fine words about industrial democracy, people began to see it was a scheme to permit business men to combine to put up prices and keep them up by direct decree or through other devious devices. The consumer began to perceive that he was getting it in the neck. Professor William F. Ogburn of Chicago University resigned as Consumers'

Counsel because he said the job was futile. Bitter slurs were flung at the Blue Eagle as a fascist symbol. A senator called it the "Soviet duck." Silk workers on strike stoned the Blue Eagle in the shop windows. Labor suddenly discovered it was getting mostly fine phrases. A wave of strikes swept the country. A battle for control of NRA between labor and capital broke out. Roosevelt went on the air and pleaded for peace. Farmers were indignant at the rising prices.

But the NRA continued to exhibit its folly in a succession of crazy antics which could proceed only from people who had lost their bearings and their heads. A tailor named Jack Magid in New Jersey was arrested, convicted, fined and sent to jail. The crime was that he had pressed a suit of clothes for 35 cents when the Tailors' Code fixed the price at 40 cents. The price was fixed not by a legislature or Congress but by the tailors. A storm of indignation swept through the country. The name of Jack Magid became for a week as well known as Hugh Johnson's. The judge hastily summoned the tailor from his cell, remitted his sentence and fine and offered to give the offender his own pants to press. The purged tailor proclaimed the NRA a beautiful thing. Each town had its own horrible examples.

The NRA was discovering it could not enforce its rules. Black markets grew up. Only the most violent police methods could procure enforcement. In Sidney Hillman's garment industry the code authority employed enforcement police.[8] They roamed through the garment district like storm troopers. They could enter a man's factory, send him out, line up his employees, subject them to minute interrogation, take over his books on the instant. Night work was forbidden. Flying squadrons of these private coat-and-suit police went through the district at night, battering down doors with axes looking for men who were committing the crime of sewing together a pair of pants at night. But without these harsh methods many code authorities said there could be no compliance because the public was not back of it.

The American people were not yet conditioned to regimentation on such a scale. It could not have been operated successfully on Americans by angels. But few angels were employed. Dr. Charles F. Roos, who was NRA's research director, has written about its staff: "... the political patronage system in vogue in all previous administrations (was raised) to new levels of impudence." He says he once asked Leon Henderson, economic advisor of NRA, for a research economist. Henderson sent him a man through the White House. "The qualifications for economic-statistical analysis," wrote Dr. Roos, "possessed by this applicant were that he had once engaged in detective work." The staff grew at the rate of 100 a day. It started with 60 and soon numbered 6,000, not including the thousands who served the local code authorities. A green doctor of philosophy fresh out of school, appointed at $1800, was getting $4500 in six months. The abler economists knew the whole thing was drifting from error to error. Dr. Roos says: "Some quit. Some stayed and criticized. Some tried to improve it." He adds that a vast amount of mail received indicated that "Mob rule and racketeering had to a considerable degree displaced orderly government."[9]

Feuds broke out everywhere. Johnson and Richberg quarreled. Richberg broke into tears.[10] Senator Borah and Senator Nye denounced the whole institution. Johnson suggested that a committee be named by the President to investigate. The senators agreed. Clarence Darrow was named chairman of the committee by Roosevelt. It held hearings and issued a report[11] in May, 1934, blasting the NRA with a merciless damnation. Some of the words used in the report to castigate it were "harmful, monopolistic, oppressive, grotesque, invasive, fictitious, ghastly, anomalous, preposterous, irresponsible, savage, wolfish, and others." Johnson denounced the report but the judgment had come from a board named by the President with a chairman suggested by Johnson. After that the life began to run out of NRA. Miss Frances Perkins began to fear Johnson wanted to be a dictator. She says she began to wonder what he was about, "whether he understood the democratic process ... and whether he might not be moving by emotion and indirection toward a dangerous pattern."[12]

By this time Johnson was a sick man. He lived at times without sleep. Senator Robert Wagner decided labor was being victimized. Johnson broke with Richberg. Johnson had to go to a hospital. NRA was blowing up, as Miss Perkins said, "from internal combustion." Papers began to say business was just about where it was when the New Deal started. The Chamber of Commerce decided that price control and production control were a mistake.

Johnson tried twice to resign. The President refused. Department heads were at war with each other. Roosevelt forced Johnson to take a vacation and while he was away, set up a board to manage the thing. When Johnson got back Roosevelt told him the board would remain. Johnson quit. Finally the Supreme Court got around to hearing and deciding the Schechter case—the famous "sick chicken" case—which involved the constitutionality of the whole thing. On May 27, 1935, the Supreme Court, to everybody's relief, declared the NRA unconstitutional. It held that Congress at Roosevelt's demand had delegated powers to the President and the NRA which it had no right to delegate—namely the power to make laws. It called the NRA a Congressional abdication. *And the decision was unanimous,* Brandeis, Cardozo and Holmes joining in it.

This brought down on the heads of the justices a bitter denunciation by all the bureaucrats thus suddenly bereft of their unconstitutional jobs. But the verdict can no longer be questioned. Ernest Lindley, who has written three books in defense of the New Deal, wrote in 1936:

> "The NRA Act was the Roosevelt administration's greatest error … From whatever point of view the NRA is approached it would be generally agreed that it attempted to do too much in too short a time. NRA was an administrative failure and it evoked a wide range of unfavorable public reactions."[13]

And Lindley admitted besides that when the Supreme Court decided the Schechter case, *the NRA was already dead.* This is the mildest comment that can be made on it.

Some cabinet advisers thought that with some changes the NRA could be saved. Secretary of Labor Perkins urged Roosevelt to consider this advice. But the President refused and rendered his own decision on the NRA which ought to stand as final. Miss Perkins writes that Roosevelt said to her:

> "You know the whole thing has been a mess. It has been an awful headache. Some of the things they have done are pretty wrong."

He felt business had started up, that it would not go back to its old wage levels and would stick to the 40-hour week:

> "I think perhaps NRA has done all it can. I don't want to impose a system on the country that will set aside the anti-trust laws. I have been talking to other lawyers besides Cummings and *they are pretty certain that the whole process is unconstitutional* and that we have to re-

study and revise our whole program. Perhaps we had better do it now. So let's give the NRA a certain amount of time to liquidate. Have a history of it written and then it will be over." (Italics supplied)[14]

But of course he had imposed it not as a temporary expedient but *as a new order* and he boasted of it. He had done his best to impose the dissolution of the anti-trust laws on the country. And everything Johnson had done *he had done with Roosevelt's full knowledge.*

It would have been impossible to invent a device more cunningly calculated to obstruct the revival of business than this half-baked contrivance which is utterly impossible of administration save in a country like Italy or Germany where obedience can be enforced by a dictator under an absolute government.

2.

There is a kind of little man who will tell you that he can't hit a nail straight with a hammer, but who loves to spread a big country like the United States out before him on top of a table, pull up a chair and sit down to rearrange the whole thing to suit his heart's desire. Through the providence of God this kind of fellow, in a country of practical politicians, does not ordinarily get into a spot where he can play this game. But occasionally one slips through and when Roosevelt was picking his cabinet in 1933 a prize specimen of this species was eased into the Department of Agriculture.

During the campaign, Roosevelt had told the voters they would see no cruel jokes like plowing up cotton or not planting wheat or buying up crops to raise prices, all of which had been urged on farmers. He had a plan, he said, which *would not cost the government a dollar.* Whatever became of that plan we shall never know. Instead Henry Wallace, as mild-mannered a man and mystic as ever knelt on a prayer rug or slit a pig's throat or burned a field of corn, became Secretary of Agriculture and came up with a plan that was supposed to be more effective and more orderly than cinch bugs, boll weevils or dust storms in providing our people with the scarcity that everybody needed.

Curiously enough, while Wallace was paying out hundreds of millions to kill millions of hogs, burn oats, plow under cotton, the Department of Agriculture issued a bulletin telling the nation that the great problem of our time was *our failure to produce enough food to provide the people with a mere subsistence diet.* The Department made up four sample diets. There was a liberal diet, a moderate diet, a minimum diet and finally an emergency diet—below the minimum. And the figures showed that we did not produce enough food for our population for a minimum diet, a mere subsistence.

How to better this may be a problem, but the last course a government run by sane men would adopt to get it solved would be to destroy a good part of what we do produce.

The AAA produced all sorts of dislocations in our economic system. For instance, we had men burning oats when we were importing oats from abroad on a huge scale, killing pigs while increasing our imports of lard, cutting corn production and importing 30 million bushels of corn from abroad.

Wallace himself said: "It is a shocking commentary on our civilization." That was not so. That kind of thing was no part of our civilization. It was, rather, a shocking commentary on the man who engineered it. It was a crime against our civilization to pay farmers in two years $700,000,000 to destroy crops and limit production. It was a shocking thing to see the government pay one big sugar corporation over $1,000,000 not to produce sugar.

Meanwhile, the plight of the sharecroppers, who got nothing out of this, became deplorable and led to a violent schism in the AAA which resulted in the liquidation of their champions.

At all events, the Supreme Court declared the AAA unconstitutional as it did the NRA. However, the administration managed to fix up a fake soil conservation scheme under which it continued to pay farmers for not planting crops upon the fiction that they were saving the soil. The real purpose, of course, was to pay money to the farmers. The war in Europe put an end to the reason for all that by opening up a world-wide market for what we raise and at the same time opening up Uncle Sam's pocketbook to pay the farmers for everything they could raise at however fantastic a price.

3.

Whatever else might be said of the latest New Deal, it was a great show. As each problem presented itself the President stepped up with a "must" bill, a message and, perhaps, a radio talk. Then the reporters would say "he pulled another rabbit out of his hat." A rapidly

extemporized legend sprang up that we need worry about no difficulty—the President could always pull a rabbit out of his hat. The reporters played along with this maker of news. They had to have a
continuous parade of rabbits. The President enjoyed it all hugely and
was always more than anxious to oblige.

As the performance proceeded the President began to exhibit one
of those amiable weaknesses which his immediate entourage looked
upon as one of the delightful aspects of his character. In the first days
of the administration the inflationists in Congress were riding high.
Before the inauguration the Democratic House passed the Golds-
borough bill to inflate the currency until prices returned to the
1921–29 level. After the inauguration the Senate came within a few
votes of passing a free silver bill. However, when the AAA act
reached the Senate, an amendment was offered to it by Senator Elmer Thomas of Oklahoma. This authorized the President (1) to issue
$3,000,000,000 of greenbacks to retire government debts, (2) to ac-
cept silver in payment of war debts up to $100,000,000, (3) to permit
free coinage of silver at a ratio to gold to be fixed by the President,
and (4) to devalue the gold dollar up to 50 per cent. Here was a four-
barreled inflationary bill which packed all the explosive power the
most ardent inflationist could ask. That night a party gathered at the
White House, including Hull, Lewis Douglas, Will Woodin, William Bullitt and Raymond Moley. Quite casually and smilingly the
President dropped the remark that he had agreed to the amendment.
Moley says Douglas and Bullitt were horrified. Hull looked as if he
had been stabbed in the back. Woodin had just heard of it before the
party, but he had not been consulted before the President made the
agreement. Moley says "Hell broke loose" in the White House and it
took all the President's tact and patience to mollify his guests. He assured them the powers granted him were discretionary. He
laughed—he would not have to use them.[15] But of course he did.

This was the weakness which his admirers spoke of as a sort of
impish or elfin quality that gave color to his personality. He loved to
flabbergast his associates by announcing some startling new policy
without consulting any of them. He usually had a good laugh over it.
The day after the incident just recorded, the President issued an order prohibiting the export of gold and transactions in foreign exchange save as authorized by the Secretary of the Treasury. Later

that innocent functionary arrived smiling as usual. Roosevelt said to him: "Mr. Secretary, I have some bad news to announce to you—that the United States has just gone off the gold standard!" Poor Woodin's eyes popped: "What? Again!" Later the President told this story to his first biographer, Emil Ludwig, with unaffected delight.[16]

The next target of this merry habit was Mr. Cordell Hull. He was a sober, solemn person, yet he was now cast for a lugubrious role in a veritable comedy of errors. An International Economic Conference had been called before Roosevelt became President. It was due to meet just as the famous Hundred Days drew to an end. Mr. Hull, as Secretary of State, was naturally named as chairman of the American delegation. He was a man of one idea. He believed in free trade as devoutly as a Tennessee plantation darky believes in ghosts. Pending the unity of the world in a state of perfect free trade, he hoped to break down tariffs as much as possible by means of reciprocal tariff agreements between the United States and other nations.

This dream was within his grasp. As a foundation for his debut on the world stage, he prepared a bill by which Congress would delegate to the President the power to negotiate reciprocal agreements without requiring Senate confirmation. The bill was on the President's desk. The President had agreed to send it to Congress and urge its passage. As Mr. Hull sailed he had a copy tucked away in his pocket to exhibit in London as evidence of his authority to make a binding arrangement there.

He had got one jolt already. The five members of the delegation going with him had been named by the President *without consulting Hull*. They were actually agreed on nothing and no sooner had they sailed than they fell to quarreling among themselves.

While at sea, Mr. Hull began to get dispatches that the President had decided not to send his reciprocity bill to Congress. As this was the basis of Hull's whole program he was shocked. Reaching London, he wired the President and got a reply saying there would be no tariff legislation at this session. Thus the President pulled the rug from under his Secretary of State. At a session of the delegates in the Claridge Hotel the members had it out hot and heavy. Hull stormed. He declared he had been humiliated by the President, that the delegation did not support him and that he would resign. Someone wired the President to appease Hull and Roosevelt sent his Secretary a message saying in effect: Do not worry, I am squarely behind you. Hull wrote later that the President was behind him in words but not in actions.

But trouble dogged poor Hull's footsteps. He prepared a speech to be delivered at the opening of the conference. In it he denounced "economic nationalism" and all the numerous "bootstrap" methods of lifting a nation out of economic trouble. He sent a copy to Roosevelt for approval. At the moment the President was up to his eyes in a program of economic nationalism. Morgenthau, Johnson, Wallace and Hopkins were piling on the controls and yanking at the bootstraps. It is not difficult to picture the President's countenance when he read Hull's blistering paragraphs. He blue-penciled, erased, interlined and changed freely. And when Hull got the President's editorial elisions he was bowled over completely. When the conference opened he was unable to appear for his speech, which had to be postponed a day.

But the conference bogged down at every point. Hull was limited in his power to the tariff and trade agreements. Stabilization of currencies and other matters were to be handled by others. The section dealing with currencies and exchange was in favor of stabilizing currencies on a gold basis. However, rows broke out in the delegation and the whole conference seemed on the point of falling apart. At this point Raymond Moley, Assistant Secretary of State, arrived in London. He was sent by the President.

Moley did not go to London to interfere in Hull's tariff plans. The President had already squelched them. He went in connection with the currency negotiations being carried on by O. M. W. Sprague and James Warburg of the Treasury. The French wanted to stabilize. American advisers did too, but at a higher ratio to the pound than the British were demanding. Roosevelt sent Moley over with full power to negotiate on that subject and he was authorized as well by the Treasury. But Moley's arrival upset Hull almost to the point of illness. Coming as an emissary from the President to a conference hopelessly at sea he was naturally received as one bearing the latest orders from Roosevelt on the only subject that remained partially alive—currency stabilization. The highest state officials went to meet him. They made a fuss over him. Hull felt himself ignored and eclipsed. He went into a pout. He ostentatiously kept himself in the background and his mouth shut, thus accentuating his futility.

Moley was authorized to agree to a dollar-pound stabilization agreement around $4.25. The President was not anxious for stabilization but was willing to take that. His technical advisers were for that too. However, they were able to get from the conferees a very much better agreement according to Roosevelt's own standard. The proposed agreement committed Roosevelt to nothing save to authorize his Treasury to cooperate in *limiting fluctuations*. Prime Minister MacDonald asked Moley "for God's sake" to plead with the President to accept the proposal which would cost the President only a meaningless gesture. It would save the conference from wreck and "repel the panic that held Europe in its grip."

Moley talked over the telephone with Baruch, Acheson and Woodin at Woodin's home where he lay mortally ill. They approved. The agreement was sent to the President. Congress had adjourned at the end of the dramatic Hundred Days. The President was on his holiday in the *Amberjack* stuck somewhere in a heavy fog off Campobello. There a destroyer got to him with the message. With him were Morgenthau and Louis Howe. It would have been perhaps impossible to find three men whose total knowledge of international exchange and currency problems and monetary theory was so thin. In London everybody awaited Roosevelt's approval. Moley was with Hull who was pouring out to him the long catalogue of the humiliations he had sustained. Later, from out of the fog over the sea came the President's reply into the fog over the London conference. The proposed agreement was rejected. It hit the conference like a bombshell and it ended the conference for all practical purposes. The delegates, including Hull and Key Pittman, as well as Moley, had to admit they didn't know what the message meant. The conference drifted along aimlessly, paper-chasing, as Hull put it, and then died.

Hull says on his return he went to Roosevelt and complained bitterly about Moley's mission. He believed the President ought to call Moley down. The President, he says, told him he was surprised at Moley's conduct and that he would transfer him to another department. Of course, Moley went to the conference with specific instructions from Roosevelt and obeyed them. And if Roosevelt told Hull he would transfer Moley—and Hull must be believed—then

Roosevelt was pulling the Secretary's leg. Roosevelt knew Moley had already signed a contract to quit the State Department and to edit a new magazine because Moley had notified him to that effect before he left for London.

As for Hull, he seemed to have a genius for getting superseded and ignored. For he made the same complaint in order about Sumner Welles, Bill Donovan and Pat Hurley at a later day. Indeed he was hardly back home when he ran into another incident of supersession. George Peek had been let out of the AAA and to mollify him Roosevelt appointed him Foreign Trade Administrator with authority to negotiate barter trade agreements with foreign countries. Hull was not consulted about this and inevitably a collision occurred. Peek made an agreement with Germany. Hull protested vehemently. Roosevelt told him to talk it over with Peek. Hull did and then wrote Roosevelt that he and every other government department were agreed against the Peek proposal. Then Hull went to Tennessee to make a speech. No sooner had he turned his back than Roosevelt sent for Peek and approved his plan. Hull was angry when he returned. He went to the White House and protested vigorously. Roosevelt reversed his approval and turned thumbs down on Peek's plan and two months later abolished Peek's office.[17]

Hull did get a clear track later for his reciprocity agreements—a policy good in principle but of little relative importance against the background of world problems. How much interest Roosevelt felt in these is problematical. Hull was important to him. The Secretary was in no sense a student of international affairs. He was favored by nature with a countenance that gave him the imposing aspect of a mid-Victorian Liberal statesman. The mind behind the countenance was that of a crusty, old-fashioned Southern politician. The President throughout his tenure had a problem on his hands in the Southern senators who disliked the New Deal intensely. They went along because they had to do it or go without their share of the vast spoils for their states which the President had at his disposal. However, the intransigence of many was deep and at times turbulent and Hull was a valuable instrument to keep his old Southern colleagues in line.

This disconcerting technique of the President in bypassing his top leaders infected some of the men under him. Secretary Woodring complained, for instance, that Morgenthau went over his head on military matters. When Morgenthau was told this he said gleefully: "I went over and under and all around him." But Morgenthau himself was a frequent target of his master's impish pleasure in these secret intrusions into his own preserves. Morgenthau was perhaps the strangest of Roosevelt's cabinet appointments, unless we except Wallace and Hopkins as Secretaries of Commerce. Morgenthau was doubtless a good man, loyal, honest, industrious, if permitted to remain on some lower level of mediocrity. As a cabinet officer he was a kind of historic specimen. Other cabinet officers looked on him with scorn. Garner said that "Wallace has crazy ideas and Morgenthau none." He said "He is servile. I do not mean loyal. I mean servile to Roosevelt."[18] He was a slow, dull youth with no capacity for study. Up to the time he was given an important post by Roosevelt he had had no success in any kind of business. His father had set him up as a gentleman farmer on an estate next to Roosevelt's home at Hyde Park and endowed him with plenty of money. That is how he met Roosevelt and he remained for life the latter's humble and compliant servitor.

In the Fall of 1933, prices were not going so well for the farmers and Henry, whom Roosevelt had made head of the Farm Board, decided to do something about it. He fell under the influence of two men—Professor George F. Warren, a farm economist from Cornell and Professor James Rogers of Yale. Another was Irving Fisher, an evangelist of the theory of a managed currency. They sold him on the idea that the country could use a little dose of inflation. Warren was the most persuasive. Like all farm economists he was an inflationist. They believe the way to hoist farm prices is to grow less farm produce and manufacture more dollars. Warren had a pet theory that the great enemy of mankind was gold, which was the worst rather than the best commodity to use as a measure of money value. He and a colleague had written a book to prove that gold is one of the most variable of all commodities in value. Fisher held that the unit of value should be a composite of commodity values and the value of the dollar moved up and down around that base.

Between them they hooked Morgenthau and he took them to Roosevelt. Dr. Warren lectured the President, explaining how the government could regulate prices very simply by regulating the price paid for gold—move the price of gold in dollars up and down to suit the government's price policy at any given time. In time a commodity index could be adopted and the government could then have a completely managed currency. Whether this is sound or not it is a thoroughly revolutionary plan. But it was inevitable that its unorthodox features would captivate the mind of Roosevelt. Warren proposed that the price of gold, which was then fixed by law at $20.67, should be raised to around $35 an ounce. It didn't take them long to sell this gaudy bill of goods to Roosevelt. He asked the Attorney-General for an opinion on his authority to act. Dean Acheson, Assistant Attorney-General, held it could not be done under the law. Roosevelt was furious. He called on Stanley Reed, then counsel for the RFC, and Morgenthau brought in Herman Oliphant, legal adviser of the Treasury. Oliphant was a lawyer whose reformist addictions overflowed into every branch of public affairs. A devout believer in rubber laws, it was easy for him to find one which could be stretched to include rubber dollars. Stanley Reed obliged with a favorable opinion. That, of course, is why he was asked for one. The opinion of the Attorney-General was disregarded and Roosevelt went on the air on October 22, 1933 and announced that hereafter the Treasury alone would buy all gold mined in the United States and all gold offered from abroad if necessary. The price would be raised and fixed from day to day by the President and the Secretary of the Treasury. The RFC would furnish the money to buy the gold. The initial price was fixed at $31.26 an ounce—giving us 66 cents of gold in a dollar. The President said: "I would not know and no one else could tell just what the permanent valuation of the dollar would be. When we have restored the price level then we shall seek to establish and maintain a dollar which will not change its purchasing power during the succeeding generation."

He declared: "If we cannot get prices up one way we will get them up another," and, most important, he told the radio audience: "This is a policy, not an expedient. *We are thus continuing to move toward a managed currency.*" Later Congress passed an act to validate what he had done, which was clearly illegal when he did it.

Thereafter each day Morgenthau and Roosevelt met, with Jesse Jones, head of the RFC, present, to fix the price of gold. They gathered around Roosevelt's bed in the morning as he ate his eggs. Then

"Henny-Penny" and Roosevelt decided the price of gold for that day. One day they wished to raise the price. Roosevelt settled the point. Make it 21 cents, he ruled. That is a lucky number—three times seven. And so it was done. That night Morgenthau wrote in his diary: "If people knew how we fixed the price of gold they would be frightened."[19]

The theory of the plan was to boost foreign purchases, particularly of farm products. But it didn't work. And it didn't raise prices as expected. Had the President called in Dr. O. M. W. Sprague, his distinguished economic adviser, Dr. Sprague could have told him that this had been tried in Britain, Sweden, Japan, Italy and France; that in England, Sweden and Japan prices had actually declined, while in Italy and France they had increased only slightly, but due to other causes. But the President knew he had a naughty economic trick in prospect and he didn't dare let Dr. Sprague know or the doctor might explain it to him and ruin the whole show. So he said nothing. Shortly after, Dr. Sprague resigned and on the door of a room in the Executive Department was painted the legend: "Dr. George F. Warren, Economic Adviser to the President." Of course, as the fairy-like dream evaporated, the good doctor, who was an honest man and a good farm specialist also evaporated out of the government.

Some time later, Senator Borah and a number of senators from the silver states went to the White House to urge Roosevelt to do something about silver. After a good deal of amusing badinage, Key Pittman finally nailed the President down to an answer. "All right," said the President laughing, "I experimented with gold and that was a flop. Why shouldn't I experiment a little with silver?"[20] Al Smith had his say about it all in characteristic language. He called this new trick "baloney dollars"—a name that stuck—and asked why the "Democratic party is always fated to be the party of greenbackers, paper money printers, free silverites, currency managers, rubber dollar manufacturers and crackpots."

Poor Henry, however, who enjoyed circumnavigating Woodring and bypassing Woodin on Treasury policy, got plenty of the same medicine from Roosevelt himself. After Roosevelt named him Secretary of the Treasury to succeed Woodin, Morgenthau prepared a tax bill with the aid of Treasury experts. Twenty-four hours before it was to go to Congress, Roosevelt had sent for one of Henry's

Treasury underlings and kept him at the White House all night working up some fad just sold to the President into a tax bill which Henry learned about only when it was ready to go to Congress. Later Henry engaged an eminent tax authority to overhaul our tax laws and plan a more rational tax system. While this was being readied, he took a rest trip to Sea Island, Georgia. During his absence, Oliphant took a bright young man to the White House and in a brief talk convinced Roosevelt to scrap the whole system of corporate taxes, to end all existing taxes on corporations and tax instead their undistributed profits. A more crack-brained scheme never got a welcome in a sober executive office. It was all settled on when Morgenthau got back and prepared to submit his own plan to the President.[21] Congress was shocked and the Democratic leaders had to make a hurried rehash of the bill, restoring the corporate taxes and using enough of the undistributed profits scheme to save the President's face.

4.

There were other plans—the Social Security Act and the Securities Exchange Act. There was no real objection to social security—everybody was for it. The Republicans had denounced the President for his tardiness in presenting a plan. In due time a bill was passed. But here we saw a characteristic of the President's mind which was to bring countless troubled hours to his Congressional leaders. One might pour a perfectly good idea into his mind at one end and it would come out the other with some fantastic twist. There is only one way to provide old-age pensions for retired workers. Those who still work and their employers must make up by contributions each year a sum sufficient to pay the pensions. The commission finally named by Roosevelt to prepare a plan brought forward just such a proposal with a "pay-as-you-go" tax—a small tax on payrolls to meet the requirements each year plus a moderate contingency fund of two or three billions. The bill, after hearings before a Congressional committee, was ready to be reported when Morgenthau was sent post haste to the committee with a scheme just sold to the President in a short talk. The plan was to make the payroll tax big enough to pay the benefits, plus enough more to create a so-called reserve of $47,000,000,000 in 40 years. It was given the fraudulent name of Old-Age Reserve Fund. The Security Board would collect the taxes each year, use a small part to pay the pensions and put the rest in the "Fund." That is, it would "lend" it to the Treasury and the Treasury would then spend it for any purpose it had in mind. At the end of 40 years, Roosevelt was told, this money could be used to pay off the national debt.[22]

Fortunately, Congress in 1938 had the courage to put a stop to this and to reduce the rates to a moderate sum. But the "reserve" idea remains. The government now collects from workers and employers four percent of the payrolls, which it promptly borrows and spends. Then it must turn to general tax revenues to pay the benefits. Thus workers and bosses are taxed twice for a "security" program with most of the funds being spent for other purposes.

The Securities Exchange Act when finally passed was on the standard New Deal model—the creation of a commission, another bureau, which has been given vast powers to make laws for the security markets. It is a good idea badly twisted. What harm it has done is difficult to appraise as yet. Before any real revival in the investment markets could appear the war intervened. But at least one thing is certain and that is that the Commission has in its hands powers it ought not to have, powers which could be used and might well be used to literally destroy the investment market in this country.

There was one thing more—the banks. When the banks had been closed and then reopened following the crisis, the next thing in order was to adopt a rational banking law that would make the abuses of the past impossible. For some reason which I have never been able to fathom the President never displayed the slightest interest in this subject. Two measures emerged. One was the Glass-Steagall Act to eliminate some of the bad features permitted under the old laws. The other was the present system of insured bank deposits. The President and his promoters took a great share of credit for these bills. Without discussing whether they were sound or not, the fact remains that the President refused to support the Glass-Steagall bill, and that the guarantee of deposits, first proposed to him by John Garner, he resolutely opposed. Both were passed without the movement of a finger by him to assist them.[23]

This is what happened to the new New Deal—the Second New Deal. The big controversial, sensational experiments which were its heart were all killed or died of their own inherent weaknesses. The

NRA, the AAA, the Gold Purchase and Managed Money plan vanished. Roosevelt was glad after they were gone to see them go, but he hated those who had opposed them and who had been proved right. He never forgave them. He had literally nothing to do with what banking reform was adopted. His spurious surplus tax plan had to be smothered by his own leaders. The taxes he promised to reduce were now higher than ever. The debt he was going to check and pay off was now nearing the point of being doubled. And the spending plan—spending by Hopkins through the WPA—had come into such bad odor that Hopkins publicly admitted it was a mistake and the President echoed this opinion by saying that spending on doles must stop—it must in the future be on useful public works.

What was left of this Second New Deal? There was one thing left, one rabbit—the Spending Rabbit—however the money might be put out. This it was which had accounted for whatever lift there was in business and for the tremendous power the President had acquired over the machinery of his party, over numerous groups in the nation and over every town, country and state government which wanted a part of that money. But the New Deal in its second edition was not in any sense a system of government polity. It was a collection of measures based on contradictory principles, the most important of which had been wiped out.

Chapter 6: The Dance of the Crackpots

The times were indeed out of joint as the New Deal moved along. Nature took a hand in the festival of disaster. The plains, long parched by drought, were swept by cruel dust storms that made life impossible. Cattle died in the fields and the despairing farmers piled their wretched belongings on their old jalopies and began that dramatic migration of the Okies to the west coast in search of food and life. Floods inundated the great river valleys, bringing death and starvation in their wake. All this was added to the dislocations produced by man in his ignorance and folly.

An old Oklahoma farmer, watching the jalopies go by across the dried fields, said: "Things are just about right now for the skies to open and for the prophets to come down off the mountain and run for office." In times of stress they never disappoint us. And sure enough, up out of the muck and misery, rather than the skies, rose the messiahs with strange voices crying in the wilderness and proclaiming gospels of many brands. Roosevelt had been having a more or less easy time with his Republican opposition. It had been working the wrong side of the street for votes. The votes were over on the other side now, where great masses of people were out of work, or busted, or land poor or old or sick or weary or brought down with despair. Mr. Roosevelt had been singing the sweet song of plenty in their ears. But now a new batch of prophets began to crowd in and to work the same side of the street as Roosevelt.

Politically this was a greater challenge to him than the Republicans. These bold champions threatened to split the ranks of the dispossessed. To those to whom the great and good President had offered a crust, some of these great promissory spirits offered a whole loaf, while some even offered cake with icing. Serious-minded men knew that we had gotten into a sorry mess through a long series of economic and social sins and that the cure lay in dealing with certain definite dislocations in the social organism and that we had to endure with patience the slow process of recovery. But such men in such circumstances can never compete with the quacks who can cure everything out of the same bottle of pills. Roosevelt, once he got into power, began, in complete violation of his Number One pledge, to spend money like a drunken sailor and then to promise the earth and the fullness thereof. He asked nothing of the people but that they vote for him.

In the Agricultural Department a vast bureau was set up with a wilderness of check-writing machines and amidst thundering mechanical noises, was pouring out a flood of checks to farmers in return for killing their stock, plowing back crops and burning grain in their fields. The hotels and boarding houses of Washington were crowded with the delegations from the farms, from villages and cities, from counties and chambers of commerce and boards of trade and colleges and trade organizations, all standing in long lines with their hats in their hands for the easy money that gushed from the

Federal Treasury at the touch of the President. Suddenly all the old-fashioned laws about gravity and the arithmetic tables seemed to have been repealed by decree of the President. The impact of all this, coming not from prairie seers with long whiskers, but from the President of the United States and many seemingly sober-minded cabinet ministers and some business men, seemed to knock loose some nut or bolt somewhere inside the social structure which keeps men on an even keel and moving in accordance with the laws of sanity.

Hence along came a great troop of prophets to compete with the President as a promiser. If his Republican realists were helpless in a contest against his new collection of sloganized promises, he now found himself in a contest with men who could out-promise him. And one effect of these weird evangelists was to give to the reckless President an aspect of conservative restraint.

Perhaps the most dangerous of these was Huey Long, that mighty madcap Kingfish from Louisiana, "the Bonaparte of the Bayous," whose brief but fiery career was to give Roosevelt no end of headaches. After a tempestuous career as governor of Louisiana, he was elected to the Senate and, before he took his seat, played a decisive role at a critical moment in the nomination of Roosevelt. Fearing neither God nor man nor the devil, he was not intimidated by the White House or the Senate. At his first meeting with Roosevelt in the White House, he stood over the President with his hat on and emphasized his points with an occasional finger poked into the executive chest. He found very quickly that he could move as brusquely around the Senate floor as he had the lobbies of the state legislature. He strode about the Capitol followed by his bodyguards. He ranted on the Senate floor. He made a 15½-hour one-man filibustering speech. He made up his mind very soon that the New Deal was a lot of claptrap and proceeded to preach his own gospel of the abundant life.

He cried out: "Distribute our wealth—it's all there in God's book. Follow the Lord." This was the prelude to his Share-the-Wealth crusade. Huey proclaimed "Every man a King" with Huey as the Kingfish. He made it plain he was no Communist despoiler. He assured Rockefeller he was not going to take *all* his millions. He would not take a single luxury from the economic royalists. They would retain their "fish ponds, their estates and their horses for riding to the hounds."

When he began, he had no plan at all. He just had a slogan and worked up from there. But by 1934 he was ready to launch the movement with Gerald L. K. Smith, a former Shreveport preacher, at its head. The program was simple. No income would exceed a million dollars. Everybody would have a minimum income of $2500. The money would be provided by a capital levy which would remove the surplus millions from the rich—which revealed that Huey really did not know any more about economics than the President did. There would, of course, be old-age pensions for all, free education right through college for all, an electric refrigerator and an automobile for every family. The government would buy up all the agricultural surpluses against the day of shortages. As a matter of course there would be short working hours for everyone, and bonuses for veterans. All surplus property would be turned over to the government so that a fellow who needed a bed would get one from the fellow who owned more than one.

Some editors who supported Roosevelt said Huey's plan was "like the weird dream of a plantation darky." It is not clear why Huey broke with Roosevelt. It is probably because it was impossible for him to endure the role of second fiddle to any man and he had come to see wider horizons for his own strange talents. Visitors to the Capitol were more eager to have the guides point out Huey Long than any other exhibit in the building. He was aware of the immense notoriety he had achieved and he believed he saw a condition approaching in which he could repeat upon the national scene the amazing performance he had given in Louisiana.

Certainly he set out to ruin Roosevelt. He declared war on Joe Robinson, Roosevelt's leader in the Senate and on Pat Harrison of Mississippi, for he had set out in a sense to annex the neighboring states of Arkansas and Mississippi to his Southern earldom. He declared war on Roosevelt and he denounced him in terms Roosevelt's beloved "Common Man" could understand. In the Senate he cried out:

"Hoover is a hoot owl. Roosevelt is a scrootch owl. A hoot owl bangs into the nest and knocks the hen clean out and catches her while she's falling. But a scrootch owl slips into the roost and scrootches up to the hen and talks softly to her. And the hen just falls in love with him. And the first thing you know—there ain't no hen."

He denounced Roosevelt on a tender point. He called him "Prince Franklin, Knight of the *Nourmahal,* enjoying himself on that $5,000,000 yacht with Vincent Astor and Royalty while the farmers starve." Farley says Roosevelt told him to give no patronage to Huey. Roosevelt's billions, adroitly used, had broken down every political machine in America. The patronage they once lived on and the local money they once had to disburse to help the poor was trivial compared to the vast floods of money Roosevelt controlled. And no political boss could compete with him in any county in America in the distribution of money and jobs.

Roosevelt went to work in Louisiana on the rebel Kingfish. He poured money into the hands of Huey's enemies to disburse to Huey's loyal Cajans. And there came a moment when Huey seemed to be on his way to the doghouse. But he was an incorrigible figure of unconquerable energy. When Roosevelt sought to buy with federal funds the Louisiana electorate and ring, Huey struck back with a series of breathtaking blows that brought the state under his thumb almost as completely as Hitler's Reich under the heel of the Fuehrer. First of all, he stopped federal funds from entering Louisiana. He forced the legislature to pass a law forbidding any state or local board or official from incurring any debt or receiving any federal funds without consent of a central state board. And this board Huey set up and dominated. He cut short an estimated flood of $30,000,000 in PWA projects. Then he provided, through state operations and borrowing, a succession of public works, roads, bridges, schools, hospitals, farm projects and relief measures. The money was spent to boost Huey instead of Roosevelt. The people were taught to thank and extol Huey rather than Roosevelt for all these goods.

He gave the people tax exemptions, ended the poll tax, cut automobile taxes, put heavier taxes on utilities and corporations. He took over the police department of New Orleans from the City Ring, threw out their police commissioners. He was followed around by troops. He gathered into his hands through his personally owned governor absolute control over every state and parish office. He got control of education and the teachers. He took over the State University and added its football team and its hundred-piece band to the noisy and glittering hippodrome in which he exploited himself. He possessed the entire apparatus of government in Louisiana—the schools, the treasury, the public buildings and the men and women in the buildings. He owned most of the courts, and had a secret police of his own. He ran the elections, counted the votes and held in his hands the power of life and death over most of the enterprise in the state.

Roosevelt was profoundly alarmed. The Democratic National Committee was astonished when a secret poll revealed that Long on a third-party ticket could poll between three and four million votes and that his Share-the-Wealth plan had eaten deeply into the Democratic strength in the industrial and farm states. Farley says there was a possibility "that his third-party movement might constitute a balance of power in the 1936 election." The poll indicated that Long could corral 100,000 votes in New York State, which could, in a close election, cost Roosevelt the electoral vote there. Long became a frequent subject of conversation at the White House.

But Fate had gone Democratic in 1932 and remained so. On Sunday, September 8, 1935, Long was in Baton Rouge issuing orders in one of his frequent political tantrums. Louisiana had been in something approaching a state of terror. Long was crossing a corridor of the state Capitol. Dr. Carl Austin Weiss, a young physician, eluded the vigilance of Long's guards and shot him. The guards filled Weiss' body with bullets—61 of them. Huey died September 10, and was buried in the presence of 120,000 weeping worshipers from all over the state. The oration was pronounced by Gerald L. K. Smith who said: "His body shall never rest as long as hungry bodies cry for food." A monument stands to the memory of this arch demagogue in the Hall of Fame of the Capitol building in Washington and his body rests in a crypt on the state Capitol grounds—a shrine to which crowds flock every day to venerate the memory of the man who trampled on their laws, spat upon their traditions, loaded them with debt and degraded their society to a level resembling the plight of a European fascist dictatorship.

The assassination of Long removed the threat of Huey from Roosevelt's side of the street, but the machine he had created still remained. It could exist only by using his techniques and trading on the immortality of the murdered leader. But of that later.

There was another who was infringing on Roosevelt's territory. An aged physician in Long Beach, California, was looking out his window one day when he saw three old women rooting in a garbage can for food. The vision set the doctor's soul on fire. Physical torture shook his body. He burst into a violent spasm of invective against a system in which this was possible. Thus inspired, he sat down to invent a plan to end it and came up quickly with the famous Townsend Old Age Revolving Pension Plan. This old gentleman was Dr. Francis E. Townsend. He was an honest man of generous impulses. But his anger led him into the mazes of modern economics which he understood as little as the poor old women whose plight had detonated his wrath.

The plan was simplicity itself. Every person reaching the age of 60 would receive $200 a month. There were four conditions: (1) that he or she retire; (2) have no criminal record; (3) have no income over the $2400 a year; and (4) spend the entire $200 each month. A man and wife over 60 would get $400 a month. There were 10,384,000 persons over 60. But the doctor estimated that only about 8,000,000 would qualify. This would cost the country $1,600,000,000 a month or about $19,000,000,000 a year. The money would be provided by a transactions tax of 2 per cent on every commercial transaction. A crazier idea never entered the brain of man. But this was a day of crackpot philosophers. It was not much crazier than Henry Wallace's hog-killing and crop-burning schemes or Roosevelt's NRA. But the minds of the people had gotten off the tracks of reality. And this alluring promise lighted up the imaginations and appetites of the aged. It spread like a prairie fire among the oldsters until millions were marching behind the good doctor as in a holy crusade. In the three months at the end of 1935 the organization collected $350,000 and it grew from there.

The commentators laughed at this pathetic host of old people trooping behind their challenging Quixote. One said it was bad enough to tell Junior there is a Santa Claus, but to lead Grandpa to believe in him was unpardonable. And another commented that the Longs and Townsends and Sinclairs and Roosevelts had set up professionally as my brother's keeper, but it was time for someone to set up as my brother's bookkeeper. It was not possible, however, to laugh off the vast horde of registered voters who took the old doctor seriously. Like Huey, he was very much on Roosevelt's mind and in his talks. For the doctor was hog-calling millions of natural New Dealers off into his Revolving Old Age Plan. The old folks were crowding the railroad stations getting estimates on voyages hither and yon. The passion for travel seized upon their imaginations as they beheld an old age of leisure and more money than the vast majority of them had ever made by work in their life times.

Nor was this all. While Huey and the doctor clamored to make every man a king or a tourist, the inflationists never relaxed their pressure for their various money plans. It began to look as if the printing presses would have to go to work. And this very well-founded apprehension exercised a profound influence upon the minds of business men who were being exhorted to expand and expose themselves to the dangerous gamble of inflation.

Meantime, out in California an almost incredible movement got under way. Upton Sinclair, an old Socialist who had stirred America thirty years before with his famous novel "The Jungle," had been living in California for years. He was an intelligent and industrious critic of the capitalist system and a writer of amazing fecundity. Novels, brochures, pamphlets, critical volumes poured from his pen, were published by himself and translated into every language in the world. He was a gentle, scholarly, deeply sincere man. Suddenly this Socialist amazed the voters of California by announcing himself a candidate for the Democratic nomination for governor against George Creel, a brilliant and courageous liberal journalist who was supported by the Democratic leaders for the place. Creel, an old Wilsonian reformer, still harboring a chimerical faith in the laws of arithmetic and gravity, was soon to learn that he, a lifelong Democrat, was no match in a Democratic primary for a lifelong Socialist with a platform for turning California gradually into a socialist heaven.

Sinclair had a tremendous weapon. We were still in a depression. Nobody seemed quite sure what to do about it. Sinclair capitalized on this. He told the voters he had a plan and he was dead certain about it. He said:

> "We can end poverty in California. *I know what I am talking about.* I am an expert in depressions. I have spent thirty years of my life studying them. I know what causes them and how to cure them. And I tell

you the only way to do this is by my plan to END POVERTY IN CALIFOR-
NIA."

From the first letters in this plan—EPIC—the movement took its
name. Creel says that overnight the people stopped talking about the
climate and began to talk about EPIC.

Like all the plans it, too, was simplicity itself. There were in California a million persons unemployed by industry or starving on the
farms. Also, said Sinclair, there were a great number of idle factories
and idle farms. The state would put up the money to start up all the
idle factories and the abandoned farms. The unemployed would be
put to work in these factories making essential goods for themselves
and all unemployed persons. Others would be set to work on the idle
farms growing food and raw materials for the factories. These unemployed are now, he said, no longer profitable customers for those in
private business. In fact they are a burden since private business must
now provide the taxes for relief. EPIC would take all the unemployed off relief, hence off the backs of the self-supporting element
in the community. The state would finance it all with a bond issue.

It would be operated by a California Authority for Land (CAL)
which would buy up the idle farms and the California Authority for
Production (CAP) which would take over the idle factories, all serv-
iced by a great fleet of trucks and a chain of stores in which would be
sold to those employed by these Authorities the clothes and food
produced by the CAL and CAP. Of course there would be a California Authority for Money (CAM) which would float the bond issues
to finance all this. The sales tax would be repealed. There would be
income taxes on incomes of $5000 and over, and tax exemptions for
homes and farms valued at less than $3500. There was more to it, in-
cluding of course a great Central Valley Water Project for power.

All these plans were called crackpot. But Sinclair's was not a crackpot plan. He knew what he was doing. Had he succeeded he would
have created in the body of the capitalist system of California a more
or less complete socialist organization operating strictly on the principle of production for use. At a blow, 10 or 15 per cent of California's
population would be transferred to a socialist economy. He undoubtedly believed, and he was right, that the success of his plan would
gradually enervate and enfeeble the capitalist system which

contained and supported it and that EPIC would gradually swallow the whole.

There were other groups—Major Douglas' Social Credit and Howard Scott's Technocrats, neither of which made much progress though they did supply to Mr. Roosevelt's great economic staff some of its top dog "economists" and statisticians. The Social Credit advocates laid out as a principle that the capitalist system does not produce enough money income to enable all producers to buy the national product of consumable goods at a profit. Stated differently, the customers of the nation do not receive enough money income to purchase at a profit what the employers produce. A powerful argument can be made for this thesis. However, the Social Credit advocates proposed that to correct this deficit in purchasing power the government would at intervals issue to all the people what they called social dividends, government-issued cash, to enable them to buy what they needed. It amounted to this: that the government would give to everybody a cash handout at certain periods in the year.

The Technocrats were the most radical of the new reformers. They insisted that we must have a continental economy—that is we must unite to the United States, Canada, Mexico and the Central American countries in order to have a self-sustaining continent. We must then liquidate the democratic system and turn the management of the system over to the only people capable of understanding it, namely the engineers, to whom they later added the economists and other technicians. This was called the Soviet of the Engineers. Next we would abolish the existing money system and base all money on the unit of energy—the erg. There is more to it, but this is enough. One of the most eminent supporters of Technocracy, and chief sponsor of the crackpot Howard Scott, was Mr. Leon Henderson, who was made statistician of the NRA and later economic adviser and research director of the Democratic party, and finally head of the Office of Price Administration—the OPA of sad memory during the war.

This dance of the crackpots all over Roosevelt's side of the street was playing havoc with his own medicine show. The election year 1936 loomed menacingly ahead. They must be liquidated or composed or appeased or devoured. And someone, aided by Fate, did an excellent job of getting all these dervishes to quit their merry hoopla and march along in the ranks of the great New Deal.

While Hoover was President, the Treasury and the Department of Justice had been pursuing the Huey Long forces on their income taxes. But when Roosevelt came into power, Justice turned her eyes away. However, when Huey went out on the warpath, Justice once again went to work on Huey and his pals. It has been said the decision to indict him on income tax frauds was made the very day before he died. But he left behind a batch of heirs who knew how to trade on the powers of the departed Saint Huey. Huey's organization showed no loss of strength. The Treasury and the Department of Justice went into action and before long there were income tax indictments against at least 25 of the Long leaders and henchmen.

Richard W. Leche was governor. In January, 1936, he was reelected by an immense landslide, thus demonstrating the survival of the Long power. But in some mysterious way the raucous chorus of denunciation of Washington by the Long machine stopped cold. According to Drew Pearson in the Washington Merry-go-Round column, a Washington reporter saw Marvin McIntyre, Roosevelt's secretary and said: "Mac, did it ever occur to you that the administration might arrange a rapprochement with the gang in Louisiana? ... I think I could be of some service to you." McIntyre said: "I think that's already been taken care of." "Then nobody has to worry?" "Nobody," answered Mac.

Not long after the United States Attorney asked the United States Court to dismiss most of the indictments against the Long crowd. Westbrook Pegler dubbed this the Second Louisiana Purchase. Harnett Kane,[24] who has written a brilliant account of this episode, says "A judicial bargain basement was set up, and men by paying $1000 fines were freed of charges which might have brought them years in prison." The civil suits were pressed and succeeded in collecting $2,000,000 in unpaid taxes. In June, just before the Democratic convention met, Roosevelt made a trip to Texas. The Louisiana Legislature was ordered by Governor Leche to adjourn and "convene" in Texas at the Centennial grounds where Roosevelt was camped. There they passed a resolution praising divine Providence for providing "a great leader, Franklin D. Roosevelt, who saved the nation from ruin and chaos," and they called on the Republican party to withdraw Alfred Landon and make Roosevelt's reelection unanimous. The State University band, Huey's pride and joy, played Huey's theme song—"Every Man a King."

As for Upton Sinclair and his EPIC plan, he got his trial by fire in an election. He beat Creel in the Democratic primaries and this lifetime Socialist, on a strictly socialist proposal, became the candidate of the Democratic party. Sinclair went to the White House and emerged in a happy mood. EPIC and the New Deal, he said, were perfectly consistent. Hopkins said he hoped Sinclair would be elected. "He's on our side, isn't he?" he asked. And when Sinclair got back to California he published a letter from Farley urging all to vote for the full ticket. Later Farley said the letter was a stenographer's mistake.

Roosevelt was ready to play with any one of these curious heresies. Ray Moley pleaded with him in September to dissociate his administration from Sinclair. Roosevelt said that Merriam, the Republican candidate for governor, was taking the support of the Townsend people and that the Townsend heresy was no worse than the EPIC heresy. Then he added "Besides, they tell me Sinclair is sure to be elected."[25] Creel at first agreed to support Sinclair on the promise that he would not push the EPIC plan in the general election, which seemed incredible as that was his whole stock-in-trade. At all events, Creel reported this to Roosevelt and Farley, who praised the bargain. But of course Sinclair had to push the EPIC plan and he did so with the same vigor he had pushed it in the primary, after which, on October 26, Creel wrote him a letter repudiating him.[26]

Francis Perkins tells that sober liberals in California were horrified at EPIC and pleaded with her to get the President to stem the tide for Sinclair while he was running against Creel. But it didn't bother Roosevelt at all. He said: "Well, they might be elected in California and get EPIC there but what difference will that make in Dutchess County, New York, or Lincoln County, Maine?"[27]

In the end the Republican candidate defeated Sinclair. And within a short time every vestige of the EPIC movement disappeared from California.

Soon the remnants of that movement were traipsing off into the new evangelism known as "Ham and Eggs"—a plan to provide everyone with $30 every Thursday, a plan, by the way, which elected Senator Sheridan Downey to the United States Senate.

Meantime Roosevelt observed to his intimates that it was necessary to steal a little from good old Doctor Townsend. For some strange reason, Roosevelt had lagged in his interest in old-age pensions. Wagner and others had been working on an unemployment insurance bill but not on old-age pensions. In the 1934 Congressional elections the Republicans denounced Roosevelt for doing nothing about this subject. He therefore appointed a commission to study the subject. But after the election was safely over he told its members the time was not yet ripe for it. It was the sweep of the Townsendites, the Share-the-Wealthers and EPIC planners that spurred his interest and resulted in the passage of the Social Security Act with old-age pensions and unemployment insurance. While Townsend agitated, Roosevelt acted. The oldsters were to learn very much later that there was not very much social security in Roosevelt's act. But feuds began to divide the Townsendites. Dr. Townsend got into a row with the House of Representatives which cited him for contempt. His leaders split. Then in June, on the eve of the Democratic convention, Farley had a conference with Gomer Smith, one of the Townsend directors. Smith told Farley that he and several others controlled seven votes in the directorate and they and not Townsend would control the organization. The meeting was kept secret so as not to compromise Smith.

Thus by the time the election came around the Townsendites, the Ham and Eggers, the EPIC planners and the Long crowd were all on the bandwagon that rolled down Roosevelt's side of the street, safely under the guidance of himself and his skillful coachman, Jim Farley.

This curious epidemic of grotesque notions sponsored by shallow and in some cases dangerous men is, of course, not an unknown phenomenon. When little men think about large problems the boundary between the sound and the unsound is very thin and vague. And when some idea is thrown out which corresponds with the deeply rooted yearnings of great numbers of spiritually and economically troubled people it spreads like a physical infection and rises in virulence with the extent of the contagion. The spiritual and mental soil of the masses near the bottom of the economic heap was perfect ground for all these promisers of security and abundance. Roosevelt prospered on that. And he was in a grave political dilemma when he found himself surpassed in the size and beauty of the promises made by his competitors.

One of the mistakes committed by the critics of the President at this time was the charge that he was drifting toward Communism. And as each new cure for the woes of the people was advertised it was called Socialism or Communism. The infusion of Communism would come into Mr. Roosevelt's New Deal in good time; but it certainly was not there yet. Some of the more radical agitators who surrounded the President and got access occasionally to his mind believed that the capitalist system and our traditional representative system were done for. But they were not Communists. Most of them were confused dilettante revolutionists, revolutionists of the chamber and not of the field or the barricades—daring enough in discussion in hospitable living rooms or cocktail lounges but having no boldness in action. What is more, few of them had the hardihood to admit themselves to be even philosophical Communists. They had cooked up for themselves that easy, comfortable potpourri of socialism and capitalism called the Planned Economy which provided its devotees with a wide area in which they might rattle around without being called Red.

That was the revolution—the Planned Economy—they were preparing for and hoping for. There was a moment, during the NRA and the AAA, when things looked good for that bold dream. But their purposes were never clearly understood by those who criticized most mercilessly the Roosevelt regime. They were never really in control though they may have seemed to be. But the time would come when they would approach much closer to their dream of a planned people. We shall see that later.

The haunting fear of these vocal and conniving dreamers broke out in full flame in 1934. Dr. William A. Wirt,[28] famous as the originator of the Gary System of public education and superintendent of schools of Gary, Indiana, since 1907, was in Washington. He attended a cocktail party at the home of his former secretary, Miss Alice Barrows. After this he wrote a letter to a number of friends, one of them James H. Rand, who read it before a House hearing. Rand said a brain-truster had told Wirt:

"We believe we have Roosevelt in the middle of a swift stream and that the current is so strong that he cannot turn back or escape from it. We believe that we can keep Mr. Roosevelt there until we are ready to supplant him with a Stalin. We all think that Mr. Roosevelt is only the Kerensky of this revolution. We are on the inside. We can control the avenues of influence. We can make the President believe that he is making decisions for himself."

This produced a storm of wrath in Congress both among those who believed and those who didn't believe Wirt. There is little doubt that the statement was made to Wirt. The man who made it said later they were all just pulling Wirt's leg. But the fact is that this belief was widely held by a large number of these so-called pink and scarlet intellectuals. They believed the great capitalist catastrophe had come. They believed Roosevelt's half-way measures would fail—as they ultimately did. And then would come revolution. But, as it turned out, it was not to the Reds Roosevelt was yielding at this time, but to the special interests, to farmers who wanted high prices and labor leaders who wanted more power, to bankers who wanted one thing or another, to city and county and state chambers and councils who wanted government money, to political bosses who wanted patronage and graft, to the poor and unemployed who wanted government money, to the crackpots who wanted various things and, generally, to any strong group that had votes enough to count.

CHAPTER 7: AN ENEMY IS WELCOMED

At what point did the Communists find the crack in the wall of the New Deal and climb in?

The critics and enemies of President Roosevelt have made, from the beginning, the fundamental mistake of always misunderstanding him and his objectives. Throughout the first administration, his political enemies denounced him as the willing or unconscious agent of Communist philosophers bent on socializing America. This was not true. There was not in Roosevelt a grain of conviction on the side of the Communist philosophy. One of the facts about him least understood is that fundamentally he was without any definite political or economic philosophy. He was not a man to deal in fundamentals. Miss Perkins, who knew him well, was sure that Roosevelt was not a political or economic radical. "He took the *status quo* in our economic system," she said, "as much for granted as his family." He had come into political life under the influence of Wilson's theories of liberal political reform. That is to say, he had voted for the Democratic candidates without any strong opinions about the subject. Roosevelt went as naturally into the Democratic party as he did into the Episcopal church. But while he was no radical, it is equally true to say of him that he was not a conservative. He was a man literally without any fundamental philosophy. The positions he took on political and economic questions were not taken in accordance with deeply rooted political beliefs but under the influence of political necessity.

Miss Perkins says he had "no theoretical or ideological objections to public ownership when that was necessary." It was a proposal upon which he could take either side without doing any violence to any basic political or economic philosophy, since he had none. Miss Perkins says that once a young reporter, in her presence, had the following conversation with Roosevelt. The reporter asked:

"Mr. President, are you a Communist?"

"No," said Roosevelt.

"Are you a capitalist?"

"No."

"Are you a Socialist?"

"No."

Then the young man asked what his philosophy was.

"Philosophy?" the President was puzzled. "Philosophy? I am a Christian and a Democrat—that's all."[29]

By a Christian he meant he was a member of the Christian church. By a Democrat he meant he was a member of the Democratic party. He was not concerned with the theories of the church or the party. These change. He could change with them. The test was the value of the theories as vote-getters. To put the matter in a word, he was in every sense purely an opportunist, and it was certainly not in accord with the opportunist philosophy to be a Communist or a Socialist or even a mild pink during Roosevelt's first administration.

Actually the one thing he did that was based on a very definite phi-losophy was the program that consisted of the NRA and the AAA. This was a plan to take the whole industrial and agricultural life of the country under the wing of the government, organize it into vast farm and industrial cartels, as they were called in Germany, corpora-tives as they were called in Italy, and operate business and the farms under plans made and carried out under the supervision of the gov-ernment. This is the complete negation of liberalism. It is, in fact, the essence of fascism. Fascism goes only one step further and insists, logically, that this cannot be done by a democratic government; that it can be done successfully only under a totalitarian regime. Of course Roosevelt did not know that he was indulging in a fascist experiment because he did not know what fascism was. In those days fascism was not defined as anti-Semitism. It was a word used to describe the po-litical system of Mussolini. Roosevelt merely did something which at the moment seemed politically expedient because it satisfied a vast mass of farmers and business men. He never examined the funda-mentals of it because that was not the way his mind worked. The NRA did not fully satisfy the technocratic groups represented by the Tugwells and their disciples in spite of the many points of resem-blance. The NRA left too much control in the hands of business whereas they would have preferred to see that control in the hands of the technicians—preferably the professors. As for the Reds, they did not move in heavily until the second term and not *en masse* until the third term, although the entering wedge was made in the first. And then the point of entry was the labor movement.

In 1935, Roosevelt had a labor problem on his hands. When the NRA was launched it contained a clause called Section 7a. This was called labor's Magna Carta. It gave to labor the right to collective bargaining through representatives of their own choosing. Labor leaders did seize upon it as a great instrument for the rehabilitation of organized labor. Membership in labor unions had sunk to a low fig-ure as a result of the depression. Some of the unions were on the verge of disintegration. As the NRA codes were launched, they rep-resented literally compulsory unions of employers, and the labor leaders went to work to expand their own membership. They soon found that the NRA was, so far as labor was concerned, a complete fraud. Employers were *required* to form into a *single* code authority in each industry. Labor was merely given the *right to organize* and it could organize into one, two, three or a dozen different unions. For instance, the steel industry was united in the Steel Institute, but the steel workers were in no unions at all or separated into as many unions as there were plants. Aside from affording the unions protection, the operation of the act did not give them much cause for satisfaction. Codes guaranteed minimum wages but generally the wage guaranteed was $14 a week. In many instances, workmen were earning less money under the codes. For instance, in Detroit factory workers had their pay raised from 35 cents to 40 cents an hour. At 35 cents an hour they worked 60 hours and made from $42 to $45 in two weeks. At 40 cents an hour they worked 40 hours under the hour limitation, and made $32 in two weeks.

The whole thing got so bad that the Wagner Labor Relations Act was passed, presumably to force some kind of solidarity in labor and to give them effective bargaining rights. Actually a good many employers favored this law. The employer who wanted to pay labor decent wages and give them decent working hours and conditions could be undercut by anti-social employers who were willing to beat labor down as far as possible. There might have been a chance for this act but for the outrageous manner in which it was administered after Mr. Roosevelt's reelection in 1936.

At all events, several ideas were set in motion at this time in the White House. First, labor had to be appeased and something had to be done to quiet the mutterings which were coming up from the masses of labor.

The second was a far more serious idea. There were men around the President at this time who saw the tremendous possibilities of organizing labor as a political force. They knew the history of the labor movement in England, which had grown so great that it had completely wiped out the old Liberal party as a political force. They believed that something like that could be done in America and they wanted the President to use his vast powers and great funds to encourage the formation of labor into a great political force. To do this it was necessary to enlarge the field of labor organization.

In America, the American Federation of Labor, which included most of organized labor, specialized in organizing only craft unions. That is, carpenters, plumbers, masons, painters, machinists, etc., were organized in unions representing these separate crafts. They constituted only a small part of the labor force. The vast majority of workers were unskilled and were employed in factories or single industries and were unorganized. There were three large industrial unions—the United Mine Workers of John L. Lewis, the International Ladies Garment Workers Union of David Dubinsky and the Amalgamated Clothing Workers of Sidney Hillman. An industrial union is one in which all the people engaged in a single industry are included without regard to the type of skills at which they work. Lewis had for a long time talked about the importance of organizing all labor into industrial unions. The Federation of Labor bitterly opposed the idea.

But the industrial union was the one great instrument by which all labor could be organized and it has been said that the President was urged to promote this idea as the starting point in building up a powerful political labor movement.

At the time there were about four million men in American unions and inasmuch as the unions finally achieved a membership of over fifteen million, it can be seen what the political possibilities were. Roosevelt sent for John L. Lewis and William Green and urged them to form industrial unions. Green, head of the A. F. of L., naturally refused, but Lewis did not need much urging. Under the leadership of Lewis, Hillman and Dubinsky the fight for industrial unions was begun. Lewis proposed that the Federation of Labor admit industrial unions to its membership. This precipitated a bitter fight between Lewis, Hillman, Dubinsky on one side and what was called the Old Guard on the other—Green, Hutchinson and Frey. It reached a crisis at Atlantic City in 1935 at the Federation convention when the Federation committee brought in a report against industrial unions. Following this, in a furious exchange of epithets, Hutchinson of the Carpenters' Union, called Lewis a bastard and Lewis hit him on the jaw. Benjamin Stolberg, in his "Story of the CIO" says "that blow resounded across the American labor movement and split it in two."[30]

Under the leadership of Lewis, a new group of unions was formed called the Congress of Industrial Organizations (CIO) which opened for business on November 9, 1935. The backbone of it was the United Mine Workers, the Ladies Garment Workers and the

Amalgamated Clothing Workers. Its total membership was a million. These unions did not withdraw from the A. F. of L. However, on August 4, 1936 the executive council of the A. F. of L. voted to suspend the CIO unions unless they disbanded within a month. And this threat was carried out. The important work of the new CIO was accomplished after 1936, but the year 1936 was a period of furious organizing work by it among the unskilled workers of the country.

A labor union is not something that can be brought hurriedly into existence by unskilled hands. Half a century of labor organization has built up a body of expert knowledge about organizing and operating a union. As John L. Lewis and Dubinsky and Hillman set about organizing millions of workers they were immediately up against the problem of finding skilled organizers to promote and manage the new unions. *It was at this point that the Red appeared on the scene.*

There had been in the United States a Communist labor organization known as the Trade Union Unity League which took its instructions directly from Moscow. It is estimated that ten or fifteen thousand Communists were in these unions. There were a large number of members who were not Communists, of course, and the Communist connection was carefully concealed. Joseph Zack represented the Communist party in the United States in charge of its labor activities from 1919 to 1934. He had gone to Russia where he was instructed in the techniques of Communist labor control.

Then in 1934, Moscow directed the Communist party in the United States to dissolve the Trade Union Unity League unions and to march the members of those unions into the American Federation of Labor. This was the beginning of their plan to bore into the American labor union movement from within. The purpose of this was not to advance the cause of labor unions or to get better working conditions for the members, but to use the apparatus of the labor union as an instrument of revolution. This is not surmise, but is proven by the testimony of Joseph Zack himself, as well as that of Benjamin Gitlow who was secretary of the Communist party of the United States and by the official minutes of the Party covering this period. The Communist party in the United States in January, 1935, passed the following resolution:

"The influx of hundreds of thousands of new workers from basic industries and mass production plants into the American Federation of

Labor unions … make the American Federation of Labor unions more militant and mass unions in character, opening up new and greater possibilities of revolutionary mass work within them.

"In view of this, the main task of the party in the sphere of trade-union work should be the work in the American Federation of Labor unions so as to energetically and tirelessly mobilize the masses of their members and the trade unions as a whole for the defense of the everyday interests of the workers, the leadership of strikes, carrying out the policy of the class struggle in the trade unions …"[31]

Shortly after came the split between the A. F. of L. and the CIO and John L. Lewis found himself in need of experienced organizers. The Communist leaders saw in the rise of the CIO a better opportunity for their own revolutionary objectives than in the A. F. of L. and instructed their members to withdraw from the A. F. of L. and go into the CIO. The CIO leaders on their part saw ready to hand several thousand trained union organizers and eagerly sought and used their talents. Some of these men were known to be Communists, but the CIO leaders imagined that they could utilize their special aptitudes for organization while at the same time suppressing their revolutionary energies. They were to learn the hard way, as we shall see.

Lewis was interested in bringing into existence industrial unions like his own, in which he had always believed. Roosevelt was interested in bringing into American labor unions as many voters as possible and in capturing their leadership to be used to build up a powerful labor faction which could control the Democratic party and which he and his allies could control through the vast power of the government and the vast powers of the labor leaders, along with the immense financial resources that so great a labor movement would have. The Communists were interested in getting into the unions, into key positions as union officers, statisticians, economists, etc., in order to utilize the apparatus of the unions to promote the cause of revolution.

I think we have to be fair in saying at this point that neither Roosevelt nor Lewis realized the peril to which they were exposing both the unions and the country. This thing called revolutionary propaganda and activity is something of an art in itself. It has been developed to a high degree in Europe where revolutionary groups have been active for half a century and where Communist revolutionary groups have achieved such success during the past 25 years. It was, at this time of which I write, practically unknown to political and labor leaders in this country and is still unknown to the vast majority of political leaders. The time came when Lewis saw the gravity of the situation and faced it frankly and dealt with it immediately. But as we shall see, Roosevelt, through a combination of events and influences, fell deeper and deeper into the toils of various revolutionary operators, not because he was interested in revolution but because he was interested in votes.

For the time being, however, he capitalized heavily on the activities of the CIO. The CIO put up half a million dollars for Roosevelt's 1936 campaign and provided him with an immense group of active labor workers who played a large part in the sweeping victory he won at the polls. But among them now were a large number of Communists in positions of great power within the new union movement, some of them actually moving close to the center of power. This was the crack in the wall through which they entered. Their power was to grow and prosper.

CHAPTER 8: THE RIDE OF THE WILD RABBIT

It was 1936 and the verdict on Mr. Roosevelt was now up to the people. As the year rolled along, an uninformed observer might well suppose that the Roosevelt New Deal was in a state of considerable disarray. One after another of Mr. Roosevelt's great adventures in social architecture had been outlawed by the Supreme Court or had fallen apart of their own weakness or both. The NRA had vanished and everyone was glad to be rid of it. The AAA had been held unconstitutional and was subject to bitter criticisms. The Warren gold plan had more or less evaporated as an effective policy. The Guffey Coal Act was declared unconstitutional. The President was being pilloried because of his enormous expenditures, his unbalanced budgets, his tremendous deficits after all his merciless attacks on Hoover in 1932. By 1935 the expenditures of the Hoover administration had been more than doubled by Roosevelt and the debt had increased by 16 billion dollars. Mr. Roosevelt's strident, staccato attacks upon Hoover as the world's greatest spendthrift were being shot back at him.

The grotesque spectacle of Harry Hopkins' shovel army, Wallace's pig killing and crop destruction and the merry dance of the crackpot spenders kicking their heels in the Roosevelt electoral parade all excited the mirth and scorn of the jokesters and the commentators.

Harry Byrd was digging into New Deal extravagances and announced that the bureaucracy had proliferated at such an amazing rate that space was rented in 107 private buildings by the government to house the bureaucrats. Senator Carter Glass leveled his harshest attacks at the administration. "The New Deal," he said, "is not only a mistake. It is a disgrace to the nation. I would rather die than live to see the disgrace of this era." Senator Bailey of North Carolina, Senator Ashurst of Arizona, Senator Copeland of New York were up in arms. Lewis Douglas, Roosevelt's first director of the Budget, James Warburg, one of his earliest champions, George Peek, Hugh Johnson, Governor Ely of Massachusetts and, above all, Al Smith were unsparing in their criticism. Al Smith declared that if Roosevelt were renominated on an endorsement of the New Deal he "would take a walk." Smith, one columnist observed, was presenting Roosevelt with the sidewalks of New York one brick at a time.

The charge that Roosevelt had been playing a game of irresponsible experimentation with the American people as the guinea pigs was pressed with such effect that Roosevelt felt called upon, in a letter to Roy Howard, head of the Scripps Howard Newspapers, to assure him that the experimental stage of the New Deal was near an end. Amid all his other difficulties, the President was presented with the soldiers' bonus bill. He vetoed that but had an arrangement with the Democratic leadership that they would pass it over his head. Thus the President could get credit for trying to kill it while the Democrats would get credit for actually passing it.

The country had been torn by strikes—over 2,000 of them. The drive of the CIO for membership in their new unions was proceeding with ostentatious energy. There was no discounting the apparent seriousness of the differences that had developed among the Democratic leaders. The Southern senators—men like Walter George and Pat Harrison and Millard Tydings and others, including Vice-President Garner—were in deep dejection at the direction in which they saw the party going. Even stalwart Democratic leaders and newspapers, along with men whose opinions could not be dismissed, were disgusted with the orgy of the relief rolls under Hopkins. The President felt it necessary to say something about that. He said that to dole out relief in this way "is to administer a narcotic, a subtle destroyer of the human spirit ... I am not willing that the vitality of our people be further sapped by the giving of doles, of market baskets, by a few hours of weekly work cutting grass, raking leaves or picking up papers in the public parks." He declared for useful public works—roads, highways, reforestation.

Tempers were frayed. Representative Blanton of Texas offered to fight all the physicians in Washington at one time. John O'Connor of New York said he would kick Father Coughlin from the Capitol to the White House. Father Coughlin, who had extolled Roosevelt at first as a great leader, now denounced him as a liar. Vito Marcantonio said he would like to meet Police Commissioner Valentine of New York in a gymnasium. The New York *Sun* suggested that the House restaurant had better take raw meat off the menu. The Townsendites got into a fight among themselves. Townsend accused Representative McGroarty, who introduced the Townsend bill, of trying to deliver the Townsendites to the Democrats. William Randolph Hearst, who supported Roosevelt in 1932 and without whose support he could not have got his first nomination, attacked Roosevelt for accepting the support of organizations alien to the American form of government, and Steve Early said Hearst was "a notorious newspaper owner" who had made a planned attempt to ruin Roosevelt. Others branded Roosevelt a Communist and Reverend John O'Brien fulminated with blazing vehemence that this was "an ugly, cowardly and flagrant calumny."

When the Republicans met they nominated Alfred Landon of Kansas for President and Frank Knox of Chicago for Vice-President. Landon as governor of Kansas had made a notable record as a budget balancer and chief executive. The Republicans adopted a platform which did not differ much from the Democratic platform of 1932. When accused of stealing the Democratic platform of 1932, the Republicans replied "Why not? The Democrats have no more use for it. Moreover it is in perfectly good condition—it was never even used." Their chief reliance was upon the charge that the

President had usurped the powers of Congress, attacked the integrity of the courts, invaded the constitutional prerogatives of the states, attempted to substitute regulated monopoly for free enterprise, forced through Congress unconstitutional laws, filled a vast array of bureaus with swarms of bureaucrats to harass the people and breed fear in commerce and industry, discouraged new enterprises and thus prolonged the depression, had used relief to corrupt and intimidate the voters and made appeals to class prejudice to inflame the masses and create dangerous divisions.

Bertrand Snell, permanent chairman of the Republican convention, said "the people should thank God for the Constitution, the Supreme Court and a courageous press." Whether one agrees with this or not, most men, I am sure, will now agree in the light of events that had there been no constitutional prohibitions and no Supreme Court, Roosevelt would certainly have gone to terrifying lengths in his course. And as an example of what Time does to slogans and anthems, the band in the GOP convention greeted the arrival of the New York delegation by playing alternately "The Sidewalks of New York" and "California Here I Come" in honor of the two bitter antagonists of the 1928 battle—Smith and Hoover.

At the Democratic convention the theme song was still "Happy Days Are Here Again." Delirious enthusiasm was lathered up by every device known to show business for making whoop-de-dee. From the moment the gavel fell to open that wild conclave to the knock of the adjourning gavel everything that was said and done or that seemed to just happen was in accordance with a carefully arranged and managed scenario. The delegates were mere puppets and answered to their cues precisely like the extras in a movie mob scene. The only spontaneous thing in the convention was an unarranged demonstration for Jim Farley, the stage manager of the great hippodrome. It was really a Farley show. A Texan rode a donkey around the hall. The screaming delegates named a queen of the convention; they roared and paraded; they abolished the two-thirds rule and, after it was all over, on Saturday night at Franklin Field before a crowd of 100,000, Roosevelt and Garner stood surrounded by Mrs. Roosevelt, Sr. and Jr., James, John, Franklin Jr., and Mr. and Mrs. John Boettiger, while Lily Pons sang "The Star-Spangled Banner" and the exhausted Democrats sang, cheered and wept.

As the campaign got under way the betting was eight to five on Roosevelt. Nevertheless the Republicans thought they had a golden chance to win. John Hamilton of Kansas was made National Chairman and he challenged Jim Farley to name six states Roosevelt was sure to carry. The Republican forecasters—and many others—were completely deceived by the group of elements and issues hostile to Roosevelt which we have enumerated—the opposition of Al Smith and the anti-New Deal Democrats, the scandals in the relief rolls, Roosevelt's complete betrayal of all his 1932 promises, the rise in taxes and prices and debt, the boisterous, angry caterwauling of the leaders of those hungry millions who wanted old-age pensions and more government handouts. Shortly after the Democratic convention, Father Coughlin, Representative Lemke and some remnants of the Share-the-Wealthers led by Gerald L. K. Smith met to form a third party. They called it the Union Party. It resolved for Social Justice, Revolving Pensions and Every Man a King. Then it nominated Lemke for President and Gerald L. K. Smith told the world it would poll 20 million ballots in November.

These amateur politicians did not know that Farley had already gathered in the Huey Long crowd and the Townsendites and that only the shells of these movements were at the Union Party convention. As for those anti-New Deal Democrats, the dopesters refused to understand the fact that the bulk of them were from the South and they just did not understand what makes a Southern Democrat tick. Carter Glass had flung a whole string of sulphurous adjectives at the New Deal. But Heywood Broun appraised that factor rightly when he said: "Carter Glass would never forsake the party if the fiend himself were nominated. He might assail Lucifer verbally, perhaps refuse to go to his house to dinner, but if the Devil were a Democrat he would never cut him on the ballot."

They overlooked the fact that the South had both arms up to its shoulder blades in Roosevelt's relief and public works barrel. National politics was now paying off in the South in terms of billions. When Alf Landon talked about Roosevelt's invasions of the Constitution, the man on relief and the farmer fingering his subsidy check replied "You can't eat the Constitution." Not only that, but the small store owner had customers now by the millions whose WPA and PWA and CCC and AAA spendings in his store made the difference between black and red on his books. Roosevelt over the radio said the whole question was after all a simple one—just ask yourself one question. Are you worse off now or better off than when we took office? He repeated the employment figures on the day of his inauguration and during this campaign. As to the public debt he said we borrowed eight billions but we have increased the national income by 22 billions. Would you borrow $800 a year if thereby you could increase your income by $2200, he asked. That is what we have done, he answered, with the air of a man who has easily resolved a tough conundrum. And though the figures were false and the reasoning even more so it was practically impossible for a Republican orator to reason with voters against these seemingly obvious and plausible figures.

Oddly, throughout the campaign, one issue seemed to obtrude itself at intervals like a distant and indefinable odor. The smell of war got into the air off in the background. The Socialist Party held its convention at Cleveland and nominated Norman Thomas for President. But a bitter struggle arose over a resolution calling for a mass resistance to war by a general strike. The resolution was passed but Louis Waldman, Algernon Lee, James O'Neal and Thomas Kreuger walked out of the convention and formed what they called the Social Democratic Federation of the United States. Thus the war issue split the Socialist Party though it was only 1936.

Somehow people seemed jittery on this subject. If there was one resolution firmly imbedded in their minds it was that they would not be drawn into another war. The Spanish revolution was in full blast and Germany and Italy and Russia were dipping their fingers in it, to the great irritation of diverse groups here. Someone wrote that this was just a dress rehearsal for that greater conflict between Russia and Germany which was inevitable. Roosevelt, exploiting every vote-getting device and perceiving this stern resistance to our participation in any possible war, chose it as the theme of his first formal address in the campaign. He told his audience that he "was more concerned and less cheerful about international world conditions than about our immediate domestic prospects." This was saying plainly that he saw ahead a possible war situation rather than any domestic crisis. He said: "We shun political commitments which might entangle us in future wars; we avoid connection with the political activities of the League of Nations." He told the audience "We are not isolationist except insofar as *we attempt to isolate ourselves completely from war.*" Then he warned that "so long as war exists on earth there will be some danger that even a nation which ardently desires peace may be drawn into that war."

He continued with emphasis: "I hate war. I have passed unnumbered hours, I shall pass unnumbered hours thinking and planning how war may be kept from this nation." The Congress, he explained, had given him certain authority to provide safeguards of American neutrality in case of war. The President had been given "new weapons to maintain our neutrality." Thus he was approving the existence of those weapons in the Neutrality Act. But this was not enough. Whether we went in or stayed out of war would depend on who was President at the time. "Nevertheless," he said with staccato emphasis on every word, "and I speak from long experience—the effective maintenance of American neutrality depends today as in the past on the wisdom and determination of whoever at the moment occupies the office of President of the United States and Secretary of State."[32]

Nothing could be clearer. At the moment three leading nations were flirting with war. That war might break. It might spread over Europe as the First World War did, which started in Serbia and then engulfed the world. Roosevelt was saying as plainly as words could say it that if the President, when the chance came, wanted to take us into the war, the Neutrality Act would not avail, but if the President wanted to keep us out, this would be an effective weapon in his hands. And, of course, the final implication was that the great chance of the American people to avoid this grave possibility was to name him President.

Then he touched a sensitive note: "It is clear that our present policy … would in the event of war on some other continent, reduce war profits which would otherwise accrue to American citizens. Industrial and agricultural products having a war market may give immense fortunes to a few men. *For a nation as a whole it produces disaster.*" Who, then, had we to fear as the war-mongers? "Let us not blink the fact," he continued, "that we would find in this country thousands of Americans who, seeking immediate riches, fool's gold, would attempt to break down or evade our neutrality." They would tell you the unemployed would find work, that America would capture the trade of the world. "It would be hard for Americans," the President said, "to look beyond—to realize the inevitable penalties, the inevitable day of reckoning that comes from a false prosperity ... But all the wisdom of America is not to be found in the White House or the Department of State; we need the meditation, the prayers and the support of the people of America who will go along with us in seeking peace."

He ended by saying that "peace will depend on their (the President and Secretary of State) day to day decisions ... We can keep out of war if those who watch and desire have a sufficiently detailed understanding of international affairs to make certain that the small decisions of today do not lead toward war and if at the same time they possess the courage to say no to those who selfishly or unwisely would lead us to war."

Of course Roosevelt was talking not about some mythical or vague threat of war. He was talking about a war in Europe or Asia. Hitler had been in power for four years. He had denounced the Versailles Treaty and the Locarno Pact. He had marched into the Rhineland. He had announced his intention to rearm Germany to the teeth. He was breathing fire and brimstone against his neighbors. When, therefore, Roosevelt referred to a possible war, it was just such a war as broke out in Europe in 1939. And he was telling the people of America that if such a crisis came the one chance to stay out of it was to name him President to be certain that the Neutrality Act would be used to the fullest extent to keep us out.

Two months after this, Jim Farley reported to Roosevelt that Senator Hugo Black, who had just made a trip through many states, had told him the President's opposition to a possible war was the most effective issue he had, coupled with the fact that he was familiar with the international situation, and Black urged Farley to induce the President to make another speech on the subject.

To those who followed the election closely the result was a foregone conclusion. But few realized it would be so sweeping. Jim Farley had predicted that Landon would carry only two states. It must stand as an all-time record in the field of political prophecy. Roosevelt got 523 electoral votes, Landon only eight. In no state, save New Hampshire, was the voting even close. Roosevelt got 27,751,000 votes; Landon 16,681,000. Curiously the election not only wrecked for the moment the Republican party; it almost destroyed the Socialist party. That party had once polled a million votes for Eugene V. Debs. It polled 884,000 votes for Thomas in 1932. In this election it got 187,000. Some 700,000 Socialist votes had been swept into the Democratic party.

After the election predictions were being freely made by various writers and political observers all over the country that the defeat of Landon marked the end of the Republican party.

The election had in it a profound lesson for those who have some familiarity with European history. What had achieved this amazing result? The President's golden voice? His oratorical power? His extraordinary personal charm? The astonishing success of his program? Obviously none of these. His program was almost all in collapse and those things which remained, such as the Social Security Act, the Stock Exchange Act, the Utility Holding Company Act, etc., had had no possible effect on the economic system yet. Men do not win elections with golden voices and personal charms. They do not win such resounding victories as these. Actually, the President was supported loyally by many men who, far from melting under his charm, hated him.

The President's victory was due to one thing and one thing only, to that one great rabbit—the spending rabbit—he had so reluctantly pulled out of his hat in 1933. This put into his hands a fund amounting to nearly 20 billion dollars with which he was able to gratify the appetites of vast groups of people in every county in America—not merely the poor and disconsolate victims of the depression, but the long deferred ambitions of every town, county, city and state for expensive and even grandiose projects otherwise hopelessly out of their reach. It enabled him to engage in that succession of grandiose and reckless adventures, which had the appearance of great daring and captivated the imagination of so many young men and women who understood little or nothing about the great laws of both nature and economics which he flouted. The meager campaign funds spent on Presidential elections in the past were so much chicken-feed compared with that stupendous barrel of billions which the President had to dispense twelve months a year. Of all those fictitious rabbits the President pulled out of his hat this was the one and the only one which survived and was any good for the great job ahead. It became a snorting steed of incredible vigor. It had become a little wild. But it was this monstrous rabbit with Roosevelt on its back that carried him on that wild ride through the polling places of 46 states and shot him breathlessly back into the White House for another four years.

Book Two:
Confusion

Chapter 1: The Coming American Boom

For the second time, Franklin D. Roosevelt faced the Chief Justice on the front portico of the Capitol to be sworn in as President. For a man who took almost childish delight in breaking precedents, he must have derived a good deal of satisfaction from the fact that he was the first President, under the new law, to be sworn in on January 20 instead of March 4. Aside from that, it was the standard type of inauguration, including the rain.

But the scene in the great wide country had changed vastly. The nation was having its disasters, but they were natural ones—rivers swollen and farms inundated—but no great economic disturbances were in sight. Roosevelt appeared before the throng as the great physician who had healed the nation. True, the patient was not wholly recovered. The national income, payrolls, industrial production were still 20 per cent under the 1929 figure and building was only about one-third of what it had been in 1929. Farm commodities were still under their 1929 price. But things were moving up.

The tremendous victory of the President at the polls had done something to his enemies. A sense of political frustration had swept over the business leaders of the country. Many of them were so beaten down by the popular endorsement of the President that the fight was taken out of them. A vague presentiment troubled them that some new condition had come which they did not fully understand and that the best thing to do was to make the best of it. Newspapers and magazines were saying that the Republican party was done.

Above the depressive undertone, however, was a rising tone of optimism. Men in Wall Street and business circles were talking about the coming American boom. Even the great steel industry, the last to feel the pull of this new life, was roaring along. I went through the steel towns before Christmas, just prior to the 1937 inauguration. As one approached the steel country the sky was ablaze with the radiance of the old beehive ovens—thousands of them brought into life again because the existing modern ovens were inadequate. At Pittsburgh a spirit of rush and movement was there again for the first time since 1929. In all the hotels and restaurants the orchestras were playing the new song "Santa Claus Is Coming to Town." The mills were working three shifts a day and the workers were getting 10 per cent wage increases. They were paying up old bills and buying new things in the stores. Spindles were humming in the cotton textile mills of New England. By March there were some business men who were afraid the boom might get out of hand and go too far.

Labor was on the march. The great drive for the steel workers, with John L. Lewis as commander-in-chief of the CIO was under way. The workers were joining up in great numbers and ahead lay the promise of a grave issue. Sit-down strikes were in progress in many plants and the whole Pacific coast was tied up in a great shipping strike. But all this somehow did not impair the brightness of the out-look to business men who were hungry for the boom.

The great victory in November had done something to Roosevelt too. Almost his whole first-term program lay about him in ruins. All the theatrical features which had excited the imagination of the peo-ple had been taken off the boards. Despite that, there had been a steady rise in recovery or at least what looked like recovery. Unem-ployment was down to about seven million and it continued to de-crease each month. The President confidently believed that he had licked the depression, but to whatever extent the country had recov-ery it was due entirely to the spending program of the administration.

This he had called "priming the pump." The pump, of course, was the great business machine into which America poured its invest-ment billions and its vast labor energies and out of which was pumped the vast flood of goods and the income to buy them. Roose-velt had poured 16 billion dollars of borrowed public funds into that pump but he had failed to do anything about fixing the pump. The pump was delivering up goods and income but only so long as he primed it. The great investment industries were idle. The building industry generally was still from a half to a third below prosperity fig-ures. Without the revival of investment there could be no revival of the economic system. The system was being supported by govern-ment spending of borrowed funds.

The President did not too clearly perceive the full significance of all this. He imagined that the pump had begun to work and that very soon he could proudly announce that he could cease priming it, that is, that he could quit spending borrowed funds and balance the budget.

He was in a gay and triumphant mood. A naturally vain man, the tremendous victory at the polls had swollen his ego enormously. Few men in public life have ever received such thunderous applause or been surrounded by so many flatterers. The reason, of course, was that no man in our history had ever had in his hands a purse so full of billions to hand out to states and to cities, to business, to workers, to rich and poor alike. Flattery drenched his uplifted head. After all, this widespread applause, these innumerable flatteries could not all be wrong. In fact, were not the results of his wizardry before him? Perhaps he *was* a wizard after all. He became more cocky and, what is more, he decided he was going to punish certain powerful elements who had defied him. To begin with he was going to bring the Supreme Court to its knees.

Aside from this, what would Roosevelt now do? If, as he supposed, the economic system was now moving rapidly towards a healthful balance, what more could be asked of him? He would have to balance the budget and, probably, reduce the debt he had created. He had given the country a Social Security Act, opened the banks, tamed Wall Street. What else was there to do?

It is not always easy to know from what Roosevelt said at any given moment just what he was about. For instance, in his 1937 inaugural address he gave the impression that there stretched before him certain great objectives—that millions of people worked at pitifully low salaries, that millions of farmers lived squalid lives, on farms worse than the poorest European farms, he said; that millions of people didn't have enough to eat. He used the phrase "one-third of a nation ill-clad, ill-fed and ill-housed" and from this he gave out the promise that he was just beginning to fight and that he proposed to use the powers of the government to put an end to all this.

Yet a short time after this he said to a very powerful senator among his own supporters that he was through with experimentation and that what he now wished to do was to consolidate his gains. This, coming a few weeks after the challenging inaugural oration, was the precise reverse of that address. Which of these points of view represented what was really in his mind?

I repeat here that until he was inaugurated as President, Roosevelt probably never entertained any doubts whatever about the soundness of our existing system. He had run with that school which believes government should put more of its weight on the side of the so-called "little people." This general attitude of benevolence to the interests of the masses, rather than to the interests of business, characterized those groups in this country who liked to call themselves liberals.

As already indicated, these were views into which he had fallen with the tide of the time in which he lived as a young man. They were the views of his associates and the party faction in which he had begun his career. It is perfectly obvious from any study of his speeches and his actions that he had not arrived at these principles through any long examination of the nature and structure of society. Looking at Roosevelt's whole program—that which he achieved and that which still remained—Raymond Moley describes it most vividly. One's astonishment at beholding it, he wrote:

> "Arose chiefly from the wonder that one man could have been so flexible as to permit himself to believe so many things in so short a time. But to look upon these policies as the result of a unified plan was to believe that the accumulation of stuffed snakes, baseball pictures, school flags, old tennis shoes, carpenter's tools, geometry books and chemistry sets in a boy's bedroom could have been put there by an interior decorator."[1]

As nearly as one can make out, Roosevelt's opinions at this moment were generally that big business was immoral, that the poor were not getting a fair break and that the depression was the result of the sins of business and that business must be punished for these sins. But it is perfectly obvious that he did not know what the sins were which had done the damage. Beyond doubt business men commit sins, singly and in organized groups. Some of the sins spring from greed. Others spring from perfectly proper motives. Some are sins of the heart; some are sins of the head without conscious iniquity in them. Some of the sins injure the whole social economy very seriously. Others, however wicked, do not have that effect—may actually help it. There is no evidence that Roosevelt ever put his finger on the real causes that make the free private enterprise system fail to work. Along with this he had drifted to the general theory, only vaguely defined, that the government must step into the situation and by the use of its credit and its regulatory power, take a controlling part in making the system work. He certainly had not explored the direction in which this theory would lead him. It is the theory of the all-powerful benevolent state toward which Europe had been drifting for fifty years and which had begun with certain small, uncertain experimental steps very much like those Roosevelt was taking. But the last thing in his mind was any suspicion that the steps he was taking would lead him as far as they finally did and as they must inevitably lead any statesman who tries them.

If he was right, he had to believe that presently the whole economic system would be moving along smoothly and that at this point he must do something to give the working man and the poorer elements in the community a better break. Furthermore, to do this he must remain in power, that is he must not merely continue to be President throughout his four years, but must have a Congress amenable to his wishes and a Court that would not balk him. To do this he must have votes all the time and particularly two years hence in the 1938 Congressional elections. Under no circumstances could he permit a recurrence of the depression.

The three forces that he wished to set in motion were under way. First, there was the great industrial labor movement. Second, the election had crushed his enemies and put in his hands tremendous power to work his will. Third, the country was rolling on in another great American boom. How would it all turn out?

Bright as it all seemed one cloud moved over this serene landscape. The great sit-down strike drive had begun. The union was encamped inside the Fisher Body plant and the General Motors plants in Detroit. Vice-President Garner was aroused at this. He went to Roosevelt. He spoke plainly. And Roosevelt assured him that he agreed that the strikes were illegal and not right. Garner got the impression Roosevelt would issue a statement against them. But he did not. Later in January, after the inauguration, Garner, Robinson and Roosevelt were discussing the legislative program. Garner talked about the sit-down strikes. They were an illegal seizure of property. If the Michigan governor did not stop it the people of Michigan were being denied a republican government. The federal government must intervene. But Roosevelt refused to move. He said any attempt to get the men out would mean bloodshed. The argument broke into an angry brawl. Garner angrily told Roosevelt: "John L. Lewis is a bigger man than you are if you can't find some way to cope with this."[2] Senator Robinson quieted the Vice-President. But from that moment on Garner was in a state of continuous disgust over the development of the labor situation. Senator Byrnes offered a resolution declaring it to be the sense of the Senate that the sit-down strike was illegal. Senator Joe Robinson, majority leader, told him he favored it, but as leader could not go along. The resolution, under Roosevelt's influence, was defeated. But this subject was to divide the Democratic party dangerously for the whole of the second term.

The outlines of the President's character now began to appear, but only vaguely. When Roosevelt became President he was very little known personally. His long illness immediately after World War I had withdrawn him from general circulation until he ran for governor of New York. He did not get around as men in public life do and he had few actual personal contacts with the men who were to deal with him later.

He appeared now before the public as a genial, happy and at times merry person, warm-hearted and generous. He had acquired the reputation of being a public speaker of extraordinary talents. But many stories got around that those famous speeches he delivered were written for him by others and his talent was rather that of an actor who declaimed them well.

In Washington, among his Democratic associates and leaders, he had begun to acquire a reputation for being a little shifty and undependable in an agreement. Garner said he was a hard man to have an arrangement with—"he would deviate from the understanding."[3] Many stories were told about the readiness with which he made promises and the equal readiness with which he forgot them. In personal conversation he was full of tall tales about himself and his prowess in laying out imaginary disputants. The public generally, however, knew nothing of this and the image of the high toned, aristocratic gentleman of unimpeachable personal integrity persisted popularly.

He was a handsome man with a colorful personality and singularly favored by nature in his physical get-up. It was not surprising that he should be a vain man. He sat, after his 1936 victory, at the topmost peak of fame. Courtiers flattered him; politicians, organizations, people of all sorts seeking some part of that vast treasure which he had been given by Congress vied with each other in extolling him. A kind of legend grew up around him from this source—about his charm, his voice, his lightening shafts of wit and such. He would have been less than human if he had not yielded to the whisperings of vanity.

For another thing, a curious laxity in the behavior of his family was causing a good deal of talk around the country. In Washington a group of senators sent one of their number to suggest to him that the escapades of some of his sons were bringing his own name under unprofitable criticism.[4] He assured the senator that he had given his sons a good education, done everything possible to put them upon the right path and he did not feel he was responsible for what they did. Magazines and newspapers printed stories about the members of his family in their efforts to exploit the White House for commercial ends. This was a source of a good deal of surprise in a family which was supposed to be wealthy. Mrs. Roosevelt's activities, her lectures and her radio broadcasts for money running into large sums were, to say the least, unusual. It took the public a little while to get used to her.

Altogether, the sum total of it was the feeling in certain quarters that the ethical standards of the family were not too high, not what had been expected of people of their standing and class. It surprised many. It disappointed and disturbed others. The tradition of the White House as an exemplar of good manners and good conduct was being subjected to some strain.

The seriousness of it lay in one fact of tremendous significance. Of that we shall see later. For the time being we may rest with the comment that already that fatal spiritual drug, Power, had begun its work upon the mind and spirit of the President. Power is an insidious intoxicant. It has produced in history some of its most appalling tragedies. Power now had come into the hands of this man. What were his moral and intellectual qualities for resisting its corrosive effects? The President's immense victory in November was a heavy dose to take, save for a soul well-armed. This thing called power had been a subject of grave preoccupation with the men who built the Republic. They had made the most elaborate arrangements to keep this dreaded cup out of the hands of presidents. Now it was in the hands of one, and filled almost to its brim—though not quite. If what follows has any lesson for history it is because it is one more clinical experiment in the effect of power upon the human mind and upon human society.

CHAPTER 2: WAR ON THE COURTS

If evidence were lacking that Roosevelt's massive victory at the polls had done something to him, he lost no time in supplying the proof. On February 4, 1937, just two weeks after his inauguration, the President sent word to Joe Robinson, his Senate leader, and Speaker Bankhead of the House to be present at a cabinet meeting that day and to bring with them Hatton Sumners and Senator Henry Ashurst, chairmen respectively of the House and Senate Judiciary Committees. The cabinet and the invited legislators were present shortly before noon, assembled around the large table in the cabinet room, and all wondering what was in the air.[5]

Presently, somewhat late, the President was led in and took his seat at the head of the table. The clerk put on the table in front of each person several documents. The President looked at his watch and said he would not have very much time. He had sent for them to inform them that he was sending to Congress a message and the draft of a bill which proposed a reorganization of the Supreme Court. The bill would give him power to appoint a justice for every member of the Court who had reached the age of 70 and refused to retire, and he could appoint as many as six additional judges. He explained that this was necessary because, due to the age of the justices the Court was behind in its work, that the method of administering the Court's docket was defective and that the same rule applied to district and circuit judges would enable him to provide enough judges to keep up with the courts' lagging business.

He made a few more brief explanations, looked at his watch again and explained that he had a press conference in a few minutes, could wait no longer and went out of the room.

The President of the United States had just acquainted the cabinet and the Democratic Congressional leaders with a plan, the boldest and most revolutionary any president had ever suggested to his party colleagues. Not a soul present, save Attorney-General Cummings, had any inkling of what was coming. No one was asked to comment or give an opinion. It was an imperial order by a man who had become confused about his true place in the general scheme of things.

This was one show that was being managed by Mr. Roosevelt himself. Up to now he had had the benefit on political matters of the astute advice and direction of Jim Farley and on Congressional matters of Vice-President Garner, Joe Robinson in the Senate, and of Bankhead, Rayburn and others in the House. But all of these men had been carefully excluded from any knowledge of this step.

The plan had been cooked up between Roosevelt, Attorney-General Homer Cummings and Donald Richberg. The Supreme Court had invalidated not only the NRA and the AAA, but a whole string of Roosevelt's New Deal laws. After all, there was and is a Constitution and Roosevelt had swept it aside in his impetuous drive for the numerous contradictory New Deal measures. His conception of the structure of the government was never really clear. The independence of the courts is something which all parties had accepted as a matter of course. Yet Roosevelt could suggest to Chief Justice Hughes that it might be well if Hughes discussed controverted constitutional decisions with him while he would discuss proposed legislation with the Chief Justice. The veriest law tyro would see the impropriety of this. Yet Roosevelt, in telling of the incident, described Hughes' coolness to his suggestion as evidence of the Court's "unwillingness to cooperate."

More than a year earlier, Tommy Corcoran had suggested to Senator Burton K. Wheeler the addition of two justices to the Court and Senator Wheeler had advised that the President quickly forget any such scheme. Corcoran reported this to the President, betraying some concern himself about the propriety of the proposal. Later, Homer Cummings took up the matter seriously and it was he who brought to the President the court-packing plan. Roosevelt was delighted and imposed on Cummings and Richberg, who was then brought into the proceedings, the most absolute secrecy. Thus nothing was known of this plan until it was thrown on the table on the morning of February 4, 1937.

The news, of course, created a sensation. Republican opposition was up in arms. But more serious, a large section of the huge Democratic majority was dismayed. The bill would be referred to the Judiciary Committees of both houses for hearings. Judge Hatton Sumners of Texas was chairman of the House committee. He had been at the cabinet meeting when Roosevelt tossed his plan before the leaders at the White House. As Sumners left the White House that morning, several newspapermen asked him what it was all about. He told them. Then he said: "This is where I cash in my chips."

The House leaders, angry though they were, reported to Roosevelt that he had a majority for the bill of 100 in the House. History, I think, will record that the House of Representatives elected in the landslide of 1936 reached the lowest level in character and intelligence of any House since the Civil War. Its members and its leaders were the compliant tools of the President and the hungry beggars for his bounties. Nevertheless, this bill was a little too much and while they dutifully expressed in the private polls taken by the leaders their readiness to go along, they muttered among themselves and they did not complain when resolute old Hatton Sumners determined that the House Judiciary Committee would not even hold hearings on the bill. The President and his subalterns considered taking a vote of the House to compel the Judiciary Committee to report the bill. They had the votes, but for some reason decided not to act, but to start hearings on the bill in the Senate.

The Republican leaders decided that it would be wise for them, after formal and perfunctory expressions of individual disapproval, to leave this bone for the Democrats. From his sickbed in Virginia, Carter Glass began hurling whole streams of epithets at the plan which, he said, was "completely destitute of all moral understanding." Harry Byrd, Millard Tydings and above all, Burton K. Wheeler sounded off and at a later meeting of the Democratic critics of the plan it was decided that Burton Wheeler should take the leadership of the opposition.

Wheeler had had a long and distinguished career as a courageous and honest champion of liberal causes. Like most liberals, he had been critical of the Court, but he was a believer in the Constitution and the American system and everything in his soul rose up in rebellion against the President's audacious plan to destroy the independence of the judiciary.

Wheeler was a Democrat—a powerful Democrat. He knew when he took the leadership of this movement he was putting under Roosevelt's hand his own political death warrant which Roosevelt would not hesitate to sign. He delivered a terrific blow to the plan on the first day of the Senate hearings. The reasons given by Roosevelt for his plan publicly were wholly lacking in frankness. He did not say he wanted to pack the Court with a batch of judges who would vote as he wished. He put it entirely on the ground that because of the age and infirmities of so many judges the Court was hopelessly behind with its work. This reason for the plan was supplied to Roosevelt by Sam Rosenman. On the first day of the open hearings, Senator Wheeler rose and read a letter from Chief Justice Hughes, in which the Justice called attention to the fact—a fact well-known to lawyers—that the Supreme Court's docket for the first time in many years was absolutely up to date. There were no cases lagging behind for any reason. Hughes had been not merely the presiding judge, but a competent and exacting administrator of the Court's affairs. This letter completely punctured the whole pretense on which Roosevelt's plan was based.

It produced consternation in the White House. Roosevelt called in his immediate White House advisers. He was angry with Rosenman, who had invented this shabby excuse which had now been completely deflated, and he poured out his wrath on Rosenman's head. One of the group, more hardy than the others, said there was nothing to do but to come out boldly and frankly with the real reason. "This," he said, "is a plan to pack the Court. You have to say so frankly to the people. Until you do that you cannot advance the real arguments which you have for the plan."

However, Roosevelt's optimism was not diminished. Taking at 100 per cent all the praise showered on him for his irresistible charm, he believed that he had the complete confidence of the voters and that he could talk them into his plan without any trouble. He said to Farley: "All we have to do is to let the flood of mail settle on Congress. You just wait. All I have to do is to deliver a better speech and the opposition will be beating a path to the White House door." He had already made two speeches—one a fireside chat in which he told the people to trust him, to have faith in him and his motives. But somehow the golden voice didn't work.

Roosevelt's first mistake was the manner in which he had announced the plan, which was an insult to the leaders. His second was the phony reason he gave for it, which was now gone. His third was in supposing that he could do anything provided he could reach the people with his voice. He was now to make a fourth.

Wheeler's plan of action in attack could hardly be improved on. He summoned before the committee none but well-known liberals, men whose standing before the country as liberals could not be questioned. Week after week there came lawyers, educators, authorities on constitutional law, writers and leaders, all of whom had been critical of the decisions of the Court, but all of whom repudiated the idea that because the Court did not agree with them our system of government should be torn to pieces and our constitutional liberties deprived of the incalculable bulwark of a free court against the aggressions of an executive. Just as Hughes' letter had cut from under Roosevelt's feet the pretense that the plan was offered to get rid of the log-jam in the courts, so Wheeler's strategy robbed Roosevelt completely of the false cry that the opposition came from the economic royalists and the tories. The more senators listened to the arguments offered day after day before the Senate Judiciary Committee, the more the people read of these arguments and the men who were offering them, the weaker and more hopeless became the President's case.

At this point the men closest to Roosevelt in managing the fight began to talk of compromises. One of these was to limit the number of new justices to two. Another was to allow the President to appoint a justice for every man reaching the age of 75, but limiting him to one appointment a year. He could have gotten this, which would have been unfortunate, but it would have enabled him to show a victory over the Court. He rejected the idea of compromise in spite of the advice of almost everybody around him.

Throughout the battle, things seemed to break against Roosevelt who, a few months before, looked upon himself as the very darling of Fortune. First of all, the Supreme Court came in with a batch of five decisions upholding the constitutionality of some recent Congressional measures; one or two of them by unanimous vote thus impairing the charge of a perversely hostile court. Next Justice Van Devanter resigned, giving Roosevelt the opportunity to appoint a judge of his own political complexion.

This presented him with another dilemma. The Senate leaders wanted Joe Robinson appointed to the bench. This had been Robinson's life-long ambition. It was Robinson's militant and unflinching defense of Roosevelt's plan that was keeping it alive. But the appointment never came to Robinson, who resented this, and a coolness developed between him and the White House. Learning of this, Roosevelt had to send his son James to appease Robinson and invite him to the White House. There Roosevelt had to make to the high-tempered senator the awkward explanation that he could not well appoint him until he had another vacancy so that he could name a well-known liberal to mitigate the objections of New Dealers who looked on Robinson as a reactionary.

Roosevelt's unwillingness to compromise now angered his own supporters who were being forced to carry this unpopular cause. In the end he had to assure Robinson that he would have the appointment, and then to crown Roosevelt's difficulties, Robinson was stricken with a heart attack in the Senate and died shortly after, alone in his apartment.

Tempers were high now. All the Democratic House and Senate leaders, cabinet officials and politicians left on a special train for Little Rock, Arkansas, to attend Robinson's funeral. The train was hot with quarrels and bickerings. It ceased to be a funeral train and became a traveling Democratic caucus seething with anger over the Court plan and all the troubles it had brought, including the splitting wide open of the Democratic party. Farley says he was "amazed at the amount of bitterness engendered by the Court issue." High on the agenda of frets and worries was the question of Robinson's successor as leader of the Senate.

Alben Barkley of Kentucky, assistant leader, was a candidate. So was Pat Harrison of Mississippi. Roosevelt, following Robinson's funeral, wished to communicate with the Democratic organization in the Senate on the Court bill. He did so by writing to Barkley—the "dear Alben" letter, which just about finished Harrison. Harrison was in arms. He said this was Roosevelt's way of tapping Barkley for the leadership job. Farley had to step into the breach. He told the President of the wrath in the Harrison camp. The President denied that he was for Barkley. He wrote a sweet letter to Harrison, but actually he was for Barkley and took pains to see that Barkley got the support that he, Roosevelt, could command in the Senate, thus electing him leader. This is an example of one of those incidents which led almost every member of Mr. Roosevelt's high command at one time or another to say that the President had misled them with obvious untruths.

Vice-President Garner, disgusted at the labor troubles which he attributed to Roosevelt, had packed up his duds and gone to Texas. Roosevelt complained that Garner had left him in the lurch on the Court fight. But he really had no right to complain. He had not taken Garner or any other leader into his confidence on the Court plan. He had set out to manage it himself. He had made an appalling mess of it and he now complained bitterly that Garner had deserted him. However, when the Robinson funeral train got to Little Rock, Garner was there. This event had fetched him out of his seclusion at Uvalde. Returning to Washington on the train, Garner got in touch with all the Democratic senators and leaders aboard. When the President got back to Washington, he was informed by those who were still fighting his battle that it was now no longer possible to get any kind of face-saving compromise.

Following this, Garner went to the White House. He was brutally frank with the President. He told him he was licked and suggested that the best course for him was to leave the matter in Garner's hands to make the best settlement he could. Roosevelt wearily agreed. Garner went to Wheeler and asked on what terms he would settle. Wheeler replied: "Unconditional surrender."

Meanwhile, the President asked Barkley to see Wheeler and to make an arrangement by which the bill would at least remain on the calendar. On July 22, in the afternoon, Senator Logan rose on the floor of the Senate. It had been agreed that the bill would be recommitted to the committee with the Supreme Court provisions left out of it. Senator Logan now made the motion to recommit. Hiram Johnson of California rose. He asked: "Is the Supreme Court out of this?" Senator Logan replied, with an element of sadness in his voice:

"The Supreme Court is out of it." Senator Johnson lifted up his hands and said: "Glory be to God!" as the galleries broke into wild applause. The Court bill was dead.

Later Roosevelt complained to Farley that Garner was blame for the defeat. He had told Garner to make the best compromise he could but, said Roosevelt, "It is apparent Garner made no effort to do so. He just capitulated to the opposition." But the truth was that Garner had capitulated to an opposition that had all the votes necessary to defeat the President.

This was in July, a little more than seven months after that avalanche of votes which had led Mr. Roosevelt to believe he was invincible and which had betrayed him into this pathetic defeat at the hands of one of the weakest and most compliant congresses in history.

There remains but one feature of this Court episode, without which its full significance is lost. The criticism of the Court among Democratic statesmen was general. They believed that some of the members were much too far to the Right and that an infusion of new minds was highly desirable. Among these critics was Hatton Sumners of Texas. But Judge Sumners was a lawyer who was also a student of the history of our constitutional system. He believed that some older judges would retire if the government made a provision for them to do so on full pay. He approached Justices Van Devanter and Sutherland on the subject and they expressed their desire to retire, but could not afford to do so on a mere half-pay stipend. Sumners discussed this with the President and introduced a bill providing for retirement at full pay.

Some of the more frenzied New Dealers promptly criticized Sumners for trying to make a soft berth for a bunch of old tories and, in disgust, he withdrew his bill. Later when the mutterings against the Court began to rise menacingly, he again offered his bill with the full assurance of two justices that they would retire when it was passed. He informed Roosevelt so, who knew, therefore, *that the way was open to him to get a majority of what he called liberals on the Court without any difficulty.* Despite this knowledge he threw away this means and sprang instead, without consulting Sumners, his wholesale grab at the Court. Only later, after a retirement bill was passed and the older justices began to resign, did Roosevelt gradually achieve his objective. He replaced them with a group of subservient judges who, by judicial usurpation, gave meanings to the Constitution which did not exist and provided the climate for the New Dealers' wreckage of our system of government.

Chapter 3: The Forgotten Depression

A month after Roosevelt's second inauguration many business men were fearful we might see a runaway boom. The war clouds had darkened over Europe. European money was in flight to America. Great Britain had just launched a $7,500,000,000 armament program and industry here was expecting to get a good slice of this war business. Our Neutrality Law did not prohibit armament sales abroad in peace-time. And Marriner Eccles and other administration officials were troubling their minds lest the rising armament industry unsettle our economy.

Throughout the year 1937 the President was busy with his misbegotten war on the Supreme Court. But there was at least a hearty draught of good cheer in the rosy reports about business that came to him from the New Deal statisticians. Despite all the fatalities amongst his glittering plans it did look to him as if his great task—rescuing the nation from the depression—was about to be completed. For a brief moment his mind wandered away from the tricky schemes of the reformers for remaking America. There were but three years to go before his White House lease would end. If he could have the nation soundly back on its feet by the end of 1938, then his chief task would be to strengthen the few institutions he had established and which had withstood the storm. He stopped talking about things like the NRA and about planning. Now he became interested in the little business man, in the enforcement of the anti-trust laws. Only a couple of years before he was delivering lectures to the newsmen with a wall chart and a pointer like a real professor, explaining how corporations and business men must be allowed to get together and write their own tickets about circumnavigating the anti-trust laws. Now he was telling the folks that he could not enforce the anti-trust laws, which the wicked Supreme Court had restored by annulling NRA, because the courts wouldn't let him. Back in 1934 the Federal Trade Commission had attacked the steel barons for their monopolistic practices. Roosevelt had rebuked the Commissioners, put them in the doghouse and cut their appropriations to the bone. Aside from this, the big thing was to balance the budget.

By August, however, while he was yet smarting under the Court defeat, signs began to appear that the vitality was oozing out of the boom. People were still talking about recovery, but the thing that makes for solid recovery in the capitalist system—the revival of real investment—had failed to materialize. The building industry was in the doldrums. Private financing was still on a hopelessly inadequate level. Much publicity was given to the large stock and bond issues. But they were issues to replace old stocks and bonds that were being recalled and did not represent any flow of new money into business.

In 1932 there were 11,385,000 unemployed. But employment improved all during the President's first term. By June, 1937 unemployment was down to 4,464,000, which was still too large. And it never got any better. It got worse and by November, 1937, there were 7,000,000 people out of work.[6] As early as July men were asking: "What has become of the boom?" The Treasury boasted that relief payments were less than in the same period the preceding year. But this was not so. The Treasury made a practice of keeping tricky books and producing phony results. It had merely shifted relief payments to other accounts. They were, in fact, larger than the year before. Stock prices began to decline and by September the unpleasant prospect could be no longer hidden. Daniel Roper, Secretary of Commerce, was putting out rosy statements about business. But the facts had seeped into the White House and on October 8, 1937, Jim Farley talked to Roosevelt about business. Roosevelt pooh-poohed it. Everything was all right, he said. It was all a move by business to discredit his policies.

This was characteristic of Roosevelt. Any unfavorable turn he attributed to a secret plot of his enemies. Any criticism of his measures he put down to some secret hatred of him personally. He was still bitter about the Court defeat. He sneered at the Senate and House. He told Farley the trouble with them, including the Vice-President, was that their thinking was still antiquated. They didn't see the importance of minimum wage and maximum hour legislation. This was a curious comment from the man who forced the Congress shortly after his first election to ditch minimum wage and maximum hour legislation which the Senate had already passed. There were some other matters, none of outstanding importance, which he wanted to see through and then, he told Farley, "then he would just ride along."

At a cabinet meeting later the same day Dan Roper undertook to say that business was all right. Roosevelt jumped on him. "Dan," he said, "you have just got to stop issuing these Hooverish statements." Roosevelt didn't disagree with Roper. He just felt the situation should be ignored and that things would right themselves. "Everything will work out all right if we just sit tight and keep quiet," he ended. The next day he told Farley there was altogether too much talking and too many press conferences. "I'm going to put the lid on," he said.[7]

But by the end of October, the grim facts about conditions could no longer be ignored. The market crashed and administration critics were saying this was the end of the New Deal. In November, at a cabinet meeting, Miss Perkins brought up a report just prepared by her statistician, Isador Lubin. It showed employment was off two per cent, she said, when it ought to be up two per cent. The heavy industries were behind and sales following the automobile show were disappointing. She feared things might be dangerous in view of conditions. Henry Morgenthau, the Milquetoast of the cabinet, got the courage to speak up. He said business was complaining that the capital gains and undistributed profits taxes were impairing recovery. Then he dared to say: "I think it would be heartening for you to show how far better off we are today."

Roosevelt shut him up with a rude rebuff: "Oh, for God's sake, Henry! Do you want me to read the record again?"

Poor Henry reddened as Roosevelt glowered at him amidst an embarrassing silence. Farley spoke up. "Boss," he said, "I think the situation would be helped if you would say something that would alleviate the fears in business. Frankly, I think you should make a quieting statement."

Other cabinet officers—Woodring and Wallace—expressed the same views. But Roosevelt was angry. He blamed the depression on Wall street. Then he burst out:

"I get all kinds of criticisms and complaints about the economic situation, but few people come into me with any concrete suggestions as to how the situation can be alleviated. It's easy enough to criticize, but it's another thing to help."

Here was the man who had blasted Hoover so unmercifully when it was Hoover's depression. Now there was a Roosevelt depression after he had spent 17 billion dollars. And he didn't like even to be told of it. He denied it at first. Then he snapped:

"I am fully conscious of the situation which exists. I have been studying it for a long time. And I know who's responsible for it. Business, particularly the banking business, has ganged up on me."

The grim specter of disintegrating business continued to haunt the cabinet meetings and to make discussion with Roosevelt difficult. Morgenthau was convinced the country was heading for another depression. After his first rebuff, he shrank from the subject. But on November 7 he wrote a letter to Roosevelt saying plainly we were moving into a depression. That night he telephoned the President and had what he describes as "a grim conversation." Roosevelt flew into a rage. He told Henry he knew "a wise old bird" who told him business was deliberately causing the depression in order to hold a pistol at his head and force a retreat from the New Deal.

At a cabinet meeting next day Roosevelt brought the subject up himself. He told the cabinet about Henry's letter. He grew angry and said: "I'm sick and tired of being told by the cabinet, by Henry and everybody else what's the matter with the country and nobody suggests what I should do."

This was indeed an extraordinary statement. Only a little over a year before he had been elected by the most amazing majority ever given a President upon the theory that he was the one man who knew what to do. And here he was now trapped in the mysterious tangles of a depression and *nobody would tell him what to do about it*. If there was one thing had been settled in his mind it was that *he, above all men, knew what to do about it*. Actually he had solved the depression. He had driven it from the land. He was in the act of putting on a few extra finishing touches to the great edifice of recovery and, lo! here is that Old Debbil Depression snoopin' 'round the White House and all the little men in the cabinet frightened to death and nobody will tell the great Depression Killer what to do about it. Apparently the depression hadn't been killed. It had just been drugged, just flattened out with 17 billion dollars' worth of knockout drops. Now in spite of everything, the damned thing was opening its eyes, breathing, even snorting again, coming to life. Could it be that all that magic medicine he had administered was no good—just a quack pain-killer?

When the President uttered his doleful complaint there was an ominous silence around the cabinet board. As Henry Morgenthau relates it, he, the meek and humble shadow of the Great Man, took his courage in his hands and, like an aroused bunny, looked the bull dog in the face. He said:

"You *can* do something about it. You can do something about the railroads. You can do something about housing. Above all, you can do something to reassure business."

Then he waited for the walls to fall in. They didn't, so he went on: "What business wants to know is: are we headed toward Socialism or are we going to continue on a capitalist basis?"

Roosevelt muttered that he had told them that again and again.

"All right," said Henry, "tell them for the fifteenth time."

Jim Farley added: "That's what they want to know."

Even Henry Wallace seconded the motion.

So Roosevelt decided to appease business. A few days later Henry Morgenthau was slated to make a speech before the National Academy of Political Science. A Morgan partner was on either side of him and spread out around the numerous tables was the elite of American business. And Henry told them. He told them the New Deal wanted to see capital go into production and private business expand. And then he used a sentence embodying an idea which never yet had gotten any real welcome in the President's head. Henry said: "We believe that much of the remaining unemployment will disappear if private capital funds are increasingly employed in productive enterprise. We believe that one of the most important ways of achieving these ends at this time is to continue progress toward a balance of the federal budget."

This sounded terribly like Mr. Hoover or Mr. Ogden Mills or Mr. Landon. Yet the whole theme of Mr. Roosevelt's New Deal had been war on business. It was a Holy War. And Roosevelt and the men around him took a delight in picturing business itself as evil and profit as criminal. Now Morgenthau was sent as the emissary of the President to deliver this belated appeal to business. The poor creature was horrified at the response. The audience first tittered and then guffawed out loud. To Oliphant, Henry's croaking New Deal Treasury legal adviser, this proved the whole New Deal case. It showed "the hopelessness of working with them."

After all, it was a little funny and no one can blame the diners for laughing. The budget was running in the red at the time to the tune of $300,000,000 a month.

The Roosevelt technique of trouncing the business man was resumed. Assistant Attorney-General Jackson and Secretary Harold Ickes in December made speeches inspired by the President raising the old ghost of the 60 families who haunt America with their controls. In January, John D. Biggers staggered the administration with his report after a survey that there were 10 million out of work. Soon it would be 11,800,000—*more than were unemployed when Roosevelt was elected in 1932.*

Pessimism spread through the cabinet. Farley wrote in his diary:

> "The days that are to follow, in my judgment, will be more important to the President than the days after the first inauguration. At that time he was trying to get us out of the depression (of Hoover) and now we are in a period that will be blamed on this administration and its policies."[8]

The dark realities of the country had sunk deeply into Roosevelt's mind now. There were just a year and six months before a Democratic convention would meet to pick his successor. All that gaudy edifice of recovery of which he was the be-medaled architect was crumbling around him. One thing was certain. The Second New Deal was a flop. The First New Deal had been abandoned, as we have seen, immediately after his inauguration. A wholly new approach and a completely unheralded series of devices were put together to the roll of the drums and the blaring of the trumpets. This was the Second New Deal. One by one all of its parts had been discarded save a few well-meaning but quite ineffectual social reforms. The President had settled down to a realization that after all priming the pump—spending billions—had by itself done the job and he hoped to skate along on that to the end of his term. But now even that had failed. Despite the billions and the debt, the depression was back. And it was not a new depression. It was the old one which had not been driven away but merely hidden behind a curtain of 15 billion dollars of new government debt. And, worst of all, he did not have a single new idea that he could use. He actually faced at this moment the appalling prospect, after all the ballyhoo, of going out of office in a depression as great as the one he found in 1932. The prospect was humiliating in the extreme, especially to a man whose vanity had allowed him to be blown up into such a giant depression-killer.

On January 16, 1938, he and poor Henry Morgenthau sat down to a sad repast. Roosevelt told him "the next two years don't count—they are already water over the dam." Then he revealed the extent of his plans—they would have to step up spending, forget about balancing the budget and get along with a two or three billion dollar a year deficit for two years. Then a conservative would come into office. That administration would do what Roosevelt had been promising he would do—quit government spending. And then the whole thing would go down in a big crash. At that point, they would have to yell for Roosevelt and Morgenthau to come back and get them out of the hole. The amazing feature of this strange confidence which Morgenthau has reported is this: Roosevelt and Morgenthau were already in a hole—the kind of hole the next administration would be in. Nobody had to call them in now—they were in. And they had not the foggiest idea what to do about getting out of the hole they were in, except to spend. Morgenthau concluded from this that Roosevelt had put out of his mind any thought of a third term. It is possible that he had.

Roosevelt was now in the center of a tug-of-war with the spenders like Harry Hopkins, Aubrey Williams, Leon Henderson and Rex Tugwell on one side and Henry Morgenthau, the frightened spokesman for the conservatives on the other. Farley reports that he had a talk on the subject with Roosevelt on March 28, 1938. It is of the first importance as revealing the precise problem that Roosevelt faced and how he solved it.

He told Farley he would have "to go in for pump-priming or relief." Farley agreed. But then Roosevelt confessed to a difficulty little understood at the time, or since. What could he spend on? That was the problem. There is only a limited number of things on which the federal government can spend. This grows out of the character of the federal system. The federal government can build schools, hospitals, roads, institutions of all sorts. But they are built in cities, counties, states and the activities which go on in these buildings are within the jurisdiction of the states. The states have to pay the teachers or nurses and staffs, have to support and maintain the roads and so on. The federal government can spend money on agricultural experimentation, on scientific research, on national parks, on power dams, etc. But in the end the outlays on these things are limited. The one big thing the federal government can spend money on is the army and navy. Roosevelt explained to Farley that he could not spend on local projects because the states and cities did not want any more buildings and institutions which they would have to support. They were having trouble enough paying the bills of those already built. Roosevelt revealed to Farley that many WPA projects approved by the government were abandoned because the states and cities could not raise the money to support them. He had to spend—but what could he spend on? The 1938 Congressional elections and Roosevelt's purge were on and of course Harry Hopkins was dishing it out as fast as he could without very much regard to utility or even decency. That was to meet a political emergency and couldn't go on indefinitely. And the whole problem was becoming complicated by the fact that inside his own official family the pressure for balancing the budget was growing embarrassing.

However, the spenders put on a vigorous winter drive and as Roosevelt went to Warm Springs, Morgenthau went to Sea Island, Georgia to work out a plan for balancing the budget. Around April 10, Roosevelt was back in Washington and Henry had a long talk with him. It was, he confesses mournfully, "a long and unhappy talk" with Roosevelt and Hopkins. Poor Henry's battle was lost. He found that the spenders had won. They had all their plans made. They had consulted no one in the cabinet, neither the Treasury nor the Director of the Budget. Secretary Ickes was to coax states and cities to borrow more. Nathan Straus was to double housing loans. They were to start a great transcontinental motor road. Morgenthau told Roosevelt the program frightened him. Immediately after Roosevelt disclosed his plans to the cabinet, Henry interrupted to say tax revenues would fall by 900 millions and the President's plans would increase the deficit to three and a half billion. The figures shocked the party leaders.

Morgenthau was so depressed that next day he told the President he "was seriously thinking of quitting." Roosevelt reproached him; refused to listen to his resignation and Henry left in a miserable state of mind.

Actually Henry didn't know the half of it. The country had now really reached a greater crisis than in 1933. The public debt, which was 22 billion when Roosevelt took office—almost all a heritage of World War I—was now 37 billion. Taxes were more than doubled. The President had a war on against the conservatives in his party and his own cabinet was split and angry. Unemployment was several thousand more than it was in October, 1932. Roosevelt knew now he was in a crisis. And he had at his disposal nothing to fight it with save a weapon—government spending—which had failed and which he felt now was a palliative and not a cure. He knew that the means of spending open to him, for the reasons explained above, were hopelessly inadequate. Yet he was now convinced for reasons which we shall see soon that he must not merely spend, but must spend two and three times as much as he had been spending. Would the country take it? He believed that the alternative was a crash of as great proportions as in 1933 and this meant, after all the wreaths that had been put upon his brow, he would go out of office in disgrace.

Roosevelt's position at this moment was singularly embarrassing. He had denounced Hoover as a spendthrift, for refusing to cut taxes and for his failure to balance the budget. Then he had proceeded to outspend Hoover, to raise taxes, to plunge the government into heavy debts, and now things were at least as badly off as when he hurled those challenges and charges at Hoover. It would be interesting to know what thoughts shouldered themselves through that carefree and comfortable mind as he saw himself now sinking under the weight of the crumbling economic system.

To a man of more humility the suspicion might have inserted itself into the secret precincts of his mind that, after all, he did not fully understand the vast organism he had set out to repair and that it might be he was a tinkerer rather than a mechanic, not so much a physician as a quack. There might have been, indeed, at least a little touch of understanding of the tremendous problem that confronted Hoover who faced the disaster at its top violence rather than after it had spent its terrible force. Certainly voices began now to speak up—voices that were lyrical about Roosevelt in 1933 and 1934—to suggest that after all Hoover may have known what he was doing, that here, nine years after the depression began and after the accidental irritants had been to some extent removed by time and gravity, the fundamental condition of the country was no further advanced than it was at the end of Hoover's three-year struggle with the disaster and that it would be very much worse but for the spending of billions of deficit government money on relief—the very thing Roosevelt himself had denounced as so shocking.

The depression which assaulted our unprepared society in 1929 was by no means a mysterious phenomenon to those who had given any attention to the more or less new studies in the subject of the business cycle. It was, first of all and essentially, one of those cyclical disturbances common to the system of private enterprise. That economic system has in it certain defects that expose it at intervals to certain maladjustments. And this was one of those intervals. Had it been no more than this it could have been checked and reversed in two or three years. But this cyclical depression was aggravated by additional irritants:

1. The banking system had been gravely weakened by a group of abuses, some of which arose out of the cupidity of some bankers and others out of ignorance.

2. A wild orgy of speculation had intruded into the system stimulated by a group of bad practices in the investment banking field.

3. A depression in Europe arising out of special causes there had produced the most serious repercussions here.

The great, central consequence of these several disturbances was to check and then almost halt completely the flow of savings into investment. All economists now know what few, apparently, knew then—that in the capitalist system, power begins in the payments made by employers to workers and others in the process of producing goods. And this must be constantly freshened by an uninterrupted flow of savings into investment—the creation of new enterprises and the expansion of old ones. If this flow of savings into investment slows down the whole economic system slows down. If it is checked severely the whole economic system goes into a collapse.

Now whatever one may think of Hoover, he at least understood this. And whatever one may think of Roosevelt, he did not have the foggiest idea of this subject. President Hoover while Secretary of Commerce had promoted a series of studies into this subject of the business cycle. The studies were made by the National Bureau of Economic Research and fortunately were directed by Wesley C. Mitchell, of Columbia University, a pioneer in stimulating research into the business cycle and the sources and behavior of national income. The results of these studies appeared in several volumes and were widely discussed at the time.

When the depression appeared, Hoover, aware of the latest available authoritative opinion on this subject, knew well that the great central problem was to reactivate the economic system by restoring conditions under which savings and bank credit would begin to flow once again into private investment. There was not too much he could do about the European situation, but there was something he could do about the banks. And there was something could be done about the correction of the whole machinery of speculation. In addition to this, there were the purely human ravages of the depression arising out of the unemployment of so many people.

The banking problem consisted in saving the banks which were threatened with destruction and in correcting the banking system, first to restore confidence in the banks and second to prevent a recurrence of the disaster. The speculative mania had been corrected, but many of the destructive tools that had been employed in the speculative markets still existed, ready to the hand of any unconscionable operator who wished to use them; and throughout Hoover's term one of these—the ruthless operation of gamblers in the stock market with the dangerous weapon of short selling—continued to add at intervals spectacular crashes in the market which intensified the declining confidence of the people.

Hoover therefore urged a reform in the banking structure and, when the situation grew worse, established the Reconstruction Finance Corporation to aid banks threatened with runs and disaster. He provoked that investigation of the speculative markets which

functioned until Roosevelt came into office and which most uninformed people imagine was set in motion by Roosevelt.

Hoover stood fast upon a group of propositions. For one, he insisted that the government expenses should be cut and he never faltered in this demand. Second, he demanded that Congress should
balance the budget, and not expose the nation's credit to the hazards
of the depression. Third, he insisted that aid to the distressed was
primarily the function of the states and local communities as well as
private organizations. The states and local governments should provide the funds. But he urged that the Reconstruction Finance Corporation should aid in this by lending federal money to the states
upon the security of state bonds. Fourth, he believed that the federal
government should stimulate the recovery of the economic system by
expenditures on public works, but that these must be essential public
works—roads, dams, necessary public buildings, etc. For that purpose, almost as soon as the depression assumed threatening proportions, he urged Congress to plan a program of public works
amounting to $600,000,000, roads' construction of $75,000,000, the
Colorado Dam at $65,000,000, river and harbors at $150,000,000.
Actually he was a pioneer in proposing government intervention in
the correction of cyclical economic disturbances. He proposed that
the governments should accumulate public works and improvements
during periods of prosperity in order not to accentuate its boom proportions and that these improvements should be launched at the appearance of a depression.

But Hoover had against him, in addition to those natural, international and social disturbances, an additional force, namely a Democratic House of Representatives which set itself with relentless
purpose against everything he attempted to do from 1930 on. It had a
vested interest in the depression. The depression seemed to come to
it as a gift from heaven. And as the campaign for the presidency got
under way in its early stages in 1931, there was nothing that could
have delivered a more staggering blow to its hopes than the success of
Hoover's plans for stemming the tide.

The Democratic leadership and Roosevelt himself, when he became the candidate, kept the air hot with denunciations of Hoover's
"failure to balance the budget," his "plunging the nation into debt,"
his mounting taxes and rising expenditures. Roosevelt called him

"the greatest spendthrift in history," spoke of his "multiplication of useless and oppressive bureaus," his "failure to deal with the banking collapses" and finally "his callousness to human suffering and the lot of the unemployed." While the Democrats were damning him for his extravagances at the very time when he refused to be drawn into extravagances, the Democratic House passed a bill appropriating $1,500,000,000 for old-fashioned pork-barrel outlays.

Roosevelt's collection of expletives picturing Hoover as the spender, the plunger, the debt-maker, the bureau builder and so on have been recalled endlessly. However, when Roosevelt came into power he proceeded to do all these things—to spend billions, to get these billions by increasing the public debt, to create bureau upon bureau and generally to do all those things he had denounced in Hoover without the slightest foundation for the charges. The nation had indeed gone into debt because in the depression tax revenues had fallen critically. Hoover had indeed spent a great deal but never so much as Roosevelt was demanding he should spend. But whatever Hoover did, this much must be said; it was done in conformity with a definite and compact theory of the cause and cure of depressions. And I think it must now be admitted that had he had a Congress in sympathy with his own theories the economic system could have been rescued from its doldrums without all that appalling train of consequences which flowed from Roosevelt's policies. There would, of course, have been much to do to put the economic system in perfectly good health and no one knew that better than Hoover. And it is entirely possible that no one knew less about that subject than Roosevelt. It would seem that the most unthinking admirer would concede this in the presence of the fact that after six years of extravagance, deficits and debt, of so many wild schemes which had to be abandoned as failures, Roosevelt should find himself in 1938 with 11,800,000 unemployed on his hands, business still showing no spark of recovery and his whole cabinet split, angry and surly.

He had charged ahead and around, like an amateur soldier at a riot, pushing and hauling and driving in every direction, without realizing quite what he was doing. Yet out of his numerous sallies a fairly clear pattern of behavior began to appear. It was always easy to sell him a plan that involved giving away government money. It was always easy to interest him in a plan which would confer some special benefit upon some special class in the population in exchange for their votes. He was sure to be interested in any scheme that had the appearance of novelty and he would seize quickly upon a plan that would startle and excite people by its theatrical qualities. That these several projects should be in eternal hostility to each other was of no moment. As a social physician he gave to his patient eagerly one pill for diarrhea and another for constipation, one solution for high blood pressure and another for low blood pressure, one to produce fever and one to allay it, stimulants and sedatives, prophylactics and poisons, each eagerly adopted on the suggestion of some quack with a theory to exploit or an organized group to benefit or delight. This was Roosevelt. And it landed him in 1938 back pretty much where he began and without a single compound left in his little satchel of remedies save spending and more spending.

But how would he spend and on what? Bridges, roads, a few more dams? These would consume a few billions at most. On what, then, could it be? He already had a definite idea in his mind on what it would be. He had denounced Hoover, among other things, for spending so much on the military establishment. He had warned that if the Republicans were not stopped, they would soon expose the people to the burden of "a billion dollars a year on the military and naval establishment." Now, looking up at the world from the hole in which he found himself, he had to swallow all that too. Half thinking aloud in a chat with Farley he said "The danger of war with Japan will naturally cause an increase in our armaments program, which cannot be avoided." He had only recently warned Americans against those politicians who would tell them that a military industry would produce work for the people and profits for business. But it would be hard, he had said at Chautauqua only two years before "for Americans to look beyond, to realize the inevitable penalties, the inevitable day of reckoning that comes from a false prosperity." Yet now he was playing with that very war motif.

But something new had happened to his mind of which his cabinet officers knew nothing. A new theory had danced across his desk—a sparkling, captivating theory—which he was to seize and hug to his heart like a man in the water whose strength is spent and who suddenly finds a powerful and lusty swimmer at his side.

Before we have a look at this brilliant idea, there was one more problem Roosevelt faced in 1938—the approaching Congressional elections.

Chapter 4: Harry the Hop and the Happy Hot Dogs

The situation as the 1938 elections loomed ahead was not the same as when the second administration began. Neither Congress nor the country were any longer at Roosevelt's feet. His party was profoundly divided and the hatreds within it were deep and poignant. He could not afford to lose any part of the subservient elements in the Congress. He had made up his mind to drive out of the House and Senate those members who had humiliated him in the Court fight and who had been grumbling at his extravagances. It was now necessary to teach them that they could not oppose his will with impunity. He was angry, resentful, vindictive. The names on the purge list were many, but heading that list were Senators Walter F. George of Georgia, Millard Tydings of Maryland, Guy Gillette of Iowa and, in the House, John O'Connor of New York. Moreover, Roosevelt felt it necessary to put every possible resource back of the renomination of his special pets like Alben Barkley of Kentucky and Joe Guffey of Pennsylvania. In Kentucky, the Governor, "Happy" Chandler, a rollicking, crooning, handshaking executive was a real threat to Barkley's reelection. Indeed it began to look for a while as if Chandler might defeat him.

Roosevelt had decided, too, that spending must be resumed. This was the only rabbit left in the magician's warren. These two projects brought closer to him the man who had done the bulk of his spending and who had accomplished it with the greatest measure of political results. This was Harry Hopkins, whom the President referred to affectionately as Harry the Hop.

Hopkins had started in Washington on the very outer rim of the New Deal, had been gradually working his way toward the center and was at this point one of the small group shouldering their way against everyone to be nearest to the all-high. It was to Hopkins that Roosevelt now turned in the campaign to repair his shattered fortunes.

The career of Hopkins began, with a kind of poetic irony, in the very heart of that horse-and-buggy age which evoked the sneers of the great lawgiver he served. His father was a harness maker in Sioux City, Iowa, where Harry was born. Later the family moved to Grinnell, Iowa, where Harry took his first steps in commercial life selling magazines, newspapers and cigarettes. His mother was a zealous Methodist who taught him to pray, to work and to avoid poverty. He went to Grinnell College, graduated and without delay plunged into the great ocean of social welfare.

He got a job as head of a small summer camp at Boundbrook, New Jersey, which brought him East and planted him close to the fountains of philanthropy and the cocktail lounges of Babylon, upon which he was to flourish. From this point on, he was committed to the many-sided life of a social worker. The social welfare world of New York is a multi-colored world in itself. It consists of the poor who are absolutely essential to the profession and of the rich who give to the poor and of the social welfare workers who are the pipeline through which the bounty of the rich flows into the hands of the poor. It is better, saith the good book, to give than to receive, and Harry Hopkins was never unaware of the pleasant consequences which inure to the profession of giving.

He began with a $45-a-month salary at Christodora House in Avenue B and arrived rapidly at the head of the Association for Improving the Condition of the Poor in New York with a salary of $10,000 a year—in the good old days when $10,000 bought a lot of the good life and one did not have to hand over $2500 in taxes to the Roosevelt-Hopkins government.

The chief function of the secretary or director of a great philanthropic enterprise is to get the money. Fortunately this world of New York poverty is a stamping ground for wealthy widows, rich octogenarians, along with the sons and daughters of the last generation of the "criminal rich" who dedicate themselves to deodorizing the family name by passing out to the poor the millions left by their "predatory" dads. The prime business of the secretary is to stalk this game. The bulk of the hard work is done by the rookie welfarers in the

slums, investigating, checking, snooping, reporting, advising and su-
pervising. But the bulk of the work of the secretary is on Park Avenue
and its environs, with frequent week-end trips to the blooded cattle
farms, golf clubs, hunting lodges and other hideaways of the benevolent rich. This life is apt to do something to the secretary. He finds
himself stretching his legs under the tea and dinner tables of the rich,
drinking rare vintage wines, eating costly viands and smoking expensive cigars. It cultivates an appetite for the good life wholly beyond
the reach of even a $10,000-a-year general secretary or director. He
finds himself after a while consuming the bonded liquors and imported caviar out of other people's pantries and watching others
picking up the checks in night clubs. Warmhearted, elderly ladies
wonder how the poor fellow gets along on his slender stipend. Extravagant males are similarly puzzled, and so one day the secretary,
who is almost certain to have had a slight case of Marxism in his
youth, finds himself taking tips from the capitalist exploiters. "Tips"
is hardly the word. That has to do with small change. It is not easy to
decide at what point a tip becomes a handout or a handout becomes a
bonus or a bonus becomes a grant or when a grant rises to the royal
eminence of an honorarium. But the honorarium becomes the thing.
It is a habit-forming drug but it enables the secretary to live in the
manner to which his wealthy companions are accustomed.

It can have another effect on a man, though there are those who resist and survive it. An important feature of his professional function
is to find and keep patrons. He must dance attendance on the
wealthy ladies and cultivate the art of saying "yes" in a dozen changing accents to the heavy-check men. This was a word which Harry
was to find highly useful in the hot political world of the White
House. It was in this gay life of giving and gratuities, the life of the
survey, the questionnaire, the supervisor and the unsteady budget,
that Harry Hopkins got his training for the great role of planetary
welfare and global boondoggling, and rose from the modest function
of distributing the meager benefits in the small neighborhood of
Avenue B to operating as grand almoner of the spendingest Haroun
al Raschid in the history of human extravagance.

Hopkins married a fellow welfare worker at Christodora House.
As we have seen, he rose rapidly and after serving in the South with
the Red Cross during the First World War, went to the Society for

Improving the Condition of the Poor as assistant director in 1924 and in that year became director of the New York Tuberculosis Association.

Then in 1928 Fate rolled up her sleeves to see just how far she could toss Harry. Al Smith was running for President and Hopkins was out helping Al when he met Franklin D. Roosevelt, who was running for governor of New York. Hopkins organized a committee of medical men for Roosevelt-for-Governor. Roosevelt liked him at once and with Mrs. Roosevelt it was pals at first sight. Roosevelt was elected governor. Then came the depression, which was to be filled with milk and honey for Harry Hopkins. Jesse I. Straus, head of the Macy store in New York, became head of the Federal Emergency Relief Administration in New York in 1931 and he named Hopkins executive director. Later Hopkins succeeded him to the chairmanship with Mrs. Roosevelt's influence. When Roosevelt became President and wanted a Federal Emergency Relief Administrator he named Harry Hopkins to this post at Mrs. Roosevelt's urging.

This put Harry in a job he understood—giving away money—but now he did not have to worry about where it came from. The NRA act had given Roosevelt $3,300,000,000 to spend. It is difficult to believe, but it is true that Roosevelt was averse to spending this money. However, Mrs. Roosevelt managed to get Hopkins to the President by the direct route, bypassing all the secretarial barriers, and there Hopkins sold the President on the idea of a moderate relief program by means of grants-in-aid to the states. Roosevelt supposed the NRA was going to bring prosperity quickly, but at the end of July the bubble burst and the great champion of the balanced budget turned in desperation to the two things he had denounced—spending and doles. He then put Harold Ickes in charge of the Public Works Administration (PWA) and Harry Hopkins in charge of the Civil Works Administration (CWA). In short order Harry had a vast army pulling weeds and raking leaves. He told the President: "I've got four million at work but for God's sake, don't ask me what they are doing."

When Hopkins began this gaudy mission he found himself in a social worker's paradise—a splendid abundance of unemployed and an endless supply of money. But he and Roosevelt made another discovery. Both profoundly ignorant of finance, they did not dream of the magic that lies wrapped in public debt. When first elected, Roosevelt naturally supposed that to spend he would have to tax, which is very unpopular. The alternative would be to borrow from the people and he knew that was difficult. He did not dream of the incredible miracle of *government* BANK *borrowing*. He did not know that the bank lends money which it actually creates in the act of making the loan. When Roosevelt realized this, he saw he had something very handy in his tool kit. *He could spend without taxing people or borrowing from them, while at the same time creating billions in bank deposits. Wonderful!*

But he and Hopkins discovered something even more important. As soon as Roosevelt got hold of this $3,300,000,000, congressmen, senators, mayors, governors, chambers of commerce, charity organizations from every state and city formed in line. Hopkins saw before Roosevelt did that the President had in his hands on a vast scale what political parties had had in the past on a very small scale. The little local bosses with their pitiful little graft and social welfare benefits from the district clubhouse were pikers. Now all the philanthropy in the country through local politicians flowed from one great boss in Washington. No district leader could satisfy the appetites of his constituents on a scale comparable to the big boss of all the bosses. Roosevelt discovered what the Italian Premier Giolitti had discovered over 50 years before, that it was not necessary to buy the politicians. He bought their constituents with borrowed money and the politicians had to go along. Everybody with a halfway appealing tale got money, but on one condition—that he play ball with Roosevelt. Harry Hopkins estimated that 25 million people got their living from WPA alone. It was not the President's widely advertised charm or his golden voice that was the secret of his amazing power. It was his streams of golden billions. This was the rabbit that produced results for the magician—the spending rabbit. Harry Hopkins was the Keeper of the Golden Rabbit and knew precisely the tricks Roosevelt wanted done with it.

The CWA had got in bad very quickly as a leaf-raking agency and so it was reorganized into the Works Progress Administration (WPA). As we have seen, Roosevelt set out to purge the men who had balked him in the Court fight and to support those who had stood behind him. In the 1938 election Senator Alben Barkley was being opposed for the Democratic nomination in the primary in Kentucky by "Happy" Chandler, then governor of the state. During the election grave charges were made in the Scripps-Howard newspapers about the manner in which WPA workers in Kentucky were being forced to support the administration candidate. A special Senate committee investigated the charges. The hearings were printed but not generally circulated. The performances of the WPA in Kentucky and various other places as outlined here are taken from that official report.[9]

In the first WPA district of Kentucky, one WPA official went to work on Governor Chandler. He took his orders from the administration political headquarters in Kentucky. He put nine WPA supervisors and 340 WPA timekeepers on government time to work preparing elaborate forms for checking on all the reliefers in the district. Having done this they then proceeded to check up on the 17,000 poor devils who were drawing relief money to see how they stood on the election. The Senate committee got possession of these forms.

In the second WPA district, another WPA official who was the area engineer, managed a thorough canvass of the workers in Pulaski and Russell counties. The WPA foremen were given sheets upon which they had to report on the standing of the reliefers in the political campaign. It became a part of Mr. Hopkins' WPA organization in Kentucky to learn how many of the down-and-out had enough devotion to Franklin D. Roosevelt to be entitled to eat. It was not sufficient for an indigent Kentuckian to be just down and out and hungry. He had to believe that the President of the United States was his redeemer and had to be ready to register that belief at the polls. The reliefers were asked to sign papers pledging themselves to the election of the senior senator from Kentucky. They were given campaign buttons and told to wear them and there were instances where, if they refused, they were thrown off the WPA rolls.

All this, of course, was in a Democratic primary where only Democrats could vote. But there were a lot of poor Republicans in Kentucky who couldn't vote in the Democratic primary so long as they were Republicans. So they were told to change their registration and become Democrats, or no WPA jobs for them.

A lady employed in the Division of Employment in WPA District 4 in Kentucky got a letter from the project superintendent asking her for a contribution to the Barkley Campaign Committee. A district supervisor of employment in District 4 talked to her, told her that the election was drawing near and that she might be criticized if she did not contribute since she was employed on WPA, that she should be in sympathy with the program and be loyal and he stated also that he was a Republican but he was going to change his registration. Then he told her she would be permitted to contribute if she liked in the amount of two per cent of her salary. Letters went out from the superintendent to practically all of the reliefers. The assistant supervisor of the WPA, who got $175 a month, sent a check for $42.50 as a result of this letter and another getting $1800 a year gave $30.

Here is the kind of letter sent out. It was from the project superintendent for whom these people worked:

"We know that you, as a friend of the National Administration, are anxious to see Senator Barkley reelected as he has supported the President in all New Deal legislation ... If Senator Barkley is nominated and elected by a large majority there is definite possibility of his being the candidate of the Democratic party in 1940. Think what this would mean for Kentucky.

"We know you will appreciate the opportunity of being given a chance to take an active part in reelecting Senator Barkley by making a liberal contribution towards his campaign expenses. Such contribution is actually underwriting a continuance of New Deal policies."

These gentlemen were nice and considerate—they allowed the reliefers to pay on the installment plan. The letter went on:

"As the enclosed subscription blank indicates, you may pay one-half of your contribution now and the balance by July 16."

Worker after worker testified that he received the above letter or one like it and had made contributions in proportion to the pay he was getting, usually about two per cent.

In Pennsylvania, where Senator Joe Guffey presided over the destinies of the Democratic party, the story was much the same. Men who supplied trucks to WPA were solicited for $100 each in Carbon County. The owners of the trucks were requested by WPA officials to visit representatives of certain political leaders at their homes. Ten or twelve at a time went and many of them contributed. In Lucerne

County it was the same. They were told to call at Democratic headquarters and make their contributions. In Montgomery County, the WPA workers got letters stating that at the direction of the senator from Pennsylvania (Guffey) and the state committeeman, a joint meeting of WPA workers would be held on a certain date and they were told "there will be no excuse accepted for lack of attendance."

The evidence showed that WPA workers in this county, including timekeepers and poor women on sewing projects, were requested and ordered to change their registration from Republican to Democratic and in many cases those who refused were fired. There was testimony that there were a number of Republicans on the WPA project near Wilkes Barre. They lived in Wilkes Barre and they thought they had a right to continue to be Republicans. They soon discovered that the right had vanished when they became wards of the New Deal and as punishment, 18 were transferred from the project near Wilkes Barre to a project 35 or 40 miles from their homes because they refused to discard their Republican buttons.

In Pennsylvania work-cards were issued by the Party entitling the recipients to employment on the state highways and these were distributed by political groups. Some of these cards entitled the holders to employment *"for two to four weeks around election time."* In one county, from September, 1935 to September, 1938, the WPA spent more than $27,000,000 on highways. What chance had any man or any party against this? Al Smith had said you can't beat a billion dollars.

Those who, in their poverty and helplessness, refused to surrender their independence, paid for it. A man in Plymouth, Pa., was given a white-collar relief job before election at $60.50 a month. He was told to change his registration from Republican to Democratic. He refused and very soon found himself transferred—transferred from his white-collar job to a pick-axe job on a rock pile in a quarry. There he discovered others on the rock pile who had refused to change their registration. This was in America, the America of the men who were chanting and crooning about liberty and freedom 365 days a year, who were talking about democracy and freedom for all men everywhere.

It was the same in Tennessee where the WPA was lighting a fire under Governor Browning. Reliefers who were for Browning—if it could be proved—were excommunicated from the payroll. They were asked for contributions—two per cent. One man was asked to put up $5. He didn't have it. He was summoned next day. The collector had decided to reduce his tribute to $3. He didn't have that. He was told to get it. He had to borrow it. Another, assessed twice before, rebelled. "You don't have to pay," he was told, "but if you don't you'll have a hell of a time getting on the WPA." Negro reliefers were made to put up 25 and 50 cents.

In Cook County, Illinois, where Kelly and Nash carried the New Deal banner, 450 men were employed in one election district and dismissed the day after election. Seventy reported to do highway work and were told to go to their voting precincts and canvass for votes for the Horner-Courtney-Lucas ticket. These 450 men cost $23,268. All of them had their work-cards initialed by the campaign manager in Northern Illinois for the Horner-Courtney-Lucas ticket.

This investigation covered four states. There is not the slightest doubt, however, that what happened in these four states of Kentucky, Tennessee, Pennsylvania and Illinois, happened in greater or lesser degree in most of the states of the Union. Of course these jobs were done by men in the field while Mr. Hopkins sat in Washington and pretended to be quite innocent of it all. Indeed, after the findings of the committee were made public, Hopkins declared he had made his own investigation and denied all the charges. But the committee said: "After still further investigation of its own, it adhered to its own findings." It also called attention to an address made by Aubrey Williams, Mr. Hopkins' chief deputy administrator, at a big WPA conference on June 27, 1938, in which he said: "We've got to stick together; we've got to keep our friends in power."

These primaries of 1938, of course, were the scenes of the great Roosevelt purge, when distinguished Democratic senators and congressmen were marked for annihilation. Raymond Moley pointed out that Harry Hopkins was directing this purge while passing out these hundreds of millions. In fact, on August 31, 1938, in the midst of this campaign, Hopkins complained that the leadership of the Democratic opposition was urging Democrats to register and vote in the primaries to help defeat the aims of President Roosevelt, not in the clear-cut general election "where the divergent views of parties are clearly understood, but stealthily, within the councils of our own party." Now consider the significance of that statement. This man was actually complaining that the Democratic opponents of the President were calling on Democrats to register and vote in a Democratic primary. It had already become a crime for a Democrat to disagree with the administration. Mr. Hopkins was making it a crime for a Democrat who didn't agree with the nominations of the administration in various states to register in his own party and vote against the administration nominee. But while he was objecting to Democrats registering as Democrats and voting in a Democratic primary unless they agreed with Roosevelt, his agents in Kentucky and Tennessee and Pennsylvania and Illinois and practically everywhere else were threatening Republican reliefers with starvation if they didn't quit being Republicans and register as Democrats and actually firing them and in some cases putting them on the rock pile.

Roosevelt was profoundly convinced that all he had to do was to let the Democratic electorate in any state or district know that a senator or congressman was his enemy and that would sound his doom. He had come to the settled conviction that the people were no longer interested in issues, that they were interested only in him, that they were for him or against him. In the 1936 campaign he had told his campaign manager there was only one issue—"myself"—and he told members of his cabinet that the people were for the Court plan because he was for it and that they would be for whatever he was for.

It was therefore a source of unmixed astonishment to him when every Democratic candidate but one whom he had marked for the purge in the Democratic primaries of 1938 was renominated. Barkley and Guffey, of course, had been renominated for the Senate, but they were not involved in the purge—their fights had been local ones. The one instance in which Roosevelt was successful was in defeating Congressman John O'Connor in New York City for renomination. In this case he committed the job to Tommy Corcoran who went to New York and with all the forces of the administration at his command succeeded in defeating O'Connor. Roosevelt regarded this as in some measure proof of his own personal political acumen, since the job of defeating O'Connor had been handled by a White House subaltern. He believed it was in some way due to his own mastery.

The odor of Harry Hopkins' performances in WPA became such that it was advisable to lift him out of that position after the 1938 elections were over. Then this cynical man, who had been living on endowments and tips all his life, who had never been in a business transaction, who despised business and business men and loved to exhibit his scorn, who in the group around the President was the most skilled in needling him against business and whose only contacts with business men had been as a beneficiary of their bounty, was made by the President—of all things—Secretary of Commerce! He spent much of his time as Secretary in the hospital. When he left the Department of Commerce a little more than a year and a half later it was to enter the White House as the officially installed and publicly proclaimed favorite of the court—not merely a friendly adviser to the President, as many presidents have had, but as a resident of the White House itself, roaming around its halls with access to the President's bedside at all hours of the day and night, a free boarder holding an office that was never created by Congress and does not actually exist, being paid a salary that was never authorized by Congress, discharging functions that were never envisioned by Congress, exercising the highest authority without being appointed in the constitutional manner, that is without senatorial confirmation, outranking cabinet officers and, indeed, sending orders to cabinet officers signed "H.H."

He would become powerful enough to keep one member of the cabinet out of the White House for eleven months—to make it impossible for a cabinet officer, a legally confirmed adviser of the President, to even see the President for nearly a year. This curious figure, operating in the shadows, became, next to the President himself, the most powerful person in the United States.

How did Harry Hopkins worm his way into this position of power? It was not by accident. It was because he had a character well-suited to the functions he was expected to discharge and a special talent for maneuver in the turgid pools of palace politics. He was rich in cunning, always devious in his enterprises and something of his personal history throws much light upon those elements in his character which fitted him for the role of intriguer.

Hopkins inhabited an area of moral and ethical life which does not correspond in its standards of behavior to the area in which most normal Americans move. He was pictured to the popular audience as one whose life was dedicated to the welfare of the under-privileged masses. He had married as a young man a fellow welfare worker. They had three sons. In 1930 his wife filed suit against him for absolute divorce in New York State, the charge being infidelity. She secured the divorce and, I am informed, an order for the payment of $5000 a year in alimony. Hopkins was making $10,000 a year at the time. This meant that one-half his salary would be retained for himself and the other half for the support of his wife and three children. It does not seem to have been an excessive provision. All this, of course, is a matter personal to Hopkins' own life, but it is germane here because of several facets of the incident. Shortly after the divorce, he took a second wife. He became WPA Administrator at a salary of $10,000 a year. Hopkins himself was a man of very expensive tastes. It took a good deal of money to keep him provided with the forms of amusement to which he was addicted and $10,000 was not enough to take care of his two families and his expensive appetites. The matter was arranged in a manner that cannot be overlooked in forming an estimate of Hopkins' character. Mr. Marquis W. Childs, in an article in the *Saturday Evening Post* of April 19 and 26, 1941, said Hopkins was hard-pressed for funds under the circumstances and was having a difficult time meeting the alimony payments to his first wife. To cure this situation, social workers were brought together to raise a fund of $5000 a year to take care of Hopkins' alimony. A number of small-salaried little social welfare workers were assessed to discharge Hopkins' natural obligation to support his own children in order to enable him to indulge in those expensive tastes to which he was accustomed. In theory the money was collected to pay him for lectures, which he rarely had the time to deliver. It was a subterfuge to mask the real purpose of the levy. And it went on for two years. Then in January, 1936, his salary was raised to $12,000 and the welfare workers were relieved of the burden of Hopkins' alimony.

It is a strange story in view of the further incident related by Mr. Childs in the same articles, that during those WPA days, Hopkins, who was so pressed for funds that the support of his children through alimony was saddled upon a group of low-paid social workers, was, with the men around him, playing poker with losses so stiff they ran to $500 or $600 an evening and that he found the time and the means to run up for week-ends to the homes of some of the malefactors of great wealth he so liked to denounce and to make frequent visits to the race tracks at Saratoga, Pimlico and Warrenton. *Life* has printed much the same stories about him.

There came then the time when Hopkins had to leave the WPA and later saw fit to end his brief career as Secretary of Commerce. For a while he found himself without any income. Hopkins belongs to that class of person who must be taken care of one way or another. Having no job, a job had to be invented for him. About this time the President created a monument to himself—a library building on his estate where future generations may make pilgrimages to honor his memory. According to Mr. Felix Belair in an article in *Life*, Post-master-General Walker and John D. Hertz, the taxicab magnate, and other millionaire friends, raised a purse to pay Hopkins $5000 a year as head of Franklin D. Roosevelt's library at Hyde Park. But of course Hopkins could not subsist on this wretched stipend. Hence when the Lend-Lease act was voted the President found a way to arrange a $10,000-a-year salary for Harry under the Lend-Lease program.

In the meantime, he had moved into the White House where he enjoyed the additional privilege of free board and lodging. His second wife had died and his daughter by this marriage lived with him in the White House. It is worth observing that still later, when he had taken a third wife and moved with her to Georgetown, his daughter, after remaining with them a while, went back to the White House. Mrs. Roosevelt tells how she fretted about the lonely life of this child and spoke to Hopkins about it. He said to her: "That's totally unimportant. The only thing that is important is to win the war." He found plenty of time, however, to pursue at intervals his favorite forms of diversions in the night clubs of New York and Washington.

Yet he had found time during this period to pursue his new courtship and marry a third wife, who was brought to the White House to live at government expense. But even with free board and lodging at the White House and free transportation and government expense accounts, $10,000 a year was not enough for Hopkins. As usual, ways had to be found to provide him with more. And so he began to appear in the magazines as a literary light, like so many others in the New Deal. Tom Beck, the head of the Crowell-Collier Publishing Company, a faithful satellite of the White House throughout the

New Deal episode, provided Harry with the trimmings for his meal ticket by paying him $5000 a piece for seven or eight articles in the *American Magazine* over a period of several years—articles written, of course, by someone else and signed by Hopkins. This was one of the favorite rackets of the New Deal "scholars."

When he married for the third time, the charge was made that the new bridal couple spent their honeymoon on a vessel which the government had taken from the owner and converted into a warship and that Lord Beaverbrook gave to the new Mrs. Hopkins a magnificent necklace of emeralds. The Hopkinses denied getting any emeralds. Later Drew Pearson printed the story that while this denial was correct, it was a necklace of diamonds which Beaverbrook had presented and it was worth $4000. Like Jacques in "The Two Orphans," he was charged with stealing a coat and replied: "You lie—it was a cloak." Why should Beaverbrook, then representing the British government, make a present of $4000 to the bride of the man who was arranging Lend-Lease shipments to England—a man he scarcely knew?

Then some time in December, 1942, Mr. Bernard Baruch gave a dinner for Mr. and Mrs. Hopkins. It was during the war, when the President was constantly calling upon the people to make more and more sacrifices as part of the war effort and to learn to do without luxuries and even many necessities. Some enterprising reporter produced the sacrificial menu at the buffet feast tendered to Hopkins and his bride. Here it is:

Bowl of Caviar with trimmings	Mousse of chicken
Pate de Foie Gras	Gallatine of Capon
Cheese croquettes	Cold tongue
Baked Oysters Bonne Femme	Beef a la Mode
Celery, Radishes, Olives, Pecans	Corned beef in jelly
Tortue Clair (En Terrine)	Turkey—Chicken—Virginia Ham
Creme au Champignon Frais	Calves head Vinaigrette
Profitrole	Russian dressing
Truite en Gelee	Mixed green salad
Homard en Aspic	Assorted cheese and crackers
Terrapin (Baltimore style)	Iced black cherries and
Chicken a la King	vanilla ice cream
Steamed Rice	Socle of Raspberry Ice
Sliced tomatoes, crisp lettuce	Petits Fours
Mayonnaise French Dressing	Demi Tasse

A Washington reporter wrote: "Throughout the function the face of Hopkins, who warned his countrymen in a recent magazine article that they will have to forego milk and tea and predicted drastic curtailment of all civilian industries except coffin-making, was wreathed in smiles."

The story of Hopkins is not complete without some reference to that pulling and hauling which went on behind the scenes for control of the great man's coattails. From the beginning of the New Deal, Felix Frankfurter had been pictured as the mysterious being who sat off in the shadows and pulled the strings that operated all the puppets who had cooked up the NRA and invented the AAA, who was the arch Red and was in fact the unseen and unheard culprit behind most of Mr. Roosevelt's dangerous enterprises. The bureaus were supposed to be filled with the satellites of Frankfurter and in good time this exclusive crew of sappers and borers came to be known as the "happy hot dogs."

As a matter of fact, Felix Frankfurter never was a Red—neither a malignant Communist nor a benevolent Socialist. He disapproved of the NRA and looked with dismay on the AAA, and above all, he condemned, though he held his peace publicly, the fight on the Supreme Court. Frankfurter appeared before the larger public less than any of the prominent supporters of the administration. Actually there was perhaps less in common between Frankfurter and Roosevelt than between Roosevelt and any of those who remained so long a part of his intellectual entourage. Frankfurter had been a life-long disciple of the social theories of Justice Brandeis and the legal philosophy of Justice Oliver Wendell Holmes. It was Brandeis who got him appointed to the Harvard Law Faculty after the First World War, where he remained until he went on the Supreme Court. One of Frankfurter's controlling intellectual passions had been for freedom of speech. He might be defined as a reformer, not a Socialist. He defended Sacco and Venzetti not because he was a Communist but because he believed no man charged with a crime tinged with political implications should be convicted and electrocuted without a competent defense.

There was, however, another side to his nature by no means as harmless as his political philosophy. He had a yearning to exercise power from the sidelines. He wished to shape affairs anonymously.

Without any ambition to hold political office, he loved to exercise power over the minds of men who did. He wrote little himself but patiently cultivated intimate association with those who did. He was beyond doubt a teacher who inspired his students. He talked to them not only about law but about history and political ideas and thus he attracted to his classes young men with lively interests in public affairs. When they left law school they went into powerful law firms and government offices. In the lean years after 1929 the flow of these energetic spirits into government increased as the demand in private practice shrank. And soon, almost without realizing it, Frankfurter found his students and his disciples in all sorts of places in Washington where they sat close to the centers of power.

As the depression deepened, Frankfurter made a more conscious effort to place his students where their weight would be felt. A Washington bureau may employ a thousand men, but only a handful are important—the administrator, the counsel, the economist, the statistician, the publicity man. These are the men who influence policy and it was policy, not jobs, that interested Frankfurter.

Frankfurter's most important move upon this board was sending Thomas G. Corcoran, one of his ablest pupils, to a place in the Reconstruction Finance Corporation while Hoover was President. Tommy had a flair for public affairs and a passion for political maneuvering.

As the New Deal began to create bureau after bureau and the number of jobs desirable to both Frankfurter and Corcoran multiplied, Corcoran proceeded to fill them with what Hugh Johnson called the "happy hot dogs." Tommy found the places; Frankfurter produced the recommendations and the Frankfurter boys were in. They were everywhere. Most of them, of course, were lawyers, but many had become economists overnight. And soon Tommy Corcoran was in the White House at the elbow of the President, writing or superintending the preparation of his speeches.

With the beginning of the second campaign—that is, after Moley had departed and Louis Howe had died—the Frankfurter influence was topmost around the White House, despite Frankfurter's grave concern about Roosevelt's drift toward the planned economy. But little by little Frankfurter's personal influence waned, particularly after the Supreme Court fight.

When Frankfurter started filling the bureaus with his lawyers and economists he didn't quite realize what he was doing. Many had been his proteges but he did not know as well as he supposed what was going on in the minds of these young men. The times, perhaps the smell and color of revolutionary activity which intrigues young minds, the absorption of these gay and truculent youths in the vague yet trenchant philosophy of the New Deal under lawgivers and philosophers who were peddling a far more tasty and intoxicating brand of liquor than had come from their old law professor—all combined to draw these fellows closer to Roosevelt than to Frankfurter. Some, in fact, had drifted into the far more turbulent waters of Communism and near-Communism where the fellow-travelers disport themselves. Probably from 1937 to 1940 Frankfurter became a minor figure so far as his influence on policy was concerned. But he came back with a real bounce when America went into the war.

In the meantime, things were not going too well for his "chief of staff," Tommy Corcoran. Tommy actually lived in the White House for months to be near his chief. But Hopkins had his eye on the spot occupied by Tommy. Hopkins set out deliberately to get possession of Roosevelt's confidence and he worked and wormed and lied wherever necessary to push away everybody and, above all, Corcoran. In this contest Corcoran was no match for Hopkins. Corcoran loves politics with a Gaelic fervor. He has opinions. He is something of a student and had his own collection of political beliefs. He was eager, doubtless, to hold his place near the throne, chiefly to influence Roosevelt's mind on the side of his own philosophy.

Hopkins had no such foolish and impractical objectives. Earlier in his life he had been a mild Socialist but at this time he had no philosophy save insofar as his opinions were influenced by his deep cynicism. His object was to become first man in power next to Roosevelt. He explained his theory about this to more than one. He said that a man must always have a clear idea of the source of his power. Some men get their power from the people. Others get their power indirectly through some other man. He confessed freely that he could not get any power whatever at the hands of the people. He must therefore fasten himself upon the man who had the power to give. The source of that power was the President and so he fastened himself upon the President. To hold that power he must cultivate the

President. It was no part of his business to argue with Roosevelt or to cross him or ever to use the word "no" definitively. He must be ever the subservient, compliant yes-man, cultivating the good graces of his master, flattering his vanity, doing his chores, satisfying his desires, cunningly divining those desires and without revealing his discovery, giving him the favors he wished, getting his own way by deviously influencing the master and by all means possible killing off the rivals for the royal favor.

It is one of the characteristics of power long held that it attracts around it men of this stamp. The man with vast powers is sure to find men like Hopkins worming themselves into their confidence if they are willing to use that kind of man. Men of high intellectual and spiritual caliber soon make themselves disagreeable to rulers who want abject subservience in their subalterns. They soon find the atmosphere of the court repulsive. They either depart or are dismissed. In the end, the only ones who remain are men of the type of Hopkins. There were men close to Roosevelt who were interested in pressing upon him their own ideas of policy. There were men who were not interested in policy but only in discerning Roosevelt's pet mental drifts and promoting them. Hopkins was of the latter breed. As the years passed, one by one the abler men with some sense of personal dignity who were unequal to the role of sycophant drifted away or were dropped. Raymond Moley, Lewis Douglas, John Hanes, Hugh Johnson, George Peek, Tommy Corcoran, Jim Farley, Stanley High and many others departed. The palace guard that survived were such men as Harry Hopkins, Sam Rosenman, General "Pa" Watson, who was a sort of court jester, Admiral (Doctor) McIntire, the President's physician who could see no wrong in Roosevelt, even in his vascular system, David Niles and Henry Wallace, who hung fast to the tails of whatever coat Roosevelt chose to wear—men who listened attentively for Roosevelt's slightest changes in desire, sensed them with the readiness of faithful animals, and ran obediently to perform whatever tricks the master wanted.

There were others like Hull, who hung on even though it was on the outer fringes of policy, willing to suffer any indignity so long as he might continue to call himself Secretary of State and promote his febrile crusade for commercial reciprocity, while Roosevelt named ambassadors, ministers and minor employees in the State

Department without consulting him and carried on our foreign affairs through Sumner Welles behind Hull's back.

CHAPTER 5: THE DANCE OF THE PHILOSOPHERS

I. THE PLANNERS

We must now have a look at some of the men who were the managers of that sparkling and seductive idea which danced across Roosevelt's desk as he wrestled with the grave crisis in his fortunes in 1938. Roosevelt had cried out in despair to his cabinet for help: "No one tells me what to do about it." As a matter of fact, he was not in the habit of purchasing his magic rabbits from his cabinet. Old Man Hull and Big Jim Farley, Dan Roper, Harry Woodring and the aging Swanson never dreamed of being in the rabbit business. Cummings had produced one—the Court plan—and it had bitten the master. Certainly Morgenthau was no breeder of magic rabbits, nor even Miss Perkins, nor Ickes who, after all, was just an old-fashioned Progressive who had been fighting the power trust and was for soil conservation and really belonged to the First New Deal to which he had added an illusion of revolution by his vitriolic tongue. Wallace, of course, could promote rabbits and, before he ended, squirrels. But at the moment he was more bewildered than anything else. It was always from the rapidly shifting membership of the kitchen cabinet that Roosevelt got his great ideas. And so it proved now.

Perhaps the most influential member of this group was always Rexford Guy Tugwell, though his influence was most powerful indirectly through those whose minds he influenced. He, more than any other man in this orbit, represented the true form of the Third New Deal which was now about to be born.

Tugwell came from a New York State farm, went from high school to the Wharton School of Business and then began as a teacher at the University of Pennsylvania, the University of Washington and finally Columbia. Ray Moley, who knew him at Columbia, drafted him for Roosevelt's Brain Trust in 1932 and when Roosevelt was inaugurated Tugwell was made Assistant Secretary of Agriculture under Henry Wallace.

Perhaps no colder heart ever beat for the Common Man than Tugwell's. Unlike some of his colleagues, he was in no sense queer. He differed from most of them in that he had a first-rate mind and wrote well, in a severely cold style with a painfully cultivated formality. He perfected himself in the fine art of being contemptuous. At college he looked at the world and found it distinctly third-class—not at all the kind he would have made. He burst into song in a poem called "The Dreamer," indicating his general intention with reference to his own tawdry country as follows:

> "I am strong.
> I am big and well made.
> I am sick of a nation's stenches.
> I am sick of propertied czars.
> I have dreamed my great dream of their passing.
> I have gathered my tools and my charts.
> My plans are finished and practical.
> I shall roll up my sleeves—make America over."[10]

And sure enough, here he was in Washington with his charts and his tools—only his tools were men, and he didn't think much of them either. As an administrator in the Agricultural Department he did not get far, due chiefly to his bad manners. Farmers who called on him were treated with scorn. But the darling targets of his contumely were congressmen and senators. He quarreled with everyone, save, of course, the President—the source of his present power. He had to be got out of Washington because of the trouble he stirred up and in due time, like many another New Dealer, he hid his scorn under a bushel while he crawled onto the payroll of one of those great enemies of the Common Man—a big Puerto Rican sugar corporation. Later he would be named Governor of Puerto Rico. Despite all this it was, nevertheless, this well-dressed, almost dandified, contumelious and disliked scholar who, as much as anyone else, indicated the lines upon which the much-bedeviled and bewildered leader of the New Deal would travel.

Before following this trail further we must reconstruct in our minds the state of political opinion on that side of controversy called the Left. Nothing has confused so perfectly the critics of Mr.

Roosevelt's various New Deals as their obscurity about the meaning of a lot of words such as Socialism, Communism, Fascism, Liberal, Conservative and so on. We must clear this up for ourselves before we can see with clarity just what happened in Washington in the next two years.

It goes back a long way and begins with the Socialists. There were all sorts of schools of Socialists. But in the United States the kind that acquired such a large influence over the minds of Americans were those democratic Socialists led by Eugene Debs, Maurice Hilquit and Norman Thomas. They were profoundly devoted to the ideal of human freedom. They believed they could, by a gradual series of alterations in the structure of our society, create a truly democratic world in which all men would enjoy not merely freedom but plenty. They believed this could never be achieved under the system of private property and profit. They did not advocate revolution, but rather a gradual acquisition by the State of all the great utilities—power, transportation, communications and the great basic industries like coal, oil, steel, etc. From this point on this partly socialized state would expand its acquisition of all other economic activities to whatever extent seemed feasible.

They dreamed of a cooperative commonwealth in which all would share suitably in the abundance created by a great productive organism owned by the people. This would end poverty, ignorance and crises. The Socialist Party once polled a million votes and even in 1932 Norman Thomas polled over 800,000 votes. But the influence of the Socialist Party cannot be measured by the number of votes it got. Its philosophy penetrated deeply into the thinking of large numbers of men who never voted a Socialist ticket and particularly into those groups loosely described as intellectuals.

The Russian revolution was essentially a Socialist revolution. Lenin preferred to call his government a Communist government though the term meant very much the same. In fact Russia became known as the Union of Socialist Soviet Republics. However, Lenin and his colleagues completely discarded the idea of a democratically controlled society and instead set up what they called the Dictatorship of the Proletariat which was in fact nothing more than a dictatorship by the Communist Party, a tiny fraction of the population. It was in fact a dictatorship by an elite—the so-called experts in the

Socialist organization. And this it has remained. This dictatorship, so complete, so cruel, so savage in fact, produced a sense of defeat or at least frustration in the minds of great numbers who had nursed the old Socialist democratic dream. This shocking example of the first Socialist state dampened the tolerance with which the Socialist dream was held by many people who never embraced Socialism but were willing to give it a free voice in the discussion of public problems.

On the other hand, semi-Socialist states rose all over Europe—social democracies they were called. They were part socialist, part capitalist, part parliamentary, but with all the defects of the European parliamentary system critically exaggerated. Perhaps it would be better to say that systems which were at least three-fourths capitalist were being operated by Socialist governments, for in most of the countries of Europe for a while at least Socialist prime ministers and partly Socialist ministries were running the show.

However, the most important thing that rose out of all this was a new approach that made a tremendous appeal to many of the same intellectuals who had dallied with socialism. I say new, yet it was not really new. Men had been flirting with the idea in Germany since the days of Fichte, who might be said to be the father of the theory of a planned capitalism. The idea was that it would be sufficient to nationalize the banks, the railroads, all means of transport, the mines and a few great basic industries—perhaps not even all of them. This would leave all the factories, stores, amusements, farms, etc., in the hands of private owners. Actually such a society would be about one-fourth socialist and three-fourths privately owned or capitalist. However, in this society the State would assume the responsibility for making the whole work; it would hold itself responsible for the well-being of all the citizens, their protection from the hazards of life—poverty, sickness, age, etc. And to make the whole work continuously without occasional breakdowns, the State would set up certain great planning agencies or boards which would continuously study and observe the functioning of the economic system and make plans covering production, prices, distribution, financing, profits, wages, hours, etc. Thus we would have what was in fact a Planned Capitalism—with the State responsible for the planning and for ensuring the carrying out of its plans through great government bureaus armed with the necessary powers to enforce compliance.

This was the perfect haven for great masses of intellectuals—students, teachers, lawyers, politicians, writers, journalists and others—who had flirted timidly with Socialism and Communism, but who did not dare admit they were Communists or Socialists because that would carry with it a certain ostracism in the schools, the journals, in the professions and in business. There was indeed a good deal of tolerance for the idea of planning our capitalist system even in the most conservative circles. And a man could support publicly and with vehemence this system of the Planned Economy without incurring the odium of being too much of a radical for polite and practical society.

There was only one trouble with it. This was what Mussolini had adopted—the Planned Capitalist State. And he gave it a name—fascism. Then came Hitler and adopted the same idea. His party was called the Nazi party, which was derived from the initials of its true name, but it was dedicated to fascism. Mussolini and Hitler, of course, realized that a system like this, which undertakes to impose a vast complex of decrees upon a people while subjecting them to confiscatory taxes to support the immense activities of the State cannot be operated save by an absolute government that has the power to enforce compliance. Actually this system had spread over Europe. For nearly 70 years all the countries in Europe, with Germany in the lead, had been experimenting with the baleful idea of the security State, the State which attempts to provide its people with jobs and protection from all the hazards of life. After World War I, the dominance of this idea over the populations of every European state became complete and every state in Europe was riding, before World War II, hell-bent for bankruptcy under the impossible burden of meeting these obligations.

Whatever it was, it was the direct opposite of liberalism. It was an attempt, somewere midway between Communism and capitalism, to organize a stable society and to do it by setting up a State equipped with massive powers over the lives and fortunes of the citizens. This may be a wise dispensation, but it is the negation of the liberal philosophy which for decades has been fighting to emancipate the people from the tyranny of all-powerful states. Yet this curiously un-American doctrine was being peddled in America as the bright flower of the liberals. Of course they did not dare call it fascism, because that had a bad name. They did not dare admit that it implied the restoration to the State of a numerous collection of those very powers which we had stripped from the State as the means of giving freedom to men. They called it the Planned Economy. But it was and is fascism by whatever name it is known. And though it may be launched under a free republic, it will wither and die because of the feebleness of the government which tries to enforce it by helpless appeals to the people. Little by little the government must be made stronger, the rights of the citizens before the government must be reduced. Little by little, if the Planned Economy is to be made to work, the free republic must wither. These two ideas—the idea of a free republic and the idea of a Planned Economy—cannot live together.[11]

But this meant little to Tugwell and his school. He wrote:

> "Planning will become a function of the federal government; either that or the planning agency will supersede the government, which is why, of course, such a scheme will be assimilated to the State."[12]

The most vocal of the open advocates of the system of the Planned Economy was Mr. George Soule, in the columns of the *New Republic*. He wrote a book on the subject in 1932 and about the same time Stuart Chase began to advocate a Closed National Economy.[13] This word Planned Economy is a very tricky one. If you oppose it you can be asked: "Do you really mean we ought not to plan our economic system?" What objection can anyone have to planning to make an economic system work? If I am asked: "Do you believe we should plan to make the economic system work?" I would answer "Yes." But what system? A Communist system? A fascist system? Or a capitalist system? I believe in planning to make our free capitalist system work. What must be the object of my planning? It must be to keep the system privately owned and free and functioning at its highest efficiency. Obviously I cannot plan for a free capitalist system the way I would plan for a Communist system. My plans must be to make the free capitalist system function at top capacity according to its own special genius.

But the Planners have something else in mind. The first thing they would do is to destroy the freedom of the system. The next thing would be to socialize about one-fourth of it. Obviously this would not be planning to make "our" economic system work. It would be planning to substitute another one. These planners mean that inside the State a great aggregation of bureaus must be set up with some totalitarian over-all bureau to decide what will be produced and how much and who will produce it and who will be allowed to produce and where and at what price he will get his materials and at what price he will sell them and what he will pay for labor and the conditions under which labor will work and so on. In foreign trade, the business will be handled precisely as it was in Hitler's Germany, through huge state cartels which will, if possible, unite with similar cartels from other countries in great international cartels which will regulate the international flow of goods. The central planning agency will control the banks and the flow of all investment, deciding where it will go and at what profits it will work. This is what they mean by planning and any man in his senses knows that when such plans are made for the guidance of a free people—140 million of them—who are not accustomed to being pushed around, they will refuse to comply unless the government has in its hands powers sufficiently formidable to compel them. This means a continual accumulation of power at the center until it becomes absolute. And whether it is good or bad it represents a complete revolution. "Planned Society" is just a soft, misleading name for a society part capitalist and part socialist run by a dictatorship of the experts.

Stuart Chase, one of the few among the Planners who stated the case fearlessly and frankly, admitted that to introduce it into a society of *laissez-faire* would be suicidal. "It can be introduced," he said, "only when governments take power and speculative profits away from bankers and business men ... New industries must be set up; old industries liquidated; industrial research for substitute commodities encouraged on a large scale; millions of potentially unemployed steered to new jobs; colossal capital shrinkage adjusted in some fashion; such foreign trade as remains rigidly budgeted by central authority. National Planning and economic nationalism must go together or not at all."[14]

Perhaps the great pioneer of planning in this country was Thorstein Veblen and it was from him that Tugwell and the others drew their inspiration. Veblen, like so many of his kind, was an unpleasant fellow. He was born in Minnesota in 1857 and went to a small western college where he got himself disliked for his incredible bad manners. From there he took his sneering mind to Johns Hopkins where he hoped to get a scholarship and where, in addition to failing in that, he involved himself in debt from a good deal of promiscuous borrowing. After a period at Yale he went back home where he lay around for several years exploiting a fake illness. Then he married a young lady of wealth and treated himself to many years of idleness. Like Marx and some other such philosophers he proceeded on the theory that the world owed him a living. At the end of this series of easy sabbaticals he decided to return to college at the age of 34. His wife, of course, eventually left him.

In time he went to the faculty of the New School for Social Research in New York. He had a brilliant though erratic mind, and his influence on young teachers with radical leanings in New York at Columbia and the New School cannot be exaggerated. In an age when it was the popular thing in college to be in revolt, Veblen supplied his followers with a steady stream of alluring and half-baked slants on the world around them. The point that stuck with them was that our democratic system of business was run by a lot of ignoramuses and that the remedy was a new structure of society in which the experts—the technicians and the professors—would take over. This was government by the elite, which is precisely what Mussolini believed in.

Veblen decided that the capitalist system was doomed because it could never produce abundance. It could not do this because the business men who dominated it were systematically engaged in sabotage—that is, the conscious withdrawal of efficiency in order to create scarcity and increase prices. The technicians alone possess the technological knowledge for producing at all times all the goods and services which the population requires. Unfortunately the experts were now under the control of the bankers and the absentee owners who forced them to curtail output. Veblen insisted that the engineers should unite, since they are few in number and could easily do this. "Given time it should not come as a surprise that the guild of the engineers are provoked to put their heads together and disallow that large absentee ownership that goes to make the vested interests and to unmake an industrial system ..."

"A general strike of the technological specialists in industry need involve no more than a minute fraction of the whole population; yet it would swiftly bring a collapse of the old order and sweep the time-worn fabric of finance and absentee sabotage into the discard for good and all."[15]

One of the men who fell under the spell of this ribald and lawless iconoclast was Rex Tugwell and it was Tugwell, of all the men who had a chance to influence Roosevelt, who resembled Veblen most in the substance of his philosophy.

Another was Leon Henderson. Around 1932 a seedy philosopher with a patch in his pants named Howard Scott appeared upon our troubled scene sponsored by Leon Henderson. Scott was full of the Veblenian philosophy. He started a squalid little movement, until Leon Henderson and some others managed to get some business men to give him a hearing at a big banquet. Henderson got him into a cheap dinner jacket and Scott then proceeded to frighten the soul out of his hosts. He was pure Veblen. The present system was going to smash. Nothing could save it but a Soviet of the Engineers. They must take over. Then we must unite the whole continent in a single economic unit in the most severe type of economic nationalism, since the United States alone did not possess all the materials essential to a self-subsisting economy. The engineers would take it all into their laps. Money would be abolished and the unit of value would be the erg—the unit of energy. The production possibilities would be colossal.

A number of academic gentlemen set up an institute at Columbia University to study the possibility of this great Continental Economy and it was promoted by Henderson and others in what was called Technocracy, Inc. Henderson was a director. But the philosophers soon disagreed and the project blew up. On January 12, 1942, Congressman Martin Dies charged in the House that Henderson had been a Technocrat. Henderson, then clowning as the boss of OPA, indignantly denied it and offered to eat the Washington telephone book on the steps of the Capitol if Dies could prove it. But the proof was simple. The New York *Times* on January 24, 1933 announced the break-up of Technocracy, Inc., as being due to the resignations of four of its eight directors, including Leon Henderson. The New York *Herald-Tribune* reported the same story, adding that

Leon Henderson defended Technocracy, notwithstanding the resignation. The trouble arose over the manner in which Scott was running things.

Not long after this adventure in continental remodeling, Leon Henderson became the economic adviser of the NRA and from that incredible explosion he moved over to become the economic adviser and research director of the Democratic National Committee.

As for Mr. Tugwell, he always maintained a close pipeline for transporting his views on affairs. These men and those like them had never thought much of that Second New Deal which in 1938 came tumbling down. Roosevelt was bewildered, asking why no one told him what to do—and these men and their confreres all the time knew precisely what to do.

However, there was still another group of philosophers, and as the sweet, discordant notes of the crumbling capitalist system, like a Shostakovich symphony made music in their ears, they were on hand with their special brand of medicine.

2. THE SPENDERS

All during the winter and spring of 1938 a group of young instructors from Harvard and Tufts were busy on a book which they called "An Economic Program for American Democracy." This little volume made its appearance in October, 1938, just as the solemn truth about the crack-up of the Second New Deal had sunk definitely into everybody's consciousness, including Mr. Roosevelt's.

These young professors had been moving under the guidance of a person somewhat more eminent than themselves—Dr. Alvin H. Hansen, professor of Economics at Harvard, who was destined before long to become the chief economic lawgiver of the New Deal in its revised Third Edition.[16]

The theory propounded by these gentlemen may be briefly stated thus. The expansion of the American economy came to an end in 1929. Before that it had grown for several well-known reasons. (1) There was a rapid increase in population due to free immigration. (2) The frontier was open to entry and exploitation. (3) Technological expansion went forward upon an amazing scale. But all this was at an end. Population is no longer increasing save at a small rate. The frontier is gone, having been exploited and settled. Technological advance at the old rate is no longer possible—the great era of revolutionary inventions is over. A basic change has come over the structure of the American economy.

Their theory continued: Government spending in the last five years had been proved to be a powerful force for promoting national well-being. Too many made the mistake of supposing that this was a temporary expedient to bring back a self-sustaining recovery. Certainly Mr. Roosevelt made this mistake. He had supposed he was merely priming the pump of business. Public spending, this new school insisted, could not bring the privately supported economic system back to full production because the private system was no longer capable of that. Public spending must be used not as a pump primer, but as a permanent additional or auxiliary pump. The old pump—private industry and business—could no longer produce the national income required for a full life. The government had to set up not a mere pump primer to prime the old pump, but a new pump to do its full share along with the old one to create abundance.

"The government," they concluded, "must assume full responsibility for maintaining national income at a sufficiently high level to assure full utilization of our human and material resource."

This must be done, they insisted, by public spending. *"The notion that public spending can be safely resorted to as a temporary emergency device must be abandoned."*

Their thesis was as follows. The people do not spend all of the income they receive on consumable goods and services. Each year they save great sums. These savings are thus withdrawn from the function of spending. They must be brought back into the stream of spending some way or the system collapses. The orthodox method of accomplishing this in the past has been through private investment. People who save and who do not wish to spend their money for food or clothes or consumable goods are willing to invest it. If they invest it they put it into what are called capital goods—goods designed to produce other goods such as houses, buildings, machinery, etc. If they do this the money is used to employ workmen, experts, technicians, etc., and this gets into the hands of people who will spend it. *To keep the capitalist system going at full tilt there must be a continuous flow of all savings into investment—into new industries and the expansion of old industries.* That is a perfectly sound theory. It has been held by most of the economists who have studied business cycle theory for many years. It was the basis of the conclusion reached by many men when they predicted the depression of 1929. It was the basis of the opinion of those who appealed to Mr. Roosevelt in 1933 to adopt a program that would encourage business expansion instead of making war on business and killing investment. These New Deal economists, however, were just learning this important principle. But they concluded that a continuous flow of savings into private investment was no longer possible. This is possible only when business men wish to borrow funds for new enterprises and expansion of old ones. But we can never hope to see this again, they said. Expansion on a sufficient scale in new enterprises and expanded old ones is hopeless because the economy has reached the end of its expansion era, as described above. The only way to avoid the inevitable collapse of the system, therefore, is for the government to step in and borrow those sums which business refuses to borrow and to spend these on all sorts of welfare, educational, social and other public enterprises.

Of course government spending had already plunged the government into debt to the tune of nearly 40 billion dollars. Continuous spending of funds borrowed by the government would mean a continuous expansion of the government debt. But to these new economic philosophers this was nothing to disturb the slumbers of the people. Government debt is not like private debt, they said. It does not have to be paid. The government can keep it afloat indefinitely by redeeming old bonds with new bonds. Moreover the interest on the government debt will not be a burden. The debt is due by the people to themselves. The people owe the debt. The people own the bonds which represent the debt. The government taxes the people to pay the interest on the bonds. It takes the taxes out of the pockets of the people and then pays it back to them in the form of interest. It is just taking it out of one pocket and putting it in the other.

The government therefore need not bother about the size of the debt. It can go on borrowing indefinitely. One of the eminent Harvard economists delivered a speech in which he assured his hearers that over the course of years the government might create a debt of a thousand billion dollars without being unduly worried. Of course a more crack-brained proposition was never promulgated in the name of higher learning. But the fact that all this was coming, not from some howling dervishes in the corn belt, but from gentlemen who took care to identify themselves as Harvard economists gave it a respectability which got for it a ready welcome in the most astonishing quarters.

About this time Mr. Tugwell and Leon Henderson engaged a couple of more orthodox economists in a discussion of the public's recovery problem. Mr. Tugwell and Mr. Henderson both admitted that the President's spending program had failed. But they insisted that it had failed because it had been on a far too modest scale. Instead of spending three billion a year, for which Roosevelt was being damned, Tugwell said he should have spent twelve billion a year.

It is not hard to understand what a happy effect this produced on the mind of Mr. Roosevelt. Always hospitable to fresh and bizarre ideas, he found himself now in a state of bitter frustration because, after what he had supposed was a spending spree, the depression was back on his doorstep. Here were men, not long-haired Populist crossroads philosophers, but honest-to-goodness Harvard and Columbia professors telling him the trouble with him was that he had not spent enough. He was like a man suffering with the jimmies from consuming a quart of rum who was being exhorted by his wife to sober up and take the pledge when along came a batch of eminent physicians and assured him his whole trouble was that he should have drunk three quarts instead of one and should keep it up as a steady diet. There was probably no suggestion that fell upon Roosevelt's mind and spirit that gave him such a lift as this, that picked him up out of a spiritual slump in which he could not see his way ahead and now satisfied him that what he had been doing was fundamentally right. He had merely been too stingy, too reluctant. That lone remaining rabbit—the spending rabbit—the rabbit he had been ungrateful enough to think at times had been wild—now he saw that the whole trouble was he had been keeping too tight a rein on him, that he had not been nearly wild enough. Now he was ready for a wilder ride than ever.

It was these two groups—the Planners and the Spenders—who now really captured his mind and made him feel that, instead of having arrived at the end of his experiment, he was in truth only at the beginning. And here at hand was the most magnificent of all objects of spending—National Defense.

He had arrived now definitely at the point at which the staggering, ramshackle parliamentary governments of Europe had arrived before the First World War. Very soon a Temporary National Economic Committee, composed of representatives of the House, the Senate and the Executive department was named to make a great study of our economic system. Senator O'Mahoney was made chairman, but Leon Henderson, one of the champions of this new school, was the actual executive director. Everybody was given a chance to air his views. But Henderson and his immediate associates steered the whole show in the direction of the new ideas. Next a National Resources Planning Board was appointed. And, true to his strange contradictory limitations, Roosevelt named as its chairman his uncle, Colonel Frederic Delano, an aging engineer who was one of the most reactionary mine owners in the whole field. But the god in the machine, the economic philosopher who was to inspire its purposes and devices was that Dr. Alvin Hansen, the chief apostle of the spenders, who was named to a place in the Federal Reserve Board from which spot he began to function as the chief economic thinker of the New Deal—the Third New Deal.

Almost all of the men who were responsible for the little book which proclaimed this theory to the world were summoned down to Washington and became economic advisers to some sector of the government. Leon Henderson became eventually head of the OPA when the war arrived, and Richard Gilbert, Hansen's principal adjutant, became its economic adviser.

Roosevelt now had a plan. The events in Europe provided him with a means of spending money in a way that would command the approval of many of his bitterest critics.

The spread of these two ideas now—the Planned Economy and the theory of Spending and Debt—ran with a thrill through all the bureaus in Washington. A pall of spiritual depression had settled over that large band of New Dealers who had been functioning so joyously up to the appearance of the economic crack-up. But now spending was resumed. Spending was to be continuous and everlasting. All around they saw the signs that the President, who had been regarded as a laggard in their great philosophical journey, was now completely converted. The money began to flow and there was the clear intention that the flow should be speeded up. Employment began to rise again. Never since the first inauguration had the new bureaucracy been so much in evidence. It sprang into a more spirited intellectual life.

In the capital one bumped suddenly and frequently into a happy and eager bureaucrat who had but recently been a tutor or professor or instructor in some college where he was eating his heart out over the futility of the professor's existence—where he presided over the destinies of two dozen youths in some small fragment of human learning, while lesser and baser men directed the destinies of the nation. Now he is in Washington and by a swift turn of the wheel of Fortune he presides over a numerous division of lesser bureaucrats, earns twice what he got as a teacher and is amazed and delighted at finding himself fabricating a policy to mold the lives of a million farmers or twice as many housewives. The sense of anonymous power sends the blood coursing through his heated brain. After a while he seems not unequal to any problem, however vast.

In certain cocktail bars or in the household salons of numerous Madame de Staals they foregather and are fascinated by what they have come to think of as the regime of the philosophers. Only two or three years ago it was the crackpots who were prancing and kicking up their heels all over the place and terrifying the men of power. But now, as in the days before the Bastille, the philosophers are whirling about in a new dance, a little crazier than the dance of the crackpots. The town is full of salons with well-stocked cellars. The little freshwater instructor finds himself standing up near a beautifully carved colonial fireplace in Georgetown, with a caviar hors d'oeuvre in one hand and a martini cocktail in the other, discussing with Assistant Secretary So and So or Commissioner What's His Name what shall be done with the potato crop or the new situation that has arisen in China. It is ravishing. It is intoxicating. The dead days of the dour Hoover are gone forever. The faltering and uncertain feeling of the Second New Deal are over. Roosevelt has seen the light—they knew he would all the time. The theory of the Permanent Crisis is now established. Oh, happy Crisis! Oh, blessed Catastrophe! At last we have set our foot truly upon the threshold of the real revolution—the perfect revolution, bloodless, worked out in charts and tables, attended by no massacres and no sacrifices, just a smooth, pleasant ascent up the flowery hills of government debt. But even the most wildly optimistic of the happy prophets had no vision of how tall the peaks would be.

Chapter 6: War Clouds

While the shadows of the depression were lengthening over America, the war clouds grew darker over Europe. The First World War was the inevitable result of 50 years of European history. It began with the invasion of Serbia by Austria, as the Second World War began with the invasion of Poland by Germany and Russia. But the invasion of Serbia was no more the cause of World War I than the invasion of Poland was the cause of World War II. In each case the rape of a small country was merely the last step in a long series of accumulating causes that made this last step inevitable.

For 70 years all Europe had been developing along the same lines—(1) extending social services beyond the capacity of the State to support; (2) using militarism as a means of employing men in the army, and in factories to supply the army; (3) paying for all this with vast government debts; and (4) the gradual extension of radical socialist ideas throughout Europe. The First World War interrupted but did not end these drifts. The new European governments moved as fast as possible into militaristic programs. The left-wing parties were powerful in the governments and used that power to develop on a greater scale than ever the Welfare State, committed to jobs and security for all. In Germany the use of militarism to support the economic system by providing jobs was delayed by the Treaty of Versailles. But Hitler cast off that chain and proceeded to do what all other governments were doing—develop the Welfare State with jobs for all, security for all and an army that would provide a million jobs in the ranks and two million in the factories to produce arms, uniforms and food for the army. Everywhere militarism was the biggest of all the industries. What Hitler did in Germany, Mussolini in Italy, Metaxas in Greece and various other dictators in other countries was merely the end result of every attempt to set up the Welfare State. It cannot work under a democratic government because it must have a dictator to enforce its harsh policies. *The welfare state cannot operate without the police state.*

Everywhere in Europe the armies were drilling; the shovel squads were busy in the forests and the poor and unemployed were getting their handouts from German, Italian, Austrian, Greek, Yugoslavian and other Harry Hopkinses. The arms factories, too, were busy, but the burden of all this upon the people was intolerable. To a degree people could be subjugated to these massive controls and exactions by the police authority of the absolute state, but one other weapon was also essential and that was fear. Neither the people of Germany nor Italy nor any other country could have been subjected indefinitely to the crushing taxation and humiliating controls unless they were kept in a state of fear. Control over the minds of men became as important to the dictator as his armies and police. And as it happened, the European militarist-welfare-police states had at their disposal two of the mightiest instruments of propaganda that the world has ever known—the radio and the motion pictures. Everywhere the hate campaigns were rolling along. Every population in Europe was being terrified by the radio and the motion pictures with fears of their neighbors. After 1933 nothing could avert war in Europe. It was just a question of how long it could be held off and at just what precise point it would break. It had to come soon. By 1936 Hitler was strong enough to denounce the Versailles and Locarno pacts and send his troops into the demilitarized Rhineland without France or England raising a hand. Mussolini had invaded Ethiopia.

As 1937 opened and Roosevelt began his second term, the smell of war filled the air from four directions—from Spain, Japan, Italy and Germany. The first shadow of the returning depression came in July in America and it was in July that Japan began, at the Marco Polo Bridge, the invasion of Northern China and within a month had taken possession of Peiping and invaded Shanghai.

Early in 1938, when Roosevelt was having so many blue days with his cabinet about the return of the depression, Hitler in a series of swift shocks sent the German columns to seize Austria and declared that Austria had ceased to exist as a nation. He had said there were ten million Germans outside the borders of Germany who must be reclaimed for the fatherland. By the Austrian coup he got seven million. But there still remained three million in the Sudetenland of

Czechoslovakia. That became his next objective and he let the world know it. All through the Spring and Summer of 1938, Hitler was storming at Czechoslovakia. France and Britain began to speak openly about fighting. By April, France made it clear she would live up to her treaty with the Czechs if Germany attacked and by the end of May the Czechs were ordered to their war stations. German armored divisions were moving up to the Czech border and the crisis was approaching. Clashes were occurring on the Czech frontier. Chamberlain and Daladier were putting pressure on Hitler. Hitler demanded the Sudeten. Bomb-proof dugouts were being rushed in Hyde Park and gas-mask stations were being set up in Piccadilly. Chamberlain, Daladier and Mussolini went to Munich on September 29, 1938 for a talk with Hitler. There an agreement was reached by which the whole Sudeten area was surrendered to Germany and Chamberlain went back to London with his famous announcement that he brought back "peace in our time." But no one believed it. Hitler immediately resumed his agitation against Czechoslovakia.

As Hitler's legions rolled into Czechoslovakia, Under-Secretary of State Sumner Welles claimed over the radio that Roosevelt had sent a personal message to Mussolini begging him to intervene and that, on this request, Mussolini had done so. As a result, Hitler had halted his soldiers and sent an invitation to Chamberlain to come to Munich. Five days later Secretary of War Woodring made the same claim. And the White House secretariat put out a record of all the messages from the President synchronized with the events in Munich to prove that Roosevelt had turned the scales for peace. Later, in the 1940 campaign, Willkie charged that Roosevelt had boasted of his part in the appeasement. Secretary Hull indignantly denied this and asserted that the President had "never telephoned to Mussolini" as charged by Willkie. However, in Mr. Hull's more recently published memoirs[17] he forgot that disclaimer and he himself boasted that the President sent a "message to Mussolini" and one to Hitler. He wrote "whether the actions taken by the President brought about these results it is impossible to say. But undoubtedly they exercised considerable influence" and he produced proudly a letter from King George VI to the President saying: "I have little doubt that your efforts contributed largely to the result." Whether they did or not the

President's office and his agents were loud in their claims that he had brought about the Munich appeasement.

Every man who followed the course of international affairs knew what Hitler was driving at. He was driving at Russia. Of course he had a claim on Poland for the restoration of the Polish Corridor and it was inevitable that he would fight for that. But that was a minor objective. Hitler had set himself up as the great enemy of Communism, which was becoming a menace all over Europe. But he had far more practical reasons for his Russian ambitions than the mere "defense" of western civilization against Communism. What Hitler really wanted was first to smash the Communist government in Russia and second to seize the Ukraine and the Caucasus with the vast resources of those regions. He intended to rip them out of the Soviet Union and bring them under German control where he would have free and complete access to their vast oil, mineral, timber, chemical and agricultural products. When Hitler would undertake this aggressive enterprise would depend upon his own judgment as to when the German armies were ready and it began to look as if they were pretty nearly ready in 1938.

These war moves were of profound interest to the American people. There was a general feeling that our well-intentioned entry into the First World War had been ill-advised, that none of the grandiose moral objectives had been achieved, that all the tall talk about ending war forever and bringing a reign of peace through the League had been a ghastly failure, that our allies had taunted us with our selfishness for making money out of the war, asked for cancellation of the war debts and called us Uncle Shylock. There was a feeling that we had been drawn into the war through the ill-considered day-to-day decisions made by the administration then in power and that we had been lured in by permitting ourselves to tap the resources of war as an opportunity for business prosperity.

Americans were generally decided that we would not make that mistake again and out of this grew the now famous Neutrality legislation. Secretary of State Cordell Hull, in his memoirs, has denounced the Special Senate Committee Investigating the Munitions Industry, which was headed by Senator Gerald P. Nye of North Dakota, for having put upon our statute books this Neutrality Act. It is possible that Secretary Hull to this day does not know how the

Neutrality Act came to be passed, since the President was in the habit—as Mr. Hull himself has demonstrated—of carrying out important projects in international affairs without consulting his Secretary of State.

The origin of the Neutrality Act has never, I believe, been made public before. The writer was in a position to know the facts and now states them for the first time. I was acting as one of the advisers of the Nye Committee. On March 20, 1935, Senator Nye brought the Committee into executive session. There he informed the members and myself that he had just received a message from the President requesting him to bring the Committee or as many members as possible, with him to the White House at once. I do not recall how many members went with Senator Nye, but they went at once and there the President proceeded to expatiate at some length upon the causes of war, based upon his own personal experiences in war.

He then declared that he thought the wise thing for the Committee to do would be to prepare an act which would guarantee, in the event of a European war, the absolute neutrality of the American people. This was the first proposal for a Neutrality Act and it came from the President of the United States, Mr. Hull's superior at the time. Several senators expressed prompt agreement. The President then said he thought William Jennings Bryan was right in 1916 on this subject. Senator Bennett Clark, whose father had been defeated for the presidential nomination by Bryan's leadership, laughed a little sardonically and said "Well, so far as I am concerned, I have no use for William Jennings Bryan or any of the things he stood for, but I do agree with him on that." This referred to the position taken by Bryan that American citizens should be prohibited from traveling on foreign ships in time of war or on American ships into the war zones.

The Committee was greatly pleased with the President's suggestion and left the White House in complete agreement with him. Senator Nye later prepared, after consultation with his colleagues, the first draft of the famous Neutrality Act, which generally was along the lines suggested by the President. It was introduced in the Senate and House and passed by very large majorities. It had a time limit of two years and at the expiration of the time limit it was passed again by enormous majorities in both houses.

The President promptly applied the law with a good deal of gusto when Mussolini attacked Ethiopia, and when the Spanish Civil War broke out and the President found the Act did not apply to civil wars but only to wars between countries, he sent for Senator Nye, requested him to have the law amended immediately to apply to civil war, all of which was done and the President promptly declared the Neutrality Act in force as to Spain.

In the 1936 campaign, in the famous address at Chautauqua already referred to, the President described the conditions which bring countries into war. He had said: "Industrial and agricultural production having a war market may give immense fortunes to a few men. For a nation as a whole it produces disaster." He described how war profits had sterilized our farms, extended monopoly, produced unjustified expansion of industry and a price level that dislocated relations between debtor and creditor. And then he said with complete approval: "The Congress of the United States has given me certain authority to provide safeguards of American neutrality in case of war" and he warned the nation that this was not enough unless the President himself was one who was willing to use the authority.

Yet for years writers dealing with this subject have referred to the Neutrality Acts as if they were something that had been imposed on the President against his better judgment and for the purpose of hamstringing him in the conduct of foreign affairs. The whole policy of the Neutrality Acts has been referred to as the "neutrality blunder" as if it were the blunder of the President's critics instead of one in which he had not only shared but which he had actually initiated. This is just one more thing the President did in the field of foreign affairs without consulting Mr. Hull and he probably never confided to him that he had originated the idea.

Roosevelt had said in his 1936 campaign that "the effective maintenance of American neutrality depends today as in the past on the wisdom and determination of whoever at the moment occupies the office of President of the United States and Secretary of State." And he had warned that in the event of war abroad we would have to be on guard against those seeking "fool's gold," those who would find it hard to look beyond, "to realize the inevitable penalties, the inevitable day of reckoning that comes from a false prosperity." We can keep out of war, he promised, *"if those who watch and desire have a sufficiently detailed understanding of international affairs to make certain that the small decisions of today do not lead toward war and if at the same time they possess the courage to say no to those who selfishly or unwisely would lead us into war.*" This is what was called isolationism.

And now war in Asia was a fact—a vast war with a million Japanese soldiers in China. There was a civil war in Spain which had aroused differing elements of our people, and Hitler's legions were mobilized for the inevitable plunge eastward into Poland and then into Russia.

The fatal moment was at hand when the day-to-day decisions of the President of the United States would lead us in one direction or the other and Roosevelt was the President. Already the war orders were coming fast. England had set up a $7,500,000,000 war preparation fund. Germany, France, England, Italy, China, Japan were all clamoring for steel, scrap iron, oil, planes, plane parts. The time was here when "thousands of Americans who, seeking immediate riches, fool's gold, would attempt to break down or evade our neutrality."

What would the President do?

Here he was with a depression on his hands—eleven million men out of work, the whole fabric of his policy in tatters, his promise only a few months old to balance the budget still fresh in the minds of the people and yet the pressing necessity, as he put it himself, of spending two or three billion a year of deficit money and, most serious of all, as he told Jim Farley—*no way to spend it.*

Here now was a gift from the gods—and from the gods of war at that. Here was the chance to spend. Here now was something the federal government could really spend money on—military and naval preparations.

Obviously, in the disturbed state of the world, something could be said for this. But Roosevelt in 1932 had denounced Hoover for spending so much on the army and navy. Now he promptly set off on an immense program of military and naval expenditures—which was proper and in which Congress concurred—but without making any retrenchment in the enormous outlays he was putting out on all the other New Deal departments of spending, all with borrowed money and more government debt. He simply increased his government borrowing. He was now committed all-out to the theory which the Planners and the Spenders had sold him, that government debt means nothing. He could now spread his wings for a grand flight under the influence of this new theory without troubling his soul about the economic consequences.

In 1936, when Mussolini attacked Ethiopia, the President had promptly applied the Neutrality Act. When the Civil War began in Spain, as we have seen he promptly urged the Act's amendment to cover that situation. But in 1937, when Japan invaded China, *we were in a depression and this time he refused to apply the Neutrality Act and permitted shipments to China and Japan from this country*. One excuse was that there was no declaration of war, which was silly. The Neutrality Act did not require a declaration of war by an aggressor; it merely required the fact of war. The other reason was that we were China's only source of defense materials, in spite of the fact that we were shipping six times as much to Japan as we were shipping to China. What the President's New Deal needed now was that war trade with Japan. The President defied the mandatory provisions of the Neutrality Act because his administration required that at this moment America should get a little of that "fool's gold" from Japan.

In September, 1937 two old gentlemen—Cordell Hull and Norman Davis—put their heads together and decided the United States was getting too isolationist. They decided "some day-to-day decisions" should be made to bring us a little closer to the brawl that was brewing in Europe. They went to Roosevelt and sold him the idea that he should make a speech on "international cooperation."[18] Roosevelt readily agreed. The two of them proceeded to write the speech. Davis undoubtedly did it because Hull could hardly write a decent speech for himself. And this speech Roosevelt delivered on October 5, 1937 at Chicago. It was the celebrated "quarantine" speech which created a sensation. He talked of "homicides raging over the world, destroying all the works of civilization." Then he said:

> "If those things come to pass in other parts of the world let no one imagine that America will escape ... that this hemisphere will not be attacked and that it will continue to tranquilly and peacefully carry on the ethics and arts of civilization ... If those days come there will be no safety in arms, no help from authority, no answer in science. The storm will rage until every flower of culture is trampled and all human beings are leveled in a vast chaos ...

> "It seems to be unfortunately true that the epidemic of world lawlessness is spreading. When an epidemic of physical disease spreads

the community approves and joins in a quarantine of the patients against the spread of the disease ... War is a contagion whether it be declared or undeclared. It can engulf states and peoples distant from the original scene of hostility. We are determined to keep out of war, yet we cannot assure ourselves against the disastrous effects of war and the danger of involvement. We are adopting such measures as will minimize our risk of involvement but we cannot have complete protection in a world of disorder in which confidence and security have broken down."

Ernest Lindley, a New Deal journalist, at a press conference asked the President if the speech was a repudiation of neutrality.[19] When Roosevelt answered there was no conflict between such a program and neutrality, Lindley replied that they seemed to be at opposite ends of the poles. Roosevelt refused to say what he meant by quarantining an aggressor.

Hull and Davis had not been responsible for the quarantine idea in the speech. The speech went further than they thought it ought to have gone, but not, of course, further than they were willing to go. They were eager for America to get into a war if it came. But they felt the people had to be drawn along a little at a time. They wanted the President to frighten the people a little as a starter. But he increased the recommended dose. The reaction was so violent that they felt it put back by at least six months the purpose they had in mind—rousing America to a warlike mood.

Two months later an American gunboat, the *Panay*, was bombed in the Yangtse River in China in the heart of the Sino-Japanese war area. Japan immediately apologized and agreed to pay full damages and to punish the guilty officers. Had the President applied the Neutrality Act, as he was in duty-bound to do—this boat would not have been protecting American oil tankers delivering oil in the midst of two warring armies in China. The purpose of the Neutrality Act was to avoid precisely an incident like this. However, following the *Panay* incident, Mr. Hull began to churn up as much war spirit as possible and through the radio and the movies frantic efforts were made to whip up the anger of the American people.

In January, 1938, I talked with one of the President's most intimate advisers. I asked him if the President knew we were in a depression. He said that of course he did. I asked what the President proposed to do. He answered: "Resume spending." I then suggested he would find difficulty in getting objects on which the federal government could spend. He said he knew that. What, then, I asked, will the President spend on? He laughed and replied in a single word: "Battleships." I asked why. He said: "You know we are going to have a war." And when I asked whom we were going to fight he said "Japan" and when I asked where and what about, he said "in South America." "Well," I said, "you are moving logically there. If your only hope is spending and the only thing you have to spend on is national defense, then you have got to have an enemy to defend against and a war in prospect."

Apparently the best hope of a war at that moment for popular consumption was with the Japs, who had just sunk the *Panay*, and as there was little chance of arousing the American people to fight around Japan, South America seemed a more likely battleground to stimulate our fears and emotions. There is nothing new about this. Kings and ministers have toyed with this device for ages and convinced themselves they were acting wisely and nobly.

Chapter 7: The Third Term

There is no doubt that Franklin D. Roosevelt toyed with the idea of a third term from the moment of his second inauguration. It was impossible that a man who took so much satisfaction from breaking so many comparatively unimportant precedents should fail to feel the urge to break this one.

However, it is possible that with the economic crash of 1937–38, he put the idea out of his mind. Henry Morgenthau has made it quite clear that Roosevelt had the hope that he could get through the remaining years of his second administration without balancing the budget and then go out of power to await the inevitable crash that would follow his departure and be the prologue to another Roosevelt term. The disastrous Court fight, the hopeless purge defeat, the deep cleavage within his party and inside his own cabinet, the failure of all his policies beyond doubt led him to look forward to a period of peace and he actually discussed with a magazine a proposal to write for them at a very large honorarium.

After the arrival in Washington of the academic champions of government spending and the rise of the war fever in Europe, which presented him almost like a fairy gift with the means of spending on a most elaborate scale, the sense of frustration that had extinguished in his breast the ambition for a third term was now gone. Now he knew he had the perfect project for spending—national defense. Now he knew, because the economists from Harvard and Tufts had assured him, that all his fears about the unbalanced budget were just old-fashioned horse-and-buggy bogies. There is not the slightest doubt, from the accounts of all who saw him frequently, that by the beginning of 1939 his spirits soared aloft. Roosevelt knew that war was coming, with a great probability that America might get into it. If America did not actually go into the war itself, she would certainly play a critical role on the edges of the war and when the war came to an end she would sit at the head of the table, perhaps as arbiter, in the making of some great and luminous peace. It must be very clear to anyone that Roosevelt could not bear the thought of surrendering the glorious experience of managing America's part in that war into other hands. It is fairly certain now that early in 1939, if not a little sooner, he made up his mind to seek a third election.

Roosevelt had a weakness that was a source of unending embarrassment and perplexity to his closest advisers. When he was bent upon some act which he was very eager to perform, yet which he believed would not stand exposure to discussion, he had a kind of childish habit of not only concealing his intention from those who ought to know but of even dissembling it like a small boy bent on mischief. Having made his decision to seek a third term, he kept the subject a complete secret from practically everyone. He realized the political difficulties involved in a third nomination. He wanted it, therefore, to be a "draft Roosevelt" movement, rising up spontaneously within the party. Certainly he did not tell any member of his cabinet or any of the sycophantic time-servers who formed his kitchen cabinet that they must not promote his nomination. There is an old Irish saying that sometimes half a word is better than a whole sentence. It is probable that to Hopkins and a few others, Roosevelt barely lisped that half word and they went with their whole souls and all their energies and most of their time into the great adventure of making sure of Roosevelt's nomination.

It was almost all done by the men who spent most of their time in and around the White House and so cunningly was this whole comedy of the "draft" carried on that Roosevelt himself was able at once to play both the coy maiden and chairman of the Draft Roosevelt movement.

Apparently some time late in 1938, Edward J. Flynn[20] discussed the third term with Roosevelt, who told him a story about his "Uncle Ted" as he called him. When Theodore Roosevelt was considering a similar situation he said to friends that the people of the United States "are sick and tired of the Roosevelts," that they "were sick of looking at my grin and hearing what Alice had for breakfast. In fact they want a rest from the Roosevelts." The people felt the same way about his own family, said Roosevelt. They were tired of looking at them.

Organization Democrats at this time were not so strong for Roosevelt to run. Certainly Garner was not and neither was Farley. Flynn says he refrained from urging Roosevelt to attempt another campaign. He felt the President was not in the best of health, that he was no longer young, that "he lacked some of the early resilience and power of quick reaction he once had." The eagerness for another term all came from the New Dealers and they were hard at work trying to get the necessary delegates, which Flynn says was not helping the cause any because they were deeply resented everywhere by the orthodox leaders. Charlie Michaelson,[21] who I am convinced was not very much in the inner secrets of either the party or the White House, says he wrote in 1938 "Of course I am entitled to a guess and my guess is that FDR would take a case of the hives rather than four more years of the headache that being President means."

Miss Perkins, who worshiped Roosevelt, says that she never urged him to run for a third term because she "had real doubt about the wisdom of third terms as a matter of principle." And she insists that the President did not really want a third term. She called on him with Daniel Tobin of the Teamsters' Union on some labor matter, but she does not give the date. Tobin told Roosevelt he must run for a third term. The President said: "No, no, Dan. I just can't do it. I tell you I've been here a long time. I am tired. Besides I have to take care of myself. This sinus trouble I've got—the Washington climate makes it dreadful ... I never had it until I came here. The doctors say I have to go into the hospital for a month of steady treatment and I can't do that, you know ... No, I can't be President again. I want to go home to Hyde Park. I want to take care of my trees. I have a big planting there, Dan. I want to make the farm pay. I want to finish my little house on the hill. I want to write history. No, I just can't do it, Dan." And then he added with a laugh: "You know, the people don't like the third term either."[22]

Tobin assured him that labor would stand by him. This might have been in 1938, during those dark months. However, Roosevelt knew enough to know that such a disclaimer would not prevent the "draft" so long as all the men in the White House, from Hopkins up and down, were running it.

At this same session Roosevelt told Tobin that John L. Lewis had come to him and urged him to run for a third term, much as Tobin had, and that he had made the same answer to Lewis, but that Lewis had suggested that "if John L. Lewis was nominated for Vice-President all the objections would disappear."[23] This statement was without a grain of truth. Besides, John L. Lewis was far too smart a man ever to go about getting the nomination for President or Vice-President that way.

In July of 1938, Fred Perkins of the Pittsburgh *Press*, at a White House press conference, asked: "Mr. President, would you care to comment on Governor Earle's suggestion that you run for a third term?" The President said: "The weather is very hot." Then Robert Post of the New York *Times* put in: "Mr. President, will you tell us now if you will accept a third term?" The President said: "Bob Post should put on a dunce cap and stand in the corner." Then Fred Perkins tried again: "Did your statement last winter fully cover the third term?" The President replied: "Fred Perkins to don a dunce cap likewise."[24]

However, Farley says that after 1938 the President became increasingly interested in the 1940 convention and that he saw his successor in every man to achieve stature in the country and that as the time approached he became more and more critical of all these would-be presidential candidates. As a rule, a president who does not intend to run to succeed himself, is bound to want to see a successor friendly to his policies and to his fame and a candidate who can win. Actually the normal behavior for Roosevelt, if he was not grooming himself, was to be looking around earnestly for someone to follow him and to assist in building up either that man or some other strong candidate. After 1938, Roosevelt pursued precisely the opposite course. Theodore Roosevelt had surrounded himself with the ablest cabinet of any in our time. He was himself a big man, confident of his own capacity to deal with other big men and was not afraid to have that kind around him. Franklin Roosevelt surrounded himself with a cabinet of perhaps the smallest stature of any president in our time. Theodore Roosevelt, anxious to be succeeded by a strong man, went to great pains to build up William Howard Taft. Franklin Roosevelt, on the other hand, never failed to knock down anybody suggested as a possible successor. The name of Paul McNutt was being urged. Roosevelt sent him as High Commissioner to the Philippines and jokingly asked: "Is that far enough?"

The four names most prominently mentioned were Garner, Hull, Farley and McNutt. Farley says that Roosevelt could not see Garner under any circumstances—"he was too conservative." He didn't want Hull because he was too slow—"thought things over too long." He could not have Farley because Farley was a Catholic and that would not be wise. From all this Farley, in 1939, wrote in his diary:

> "I am satisfied in my own mind that the President will not be a candidate for reelection, *but might be willing to listen to argument.* I don't know if he has anyone in mind definitely to succeed him. If he had to make a selection at the moment I believe he would select Harry Hopkins, Robert Jackson or Frank Murphy in the order named."[25]

It has been said that Jim Farley's break with Roosevelt was occasioned by Roosevelt's determination to run for a third term and thus blast Farley's ambition to be President. But a careful reading of Farley's memoirs makes it pretty clear that he had no idea of being nominated for the presidency, that he was flattered at the suggestion but what he thought he might get was the nomination for the vice-presidency. For instance, he wrote in 1939: "There isn't any doubt in my mind if I assist in bringing about Garner's or Hull's nomination, I can have second place with either man if I want it."

In February, 1939, Farley made several long trips to sound out party sentiment. He wrote: "My own opinion is that the leaders of the party with few exceptions do not want Roosevelt to run for a third term." He noted that they were sick of Wallace, Hopkins, Corcoran and the rest and did not relish the idea of a bitter campaign defending a third term candidacy. This, he said, was the opinion of every responsible leader he talked with except Olson of California and Kelly of Chicago. Farley noted that after this, in frequent conversations with Roosevelt, as different names appeared in some connection wholly removed from the election, Roosevelt would dismiss them with "he wants to be president" as if this were an offense. He was angry that McNutt should even permit his name to be discussed for the presidency. He told Farley: "I consider it bad taste on his part to be letting his name be used when he is still a member of my administration."[26] This meant that any Democrat with the Roosevelt administration could not permit his name to be discussed for the presidency without resigning.

In June, Garner told Farley that under no circumstances would he support a third term. Farley agreed and confided: "The two of us can pull together to stop Roosevelt." Garner told Farley he had committed the sin of becoming popular and that was something Roosevelt would not tolerate in anyone. He said: "He is jealous of Hull for his standing before the people. He is jealous of me for my popularity with Congress. He ought to be glad to see men in the party coming along but he doesn't like it."

This was in June of 1939 and a short time afterwards Cardinal Mundelein sent for Farley and urged him to support Roosevelt for a third term. Mundelein had come directly from the White House. Roosevelt had not consulted Farley on an appointment for a year and a half and after this, his visits to the White House grew fewer. Then some time during the summer, Roosevelt asked Farley to come to Hyde Park. He talked about the 1940 campaign and the candidates. There was Garner—he's just impossible. Then Wallace—"he hasn't got 'it.'" Then McNutt—he turned the thumb of his right hand down. Then he got around to the third term and after a pause, he leaned over and in a low voice of great confidence he said: "I am going to tell you something I have never told another living soul," and then almost in a whisper: "Of course I will not run for a third term, but I don't want you to pass this on to anyone because it would make my position difficult if the fact were known prematurely." Farley pledged his silence.

After allowing this to sink in, he told Farley that while he would not run, he did not want to campaign for a losing ticket. Farley asked what kind of candidate he wanted. He said: "Pick someone who is sympathetic to my administration and will continue my policies." It is perfectly clear from what Farley wrote at the time that he did not believe Roosevelt. Many men, enemies of the President, had accused him of being, to put it mildly, untruthful. Farley had been politically his most important lieutenant from the time he was nominated for the governorship. Roosevelt was now, under the veil of secrecy, making a firm statement to Farley about a matter of the supremest importance to both men. And Farley didn't believe him.

After this Farley went to Europe. While he was away, Hitler drove into Poland and the British and French declared war. When he came back the whole problem had been solved for Roosevelt. Farley found him in a state of the highest excitement. They had lunch and Farley said: "*We are to all intents and purposes in a state of war.* I think at this time politics should be adjourned. The people aren't interested in politics. They are interested in their country and their families." To which Roosevelt replied: "Jim, *you have hit the nail on the head*," which corresponds with Frances Perkins' statement that for Roosevelt the war years began in September, 1939.

Still later, at a dinner party at the White House, Roosevelt said to Farley's wife that he was having a terrible time. People were trying to make him run and he didn't want to. To which she replied: "Well, you're the President, aren't you? All you have to do is to tell them you won't run." He looked very much surprised and turned to the lady on his right. It was at this point that Farley knew definitely that Roosevelt was going to run again and after this the President virtually ignored Farley, and a White House assistant secretary was ordered not to assist Farley in a speech he was about to make. Cordell Hull says that from 1938 to July, 1940, Roosevelt told him definitely that Hull would be his successor. But all the time he was laying his plans for a "draft"—and acting out the comedy with Hull, who apparently still believes Roosevelt wanted him to run.

The whole story is a chapter of duplicity, in which Roosevelt, who had definitely decided to run if he could make it, was putting on before Farley the pose that he didn't want to run and before Hull the pose that Hull was his candidate, while all the New Deal agents, with his full knowledge and approval, were scouring the country for delegates and Roosevelt was using every artifice and pressure he could command to kill off every possible contender for the nomination. Saved now by the war from the disaster which overtook his administration in 1938, completely converted to the golden theories sold him by Hansen and Tugwell of eternal deficits and spending of billions on the greatest of all WPA projects, he could now rise out of the ashes of a mere New Deal leader to become a modern St. Michael brandishing his sword against Hitler and all the forces of evil throughout the world.

Chapter 8: The Shock Troops of the Third New Deal

With the invasion of Czechoslovakia and the European war a certainty, Roosevelt was now ready to go to work to get himself elected.

The whole conservative wing of the Democratic party was angry, from Vice-President Garner down. It was angry about the radical labor power inside the party, about the attacks on business and about the Court fight and the purge. Nevertheless, the President had in his hands control of the party machinery.

In the 1932 convention, Roosevelt had had the hostility of the party machines in the big cities. They had been hostile at first but had been held in line by Jim Farley. They were unwilling friends in the 1936 election, but now they had been conquered completely by Roosevelt. In addition to them, he had the vast legions of organized labor which, by 1939, were being directed from the White House through the masterful leadership of Sidney Hillman. He had the immense payroll army of the New Deal government which included millions. And he was now to cultivate those racial and religious groups whose emotions had been inflamed by the outrages committed in Europe upon the inhabitants of their old homelands.

I. THE RIGHTEOUS BOSSES

There never has been in American politics a religion so expansively and luminously righteous as the New Deal. From the beginning to the end it was constant in one heroic enterprise—war to the death upon evil, upon greed, poverty and oppression. It had, in fact, one monstrous enemy against which it tilted its shining spear seven days a week and that was SIN. If you criticized the New Deal, you were *for* sin.

Yet it must be conceded that amongst the warriors of the New Deal were many whose presence in the army against sin was a little surprising. One such collection of men were those who are called leaders by their friends and bosses by their enemies in the big cities. What were the leaders of these great grafting organizations doing on the side of the angels?

In New York City, Tammany Hall was the organization that managed the Democratic hosts of the city. It had a long and at times unsavory existence. Its motto was "To the victor belongs the spoils" and the spoils consisted not merely in jobs that went to the party workers, but those great enterprises that feed upon the state and that are included under the name of graft. Illegal graft was the levying of extortion upon contractors, gambling houses, commercial prostitution, commercial vice of all sorts. There was, however, an area known as legal graft that consisted in various kinds of profits which organization leaders and favorites made out of ordinarily legal business but which they were able to collect because of political power and pressure. For instance, a Tammany leader might have a silent partner in some firm handling contracts with the city. In cities, the bonding and insuring business is an important element in all kinds of activities—bonds in the courts, bonds of office holders, insurance and bonds of city contractors and the insurance business of large firms that depend heavily upon city business or the favor of the administration in power. Always there were Tammany leaders with an interest in an insurance firm either directly or through their relatives.

With the advent of Charlie Murphy as the leader, there was a marked moral change. Murphy, like many of his contemporaries, was a good family man and a steady church member. He began as a saloon owner but left that and as he grew older became aware of the vicious aspects of organized vice and its partnership with machine politics. When John Hylan became mayor of New York, strongly under the influence of his religious wife he made up his mind to end the toleration of commercial vice in New York City. Murphy supported him in that and whatever critics may say of Hylan and Tammany, he put that policy into effect and drove these industries out of New York City into New Jersey, where they found a hospitable welcome.

I do not mean that the leaders of Tammany Hall put on wings. There remained always a few leaders who resented this flight to grace and there were areas of so-called legal graft which were extensively cultivated. But another factor had intruded upon the scene. Al Smith loomed as a candidate for the presidency. Murphy nursed the ambition of electing an authentic Tammany man to the White House and as part of that plan he began to enforce a more exacting code of good conduct on Tammany leaders, some of whom, to be sure, chafed under it. But Murphy said Tammany could not afford a bad name to stain the good repute of Al.

One other point about Tammany must be noted. It was primarily a political organization, but one activity of the organization was social welfare. Tammany lived on the support of the masses of voters. In each city district was a Tammany club. It was the headquarters of the political life of the district, but it was also the center of certain social services. Every night the boss was there, surrounded by numerous city employees from the various departments of the city—school board, magistrates' courts, public works, health, etc.—and to this club every evening came a steady stream of people in the district looking for aid—a woman who wants her teacher-daughter brought to a school nearer home, another who wants help in the magistrate's court for her erring son, a whole collection of victims of the eternal traffic violation ticket who want it fixed, a poor woman who wants a little coal or a few dollars or a word to the commissioner of welfare for a relative, and various others seeking many other kinds of help.

The cost of all this so-called social welfare to the district boss was not very great. The personal services were performed by the faithful on the city payroll and the actual money outlay was modest and met out of the boss' own funds and funds levied on city employees and contractors and others who enjoyed the favor of the leader. But it was the most powerful source of the hold that Tammany Hall and its affiliated organizations in the other boroughs of the city had upon the people of New York.

The worst of these city machines were the Kelly-Nash machine in Chicago, the Hague machine in Jersey City and the Pendergast machine in Missouri, although there were many others in the great industrial cities. When Roosevelt was a candidate for the nomination in 1932 all these machines were opposed to him. They continued to sneer at him after he was elected and he continued to snipe at them. He directed Farley, for instance, to fight the nomination of Ed Kelly for mayor of Chicago. In New York he committed against the Democratic organization which had helped elect him the unpardonable political offense of promoting the candidacy of LaGuardia for mayor, who was elected on a Republican ticket supported by disaffected New Deal Democrats.

When Roosevelt became President, as we have seen he began spending vast sums of money on relief and public works. Into a Tammany district, for instance, now flowed not a few thousand dollars passed around in the methodical and economical manner of the boss, but hundreds of thousands, even millions, of dollars for all kinds of aid including jobs for those who wanted work and generous handouts from relief agencies. The handouts, of course, were coming from New Deal agents. The Tammany chieftain in the district could no longer compete with the extravagant hand of Roosevelt's dispensers of bounty. The only hope of the Tammany leader to hold his place in the district was to do business with the man in Washington who commanded these golden streams. He had to be the agent in the district for controlling the flow of this money or he was out, because the national government could install in every district a benefactor who could out-spend the boss not ten to one but a hundred to one.

Roosevelt did not do business with leaders directly. They had to do business with Roosevelt's man in Tammany and, as it turned out, he was probably the worst of all the leaders in that organization. Tammany men knew all about him and he became after that the model and pattern to which Tammany conformed. He was Jimmy Hines, the leader of the Eleventh District.

Prohibition in its way had done something to Tammany as it had to everything in America. It had brought the speakeasy, the illegal liquor business and the criminals and gangsters who preyed on them.

With the appearance of Jimmy Walker as mayor of New York the organization began to sink back again into its old frailties. Graft upon all sorts of commercialized vice got to be big business again. More than one district fell into the hands and under the control of men who were leagued with these enterprises. Jimmy Hines was the worst of them all. He had a partnership with Dutch Schultz, a notorious gangster and murderer.

How he became Roosevelt's right-hand man in New York is not difficult to understand. Years before a young man out of law school, wishing to get along, decided to become a Democrat. His name was Samuel I. Rosenman. After he graduated from Columbia, he went to Mr. Hines and told him of his ambitions—he wanted to go to the legislature. Hines sent him to one of his trusted advisers, an old Tammany judge, for examination. The judge found that Sammy knew his lessons and so Rosenman went to the legislature and in good time wormed his way into the good graces of Franklin Roosevelt as governor and became the first member and the last survivor of his Brain Trust. He remained always one of the close political friends of his sponsor, Jimmy Hines, while he lived in the spotlight of the purity and holiness of the New Deal, and he was able to make Hines Roosevelt's right-hand man among the bosses of Tammany.

In 1933, LaGuardia came into power in New York City and for the next ten years Tammany lost its hold upon the political machinery of New York save through some of the borough governments and by 1942 lost its hold in the state when Dewey became governor. Tammany was now strictly on the outside. It had lost the jobs and the rich perquisites of office. Many of the club houses were closed or became the cold and dreary haunts of men who no longer attracted the hungry, the poor and the dispossessed in search of help. Tammany had sold its famous old hall in 14th Street and had built a new Tammany Hall on Union Square near 14th, but after a few years of struggle it was no longer able to maintain itself there or pay the interest on the mortgage and had to sell out. Old Tammany sachems and other devout members of that dwindling congregation took refuge in tears over at Luchow's Restaurant the day Jimmy Walker, representing Tammany Hall, stood on the stage of the Hall and handed the deeds to the new purchaser—David Dubinsky, head of the International

Ladies Garment Workers Union, a socialist-dominated labor organization that strung along with Roosevelt.

Little by little the Tammany leaders who were growing older were being succeeded by newcomers who were ready to scream their heads off for Roosevelt and the New Deal. There is no vast sum of money in holding office. The riches are in the perquisites, the graft, legal and illegal, often collected by men who do not hold office but who do business with those who do. Some Democratic chieftains of the newer stripe began to drift into vice rackets of various sorts. Frank Costello, the most notorious racket manager in the country, became the most powerful factor in that once proud organization. Many district leaders were running night clubs and hot spots and little by little large sections of Tammany fell into the hands of criminal or near-criminal elements.

It was this Tammany at its lowest level which surrendered to the New Deal and became finally the political tool of Mr. Roosevelt in New York. From an old-fashioned political district machine interested in jobs and patronage, living on the public payroll and on various auxiliary grafts, some times giving a reasonably good physical administration of the city government, some times a pretty bad one, some times very corrupt, some times reasonably honest, it became a quasi-criminal organization flying the banner of the Free World and the Free Man.

In 1932, Illinois sent a delegation to the Democratic convention headed by Tony Cermak, a crude political genius who had emigrated from Bohemia, started with a pushcart, became a precinct captain, grew rich on graft, organized the Poles, Czechs, Lithuanians and Slovenes in Chicago into a powerful racial bloc called the United Societies, became boss of the Twelfth Ward, rounded up the underworld for Brennan when he was boss and when Brennan died, succeeded him as Democratic leader and became mayor of Chicago.

Cermak fought Roosevelt's nomination at Chicago, and went to Miami in February, 1933 to make his peace with Roosevelt where the bullet intended for Roosevelt killed him. Ed Kelly, Cermak's chief aide and the chief engineer of the Sanitary District in Chicago, became mayor and thereafter Ed Kelly and old Pat Nash became the twin bosses of Chicago and of Illinois Democrats.

The story of the next eight years was an incredible one. The Capone gang, robbed of their Prohibition racket, had gone into business—horse parlors, gambling houses, bawdy houses, with special rackets in barber shops and other places. The Capone rackets were operated by Jack Gusik, Chew Tobacco Ryan, Loudmouth Levin, Harry Greasy-Thumb Gusik, Frank Diamond (Capone's brother-in-law), Charles and Rocco Fischetti (Capone's cousins), Eddie Vogel, slot machine czar and Billy Skidmore with whom everybody had to do business in Chicago to keep out of jail. There were crooked labor rackets on an unbelievable scale. At one point a rumor got around that some important person had been nailed for a $100,000 income tax evasion. It turned out to be Kelly, the mayor. Roosevelt had tried to prevent his nomination but didn't succeed. In the three years that Kelly had been Sanitary District commissioner he had failed to report $450,000 in income. The Treasury went after him but allowed him to settle. He refused, however, to divulge where the income came from. He settled for $105,000.

Like the Tammany Hall machine, the Kelly-Nash machine was subdued to the Roosevelt power and the countless millions it dispensed in Illinois. And as the time for the third-term movement came along, Ed Kelly was one of its principal leaders, beating the drum for "Roosevelt and Humanity."[27]

Nowhere in America was there a political ring more widely known for its brash defiance of law, decency and principle than the notorious machine of Frank Hague in northern New Jersey. Hague ran up his career from janitor of the city hall to mayor in ten years. In 1932 he had been mayor for 14 years. He was the undisputed boss of the state and he carried its national convention delegates around in his pocket, all of which he was able to do because of a reliable 100,000 plurality he could run up in Hudson County—enough to swamp any hostile majority for his candidates in the rest of the state. Hague grew in arrogance. He bullied, bellowed and bawled out his critics as well as his opponents at the polls. He didn't like Roosevelt. He didn't like the New Dealers around Roosevelt and above all he hated the pinks and the Reds.

The year 1938 was, as we have seen, a disastrous one for the Roosevelt New Deal. The national convention was only a year and a half away. In this year Judge William C. Clark, an authentic New Dealer, became the subject of Hague's concern. Clark had put the brakes on some of Hague's more blatant and offensive attacks on freedom of speech in his bailiwick. In 1938, Clark was the judge of the U. S. District Court in Hague's district and in that year was elevated to the U. S. Court of Appeals in New Jersey. That suited Hague fine. He had a candidate for the place left vacant by Clark and the appointment was in Roosevelt's hands. His candidate was T. G. Walker who had been elevated from a seat in the assembly to be a judge of the highest court in the state—the State Court of Errors and Appeals. Hague wanted Walker appointed to succeed Clark in order to make room for his son in Walker's place. It took a good deal of maneuvering but Hague, with Roosevelt's aid, worked it out. He got his enemy Clark from the spot where he was most offensive, put Walker into that place and young Hague, who had failed to graduate from law school, on the highest court in the state.

Hague had got what he wanted from Roosevelt. Later Roosevelt wanted something from Hague. Secretary of the Navy Claude Swanson, who had held that post since 1933, had for years been in a state of great feebleness. Charles Edison was Assistant Secretary of the Navy and because of Swanson's illness, actual Secretary. When Swanson died, Edison rated the promotion but Roosevelt for some reason didn't want him. He urged Hague to make Edison governor or senator from New Jersey. Hague agreed to do so. Then Roosevelt appointed Edison Secretary of the Navy and later Hague nominated him for governor of New Jersey. It was a bad day's work for Hague, as Edison after election got the notion that he and not Hague was governor, which precipitated a long and bitter fight between these two men, one representing bossism, machine politics and political corruption at its lowest level, the other representing the spirit of rational and democratic reform and honesty in elections and government. In this battle, which came after the election of 1940, Roosevelt threw his influence and power on the side of Hague.

These were three of the most notorious of the big city bosses, but there were similar smaller bosses of the same type all over the country. In 1939, although most of them hated Roosevelt, they had been completely subjugated to his will by the great sums of money which he was able to either spend or withhold from them in their respective districts. And they continued to play an increasingly important role in this righteous thing known as the New Deal. By 1940 they were among the most ardent Roosevelt men.

2. SIDNEY HILLMAN

Beginning with the second term, events began their work on the cast of characters of the New Deal. One after another power was slipping out of the hands of one set of men and dropping into the hands of others. Up out of the leadership of labor the head of Sidney Hillman began to rise higher and higher and his shadow grew longer around the White House. This would go on until Hillman would become one of the two or three most powerful men in America. By the beginning of 1937 the new labor movement, the CIO, under the leadership of Lewis, Hillman, Dubinsky and Murray, was marching forward. As Roosevelt was inaugurated, the big strike against the General Motors plants was under way with 113,000 men out. It was a bitter struggle marked by violence on both sides, but chiefly by the famous sit-down strikes.

On March 1, John L. Lewis and Myron Taylor startled the world with an agreement between U. S. Steel and the Association of Iron and Tin Workers and in two months 260 steel companies followed suit. By 1938 almost 450 firms had signed up with over 450,000 workers. But the CIO lost its fight with Little Steel. The big fight between Ford and the unions became the bitterest of these struggles. The CIO spread its activities over the white collar groups—the Newspaper Guild, even the lawyers, salespeople, retail clerks, architects, chemists, technicians and government workers. In the early part of 1938, over three million workers had been organized.

When the NRA was scrapped by the Supreme Court, Congress passed the Wagner Labor Relations Act to take the place of Section 7a, but with many more teeth in it and then began not merely the war between capital and labor but the war within labor, between the AFL and the CIO for jurisdiction over 30 million American laborers. Under the Wagner Act elections were held in plants to determine what union would be the spokesman for the workers and in the warfare between the AFL and CIO the workers in some places actually met in armed conflict with each other. But in addition to the war between capital and labor and the war between the CIO and AFL, there was another war within the CIO. It grew out of several elements of discord. One of them was the extent to which the Communists had penetrated the CIO. The other was the extent to which the CIO was being used in politics for the interests of Roosevelt. The third grew out of differences about policy and methods and the inevitable clash of strong personalities.

From the point of view of labor and the public, however, the most serious of these elements of discord was the penetration of the CIO by the Communists. On August 13, 1938, John P. Frey, president of the Metal Trades Department of the AFL, appeared before the House Committee Investigating Un-American Activities. Frey, in a presentation lasting several days, laid before the Committee a completely documented account of the penetration of the CIO by the Communist Party. He gave the names of 280 organizers in CIO unions under salary who were members of the Communist Party. He charged that John Brophy who was the director of the CIO, was expelled by the United Mine Workers some years before for disloyal activities and while he was not directly a member of the Communist Party, he was assisted in his work by two active members of the Party. He had gone to Russia as a member of a delegation sponsored by the Party and approved by Moscow and when he returned the UMW accused him of being a paid agent of the Soviet government. Brophy at a meeting said that the condition of workers in the Soviet Union "should be a source of inspiration to workers in America."

Frey named union after union in the CIO, giving the names of the Communists who were holding positions of leadership and trust. He charged, for instance, that they dominated the United Office and Professional Workers Union, that the president of that organization was a member of the Communist Party and through that organization they had infiltrated the government with numerous Party members in almost all the bureaus in Washington.

At the time of his testimony Frey, an old and highly respected labor leader, became the object of one of the most brutal and angry blasts of denunciation at the hands of all the New Deal writers and organs all over the country. The day after Frey's first appearance before the Committee, Martin Dies, the chairman, went to the White House in connection with some matter in which Texas was interested. When he got there the President treated him with studied discourtesy. He said sharply to Dies: "What is your idea of letting this thing turn into a denunciation of the CIO?" And he wanted Dies to put an end to Frey's testimony.

Dies explained the Committee had summoned all sorts of people to give their views on the subject of subversive activities. Dies had invited the CIO and the AFL to send representatives. The CIO refused, but the AFL sent John Frey. However, this did not satisfy the President, who became very angry. He said to Dies: "Well, there's no one interested in Communism, no one at all. I've heard it all my life. There is no menace here in Communism. The great menace in this country is in Nazism and fascism. There's where you can do a good job. As far as labor leaders are concerned, I've known both these groups. The AFL is tory and reactionary, but John L. Lewis is the most progressive, liberal labor leader I've known in my life." Of course, no one had charged Lewis with being a Communist. At that time the split between Lewis and the CIO was already in progress. It was not John L. Lewis who was harboring the Communists. The studious reader might be interested to go back to the report of the Committee on Un-American Activities in 1938 and read the testimony of John P. Frey who was saying in 1938 what the Attorney-General of the United States was saying ten years later and what the whole country came to recognize not merely as a fact but one of the gravest facts in the structure of our economic life.

It was the Communists who were engineering the sit-down strikes and who instigated and organized the Lansing Holiday when a mob of 15,000 blockaded the state capitol and 2,000 of them, armed with clubs, were ordered to march on the university and bring part of it back with them. At the *Herald-Tribune* forum in New York City about this time the President delivered one of the bitterest attacks he had ever made on a government official. It was against Martin Dies for investigating these Communist influences in the sit-down strikes.

Before this ended, Dubinsky and Lewis would be out of the CIO and Sidney Hillman would become not only its dominating mind but Roosevelt's closest adviser in the labor movement and in the end, though not himself a Democrat, the most powerful man in the Democratic party.

Sidney Hillman[28] was born in Zargare, Lithuania, then part of Russia, in 1887. He arrived here in 1907 after a brief sojourn in

England. Hillman never worked as a laborer or mechanic of any kind. Ben Stolberg says he was the only outstanding labor leader who never was a worker. He began his labor career as one of the organizers of the Amalgamated Clothing Workers of America and at 27 became its first president. He held that post to the day of his death and during that time was the unquestioned czar of this union.

Hillman was never a member of the Communist Party. He never permitted Communists to get into the Amalgamated Clothing Workers. Far more than John L. Lewis he understood the Communist Party and its methods and he was far too astute a man ever to permit his own union to harbor groups that would take their orders from other sources.

But what Sidney Hillman's precise political and economic philosophy was is not easy to say. The membership of his union was overwhelmingly Socialist but his union members were the employees of a very large number of small and a few large garment manufacturers who were themselves little capitalist employers. They lived within and on the fruits of the capitalist system and Hillman, as an intelligent labor leader, accepted that situation and sought to get for his own membership as large a share of the revenues of the garment industry as possible. Outside of that, however, it is entirely probable that Hillman, while not a Communist, was at all times sympathetic to the Communist philosophy. He was a revolutionist and it is probable that if a revolutionary mood were to have taken hold of America at any given moment, Hillman would have been among the ablest and most vigorous of its leaders.

Whether a man is a Communist or not is a difficult thing to determine if he is not a member of the Party. First of all, there are all kinds of Communists, just as there are all kinds of Socialists. There are the Stalinists and Trotskyites and Lovestoneites. The Trotskyites and the Lovestoneites are as violently anti-Stalinist as the Socialists and because of their war on Stalin they got a good deal of tolerance amongst anti-Communist groups in this country of which they formed no rational part.

It is certain that the Russian revolution set off a very vigorous flame in Hillman's bosom. In 1922 he hurried over to Russia with a plan. He had organized here what he called the Russian-American Industrial Corporation with himself as president. Its aim was to operate the "textile and clothing industry of Russia." Hillman's corporation sold to labor organizations at $10 a share a quarter of a million dollars of stock. The circular letter of the corporation soliciting stock sales among labor unions said: "It is our paramount moral obligation to help struggling Russia get on her feet." Hillman went to Russia to sell the idea to Lenin. He cabled back from Moscow: "Signed contract guarantees investment and minimum 8 per cent dividend. Also banking contract permitting to take charge of delivery of money at lowest rate. Make immediate arrangements for transmission of money. Had long conference with Lenin who guaranteed Soviet support."

When the Amalgamated Clothing Workers met in Chicago on May 8, 1922, a message was sent from Moscow by W. Z. Foster, then national chairman of the Communist Party. It read: "The defeat of the employers is the natural result of the splendid spirit of the Amalgamated. Many times in my present tour speaking to your unions I marveled at this growing spirit but since coming to this country I marvel no longer. It is the spirit of the Russian revolution, the spirit that will lead the workers to emancipation." This was read to Hillman's convention and printed in its proceedings. The message sent back to Russia read: "We thank you heartily for your inspiring message."

When the Congress of Industrial Organizations was formed all the leaders were aware, as already pointed out, that certain Communist unions were moving in. But no man among the top leaders was as aware of the full meaning of this as Sidney Hillman. Before the New Deal, the bulk of the Communist unionism was in New York and its environs. Lewis, whose unions operated in the coal fields, was very little troubled by the Communist influence. To labor leaders around the country generally it was a minor feature, but this was not so in the case of Hillman and those labor leaders in New York, particularly the unions dominated by Socialist memberships, who were keenly aware of the pro-Communist labor movement and the men who were its leaders. Hillman was in no doubt about Michael Quill and Joseph Curran and Harry Bridges and Ben Gold and Abram Flaxner and numerous others who had moved into the CIO. And Sidney Hillman knew as well as any man that Communists in labor unions are interested not in the welfare of the members but in the use of the labor union apparatus for revolutionary activities. He knew, too, that they take their orders from the Communist Party and not from the membership of the union.

Hillman was never an outright exponent of Communist objectives. He was, however, deeply sympathetic to the Communist cause in Russia and to the extreme left-wing ideal in America, but he was an extremely practical man who never moved upon any trench that he did not think could be taken. He never pressed his personal philosophy into his union and his political activities any further than practical considerations made wise.

He was a resolute man who shrank from no instrument that could be used in his plans. He was a cocksure, self-opinionated man and he was a bitter man, relentless in his hatreds. He had perhaps one of the best minds in the labor movement—sharp, ceaselessly active and richly stored with the history and philosophy of the labor struggle and of revolutionary movements in general. When Lewis and Dubinsky at a later date would leave the CIO, Hillman would be supreme and would reveal somewhat more clearly the deep roots of his revolutionary yearnings that had been smothered for a while under the necessities of practical labor leadership.

There is no doubt that Hillman was one of the first labor leaders to use the goon as part of his enforcement machinery. In 1931 a garment manufacturer in Brooklyn named Guido Fererri got into a bitter quarrel with Hillman's Amalgamated and was threatened by one of its officials. A few days later Fererri was found shot to death on the street. At the time a notorious character named Louis Buckhalter, known as Lepke, was officiating as slugger and goon for a labor union and Lepke was suspected of this crime. Some time later a Brooklyn jury found this same Lepke guilty of murder in the first degree for killing Joseph Rosen in a Brooklyn candy store on November 30, 1936. He was sentenced to be electrocuted but Lepke was in Leavenworth Penitentiary serving a term of 14 years as the master-mind behind a ten-million-dollar narcotics ring and another term of 30 years for labor racketeering, both of which would keep him in Leavenworth until 1980. Governor Dewey of New York demanded delivery of Lepke in order to execute him for the Rosen murder. He demanded delivery four times but each time Attorney-General Biddle refused. Thus, by insisting Lepke serve his long prison term for comparatively minor offenses, he was saved, for a long time, from execution for the more serious offense of murder. Why? On the night Fererri was killed, Lepke was seen by a policeman on the streets in that neighborhood in Brooklyn. He told Lepke: "You're too close to where a murder has been committed, so you better come with me." The officer took Lepke to the police station. Lepke telephoned from the station to Hillman, who shortly after arrived at the station house with Fiorello LaGuardia, his lawyer. Nothing more was ever heard of this nor was anyone indicted for the Fererri murder.

As matters stood in December, 1941, Lepke was in Leavenworth and Governor Dewey was trying to get hold of him. William O'Dwyer, later Mayor of New York, was the district attorney of Brooklyn and full of ambition. He was investigating every phase of the murder ring of which Lepke was the head. His chief investigator was a captain of the Police Department and stories were leaking out that he was making progress. But this time, Hillman's counsel, Fiorello LaGuardia, was Mayor of New York. He was the commander-in-chief of the Police Department and hence the superior of O'Dwyer's investigator. At LaGuardia's order he was told to give to his superiors a complete report on the activities of every member of his staff for every hour of the day for the preceding eight months and thereafter was to continue to report hourly on their activities. LaGuardia was clearly trying to find out what O'Dwyer was investigating. O'Dwyer ordered his chief investigator to refuse to comply with the order, and he did refuse, which made it practically necessary for him to resign from the police force. It created a sensation in New York.

Why did the Mayor want to know what was being investigated? The papers began to speculate and the very cautious New York *Times* reported that it was admitted O'Dwyer was investigating the Fererri case and that the investigation involved a high-ranking New York political leader and a labor leader of national reputation and had to do with Lepke's activities as a goon for a labor union. O'Dwyer denounced LaGuardia for trying to scuttle the investigation and there the matter stood when the Japanese struck at Pearl Harbor and it all disappeared into the blackout of almost everything that followed. O'Dwyer also disappeared into the Army as a general.

Why should LaGuardia want to scuttle the investigation of a notorious murder? Why should the President of the United States refuse to deliver Lepke to Dewey and thus save him from going to the chair? Why save the life of a man convicted as the leader of a murder syndicate? Who was the leading politician supposed to be involved? Who was the nationally known labor leader?

The murder for which Lepke was convicted and wanted for execution by Dewey and shielded by Roosevelt was, as we have seen, that of Joseph Rosen. Rosen was a trucking contractor who was hauling to non-union factories in other states for finishing, clothing cut under union conditions in New York. He was put out of business by Lepke in the interest of a local of Hillman's Amalgamated and Rosen was threatening to go to the district attorney and tell how this was done. To silence him, Lepke got him small jobs and in 1936 he opened a small candy store and the members of the local were ordered to spend some money in the store. This local was controlled by Lepke and a vice-president of the Amalgamated. Apparently Lepke never trusted Rosen while he was alive and decided to murder him. The highest court in New York State, in its decision on the Rosen case, said that Lepke had supported the faction which gained control of the local and that Paul Berger, the finger-man in the Rosen murder, was an intermediary between Lepke and the Amalgamated. In the end, Rosen, like Fererri, was murdered.

It was undoubtedly the belief of Governor Dewey that if Lepke was delivered to him he might, in the hope of saving his life, tell the whole story of the Fererri and Rosen murders. Finally in 1944 the federal government surrendered Lepke, who was questioned by the district attorney of New York and Governor Dewey, but Lepke never "sang" and went to his death faithful to the gangster's code of not revealing his story.

It is necessary to observe here that there is no intention of making any connection between the President of the United States and the gangster Lepke. The whole purpose is to reveal the connection between Lepke and Hillman. There is, in fact, no intention to charge that Hillman ever hired Lepke or anybody else for the purpose of murder. But Hillman did do business with Lepke and Lepke was a gangster, a ruffian and a murderer. The purpose is to throw some light upon the character of those groups which made up the strength and support of the New Deal, which was appearing before the public in the light of a great, noble and righteous army in the cause of justice and the common man. There is no intention, either, of implying that labor leaders and their unions are lawless organizations run by gangsters and murderers. The mass of labor union membership had no more knowledge of these things than anyone else and the great majority of labor leaders were generally honest, hard-working and modestly paid agents of their unions. But for some reason there rose to the surface at this time a lawless element, some of them criminal, some of them lawless in the excess of their revolutionary zeal, some of them just plain grafters. And these elements constituted the most powerful section of those groups that were supporting the President. This was in no sense the Army of the Lord, as it was so widely advertised.

3. RACIAL AND RELIGIOUS MINORITIES

A new element now made its appearance upon the political map. In America, particularly in the more populous states, are large masses of people who were born in Europe or whose parents were born in Europe and who were still touched deeply by their old racial and religious origins. This has always been true and it is perfectly natural. We have always recognized in this country that men could be perfectly good Americans without divesting themselves of their sentimental attachment to the lands from which they or their forebears came. In elections these groups could be found voting for all kinds of candidates and all parties. Here and there they might be corralled under the leadership of some able and adroit politician as in the case of the Czechs under Cermak in Chicago. But it could hardly be said that any one party had any sort of definite claim upon the affections of any of these groups as a whole.

However, from 1938 on and particularly around the beginning of 1939 the ambitions of Hitler and the treatment received by the various races and religions inside Germany produced powerful and fevered reactions in this country among the peoples most affected. Certainly all Americans were aroused at the performances of Hitler—at his persecutions of the Jews, his invasions of the rights of other churches, his aggression in Austria and his clearly planned aggression against the Czechs and the Poles, the Lithuanians and other

Baltic peoples, to say nothing of the peoples in the Balkan countries. Most Americans, with few exceptions, sympathized with these peoples and shared with them the emotional excitement they experienced. But here was a perfect mass of inflammable material ready to the hand of any politician unscrupulous enough to use it.

Every politician in America had now to concern himself with the problem of the approaching war. Every politician knew too that no man in his trade could become at this point an advocate of entering into any war that might break out in Europe. On the other hand, they were aware of the votes that might be picked up by assuming the role of the uncompromising enemy of Hitler. How far they could go to get votes and yet resist resolutely all efforts at involvement in the approaching war was a delicate problem. As it happened, the votes of those groups most seriously affected by the war were to be found congregated in limited areas. Thus, for instance, the Polish people were to be found mostly in six or seven northern states, particularly in New York. Roosevelt had spoken out against getting into a European war more vocally and positively than any other man in public life. He had been among the first to warn the people against all attempts to involve them and he had warned them to have an eye upon either politicians or business men who, when the war drums sounded in Europe, would attempt first to make money out of the war and then to draw us one step at a time, through small day-to-day decisions, into the war.

But Roosevelt was above all things else a politician and he had not the slightest intention of surrendering into the hands of whoever might be his adversary the support of these numerous groups who were the special target of Hitler's oppression. From that moment in March, 1939, when Hitler moved into Czechoslovakia and began thundering against the Poles, Roosevelt stepped out in front as the champion, above all others, of the threatened victims of Hitler's aggressions.

During the campaign he directed his aides to have speeches made by the ministers and ambassadors of the oppressed nations who were still in this country. He thought they could speak out effectively in cities where were congregated a goodly number of inhabitants of the countries from which they came. He wanted ambassadors from their own countries to tell them that other governments were "looking to

Roosevelt as the savior of the world," as he put it himself. Farley admits this was done and says it was a mistake and that he said so at the time.

Roosevelt also had told his national chairman to organize a Committee of Twelve, and said that there should be five clergymen on it—a Catholic, a Presbyterian, an Episcopalian, a Baptist and a Jewish rabbi. Farley noted the omission of the Methodists. Roosevelt suggested they put on a Methodist and drop the Jew and then corrected himself by saying there are more Jews than Episcopalians, so keep the Jew and drop the Episcopalian.[29] Thus racial and religious minorities became mere pawns to be moved about on the chessboard of politics. Their fears and hopes were to be exacerbated. To Roosevelt they were just so many votes.

4. THE PAYROLLEES

Back in the days before the New Deal the employees of government in the United States were chiefly on the payrolls of the states, counties and cities. It was the local organizations and machines with what was then considered their large payrolls which enjoyed this element of power in elections. The federal payroll was small and the number of persons affected by it quite insignificant. With the rise of the New Deal, however, a vast army of persons appeared on the payroll of the federal government and because some of the payrolls were flexible and had no connection whatever with the Civil Service, it was a simple matter for the government to use this ancient but now enormously enhanced tool to control votes in particular localities. Benefits paid to farmers, subsidies of all kinds could be timed in their delivery to correspond with the moment when farmers were making up their minds how to vote. Relief rolls could be expanded in doubtful counties and doubtful districts and this was done, as we have seen in the story of Hopkins' activities in the Democratic primaries of 1938.

Thus Roosevelt did not doubt his ability to get himself nominated, despite the long tradition of his party and the country against a third term. There remained the problem of getting himself elected, which seemed simple enough. After all, there were 531 electoral votes. All he had to get was a majority—266. He could count on 157 from the South (including Oklahoma and Arizona). He would need only 109 more from the North. The North had 374 electoral votes. He would need, therefore, only a little over one-third of the northern votes and four states could supply this—New York, New Jersey, Illinois and Massachusetts. He made up his mind that with the support of the Southern states which were congenitally Democratic, the city bosses in the big industrial centers who had been brought under his thumb, the labor vote which had been mobilized under unions that were predominantly political, the votes of the disturbed racial and religious groups affected by the war, and that immense and vital and active army of payrollees, he could hurdle over the difficulties of a third-term election. The story of the third-term campaign which we shall now see is the story of dealing with all these groups, and the feasibility of doing so successfully was enormously enhanced by the fact that in September, 1939, just about the time the active work for the coming convention was under way, Hitler marched into Poland.

Chapter 9: Roosevelt Breaks with the Past

On July 17, 1940, Franklin D. Roosevelt was nominated for the presidency for the third time. The prologue to this event was supplied by Europe.

After months of raging at the Poles and while Britain and France were negotiating with Molotov for an alliance against Hitler, on August 23, 1939 the whole western world was shocked by the news that Hitler and Stalin had made a deal. A week later, on September 1, Hitler sent his panzer divisions and his motorized infantry into Poland in a new kind of war. While Hitler was taking western Poland, Stalin was occupying eastern Poland in accordance with the agreement they had made. Stalin took the three Baltic states into "protective custody." Two days later Great Britain and France declared war on Germany. French armies moved to the German border and an English army appeared in France. There were skirmishes and minor actions. But the Maginot Line was supposed to be impregnable and the hostile armies settled down on both sides of it for that long stretch of inactivity which was called the "phony war."

Then on April 9, 1940, out of the quiet of this sleepy western front, the German army erupted into Denmark, while the German navy seized Norway. A month later the Nazis took Luxembourg in a day, the Netherlands in four days and Belgium in 18 days. The attack on France was launched with terrifying fury. The British were driven swiftly into a corner at Dunkirk from whence their entire army was forced out of France—335,000 men, leaving all their equipment on the beaches of Dunkirk. The Nazi panzers were thundering along various French routes, past the Maginot Line and into Paris by June 14. The French cabinet resigned and on June 21, French officials went through the melancholy ceremony of meeting Hitler and his marshals in the Compiegne Forest in that same military dining car in which Marshal Foch had received the surrender of the Kaiser's army in 1918. Having witnessed this, Hitler ordered the historic car sent to Germany. At that moment the delegates to the Republican Convention were arriving in Philadelphia.

As the convention assembled, therefore, the war was the supreme issue. The government had already appropriated billions for defense. Business was surging upward. The war contractors were crowding into Washington. There was no longer a question of unemployment, low prices or depression. The great question was: Are we going into the war or not? The Gallup poll showed an overwhelming vote against going in; but almost as big a vote for aiding the allies short of war.

The leading candidates before the Republican Convention which met on June 24 were Governor Dewey, Senator Robert A. Taft, Senator Arthur Vandenberg and Wendell Willkie. When the convention met, Willkie seemed the most unlikely of these candidates, but his strength grew. Dewey was eliminated on the fourth ballot and on the sixth, in a contest between Taft and Willkie, the latter was nominated in one of the most amazing upsets in convention history.

The Democrats believed that Willkie would make a formidable opponent. But from the moment he was nominated the result of the election could no longer be in doubt. Charles McNary, Republican leader in the Senate, was nominated for the vice-presidency. The joining of these two men—Willkie and McNary—was so impossible, they constituted so incongruous a pair that before the campaign ended McNary seriously considered withdrawing from the race.

There was a moment in that convention when one voice was lifted in solemn warning, the full meaning of which was utterly lost upon the ears of the delegates. Former President Hoover, in a carefully prepared address, talked about the "weakening of the structure of liberty in our nation." He talked of Europe's hundred-year struggle for liberty and then how Europe in less than 20 years surrendered freedom for bondage. This was not due to Communism or fascism. These were the effects. "Liberty," he said, "had been weakened long before the dictators rose." Then he named the cause:

"In every single case before the rise of totalitarian governments there had been a period *dominated by economic planners*. Each of these nations had an era under starry-eyed men who believed that they could plan and force the economic life of the people. They believed that was the way to correct abuse or to meet emergencies in systems of free enterprise. They exalted the State as the solvent of all economic problems.

"These men thought they were liberals. But they also thought they could have economic dictatorship by bureaucracy and at the same time preserve fee speech, orderly justice and free government. They might be called the totalitarian liberals. They were the spiritual fathers of the New Deal.

"These men are not Communists or Fascists. But they mixed these ideas into free systems. It is true that Communists and Fascists were round about. They formed popular fronts and gave the applause. These men shifted the relation of government to free enterprise from that of *umpire* to *controller*. Directly or indirectly they politically controlled credit, prices, production or industry, farmer and laborer. They devalued, pump-primed and deflated. They controlled private business by government competition, by regulation and by taxes. They met every failure with demands for more and more power and control … When it was too late they discovered that every time they stretched the arm of government into private enterprise, except to correct abuse, then somehow, somewhere, men's minds became confused. At once men became fearful and hesitant. Initiative slackened, industry slowed down production.

"Then came chronic unemployment and frantic government spending in an effort to support the unemployed. Government debts mounted and finally government credit was undermined. Out of the miseries of their people there grew pressure groups—business, labor, farmers demanding relief or special privilege. Class hate poisoned co-operation."

That was a perfect description of Europe in the years immediately preceding and following the First World War. And out of these vexations and dislocations came Communism in one place, fascism in others and social-democracies, so-called, in others, which were really societies one-fourth socialist, three-fourths capitalist, administered by socialist ministries winding the chains of bureaucratic planning around the strong limbs of private enterprise.

Mr. Hoover then undertook to describe the progress of this baleful idea here in a series of headlines: Vast Powers to President, Vast Extension of Bureaucracy, Supreme Court Decides Against New Deal, Attack on Supreme Court, Court Loaded with Totalitarian Liberals, Congress Surrenders Power of Purse by Blank Checks to President, Will of Legislators Weakened by Patronage and Pie, Attacks on Business, Stirring Class Hate, Pressure Groups Stimulated, Men's Rights Disregarded by Boards and Investigations, Resentment at Free Opposition, Attempts to Discredit Free Press.

This, of course, was the great problem before the country. The onset of fascist governments in Europe as described by Mr. Hoover corresponded precisely with the schemes of the Tugwells and Hansens and Hendersons and Hillmans and Wallaces and Hopkinses which had now become the motif of the Third New Deal—not Communist, not fascist, but a common program on which for the moment Communists and fascists and various grades of pinks could unite under the great goal of the State Planned and Managed Capitalism for abundance. But nobody was interested in this now. The billions were flowing again, everything was going up—wages, prices, sales and—*government debt*. But it didn't matter because now we had learned from the Harvard and Tufts economists that government debt is a mere nothing—something we "owe to ourselves." We were all off on a grand crusade to save the liberties and the "democracy" of Europe, now caught in the great final disaster which marked the climax of all those crazy ideas that had bred fascism and Communism in Europe and which were now being introduced into America by the same kind of minds that had given them to Europe.

The Republican party platform denounced Roosevelt for fanning the flames of class hatreds, bringing the judiciary into disrepute, fomenting war between capital and labor and for the mounting taxes and debt and the expanding regimentation. There were in the Republican convention, however, a number of delegates, chiefly from the East, whose position on the war was not very different from that of Roosevelt. And they made an all-night fight in the resolutions committee for a strong plank committing the party to a course similar to Roosevelt's. This was defeated. The war plank adopted read:

"The Republican Party is firmly opposed to involving this nation in foreign war.

"We are still suffering from the ill effects of the last world war, a war which cost us a 24 billion dollar increase in our national debt, billions of uncollectible foreign debts and complete upset of our economic system in addition to loss of human life and irreparable damage to the health of thousands of our boys."

The Roosevelt administration was denounced for the poor use it had made of the vast sums appropriated for national defense and then the platform declared:

"We declare for prompt, orderly and realistic building of our national defense to the point at which we shall be able not only to defend the United States, its possessions and essential outposts from foreign attack but also efficiently to uphold in war the Monroe Doctrine ... In the meantime we shall support all necessary and proper defense measures proposed by the administration in its belated effort to make up for lost time; *but we deplore explosive utterances by the President directed at other governments which serve to peril our peace and we condemn all executive action and proceedings which might lead to war without the authorization of the Congress of the United States.*"

The plank expressed sympathy for all unoffending nations whose ideas most closely resembled our own and favored the extension to all peoples fighting for liberty or whose liberty is threatened "of such aid as shall not be in violation of international law or inconsistent with the requirements of our own national defense."

Before the convention assembled, Roosevelt executed a political maneuver that beyond doubt caused great embarrassment to the Republicans. He announced the appointment of Henry L. Stimson, who had been secretary of State under President Hoover, as

Secretary of War, and Frank Knox, candidate for Vice-President with Landon in 1936, as Secretary of the Navy. Both Stimson and Knox were eager and ardent supporters of Roosevelt's war policy. There were some features of this curious episode which, so far as I know, have never been fully told. We will come to them in the events of a few weeks hence.

On July 15, the Democratic National Convention opened in Chicago to name a "successor" to President Roosevelt. The great question before this convention, of course, was the nomination of the President for a third term. Some years later many of those who played leading roles in that noisy and truculent comedy told their several stories of what happened so that now it is possible to tell how the business was managed.

In a previous chapter we have seen how Roosevelt, in the summer of 1939, had confided in the deepest secrecy to Jim Farley at Hyde Park that he would not run for a third term. Nevertheless, Farley had begun to gather that Roosevelt would run and that he was laying his plans in that direction without taking Farley, Garner or any of the other leaders into his confidence. He was laying his plans cunningly to have himself "drafted." The movement began some time in 1939 and the leaders in it were Ed Kelly of Chicago and Frank Hague of New Jersey. Some time later, Harold Ickes and Harry Hopkins uttered public demands for Roosevelt's nomination and later Attorney-General Jackson and Senator Joe Guffey joined in the public clamor. Guffey, Hopkins and Tommy Corcoran began contacting the state leaders. It is entirely probable that Roosevelt did not confide fully in any of these people save perhaps Hopkins, but Ickes, Hopkins, Wallace, Corcoran and Jackson were a part of the White House political entourage and they carried on the campaign without hindrance from the President and knew, without being told, that they were operating in accordance with his wishes.

In August, 1939, at a meeting of the Young Democrats, Roosevelt said that if the nominee were a conservative or one who just gave lip-service to the New Deal on a "straddle-bug" platform he could not offer active support to the ticket and indicated what kind of candidate he would support. Arthur Krock in the New York *Times* said "his description of the ideal candidate seemed like a self-portrait." And a day or two later Mayor Kelly told the Young Democrats "they must not take 'no' from Roosevelt." By December, 1939, Vice-President Garner had decided that Roosevelt would be a candidate. He had declared himself unalterably opposed to the third term and he announced his own candidacy as a public protest against that idea. Curiously enough, Garner's announcement did not bring him an offer of support from a single party leader. In Illinois, Ed Kelly after talking with Roosevelt, entered the President's name in the Illinois primary. Roosevelt did not withdraw it. And then on March 23, 1940, Farley declared that he had consented to have his own name entered in the Massachusetts Democratic primary.

On July 1, 1940, two weeks before the convention was to meet, Roosevelt asked Farley to visit him at Hyde Park. When Farley reached the house he was greeted by the President's mother. The morning papers had a story that Jim was going to resign from the national committee chairmanship and go into business. The old lady greeted him cordially and wanted to know if there was any truth in these stories. "You know," she said, "I would hate to think of Franklin running for the presidency if you were not around. I would like you to be sure to help my boy." Inside the house, Mrs. Eleanor Roosevelt met Farley and said she was shocked at the thought of him not directing things in the coming campaign. There was no doubt in Roosevelt's home who the candidate would be.

After luncheon, Farley sat down with the president in his study. Roosevelt began by explaining that he had not written a letter indicating that he would not be a candidate around February 1, as he had promised the preceding summer. He said the war had started and to have issued the statement would have nullified his position in the world and handicapped the efforts of this country to be of constructive service in the world crisis. As we shall see, Roosevelt was putting on a carefully studied act with Farley. He shook his head dolefully and said: "I still don't want to run for the Presidency."

He repeated: "I don't want to run, *and I am going to tell the convention so.*" He suggested various ways in which he would do this, but the implacable Farley, who apparently was not falling for the little comedy, told him he should not have waited so long, that he had, by his own maneuvers, killed off every other candidate and that the leaders were afraid to be against him lest they suffer punishment and that if he didn't want to run he should do what General Sherman did many years ago—issue a statement saying: "I will not run if nominated and will not serve if elected." Plainly Roosevelt did not expect this reply. He fell into a reverie for a moment, explained to Farley that if nominated and elected he could not in these times refuse to take the inaugural oath even if he knew he would be dead in thirty days. That ended the subject so far as Farley was concerned. He knew that Roosevelt was going to be nominated and run. He told the President he had made up his mind he was going to allow his own name to go before the convention.

After this the conversation proceeded in the most singular manner with literally three persons present—Farley for one, Roosevelt the man who was not going to run as the second and Roosevelt the man who had decided to run as the third. In one breath he began to discuss vice-presidential candidates. He dismissed Lucas and Stark. He dismissed Bankhead because he was too old and not in good health—because the man running with him must be in good health because there was no telling how long he could hold out. "You know, Jim," he said, "a man with paralysis can have a break-up any time." He seemed to think it was all right for a presidential candidate with a strong expectancy of death to be elected, but that the vice-presidential candidate had to have good health. He dismissed Maloney of Connecticut and Jesse Jones because his health was not too good either. He was against Rayburn or James Byrnes or Garner. Thus having discussed who would run for vice-president on the ticket with him, he then began to outline the letter he would write to the convention telling them he didn't want to run and at what point he should send the letter. Then having gone into details about how he would eliminate himself he said, "Undoubtedly I will accept the nomination by radio and will arrange to talk to the delegates before they leave the convention hall."[30]

Miss Perkins says that she was never sure just when Roosevelt made up his mind to run, but that Frank Walker and others responsible for the campaign knew around March or April that he would be willing "if it could be handled properly" but they were pledged to absolute secrecy. She said that Harry Hopkins had been selected to take charge of Roosevelt's headquarters because he had got acquainted with a lot of Democratic politicians while administering relief.[31] He was to make all the decisions in Chicago and have a private wire to the White House.

Cordell Hull[32] says that Roosevelt, during all this time, had been urging him to run for the presidency. But Hull had insisted that he did not wish it. We must keep in mind that Miss Perkins said Walker and some others knew of the President's plans as early as March. Jim Farley had seen through the President's comedy a long while before this. Then on July 1, Roosevelt told Farley he didn't want to run and was going to tell the convention so, mixing up with all this talk a discussion of his plans to run, who his vice-presidential candidate would be and how he would accept the nomination by radio. On June 20 Hull saw the President who again urged him to run. And then on July 3, two days after he told Farley how he would accept the nomination when it was made, Roosevelt invited Hull to lunch. He told Hull how he was going to tell the convention he did not desire to run, whereupon, said Roosevelt, "they will nominate you." He asked Hull's opinion of the letter he proposed to write. Hull said such a letter would not delay Roosevelt's nomination more than a minute. Whereupon Roosevelt began immediately to discuss his own chances of being elected and there ensued a bizarre conversation in which he talked alternately of who would run for vice-president with Hull and of his own plans to run. Hull says he now knew the President had made up his mind to be a candidate.[33] Hull did not know that Roosevelt had said to more than one that Hull wouldn't do, that he was "too much of a free trader" and that "he was too old and too slow."

Roosevelt fooled no one. But why did he try? He was building up the "draft" illusion and seeking to create witnesses to that pretension.

The convention opened in a somewhat somber mood. Jim Farley was there, still chairman of the national committee, calling the convention to order. The delegates, with few exceptions, were mere pawns in the hands of the leaders and the leaders mere puppets in the hands of the President. Nevertheless, most of the delegates did not know what the intention was. They didn't know for whom they were supposed to vote. And they didn't like the situation. Miss Perkins was shocked when she got to Chicago at the bitterness around the corridors as the prospective candidates for the Presidency and the delegates who were for them began to believe that the President was really going to run. The leaders, she says, didn't know what was going on. They were angry about the purge. Many of them were deeply disturbed about the Supreme Court fight. Many thought that we had had more than enough of the New Deal. The delegates knew that John Garner had refused to run for a third term as vice-president. He wasn't even in Chicago.

Edward J. Flynn, who would succeed Farley as national chairman, said "The convention in Chicago was not a very cheerful gathering," and that "the political leaders thought a mistake was being made, that never before had the third-term issue really been brought to a test." They didn't know how it would go. They thought the "President's ambition for a third term was being supported largely by the political machines." He described the organization leaders as bitter. "I think it is only fair to say," he said, "that the majority of the delegates in Chicago were not enthusiastic for the renomination of the President although they felt that if they did not go along the party would be so hopelessly divided that no candidate would have a chance of winning." Looking back over the events, he felt sure that the leaders "did not support Roosevelt because of any motive of affection or because of any political issue involved but rather because they knew that opposing him would be harmful to their local organizations."[34]

Harry Hopkins, of course, was present but not very much in sight. His headquarters were in Rooms 308–309 of the Blackstone Hotel, with a direct wire to Roosevelt. He was in constant communication with the President on every move that was made. With him were such ill-assorted collaborators as Boss Ed Kelly and Boss Frank Hague and David K. Niles, a White House attache and long-time left-wing hater of people like Kelly and Hague. To Hopkins' rooms went a steady stream of state leaders to find out what they were expected to do. According to Miss Perkins, the job of contacting the leaders and communicating to them the President's intentions was in charge of Frank Walker. The President was not a candidate but was to be "drafted," which of course all the delegates knew was a pure comedy.

As the convention opened with the band playing and Farley pounding the gavel, most of the delegates' seats were empty. A lone voice yelled "We Want Roosevelt." Farley presented Mayor Ed Kelly of Chicago who would welcome the delegates officially. The mayor ended on the words "Our beloved President, Franklin D. Roosevelt." A delegate in a white suit from Oklahoma jumped to his feet, waved his straw hat and about half the delegates stood and cheered.

The following day the real fireworks began. Senator Alben Barkley, named permanent chairman of the convention, delivered his address. When he finished the formal speech, he cleared his throat and said: "And now my friends, I have an additional statement to make on behalf of the President of the United States." A hush fell over the convention. Farley knew what was coming. The President had telephoned him the night before and said: "I wanted to tell you that Alben has the statement we talked about. I decided it was best to release it after the permanent organization was set up."

Barkley continued:

> "I and other close friends of the President have long known that he had no wish to be a candidate again. We know too that in no way whatsoever has he exerted any influence in the selection of the delegates or upon the opinions of the delegates to this convention. Tonight at the specific request and authorization of your President I am making this simple fact clear to this convention.
>
> "The President has never had and has not today any desire or purpose to continue in the office of the President, to be a candidate for that office or to be nominated by the convention for that office.
>
> "He wishes in all earnestness and sincerity to make it clear that all the delegates to this convention are free to vote for any candidate. That is the message which I bring to you tonight from the President of the United States by the authority of his word."

Not a syllable about *not being willing* to run, not a line telling the delegates to *select another candidate* and taking *himself completely out of the race*; merely that he has not "any *desire* to continue in office or to be nominated." The delegates were all set free to vote for any candidate while every man in the convention knew that Harry Hopkins, a resident of the White House and the President's alter ego, Frank Walker and members of his cabinet present were all assuring the leaders that if the President were nominated he would run. There were 1094 delegates to the convention, that is there were 1094 politicians who understood the language of politics when they heard it. It was not necessary for anybody to translate for them. Just as Jim Farley knew on July 1 when Roosevelt told him he didn't want to run that he had really decided to run, so all these delegates en masse, some of them instantly and others after a moment's reflection, knew precisely what the President meant and what they were supposed to do.

However, the managers had taken no chances. Ed Kelly had been entrusted with the job of managing the demonstrations. On the floor, of course, over the heads of each delegation, stood the standards of the states with the states' names on them. Kelly had prepared a collection of duplicate standards and a bunch of choice spirits, well-muscled, from the stockyards and other districts of Chicago, were mobilized off in the shadows. Loud speakers were distributed around the hall, the wires of which led down into the bowels of the Chicago Stadium under the earth where there was stationed Chicago's Commissioner of Sewers. As Barkley finished the message, it took a moment for the delegates to get it, but only a moment. In that moment, the Voice of the Sewers went into action and from out the loud speakers all over the floor burst the voice "We Want Roosevelt." It continued: "Pennsylvania Wants Roosevelt! Virginia Wants Roosevelt! New York Wants Roosevelt! Massachusetts Wants Roosevelt!" and so on through the states. And as the Voice boomed, the goons emerged from the shadows with the fake standards of the states and began parading around the hall. The delegates, now shouting and cheering, fell in, except certain delegations which resented the appearance of the fraudulent standards of their own states marching around the floor. A number of fights were set off as attempts were made to grab these standards, but the marching goons with their spurious banners started filing by the platform in front of the smiling Senator Barkley who had really just nominated Roosevelt for the presidency, and as each standard went by Barkley leaned over and kissed it. It was really all over then and the delegates, by their quick translation of Roosevelt's false disclaimer, registered their understanding of the man perfectly.

The next problem confronting the managers of the "draft" was how to put it over. They didn't want to have Roosevelt formally nominated. That might present him with the necessity of refusing. Their first scheme was to have some delegate rise on the first roll-call, when Alabama was called, and move to dispense with the roll-call and nominate Roosevelt by acclamation. But Farley ruled that out on the ground that it would be a violation of the rules and furthermore, looking rather significantly at the proposers, he said "If you do that it won't be necessary to have an election." Various other plans were suggested. Finally they were compelled to have a formal nomination which was made by Senator Lister Hill of Alabama.

Senator Wheeler had a headquarters as a candidate for the presidency but Wheeler's chief purpose was to get a plank in the platform which would give some hope of keeping out of the war and he did get a plank which satisfied him, whereupon he withdrew. Farley, however, went through to the bitter end. He was nominated by Carter Glass, now a venerable patriarch of the party, who was hooted and booed as he made the nominating speech. Ed Flynn had tried to get Farley to withdraw. Farley refused. He said: "Don't get the impression that I am running for the presidency. Everyone knows the President has the votes but what they are trying to do is to put on an act to make it appear to the world that this is a unanimous draft. I am determined to let the people know I am opposed to a third term and this is the only way I can do it."

Roosevelt, of course, was nominated. On the roll-call the vote was 946½ for Roosevelt, 72½ for Farley, 61 for Garner, 9½ for Tydings and 6 for Hull. Farley, at the end of the roll-call, and before the vote was announced, moved to make it unanimous. Thus was the President "drafted" by his party.

But now came the most disturbing feature of all—the selection of a vice-presidential candidate. There were a number of hopefuls—Senator Bankhead, Speaker Rayburn, Paul McNutt, Jesse Jones, Governor Lloyd Stark of Missouri and others. The delegates thought this at least was an open race. Before Miss Perkins[35] left Washington she had discussed the subject of the vice-presidency with Roosevelt and after various names had been dismissed, she asked Roosevelt if he thought Henry Wallace would do. Roosevelt thought it over and said he thought Wallace might strengthen the ticket and that he would be a good man if anything happened to the President because he was not an isolationist.

However, at the convention nobody seemed to know who Roosevelt wanted for vice-president. The battle royal between the vice-presidential candidates got to be pretty bitter. Coming on top of the nomination, in which the delegates felt they had been used as mere pawns, the disaffection of Garner, the withdrawal of Jim Farley, they were in a black mood. Miss Perkins says the feeling was sour, which is putting it mildly. She said that Bob Allen (of the columnist team of Pearson and Allen) came to her in great excitement to say that the situation was terrible. It will end in a terrific rise of Roosevelt haters in the Democratic party, he said, and he wanted her to call Roosevelt and urge him to come out to the convention.

She called Roosevelt, told him about the bitterness, the confusion, the near fights and urged him to come to Chicago and address the delegates. He refused but suggested that Eleanor might come, which she did. He asked about the vice-presidential race. She told him of the confusion and ill-feeling there and urged him to make up his mind and settle the fight. He said he hadn't made up his mind and asked about Wallace. There was no sign of a Wallace campaign around but she urged him to try it. He began talking it over, more or less to himself and ended by saying: "Yes, I think it had better be Wallace. Yes, it will be Wallace. I think I'll stick to that," and he told her to give the news to Harry Hopkins. Hopkins was surprised when he heard it. He called the President for verification and then told the newspaper men it would probably be Wallace. On the morning of July 18, Roosevelt called Farley and gave him the news. When this got around it set off another conflagration. Ickes said it was a damned outrage. Jesse Jones was sore. The other candidates were indignant. The delegates didn't want Wallace and they were very ugly about it. Ed Kelly called the White House and urged the nomination of Byrnes but the President objected. A lot of the leaders wanted to fight it out but one by one the candidates withdrew in disgust. As Wallace was nominated the delegates booed and they booed every time his name was mentioned. Ed Flynn took the floor and told the delegates that the President wanted Wallace. Senator Lucas said the same thing in a speech and both were greeted with boos.

About this time Mrs. Roosevelt arrived by plane and Farley introduced her to the convention. She made a gracious speech very generously expressing her deep gratitude to Farley for all he had done—something Farley said he had never heard from the lips of Roosevelt. When Mrs. Roosevelt arrived, however, she agreed that the nomination of Wallace was a mistake. Elliott Roosevelt put in an appearance to protest against the nomination and told Farley that if

Farley would nominate Jones he would make a seconding speech. Mrs. Roosevelt telephoned her husband. She told him she agreed with Farley that Henry Wallace just wouldn't do. Roosevelt told her to put Jim on the telephone. He said to Farley: "I've given my word to Wallace. What do you do when you give your word?" That was a terrible question for Roosevelt to put to Farley. Farley snapped back like a blow in the face: "I keep it!"[36]

This convention was now on the edge of rebellion. It had not yet heard from Roosevelt whether he would "consent" to be "drafted." Back in Washington, at the White House, with Sam Rosenman Roosevelt was preparing the draft of the speech he would deliver over the radio accepting the nomination. Through Steve Early, it was announced at the White House that the President would not make any statement or deliver any address until the convention's work finished and by that, Early admitted, he meant not until Wallace was nominated.[37]

The voting started in an uproar. The delegates and spectators got out of hand. The ballot was conducted in the midst of boos and catcalls. But in the end the lash of the Boss did its work. Wallace got 627 7/10 votes, Bankhead 327 4/15. There were scattered votes for Farley, Lucas, Jones, Barkley and others. Wallace had prepared a speech of acceptance but the feeling was so bad he never delivered it. He kept away from the convention.

Apparently Roosevelt's decision on Wallace was really an eleventh hour one. There is good reason for supposing that he wanted Hull for vice-president. This would have served a double purpose. He would have liked to have been rid of Hull as Secretary of State but would be glad to have him as vice-president in the Senate, where he could serve his political use more effectively in keeping the Southern senators in line. But Hull thought he ought to be President or nothing. Hull told Farley that he believed he "was unfairly treated by that fellow in his not letting my name go before the convention." Hull said: "He tried everything he could think of to get me to take the vice-presidency. He argued and smiled. Then he smiled and argued. I said No, by God and by God, no and that's all there was to it. I felt he was trying to kick me upstairs."[38]

As for Farley, Ed Flynn and others tried to get him to stay on as national chairman but he resolutely refused and quit both as national chairman and as Postmaster General. Ed Flynn was made national chairman and Frank Walker got the cabinet post.

Roosevelt was elected. To the uninitiated the Republicans seemed to have a golden opportunity—the Democrats divided, many leaders declaring they would "take a walk," still others supporting the Republican candidate, the natural resistance to a third term, the failure of all the Roosevelt policies, his violation of every promise, his taxes and debt along with the anxieties created by his labor policies to say nothing of the split in labor itself, with John L. Lewis urging his miners to vote for Willkie. But all this ignored the new line-up. Roosevelt had the South and he needed to get only 109 electoral votes out of 374 in the North. And he could get this in four states and in these states were those numerous minorities who had been captured completely by Roosevelt on the war issue. This, with the payroll vote and the big city machines in those states was enough to do the job. Roosevelt got 449, Willkie only 82 electoral votes. For all that, the election was closer than appears in the electoral vote. Many big states were carried for Roosevelt by modest or even small majorities. There will always be a question as to what might have happened had someone other than Willkie been nominated.

There was one incident in this fight which illustrates with startling vividness how far a man who is under the influence of an overdose of ambition and power may go and how near he can come to succeeding in a seemingly preposterous objective. When Hitler struck at Poland in September, 1939, Roosevelt summoned the Democratic and Republican congressional leaders to the White House to consider legislation and he invited Alfred Landon and Frank Knox, the Republican nominees in 1936, to attend. While in Washington, Landon learned that Roosevelt was planning to invite him and Knox into his cabinet. A few days later Landon issued a statement saying Roosevelt should take himself out of the third-term race in the interest of national unity. Shortly after Knox was offered a cabinet post, but the invitation to Landon was not made. Knox said he would not go into Roosevelt's cabinet without Landon but he continued to visit with Roosevelt.

On May 13, 1940, three weeks before the Republican convention, Frank Altschul, brother-in-law of Governor Lehman, called Landon and asked him if he would accept an invitation to the White

House to talk with the President. Landon agreed and next day General "Pa" Watson, Roosevelt's military aide, wired an invitation to Landon to lunch with the President on May 22. Landon told Watson, however, he was sending him a copy of a speech he was about to make criticizing the President's foreign policy and he felt the President ought to see it. He sent the speech. Frank Knox was shown a copy of it. He phoned Landon. He said you will ruin yourself and your party if you make that speech: *you should not criticize the President.* However, Landon made the speech and got another wire from Watson confirming the luncheon. He left for Washington, stopping first in New York. There he dined with four well-known political reporters. They said: "We don't know whether you know it or not, but the Republican party is facing a debacle." The debacle was the plan Roosevelt was engineering to literally put the party out of business by inducing its leaders not to contest his election. Commentators like Dorothy Thompson and H. V. Kaltenborn and other pro-war writers were calling on the Republicans not to contest the election. And Roosevelt schemed to induce the presidential candidates of the party in 1936 to become Secretaries of War and Navy respectively in his cabinet. This he believed would so completely demoralize the more aggressive party leaders that those who were plugging for an all-out war would be able to force the party to let the election go by default. The idea had undoubtedly been sold to Frank Knox. He was in frequent touch with Roosevelt and was using all his influence to persuade Landon to go into the cabinet and he told Landon he should not criticise the President.

As this situation dawned on Landon he prepared a statement for the newspapers at once that at all hazards an election must be held. The reporters said: "You know this will end your luncheon appointment." And when Landon got to Washington next day he got a telephone call from Mr. Altschul saying General Watson had called him and asked him to get in touch with Landon and request to cancel his luncheon appointment with the President. He wanted Landon to take the responsibility of cancelling the luncheon. Watson had suggested that Landon could say he was taken suddenly ill and leave at once for home. Landon replied: "I won't do any such damn thing." And he gave Arthur Evans of the Chicago *Tribune* a statement saying: "I came here at the invitation of my President and I am going back home at his invitation. I will come again when my President wants me." He then called a press conference for 10 AM. As that got under way, a telephone call came from the President. Roosevelt said: "Alf, between Altschul and Watson, they have got us all bawled up." He told Landon to come over to lunch. Roosevelt, of course, did not offer Landon the cabinet post, but he talked about making new appointments. Then Landon had lunch with Knox. Knox talked about the terrible Nazi threat to our institutions. Landon said: "I think a third term for the President is a greater threat to our institutions than anything from the outside. If we go into the cabinet we might as well call off the elections. But there should be a *quid pro quo*. NO THIRD TERM." Knox said, "Alf, he can't run again. He's in a terrible shape physically. The President said to me last week: 'Look at me, Frank, I couldn't run for a third term if I wanted to.'" And Knox held out his hand to illustrate how Roosevelt's hand shook.[39]

However, Roosevelt did not give up his plan. But the idea of getting an uncontested election had to be abandoned. With their 1936 candidates for President and Vice-President gone over to the President's camp the Republicans would have been in a very embarrassing position. But just as the Republican convention was about to assemble Roosevelt announced the appointment of Stimson and Knox as Secretaries of the War and Navy. To do this Roosevelt had to use some high-handed methods in his official family. Around June 16 he sent Watson to Woodring to say he wanted Woodring to get together with Morgenthau to sell or transfer a number of army planes to Britain. Woodring said he could not do this unless it could be done without affecting our defenses. Woodring discussed it with the Department and the generals and he promised them he would stand his ground. When Watson's request was repeated, Woodring refused to see Morgenthau. About the same time, at a cabinet meeting the President proposed to transfer 50 destroyers to Great Britain. Roosevelt told the cabinet he had cleared the subject with the Attorney-General. At the cabinet meeting, Secretary of the Navy Edison protested, to the great annoyance of the President. John Garner, describing the incident afterward, said Attorney-General Jackson came to him (Garner) after the meeting and said that "in spite of the statement made that he had approved the sale and held it to be legal he had not made such a decision." Garner told him he should have spoken up.

However, Woodring's refusal to approve the plane transfer and Edison's protest at the destroyer sale sealed the fate of both. Watson wrote Woodring a letter saying the President would like to have his resignation. Woodring sent the resignation and a long letter, the contents of which have since been carefully guarded. Roosevelt, disturbed by the letter, offered Woodring an ambassadorship, which Woodring refused. Roosevelt wrote him again and Woodring never answered that letter. The President got Hague to nominate Edison for governor of New Jersey. This cleared the way for naming Stimson and Knox.

CHAPTER 10: HENRY WALLACE

What of the man who had just been made Vice-President of the United States, second in line for the presidency held by a man whose health was a matter of question even to himself? About the only thing Henry had that qualified him for Vice-President and President was his health.

Where did the pressure for Wallace originate? Miss Perkins thinks she first proposed him. Edward J. Flynn says the matter was discussed before they left Washington and agreed on. Miss Perkins, who is truthful, cannot be wrong when she says she telephoned the President from Chicago and that he had not yet made up his mind about Wallace. Her whole account leaves the impression that he was not too sure and many other things strengthen the suspicion that the pressure had come from other sources and that Roosevelt was yielding with some misgiving. We might conclude from Hull's testimony that Roosevelt's real candidate was Hull, who says the President literally harried him to run. Hull was a natural. This would get him out of the State Department where he was a nuisance and put him in the Senate where he would be useful. Doubtless Roosevelt settled on Wallace when Hull said no.

Wallace was a being who took himself very seriously. And yet there was a good deal of the element of stage comedy in him—wide, queer streaks in his make-up that would excite laughter in the theater but which do not originate in any merry or comic sense in his own character and which cannot by any stretch of the imagination be regarded as funny against the dark background of the events of the time. He has been pictured as a vague and impractical mystic, half scientist, half philosopher, with other ingredients that approach the pictures in the comic strips of the professor with the butterfly net.

Wallace was born in 1888 on an Iowa farm, but it was the farm of a wealthy farmer who had a house in town as well as another in the corn fields. He went to the State Agricultural College, came out at the age of 22 and worked on the staff of *Wallace's Farmer*, which had been founded by his grandfather. His father went to Washington in 1921 as Secretary of Agriculture and Henry became editor of *Wallace's Farmer*, a rich editorial property. He remained editor until 1931 when the paper, overloaded with debt, passed out of the family's hands, leaving Henry without a job. Two years later he was made Secretary of Agriculture by Roosevelt. Thus he began his political career at the top. He had no standing in the country, had given no evidence of eminence as an editor, a writer, a business man or a politician which gave him any claim on this strange appointment—which is all the stranger from the fact that he was a registered Republican. When he went to Washington he was looked upon as an impractical person who had been something of a failure, given to strange ideas and there was a rather general agreement with the opinion of the Baltimore *Sun* that he "was one of the most admirable and ridiculous figures of the New Deal."

The Agricultural Adjustment Administration—the AAA—was peculiarly Wallace's child and it contributed as much as the NRA to bringing discredit and even laughter down upon the Roosevelt administration. It would not be true to say that Wallace, at this time, was a left-winger. The man was almost without strong political opinions. He was certainly not a Republican or a Democrat of the orthodox school. His Republicanism was a mere inheritance from his father and grandfather. A distinction must be drawn between the philosophy of many men who rush to strange and bizarre experiments in economic life and the philosophy of the modern

Communist or Socialist. But Wallace brought men like Tugwell into the Department as his Under-Secretary of Agriculture. One thing about Wallace which is quite definite is his laborious pose of intellectualism. And with Tugwell he had now come into contact with a mind that was keen, busy, and widely enriched with economic and social history and dead sure of itself. It is very clear that Wallace's mind, wandering around in uncertainties, became slowly infected by the far abler Tugwell with the theory of State Planning for the well-being of all the people. It is equally clear that he did not perceive at this time the essential affinity between state planning, fascism and Communism; did not realize that all belong to one great generic philosophy. Having once taken this position, Wallace moved slowly and gropingly, little by little, toward the philosophy of the planners without, I think, giving himself up to it wholly until just before his nomination as Vice-President, and without realizing at the time the full implication of that drift. Farley says that Wallace, just before the 1940 convention, expressed some fears that Roosevelt was going too far to the left. This was probably due to the fact that Wallace did not realize that the advocates of state planning were so seriously to the left. But from here he was to move fast. Given to rapid changes in philosophies, Wallace could catch a new one like an acrobat leaping on a flying trapeze in mid-air and swinging with it full tilt from the moment he grasped it.

To understand what made this thoroughly dangerous man tick it is necessary to look at another widely advertised side of his nature—his interest in mysticism. There is a broad streak of the religious in Wallace. His early life had run through the Presbyterian church, but at college he became for a while somewhat skeptical—but only for a brief interval—and turned again to what he called "the necessity of believing in God, imminent as well as transcendental." He thought the severely logical and critical Presbyterianism was unsuited to his yearnings and he began attending the Roman Catholic Church, attracted by its rich ritual and the devotional attitude of the congregation. He liked the genuflecting, the kneeling, the sign of the cross, the silent adoration and he began to look into the dogmas. These repelled him after a while and, interestingly enough, it was what he called the scholastic method of reasoning, with its unyielding insistence upon the severe processes of logic, that repelled him and so he made one more move to the High Episcopal church where he found the warm, seemingly ritualistic atmosphere without the hard and fast insistence on the dogmas behind the ritual.

It is quite certain that his soul did not by any means come to rest in the pleasant and assured comfort of the High Church either and so he began wandering around from cult to cult, sampling them all, looking for some sort of god he could get close to and commune with and feel. In fact, he is supposed to have come upon the ever-normal granary plan while studying the economic principles of Confucius. Several journalists who have written about him say that he had probed into Buddhism, Confucianism and the mysteries and beliefs of the Orient, and that he had studied astrology and knew how horoscopes were drawn.

In the meantime, he was fiddling around on the edges and surfaces of economics. Mordecai Ezekiel, who believed in state planning as thoroughly as Adolf Hitler did and who had a plan for $2500-a-year for everybody, jobs for all and security from the cradle to the grave, was his economic adviser in the Agricultural Department. It was not surprising, therefore, that after Wallace had been Secretary of Agriculture for a while, exposed to the Tugwells and Ezekiels and to the inner urges of his own mystic hunger, he should have told the Federal Council of Churches on December 7, 1933 that perhaps the thing we should be moving towards was something like the theocracies of old. He thought, however, that the times would have to get more difficult in order to soften the hearts of the people and move them "sufficiently so they will be willing to join together in the modern adaptation of the theocracy of old." The thing he didn't like about Socialism and Communism was their spiritual dryness. "The economic and business machines," he said, "should be subjected more and more to the religious and artistic and the deeper scientific needs of man" and apparently the end of this development would be some version of the ancient theocracy. Undoubtedly Wallace believed this at the moment he was uttering it to a religious meeting. Whether he really believed it or not, whether it came out of any really studied conviction or was nothing more than a passing oratorical fancy, we cannot say.

Some time in the 'twenties, a gentleman by the name of Nicholas Constantin Roerich appeared on the American scene. Roerich was a highly self-advertised great philosopher on the Eastern Asiatic model. He gathered around himself a collection of admirers and disciples who addressed him as their "Guru"—a spiritual and religious person or teacher. He dispensed to them a philosophic hash compounded of pseudo-Yogism and other Oriental occult teachings that certain superior beings are commissioned to guide the affairs of mankind. Roerich wrote a long string of books—"In Himalaya," "Fiery Stronghold," "Gates Into the Future," "The Art of Asia," "Flame in Chalice," "Realm of Light." He founded the Himalayan Research Institute of the Roerich Museum at Nagara, India and was the founder of the Roerich Pact and Banner of Peace, signed by 22 countries in 1935. This ceremony took place in the White House. Wallace arranged for the presentation and was named the American plenipotentiary to sign the pact. At the ceremony Wallace said: "I am deeply grateful to have been named by President Roosevelt to sign for the United States this important document *in which I have been interested for many years* and which I regard as an inevitable step in international relations. The Roerich Pact which forms this treaty provides that all museums, cathedrals, universities and libraries be registered by the nations and marked by a banner—known as the Banner of Peace—which designates them as neutral territory respected by all signatory nations." And on this occasion Wallace described Roerich as "a great versatile genius" and "one of the greatest figures and true leaders of contemporary culture."

When Roerich, with his long white beard, got going here, a wealthy broker named Louis L. Horch became the most ardent and reverential disciple of the Guru Roerich. He raised the money, putting up much of it himself, to erect a beautiful building worth several million dollars at 105th Street and Riverside Drive in New York City, called the Roerich Museum, which Westbrook Pegler, who has brought much of this material to light, refers to as Roerich's Lamasery or Joss House. Roerich was a prolific painter of obscure and symbolic canvases and the first floor of the Roerich Museum was given over to the exhibition of these canvases. The remaining stories of this building served as apartments and offices for the elect or for friendly or useful souls.

Roerich's pictures were believed to possess a peculiar power over the minds of those who would sit quietly before them and contemplate them. Many disciples of his cult visited the building and did precisely that, in search of some kind of "world awareness" hidden away in these obscure daubings. Those who followed Roerich looked upon him as a great spiritual leader. Horch in addressing him, spoke of him as "our beloved master" and ended his letters "in love, beauty and action forever united, your Logvan." Logvan and Logdomor were the names by which Horch was known in this mystic circle.

Horch put $1,100,000 into the Roerich program and he said "it was our joy to give without a thought of ever receiving back the principal or interest." After Wallace became Secretary of Agriculture, at some point Horch went to the Department as the senior marketing specialist of the Surplus Commodity Corporation. This queer bureau was precisely the place for Horch. It was organized and directed by a gentleman named Milo Perkins from Houston, Texas, an ex-theosophist preacher who would grow to enormous dimensions in the New Deal before the whole comedy ended.

Roerich had decided that he wished to lead an expedition into Asia. Horch says that he expected to set up a new state in Siberia of which he would be the head. To make this possible, Wallace commissioned Roerich to go to China to collect wild grass seed. But stories in English-language newspapers in China indicated that Roerich applied to the 15th U. S. Infantry in Tientsin for rifles and ammunition and that the expedition had mysterious purposes. Of course, Roerich was not a botanist, and had no special qualifications for hunting wild grass seeds. Horch was now out $1,100,000 and began to lose faith in his teacher. Wallace apparently backslid at the same time and fired Roerich incontinently while he was in Asia. Subsequently Horch filed suit to recover his unhappy investment in the future and got possession of the building. In 1942 Horch was transferred from the Department of Agriculture to the Board of Economic Warfare of which Wallace was the head and of which Milo Perkins was executive director, and when Wallace became Secretary of Commerce he made Horch chief of the supply division in the New York office of the Foreign Economic Administration.

A controversy about this whole subject has been raging for some time between Westbrook Pegler, columnist, and Henry Wallace, with all the raging being done by Pegler. Pegler has in his possession a batch of letters written by someone to Roerich in which Roerich is addressed as "My dear Guru." The contents of these letters are silly to the point of being imbecilic. Pegler has charged that some of these letters, which are in handwriting on Department of Agriculture stationery have been submitted by him to three of the leading handwriting experts in the United States whose names he gives and that these experts have declared and are willing to take the stand and testify under oath that the letters were written by the same person who wrote two letters in Pegler's possession addressed to him by Henry Wallace and signed by Wallace. Pegler has hammered on this subject for several years. He has presented the testimony in the case in the most elaborate manner and in great detail. He has called upon Wallace to either affirm or deny the authenticity of the letters and his connection with them and to this day Wallace has refused to make any reply. Pegler's point is that the man who wrote these letters was unfit to be the Secretary of Agriculture or the Secretary of Commerce and that it was nothing short of a crime against the nation to make him Vice-President of the United States, and that Roosevelt knew when he did this of the Roerich incident. Pegler finally published a batch of these incredible letters, challenging Wallace to deny them. Wallace ignored that challenge.

Wallace was indeed as odd a bird as had ever perched upon a cabinet post. He loved to exhibit himself primarily as a deep thinker. Hugh Johnson said of him: "It is a pleasure and wonder to listen to the naive and somewhat sweet but superficial simplicity of Henry's scholarship. He will tackle almost any subject on either the scientific or literary side. He once uttered a dissertation on great books and their influence on human destiny. At the same time, with his usual frankness, he conceded that he had read very few of them." At first he was a specialist on his own soul, his health and the corn farmer. Even this limited group of interests took him off into numerous far flights into the airy world of the cultist. He made a kind of tourist trip through the various religions; he tackled corn somewhat more realistically; tried on himself all sorts of diets settling down as a vegetarian, and experimenting with all sorts of odd athletic pastimes such as boomerang throwing and Indian wrestling. But once in the Department of Agriculture the circle of his interests expanded. There was no national problem which did not excite his interest—and once interested he became concerned, and once concerned he became embattled. In all these questions, however esoteric, there had to be a cast of characters of good people against bad people. However, he was still a nationalist and he was certainly not a Socialist. In the Department in his first big battle he took sides with those who were called reactionaries—George Peek, *et al.*—against the soldiers of the Lord—Jerome Frank, Gardner Jackson, Lee Pressman and Rex Tugwell—on the plight of the sharecroppers as against the landowners. He staged the first purge of the radicals in Washington, driving Frank, Pressman and Jackson out of the AAA.

But by the time the war got under way, Wallace's range of interests had expanded. And it continued to expand until it encompassed the cosmos. Now he could give full rein to his flair for thinking. He liked to tackle something big—like the world, for instance. It is, after all, one of the smaller planets, yet it was big enough to start with. As someone observed, he set himself up "as the conscience of the world." He was now in a medium where his soul was at home—the vast, immaterial, boundless field of world morals. Down on the ground where there are men, trees, buildings, organizations and machines to clutter up the landscape so that a man had to do a little careful navigating to keep from getting crushed, life was difficult. But once Wallace spread his pinions and took off into the vast circumambient spaces of world morals he was happy.

He cried out in an ecstasy in a speech: "The people's revolution is on the march and the devil and all his angels cannot prevail against it. They cannot prevail because on the side of the people is the Lord." Now he was fighting not George Peek and Hugh Johnson and Harold Ickes. He was fighting the devil and the bad angels. And he had on his side the lord, Franklin D. Roosevelt, and the good angels—the Democrats and the CIO and, in good time, he would be joined by Joe Stalin and Glen Taylor, the singing Senator from Idaho. He would begin making world blueprints—filling all the continents with TVAs, globe-circling six-lane highways, world AAAs, World Recovery Administrations, World Parliaments and International Policemen.

This was the man chosen for Vice-President by Roosevelt who had warned that his health was not too good and who forced this strange bird upon his party in the face of a storm of angry protest.

BOOK THREE:
BETRAYAL

Chapter 1: A New Show Opens

On January 20, 1941, Franklin D. Roosevelt, on the front steps of the Capitol in keeping with tradition since the early days of the Republic, was sworn in as President of the United States for the third time—in defiance of a far more important tradition. The President addressed himself to those who doubt democracy. He pointed out how under his leadership democracy had survived a crisis at home here in America. And then he said: "No! Democracy is not dying ... We sense it still spreading on every continent." At that very moment it was dying on every continent and had been profoundly weakened in America. The address was couched on a high spiritual note intended to be a document for the ages. Who wrote it is not known. Certainly Roosevelt did not. It bears none of the stigmata of Roosevelt's own style save perhaps in the last four brief sentences, and was worlds below the quality of his first inaugural. Actually it said nothing and did not mention the war. Already men were being called into the military services by conscription. Eighteen billion dollars for national defense had been appropriated. The *Times* noted that the federal debt apparently had been forgotten. Men were moving in great numbers into the factories all over the land. There were no victory balls, no marching groups, but the index of business activity was marching up week after week until for the first time it would top the great peak of the highest prosperity in 1929. Millions of men were already in jobs or moving into jobs who had not worked in years. Two hundred and twenty-five flying fortresses and pursuit planes staged a great show over the White House. The soldiers who marched in the inaugural parade were real soldiers now. General Marshall, as chief of staff, rode at the head of the parade. Over in England, Harry Hopkins was being presented to crowds of workers who yelled: "Harry, Harry, Harry!"

All the important issues that had been agitating the people's minds were now buried under the rush of the war. The day before the inauguration, Roosevelt received Wendell Willkie, gave him a letter to Churchill and off he went to England. Roosevelt wished him godspeed and this began the movement to take Willkie into Roosevelt's camp, as Stimson and Knox and other Republicans had been taken.

At the moment, on the war front Hitler's forces were poised for what they hoped would be the final knockout blow, while in America Congress was debating the Lend-Lease bill. The House Committee on Foreign Affairs was preparing to hold hearings. The headlines in the newspapers were of the most alarming character. Four days before the inauguration the New York *Times* carried a headline in big black type: "HULL URGES FULLEST AID TO BRITAIN LEST WE MEET FATE OF NORWAY." Next day it was: "STIMSON SEES DANGER OF IN-VASION IF BRITISH NAVY BE BEATEN OR TAKEN." The following day: "CHURCHILL CALLS FOR U.S. WEAPONS, NOT BIG U.S. ARMY IN '41"; "STIMSON SEES CRISIS IN 90 DAYS." On Sunday, the 19th, the head-lines read: "KNUDSEN URGES FULL AID TO BRITAIN"; "WILLKIE SEES PARTY RUIN IN ISOLATION." And the next day Willkie left as a kind of unofficial envoy of Franklin Roosevelt to Churchill. In a little over ten months the blow would come at Pearl Harbor and the United States would be in the war. What followed in the next three years would be the story of America at war. All other issues—the issues of taxation, of debt, of labor, of the struggle between the federal and the state powers, the powers of Congress and the President, the bureauc-racy—all became merely subsidiary questions to the question of the war.

The great theatrical success—the New Deal—was to be taken from the boards. The President himself would say he was slaying his popular hero. "It will be no longer Dr. New Deal," he said. "It will be Dr. Win-the-War."[1] It was to be an even more grandiose produc-tion—the great drama of the salvation of the world.

CHAPTER 2: THE WHITE HOUSE GOES INTO BUSINESS

It is now necessary to pause for a moment to have a look at the White House and its tenants. The result of this inspection cannot possibly be very agreeable to Americans. As men rise the steep ascent of public life the people instinctively expect from them a progressively more exacting code of public and private conduct. At the top, the White House is held to the highest standard of all. It must be so. The standards of conduct of the President and his family will inevitably shape the conduct of all the orders and levels of public office below them. The nation elects the President. It does not elect his wife or his children. But an unwritten law, rooted deeply in the mores of the people, demands of the President's wife the same high ethical standards as it does of him. There can be no such thing as the President putting his conscience in his wife's name. This canon of *noblesse oblige* extends its reasonable requirements over the President's whole immediate family. And it must be said for the long line of men and women who have lived in the White House that, so far as their immediate families were concerned, they have sustained the high tradition.

The Roosevelt family entered the White House under the universal assumption that they represented the very best in the traditions of an American family. They were descended from a long line of supposedly fine stock. They were wealthy. The President himself had inherited from his father and step-brother around $600,000. He was an only son and his mother was worth more than a million.

He was supposed to be a reformer. While he was Governor of New York the country was seemingly shocked by a long series of petty corruptions among various Tammany leaders. Sheriff Tom Farley was exposed by Samuel Seabury as having kept a good deal of cash in a secret "tin box." The "tin boxes" of leaders got a sudden serio-comic fame. Sheriff Farley was put on trial before Governor Roosevelt, who removed him from office. In doing so he made the following statement:

> "Passive acquiescence by unthinking people in the actions of those *who shrewdly turn to personal advantage the opportunities offered by public office* is out of step with modern ideals of government and with political morality. Such personal gain is not to be excused because it is accompanied by the respondent's popularity of person and great public generosity. Public office should inspire private financial integrity.
>
> "*The stewardship of public officers is a serious and sacred trust. They are so close to the means for private gain that in a sense not at all true of private citizens their personal possessions are invested with a public importance in the event that their stewardship is questioned. One of their deep obligations is to recognize this not reluctantly or with resistance but freely. It is in the true spirit of public trust to give when personally called upon, public proof of the nature, source and extent of their financial affairs.*" [2]

This declaration, doubtless written for the President by Raymond Moley, his adviser in the trial, was hailed as a great moral trumpet blast representing a sane standard of public morality. It may not be so well known, but it is a fact that it is a standard followed by thousands of men in public life, in high and low positions—fortunately for this country. There is not much profit in the salaries of public office. The profit is in the graft. Graft is a slang term to describe "preying on the public either against the law or under it." It consists in "advancing one's position or wealth by dishonest or unfair means as *by utilizing the advantages of an official position for one's gain*." Those who make most money out of politics are, usually, those who hold no public office. Contractors, insurance brokers, lawyers, gamblers and such are able, through their official connections, to feather their nests handsomely, not necessarily by dishonest, but by unfair means—unfair to the public. On a few occasions, presidents have been embarrassed by some distant relative seeking to use his relationship for profit. And in only two or three cases have cabinet officers been involved. In Grant's administration and in Harding's, friends used their connection with the President for their own profit. But the Presidents' immediate families remained unscathed. When the Roosevelt family moved into the White House they had before them the example of a long line of predecessors and the code of honor the President himself had proclaimed.

I.

While Roosevelt was yet governor of New York, his oldest son James, still a student in Boston, was offered a job by an insurance company at $15,000 a year. Jimmy, in a magazine article[3] wrote later: "I wasn't being kidded. I knew perfectly well they were paying me for my name. I ... needed the money." His duties, as he described them, were to sit at a big desk and do nothing. Herbert Hoover's son, during his father's presidency, was offered a job with a big salary. He, like Jimmy, wasn't being kidded either. But he refused the job, saying: "My father's name is not for sale." Jimmy made $19,000 in 1932 and $21,000 in 1933, his first years at work, which he received for the use of his father's name.

About this time a gentleman named John A. Sargent, in Boston, who was making $7500 a year—the hard way—as an insurance salesman, saw the possibilities in Jimmy. He managed the formation of an insurance firm called Roosevelt and Sargent. Sargent knew how to capitalize on it to the limit. Jimmy's first big account was the American Tobacco Company of which George Washington Hill was chairman. Hill wanted some favor and the President invited him to Warm Springs. Jimmy sent a telegram to Warm Springs: "Tell father to be nice to Mr. Hill."

Jimmy got business from or through the following, among others: the Port of New York Authority, Columbia Broadcasting System, subject to control of the government, Ames Baldwin Wyoming Shovel Co., Transcontinental and Western Airlines, West Indian Sugar Company, National Distillers Products, Associated Gas and Electric Co., Armour and Co., National Shawmut Bank of Boston, First National Bank of Boston, Eastern Steamship Co., Pennsylvania Dixie Cement Co., New England Power Association, Ritz-Carlton Hotel of Boston, Roxy Theatre in New York, Waldorf-Astoria Hotel in New York, the Boston Braves, Stone and Webster, Detroit Edison Co., Pressed Steel Car Corporation, Federal Office Building at Vesey St., New York.[4]

Why should Roosevelt and Sargent, a Boston insurance agency, get all this business, from all over the country? William Gibbs McAdoo was made $25,000-a-year head of the American President Lines. The United States government owned 90 per cent of the Lines. The RFC granted these lines a loan of several million. The Maritime Commission agreed to give an annual subsidy of three million for five years. After that the insurance on this firm was transferred to Roosevelt and Sargent.[5]

In 1938, the government forced Southern sugar planters to plow under sugar cane. The American growers fought this. The Cuban planters favored it because they were allowed to plant four times as much as the Southern planters. The West Indies Sugar Company was the big beneficiary. Its profits were enormous. This one company exported to the United States as much sugar as all growers in Louisiana and Florida together produced. And Jimmy got the West Indies Sugar Company insurance.[6] Fifty million dollars' worth of cotton was shipped to China through an RFC-government loan. And Jimmy got the insurance. The clipper ships of the Pan American Airways had to be insured. Admiral Land of the United States

Maritime Commission said the Commission "was diverting more and more insurance to American firms." Plenty of this insurance was going to the youthful Jimmy. The Columbia Broadcasting Company was subject to a federal commission. Jimmy got its insurance. Walter Horne, an insurance broker, owned property on which the Fox West Coast Theatre building stands and the lease provided that he should have the insurance. At the time Joe Schenck, the movie magnate whose concern was interested in this theater was in jail and applying for a federal pardon. Horne was told that the $315,000 policy on this property had to be shifted to Jimmy.

This young man did well for himself. Alva Johnston wrote in a *Saturday Evening Post* article that he had made a million dollars out of this business. Jimmy replied in *Collier's* that this was untrue. He hadn't made a million. But he confessed what he made. In 1934 his insurance earnings were *only* $37,215. His total earnings for the year were $49,167. They were $44,668 in 1936. By 1937 they were $61,000 for the year. And in 1939 they were $100,000, or $25,000 more than his father got as President of the United States.[7] The Roosevelts were satisfied with the defense that Jimmy had made not a million but only a quarter of a million.

This was graft. Let us be honest about it. That is the name for it. It was graft fully known to the President. Dudley Field Malone, Assistant Secretary of State under Wilson, called on Roosevelt to investigate his son's insurance business. The President's answer was that he would do nothing to prevent his son earning a living.

Roosevelt had a very different attitude towards others earning a living. Arthur Mullen, national committeeman from Nebraska, was floor manager for Roosevelt in the 1932 Democratic convention. In 1932 when Mullen told Roosevelt he was going to open a Washington law office, Roosevelt approved and said "he might let it be known that he had the friendliness of the administration." Early in 1934, Senator James F. Byrnes on the radio criticized national committeemen who practiced law in Washington. Roosevelt told Mullen it would be bad for him (Roosevelt) if national committeemen practiced before the courts in Washington.[8] And this at the same time that he approved his son's soliciting insurance from firms all over the country which had business with the government. Oddly enough, Jimmy would himself become a national committeeman from

California without in any way relaxing his business activities. And around 1937 Jimmy became his father's private secretary. He solved the delicate ethical problem which this presented by resigning from the board of directors of Roosevelt and Sargent, without, of course, withdrawing from the firm, and substituted his mother on the board. Here was something really brand new in American political commercial adventure. And as the war arrived, with the vast business of the government running into countless millions with big corporations all over America, the insurance business of Roosevelt and Sargent grew by leaps and bounds. What its earnings were no one knows.

After all, suppose you were the head of a big corporation with millions in contracts from the government and a score of government bureaucrats continually prowling around your plants and over your books and then one day the telephone were to ring and a voice were to say: "This is the White House" or "This is James Roosevelt of Roosevelt and Sargent" and then proceeded to solicit your insurance? What would you do? You might tell young Mr. Roosevelt you were shocked or that you would bring the matter to the attention of his father or that you would publicly denounce him. But you would know that his father's government was on your neck through a dozen New Deal bureaus, that life under these restraints and directives was almost intolerable anyhow. It is not a pretty picture and it is a little difficult to believe and is literally impossible for many honest Americans to credit who have been fed upon the story of the purity and nobility of the Roosevelt regime.

Jimmy did not confine his operations to insurance. In July, 1935 he became president of the National Grain Yeast Corporation, which was organized during Prohibition. In 1929 this company was refused a permit to make alcohol because its backers were not revealed. Jimmy later referred to a Frank J. Hale as president of the company. Hale had been a prohibition agent. Before Hale became an agent, his bank deposits ran around $300 but after his appointment he deposited more than $155,000 in two banks in a year—all of it, save $5000, in cash. Why did this company hire the President's son, then only 28 years old, with no experience in this business, and pay him $25,000 a year?[9]

Around the latter part of 1938, the Department of Justice was preparing its case against the movie companies under the anti-trust laws. Jimmy resigned his job as his father's aide to take a job with Samuel Goldwyn. In thus becoming an officer of one of the indicted companies, Jimmy's name had to be added to the list of defendants under the indictment. He was given $50,000 a year. Later he went into producing on his own account.

Jimmy was thus an extremely busy man and it is not surprising that his health should be impaired. In 1938 he went to the Mayo Clinic and after being there a short time he fell in love with his nurse. In 1940 his wife asked for a divorce, saying that in 1938 Jimmy had asked her for a divorce and demanded that she leave California with their two children. She refused and he deserted her. She got her divorce in 1940 and a settlement involving a very large sum of money for so young a man. The divorce was granted in March and in April Jimmy married his nurse. This was in 1940 and by that time the country had gotten used to the marital adventures of the Roosevelts.

2.

Among this flock of Roosevelt lambs, Elliott was quite the darkest. His brother Jimmy could not make the grade at law school. Elliott had no interest in school and didn't even bother to go to college. He grew up a little on the weed model. And when his father became President, and with the example of his older brother before him, Elliott clearly considered his relationship to the White House a franchise to get rich quick as fast as he could.

He made for Texas in 1933, where he remained for seven years in which time he had earnings larger than his father's as President. Although still a very young man, he started his career in Texas with a new wife. He was divorced from his first in Nevada four months after he landed in Texas and five days later he married a Texas girl by whom he was to have three children before he changed his base of commercial and marital operations.

Elliott was a schematic business man and his mind turned to deals and promotions. One of Roosevelt's early acts in foreign affairs was to recognize Soviet Russia. Three months later—February 28, 1934—Elliott went into a deal with Anthony Fokker to sell the Soviet government 50 military planes for a price which would leave a commission of half a million dollars for Elliott and the same for Fokker, who told a Senate committee the price was excessive but that Elliott had enough influence with the Export-Import Bank and the Russian Purchasing Commission in this country to swing the deal at this price. Elliott was only 23 at the time.[10]

The next year he moved into radio. A Texas business man owned five stations. He gave Elliott a job as vice-president at $30,000 a year. Elliott sold four of these stations to William Randolph Hearst. But Mr. Hearst was *persona non grata* with the New Deal, and of course the Federal Communications Commission was not going to allow him to get these stations. In May, 1936, Elliott Roosevelt arrived at the White House from Texas and promptly applied to the Federal Communications Commission to have these four stations transferred to Mr. Hearst. One Commission member objected but the two Democratic members were for instant approval without a hearing. The objecting member didn't like the idea of the President's son appearing before the Commission which his father had appointed. Then in a month or two the summer arrived and the objecting member left on his vacation. As soon as he was out of town and on only an hour's notice the remaining two called a snap meeting and approved the transfer. A member of the President's family called from the White House to urge the transfer "because it meant so much to Elliott." It did indeed. He got a large sum for each of the stations transferred and was engaged as vice-president of the operating company at a large salary.[11] Thus Elliott began his radio career. His subsequent adventures in this field are such that we shall defer looking at them until a little later.

Elliott got himself involved in all sorts of deals. His name was constantly bobbing up in connection with some unsavory promotion or other. For instance, there was an electric transmission cooperative in Texas on the Brazos River. Harry Slattery, the Rural Electrification Administrator, refused to approve a contract for the sale of power and its operations were held up for three months, resulting in a $180,000 loss. Elliott wrote a letter to Steve Early, his father's secretary, to delay action on the project. That letter is in evidence and is attributed to Elliott's connection with a private electric power company which paid him $12,000 a year as its advertising agent—a mere side issue.[12]

As the war got under way Elliott leaped into the army as a captain and he was sent, of all places, into the procurement division at Dayton, Ohio. In quick succession he rose to be a major, a colonel and then a brigadier-general, while able officers who were colonels when the war started, who began at West Point and had long and honorable careers were kept at that grade throughout the war. While he was in the army he deserted his second wife and her children as he had his first and married after a brief acquaintance a young actress who promptly entered the White House circle and proceeded to capitalize on that. The wedding was staged under circumstances which might be said, by now, to be in the best Rooseveltian manner. Elliott by this time was hobnobbing with Howard Hughes, the military plane builder, who had contracts from the army. Elliott "plighted his troth" at a resort on the rim of the Grand Canyon. Johnny Meyers, the notorious publicity man for Hughes, gave the bride away and Jack Frye of the Hughes Airplane Company was the best man. The bills for this shindig were paid by the Hughes company. Hughes got a $22,000,000 photo reconnaissance plane contract from the government on the recommendation of Elliott after two major-generals charged with passing on this contract had rejected it. Hughes' publicity man testified under oath that in a period of two years he had spent over $5000 entertaining Elliott, that Elliott had borrowed $1000 from him—but paid it back—and that at the very time Elliott was in California on the subject of this contract, his hotel bills were paid by Hughes.[13]

Did President Roosevelt know of the activities of his sons? We know that men high in the party warned him and it is not to be believed that the numerous newspaper attacks on both Elliott and Jimmy never reached White House ears. However, the President had more direct information than that. While Elliott was still in Texas his father made a trip to Fort Worth. At the time a number of "hot oil" indictments were pending. The President eluded the newspaper reporters at Fort Worth and made a trip to a fabulous island in the Gulf of Mexico. There he met a numerous party, chiefly oil men and among them several who were under indictment in the "hot oil" cases. Within a week after this the hot oil indictments were settled after the defendants pleaded *nolo contendere*. From one of the men interested in these cases and present at that island party, Elliott borrowed $40,000. This man asked Elliott if he could do anything with Henry Morgenthau and Elliott assured him he could not, but he did better. He got an appointment with his father at the White House, summoning the oil man as a counsellor on the problems of the independent oil operators. Elliott got in pretty bad with all these people before his career in Texas ended and, in the final settlement, this $40,000 loan was paid.[14]

What had become of that code of public official honesty which Roosevelt had set up when he was governor and running for the presidency? What about the public official who allows a member of his family to obtain favors or benefits through his political connections? These words were not used idly. They are Franklin D. Roosevelt's own words. When he dismissed Sheriff Farley, he said: *"What of a public official who allows a member of his family to obtain favors or benefits through his political connections?"*

The Chicago *Tribune* estimated that Elliott's earnings from 1933 to 1944 inclusive amounted to $1,175,000 or roughly $100,000 a year and practically every dollar was made on the strength of his White House connection.

3.

One of the most curious of all the phenomena of the New Deal was the wife of the President. She had this quality: that she was something quite new. The people elect a president. In the nature of things, presidents have wives and children. The President's life history, his personality, habits and opinions are all legitimate subjects, usually fully explored during the campaign. But the President's wife and children are thrown in with the package and it is rare indeed that the people have any suspicion of what they are getting. The White House is the President's home and his place of business and the President's wife is its general manager. The family lives, in a sense, upon a hill and the hill belongs to the people, so that the President's wife and his immediate family have a definite official status during his incumbency. Besides, the wife gets elected, by virtue of his election, to a life-time annuity of $5000 for being the President's wife if she should survive him.

Obviously it would be a violation of the proprieties were Congress to pass a law requiring that the President's wife and his children should behave themselves. A hundred and fifty years of history have proved that, save in a single administration, such a law would be quite unnecessary. Presidents and presidents' wives could be counted on to preserve the proprieties governing this peculiar half-private, half-official status and to obey these proprieties and to exact from their children some respect for them.

Mrs. Eleanor Roosevelt was born in 1884. She was the daughter of Elliott Roosevelt, a younger brother of Theodore. He apparently was a gay, carefree, happy sort of man who had done little in his life save to follow his inclinations. He left St. Paul's School when a boy without going to college, went West for his health, took part of his inheritance and went around the world, hunted big game, came back to America and married Anna Hall, whose father lived entirely on what his mother and father gave him. Thus on her mother's and father's side she came from two old New York families who lived wholly on their inheritance and had never done a day's work for pay.

The facts about her early family life are such that I would leave them severely alone save for the fact that Mrs. Roosevelt has written a book telling all about these unhappy maladjustments. She writes that her father was a drunkard and died in a sanitarium. I did not rake up this family scandal. I note it only for the light it throws on his daughter who saw fit to rake it up in order to portray the bleakness of her girlhood out of which she emerged into so much light. The father spent most of his time away from the family home, either in Europe or in Virginia in a sanitarium. Her mother died when she was a small child. After this she and two other younger children were turned over to their maternal grandmother Hall, where she lived under a regime of the most solemn and exacting discipline. Until she was 15 years old she had no schooling save for a brief period when she was about six in a convent in France.

She described herself as a dour, homely child, with a lack of manners and an inordinate desire for affection and praise which she never got. She left the school in France, as she says, in disgrace because she told some childish fairy story about having swallowed a penny in order to get some attention. The Mother Superior insisted that she go "because they could not believe her." She had very few companions of her own age. Finally in 1899 when she was 15 years old she was sent to a school called Allenwood, outside of London. It was a French school kept by an old pedagogist named Madame Souvestre who had taught Eleanor's aunt in Paris before the Franco-Prussian war and was now, in her declining years, running this small school for girls of high-school age from well-to-do American and English families. Save for a summer vacation in Long Island, she spent the next three years in London at Miss Souvestre's school, with occasional travels on the continent. She was 18 when she came home, with literally no knowledge of America or her country or what it was all about and scarcely no acquaintances of her own age. All these facts are revealed by her in one of her own books.[15]

She returned to the home of her aging grandmother and to a house where she was kept, by reason of unfortunate circumstances, in great isolation. She herself is authority in this curious book for the cause of this. Her mother's brother was also a drunkard. Young people were not asked to the house. Once when two of her friends were invited to remain for a few days, Eleanor lived in such terror lest some unfortunate incident occur that none was ever invited again unless she felt free to explain to her visitors that they might have an uncomfortable time. Later she moved with an unmarried aunt to a town house in 37th Street, undoubtedly to be away from the atmosphere of this isolated and disturbed home.

This is all she knew of life when a year later she married young Franklin D. Roosevelt, a cousin, after a very brief acquaintance and courtship while he was still in Harvard College. She herself says that she scarcely knew what marriage meant. As she put it herself, her grandmother asked her if she was sure she was really in love and she answered: "I solemnly answered yes; yet it was years later before I knew what love was or what loving really meant." Why this singular woman should choose the moment when she had just become the mistress of the White House to write and sell these accounts to the American people I do not of course know. But her record of these early years makes it abundantly clear that one of the guiding urges of her life, once she was emancipated from the isolations and constrictions and bewilderment of her first 20 years, was an insatiable craving for attention. It amounted to little less than a phobia, as Americans now know.

Mrs. Roosevelt had not been in the White House very long when she appeared on the radio on a commercial program for which she was paid a large sum of money. It was a little startling to have the President's wife gushing over the air for toilet preparations, mattresses and other products. She was getting from $1000 to $4000 an appearance not because she was Eleanor Roosevelt but because she was the wife of the President. The Manhattan Soap Company, makers of Sweetheart Soap, began a campaign in 80 newspapers offering three cakes of soap for the price of one cake plus a penny and the campaign was built around the broadcasts of Mrs. Roosevelt and Jack Burch.

The Pan-American Coffee Bureau was supported by eight Latin American countries. It looked out for the interests of their coffee exporters. Some of the countries paid the bills out of their treasuries, others out of a tax paid on every bag of coffee exported to America. An advertising agency in which Harry Hopkins' son was employed offered Mrs. Roosevelt as an "attraction" to this coffee bureau and the offer was accepted. Here was the wife of the President getting $1000 a week from a group of foreign countries. One of the countries involved assumed that the President was in on it. The proposal to hire the First Lady to ballyhoo coffee for eight South American republics was submitted to the State Department. There, it is said, Sumner Welles, who had held the lady's train when she married, objected. He said it would not look good to our southern neighbors. But Mrs. Roosevelt said yes and the advertising account of the coffee bureau was taken away from one advertising company and given to the one in which Hopkins' son was interested.

During the war the candy manufacturers were fearful that candy might be classed as "non-essential." They organized the Council on Candy as Food in the War Effort. They wanted names on their radio program. They got Wallace, McNutt, some generals and admirals who broadcast without pay. They also got the President's wife but she charged $1500 each for the first two and $2500 for the third appearance. What else than this could Franklin D. Roosevelt have been referring to when as governor he talked about the families and wives of officials using their positions to make money? It had seemed pretty serious in the relatives of little Tammany officials. It apparently had become all right in the wife of the President.[16]

This versatile lady took a fling at the movies, making a series of shorts with Dave Ellman, the Hobby Lobby man. With Ellman she appeared painted up like a Cherokee Indian and told about the hobbies of her husband and her children. And, as the world knows, she has been a prolific writer for magazines and newspapers and of books. She wrote a daily column called "My Day" which was syndicated to numerous daily papers and which seldom rose in literary form or intellectual content above the level of a high-school composition. She has written a monthly magazine department and all in all has written for magazines over 160 articles on almost every subject under the sun. She has lectured in almost every city in the United States, getting $1000 or $1500 per lecture, depending on what the traffic would bear. It is estimated that she has received during the 15 years since she entered the White House at least *three million dollars*—which is not very bad for a lady who had no earning power whatever before she moved her desk into the Executive Mansion, a lady whose husband spent a good deal of time denouncing the greed of men who made less for directing some of the greatest enterprises in America.[17]

At first it was said in extenuation of Mrs. Roosevelt's sudden burst of prosperity that she gave a great deal to charity. So does every ward boss. The point at issue is not what use she makes of the money but what canons of public decency she has fractured in earning it. Besides, the defense that she pours it out to charity has been pretty well exploded.

Nevertheless, in spite of these defiances of all the amenities, all the laws imposed by decency, all the traditional proprieties and all that body of rules which high-minded people impose upon themselves, the Roosevelt family, through a carefully cultivated propaganda technique not unlike that which is applied to the sale of quack medicines, imposed upon the American people the belief that they were probably the most high-minded beings that ever lived in the White House. Behind this curtain of moral grandeur they were able to carry on in the field of public policy the most incredible programs which our people, unaccustomed to this sort of thing, accepted because they believed these plans came out of the minds of very noble and righteous beings.

Franklin D. Roosevelt, while he was governor and was judging the conduct not of a president or his wife, but of a Tammany politician, made this further statement: "As a matter of general sound public policy I am very certain that there is a requirement that where a public official is under inquiry or investigation, especially an elected public official, and it appears that his scale of living or the total of his bank deposits far exceeds the public salary which he is known to receive he, the elected public official, owes a positive public duty to the community to give a reasonable or credible explanation of the sources of the deposits or the source which enables him to maintain a scale of living beyond the amount of his salary."[18]

Of course there has been no investigation of the President's earnings but the moral formula which Governor Roosevelt proposed here must apply to President Roosevelt far more than to a Tammany county sheriff. It cannot be escaped because his wife rather than he himself is the instrument of making these vast sums—his wife who until he became president earned nothing. The President specifically closed this loophole when he insisted that the rule noted above applied not merely to the public official himself but to his family who profited out of his trust. And he said again: "The state must expect compliance with these standards because if popular government is to continue to exist, it must hold its stewards to a stern and uncompromising rectitude. It must be a stern but a just master."

I think it is a fair statement that the history of public office in the federal government in the higher levels exhibits no such instance of a president's or a cabinet officer's wife suddenly blossoming forth as one of the largest earners of money in the country. As an example to future chief executives—and we cannot know what kind of men will come to power in troubled times—there must be a full and complete investigation of the earnings of every member of the Roosevelt family which can be traced by any stretch to the political influence of that family while Roosevelt was President of the United States.

Why did the President permit his wife to carry on in this fantastic manner and why did the Democratic leaders allow her to do it without a protest? You may be sure that whenever you behold a phenomenon of this character there is a reason for it. The reason for it in this case was that Mrs. Roosevelt was performing an important service to her husband's political plans. We have already seen the unusual conditions out of which Mr. Roosevelt's majorities were fashioned. We must remember that the New Deal, by which I mean that collection of policies we call the New Deal, was as far removed from the political philosophy of the Southern Democrats as it was possible to be. There were never enough people in the country belonging to the more or less orthodox Democratic fold to elect Mr. Roosevelt. It was necessary for him to get the support of groups outside this Democratic fold. One of these groups, of course, was the radical element in the large cities, particularly in New York. For instance, in the 1940 election, Mr. Roosevelt was the candidate of the Democratic Party but he did not get enough votes on the Democratic ticket to carry New York State. He was also the candidate of the American Labor Party which provided the necessary votes to overcome the Republican lead over the Democrats. The American Labor Party at first was a conglomeration of radicals of all kinds ranging from light pink to deep red. But by 1944 the Communists had taken over the American Labor Party completely. In the election of 1944, Governor Dewey got nearly half a million votes more on the Republican ticket than Roosevelt got on the Democratic ticket, but Roosevelt was the candidate of two other parties—the American Labor Party of the Communists and the Liberal Party which was a collection of parlor pinks, technocrats, pious fascists and American non-Stalinist Communists. These two parties gave him over 800,000 votes and it was this that made up his majority in New York. The same thing was true in Illinois, in New Jersey, Connecticut, Massachusetts, and other large industrial states, although the fact was not so obvious because the radicals operated inside the Democratic party where they could not be so easily identified.

It was in this field that Mrs. Roosevelt performed her indispensable services to the President. It was she who fraternized with the Reds and the pinks, with the Red-fascists and the technocrats and the crackpot fringe generally, gave them a sense of association with the White House, invited their leaders and their pets to the White House and to her apartment in New York, went to their meetings, endorsed their numerous front organizations and generally made herself a thorn in the side of the Democratic organization when it confronted its orthodox members, but did her part in holding in line the Red faction without which Roosevelt could not have been elected after the second term. Bizarre as her performances were, offensive as they were to so-called sound Democrats almost to the point of nausea, they were indispensable and this is why she was tolerated, even though in carrying out this mission she violated all of the proprieties and shocked even some of the least sensitive persons in the Democratic party.

Let us see just how she did this job and let us be fair in passing judgment on her. We have to remember that she was a woman of very limited intelligence and of literally no information about the philosophy of the various groups she toyed with.

After Roosevelt was stricken with infantile paralysis in 1921, she suddenly found herself for the first time in her life in a position approaching power on her own feet. While she, with her rather stern sense of formal responsibility, made every effort to bring about her husband's recovery, she also saw the necessity of keeping alive his interest in public affairs and his contacts and she set herself about that job. She had already fallen into acquaintance with left-wing labor agitators and she brought these people as frequently as she could to her imprisoned husband where they proceeded to work upon a mind practically empty so far as labor and economic problems were concerned. The moment a person of Mrs. Roosevelt's type exposes herself to these infections, the word gets around radical circles, whose denizens are quick to see the possibilities in an instrument of this kind. During Roosevelt's term in Albany she was extensively cultivated by these groups, so that when she went to Washington in 1933 they had easy and friendly access to her.

I think it must be said for her that at this point—in 1933—the country, including its public men, were not too well-informed about the peculiar perils involved in Red propaganda activities. The Reds seized upon three or four very popular American democratic cults—(1) freedom of speech, (2) the defense of the downtrodden laborer—the forgotten man, (3) the succor of the poor. They also began to penetrate the colleges in both the teaching staffs and the student bodies through their various front organizations dominated by Reds. The first attempt to expose these designs was made by the House Committee on Un-American Activities. The attacks upon Martin Dies and the Dies Committee, as it was known, were engineered and carried out almost entirely by the Communist Party. But the Communist Party itself was powerless to do anything effective and it used some of the most powerful and prominent persons in the country to do its dirty work. All through the first and second terms of the President, Mrs. Roosevelt was industriously cultivated by the Communists and their various front organizations. There is no room here to go into the whole story. But she served their purposes well, while at the same time keeping them in the New Deal fold.

Throughout 1939 the President was busy laying plans for his third-term nomination, while pretending to be adverse to a third term. And all through 1939 Mrs. Roosevelt was tireless in promoting the friendships of these Communist groups. One of the Communist outfits was the American Youth Congress. It was dominated by Communists through the Young Communist League and a group of workers including William W. Hinckley, Joseph Cadden who succeeded him as executive secretary and Joseph P. Lash, one of the leaders of the movement. The Dies Committee began investigating these organizations, although the President had sent for Martin Dies and ordered him to quit investigating the Communists.

When the Un-American Activities Committee was investigating the American Youth Congress, a crowd of adolescent pinks marched into the committee room. They were headed by the wife of the President of the United States, and there they put on a three-ring circus, hopping about, distributing pamphlets, buttonholing congressmen and making themselves generally a disgraceful nuisance. Joseph P. Lash, who was the executive secretary of the American Student Union, put on a show. He sang a little song for the benefit of the committee from a skit which the little pinks had put on in New York. It ran:

"If you see an un-American come lurking your way
Why, alkalize with Martin Dies and he will disappear."

This was delivered to little squeals of joy from the assembled pinks and pinklets in attendance and to the smiling approval of their impresario, Mrs. Eleanor Roosevelt. At this very moment, Joe Lash was living in the White House as Mrs. Roosevelt's guest, while Joe Cadden and Abbot Simon were occasional boarders there. When the show was over, Mrs. Roosevelt led all of her young guests into two White House cars and carted them back to the White House for entertainment. The next day in her newspaper column she gave the Dies Committee a good going over. She went so far as to send for one of the members of the committee privately and ask him to see that the American Youth Congress was not branded as a

Communist-front organization. Here was the wife of the President of the United States, a separate department of the government, using the White House as a lobbying ground for a crowd of young Commies and Pinkies against a committee of Congress.[19]

Things were happening in the world about this time. Hitler had invaded Poland and at the same time Russia had jolted its American stooges by joining with Hitler in the invasion of Poland. Joe Lash had been the leader of the movement in the American Student Union inspired by the Communists to keep America on the pacifist side. Lash had been a member of the Socialist Party. He resigned in 1937 and published his letter of resignation in the Communist *New Masses* where he extolled the vigorous leadership of the Soviet Union. Lash worked in collaboration with the Communist Party. After this, the American Student Union became a mere tool of the Red organization in America.

Following the pact between Hitler and Stalin, the American Student Union, after an address by Earl Browder, then head of the Communist Party, denounced the war between England and France on one hand and Germany on the other as an imperialist war and they pledged themselves "to mobilize the American campus to defeat every effort to involve this country in war between Britain, France and Germany or against the Soviet Union." However, when Hitler invaded Russia, they repudiated that position and pledged themselves wholeheartedly to the defense of Russia.

The war in Europe had already begun when Mrs. Roosevelt made a spectacle of herself with her adolescent revolutionists in the House office building. In the Spring of 1941, the American Youth Congress held a convention in Washington where Justice Jackson and other officials addressed them. They ended with a get-together on the White House lawn. Germany and Russia were still allies at this time. The President, from the White House porch, addressed these young philosophers spread out on the lawn. Referring to Germany and Russia he asked them to condemn all forms of dictatorship and at this point, to his amazement, the assembled young philosophers gave the President and Mrs. Roosevelt a hearty Bronx cheer. And now, of course, Mrs. Roosevelt felt they were Communists, although she had rejected all of the overwhelming evidence before that. Booing the President suddenly turned them into Communists.

Her protege, Joe Lash, was now in a terrible position. Obviously he could not continue with an organization that had booed his host and hostess for he was living rather regularly in the White House. Mrs. Roosevelt therefore sponsored a new organization called the International Students Service. Joe Lash, the Commie stooge, turned up under her sponsorship as the secretary of that at $4200 a year. A member of Congress, an ardent New Dealer, visited the White House one morning. While there he saw Abbot Simon of the national board of the American Youth Congress, come out of one of the bedrooms. He couldn't believe his eyes. He asked the White House usher if he was mistaken. The usher assured him he was not, that this little Commie tool had been occupying that room for two weeks and sleeping in the bed Lincoln had slept in.

Lash still continued in the White House as a guest and as a symbol to every Red in America. Some time later the American Peace Mobilization, another Communist-front organization, began to picket the White House. Joe Cadden, who had been sleeping in the White House only a short time before, was now parading with the picketeers outside his old boarding house while Joe Lash, parted from his old buddies, looked out at the pink peace mobilizers and his friend Cadden from the security of the White House windows.

This whole subject is a little complicated. When we speak of Communists in American politics the word has to be explained. There is the Communist who is a member of the Communist Party and who admits he is a Communist and glories in it. These are probably not more than 80,000 or 90,000 in number, if that. But there are several hundred thousand, perhaps half a million, men and women in America, but chiefly in New York and the large eastern industrial states, who string along with the Communists without being members of the party. Most of them are confused. They are generally agreed on two things only—first that the capitalist system and the democratic form of political life are done for and ought to be abolished and, second, that the Socialist Party headed by its old democratic Socialists is impossible, hopelessly weak and outmoded. At that point they branch out into a variety of groups, some being 100 per cent Communists without being Stalinists—that is, they believe that an American Communist ought to be an American and fight for American Communist revolution regardless of Russian interests.

They then fade off into varying shades of red down to a sickly pink. While the official Communist Party was compelled by its Stalinist master to support Russia after the Hitler-Stalin pact the greater number of Commies and pinks outside the party refused to go along with the Stalinist line. Most of them believed that the Hitler-Stalin pact was purely temporary and that as soon as Hitler had knocked off France he would turn against Russia. They were confused but they were still Red and pink and they were still good for votes around the polls in 1940 and it was Mrs. Roosevelt's job to keep them in line. After Hitler's invasion of Russia in 1941 of course the situation cleared up beautifully for them and she was then able to resume on a still larger scale her White House liaison with her Red friends. How much she realized the gravity of what she was doing must be open to question but she did realize that she was making votes for Franklin D. Roosevelt and as this automatically included herself and all the rich pickings of the White House, she worked at this job seven days a week.

Mrs. Roosevelt's long residence in the White House and the long indulgence of the people toward the numerous journeys by the family across the borderline of good conduct had badly confused her sense of the proprieties. The unwritten law for Presidents and their families is that they shall be more meticulous than any in the observance of the ethical and social restraints enforced upon the population in times of stress. But Mrs. Roosevelt felt that her position in the White House entitled her to an exemption from these restraints.

While American citizens were being deprived of gasoline save for the most essential purposes, Mrs. Roosevelt was running around the country lecturing and pursuing her money-making activities, her politics and her personal diversions regardless of the law. The OPA announced that gasoline ration books would be taken up if automobiles were found near places of amusement. Mrs. Roosevelt used her car freely to go to such places and got publicly pilloried for this when she drove from the White House to a Marian Anderson concert in Washington.

She allowed her housekeeper to drive back and forth to her home in Maryland every day in a White House car when she might have traveled as other private citizens did. She made a 26,000-mile junket in an Army transport plane to the Pacific and came back in a specially fitted Army plane. She went out in a big four-engined bomber manned by two captains, three master sergeants and a staff sergeant and attended by a Washington journalist—a major in the Air Transport Command. She dressed herself up as a field service worker of the Red Cross for the duration of this trip—all this in spite of the fact that Roosevelt had warned the people that a flying fortress consumed enough gas in a single bombardment to drive your car five times across the continent. Her trip consumed the equivalent of 138,000 A coupons or 185 trips across the continent in your car. The plane was remodeled inside and fitted with a comfortable bed for the lady and while she was in the Pacific she made a special trip to an island to visit her political protege, Joe Lash. About this time the Office of Defense Transportation put on a big campaign for a renewed check on civilian travel and the government had actually cut down deliveries of milk to save gas. Mrs. Roosevelt, commenting on this, said "we must learn how we can go get things ourselves instead of having them delivered."

She accepted the most expensive gifts from private concerns and from foreign governments seeking favors—a $10,000 mink coat from Canadian fur breeders, a gold bracelet from Emperor Haile Selassie, a gold crown from the Sultan of Morocco, and gifts from various American trade organizations. She said flippantly: "The President cannot take a present from a foreign government, but I can accept a present from anybody." No law should be necessary to restrain a President's wife. Theodore Roosevelt had a standing rule that presents of food to him should be sent to charitable institutions and all others returned to the senders. But with the Franklin D. Roosevelts the rule seemed to be to "get while the getting is good."[20]

CHAPTER 3: WHAT MANNER OF MAN?

I.

What sort of man was this who permitted his family to make the White House into a headquarters for their commercial operations? The picture as it was does not resemble even remotely the vision of the statesman who stood upon a moral plateau far above the time-serving lesser men in Congress.

In good time someone will undertake an inquiry into the early personal life of Roosevelt sufficiently objective to enable us to form some opinion of the origins of the mental and moral urges that drove him along the course he took in the Presidency. All we have now is a handful of surface facts gathered chiefly from his mother, his wife and family. These are meager and pathetically distorted.

Part of the Roosevelt legend is the concept of a fine old aristocratic family that became the friend of the common man. It is unimportant, perhaps, but it serves to illustrate the glittering crust of fable which overlays this whole Roosevelt story. The President's father was a sixth generation Roosevelt who played out decently the role of a Hudson River squire. He was a dull, formal and respectable person moving very narrowly within the orbit set by custom for such a man. By 1900, however, the name Roosevelt had become a good one for promotional purposes, because it had become illustrious by reason of Theodore Roosevelt who belonged to a very different branch of the family.

On Franklin D. Roosevelt's mother's side there was certainly nothing distinguished in the blood. Her father was a crusty old China Sea trader and opium smuggler. The family had much of its fortune in soft coal mines in West Virginia and Frederic Delano, brother of the senior Mrs. Roosevelt, headed that enterprise, with as dark a social history and as harsh and grinding a labor policy as any in the region. This, so far as Franklin Roosevelt is concerned, is sufficiently unimportant, save as it contradicts the spurious legend that has been fabricated by his extravagant shirt-stuffers. His mother was, however, a woman of great beauty and force of character and whatever of good looks and positiveness there was in Roosevelt's make-up came from her.

Roosevelt was born and grew up in the midst of a baronial estate, surrounded by numerous acres and many servants and hemmed about with an elaborate seclusion. What sort of boy he was we do not know, save that he was carefully guarded from other boys and grew up without that kind of boyhood association usual in America. A sample of the mass of fraudulent "history" which is being served up about him is found in one of the few formal biographies published so far. It is by Alden Hatch[21] and though it is widely quoted, is as silly a performance as has ever come from any pen since old Parson Weems wrote his book about Washington. Referring to his childhood, Hatch says, explaining "his understanding of people—not just Americans but people everywhere" that "he played with English children on the lawns of English castles or the streets of London" and that he knew "German boys in the *Volkschule* at Bad Nauheim and French ones in the parks of Paris." As a matter of fact, Roosevelt as a boy was severely isolated from other children. His first schooling was at the age of seven when he and the Rogers boy formed a class for a brief time at the Rogers' home adjoining Hyde Park, with the Rogers' governess as teacher. He was taken abroad on summer tours by his parents from the time he was three years old. He went along in the care of a governess as the parents traveled to France and London and Berlin, following the usual track of American visitors of that day. In London his parents made visits to various people. When the boy was around 12 years old he made a bicycle trip of a few weeks around German cities with his tutor. He spent a few weeks, perhaps something over a month at most, in a small German school while his parents were at Bad Nauheim. This was all the schooling he got save from a governess until he was 14, when he went to Groton.[22] We are asked to attribute part of his wide understanding of Americans and Europeans to the story that this summer wayfarer between the ages of three and 12 "played in the London streets and Paris parks," which of course he did not do, and with a couple of boys on a neighboring estate under a governess.

At Groton, a severely exclusive school, the boy was an indifferent student and at Harvard later the same was true. He wore a Phi Beta Kappa key on his chain in later life, but this was a purely honorary one presented to him by a small women's college when he was governor.[23] He was interested in sports and was active on the Harvard *Crimson* of which in his final year he was editor. His career as a student was without distinction. After leaving Harvard he studied law at Columbia University where he failed to graduate. This record must not be taken as evidence that he was not very bright. But it is evidence of what everyone knew of him, and that is that he was not a student.

He had little interest in books. Friendly biographers say, as if it were some sort of special genius, that what he knew he "absorbed from others" rather than from books. However, one does not "absorb" history or economics from others in chats. They must be patiently studied over long periods out of the only sources that are available—the appropriate books. Miss Perkins, who knew him from his early manhood up to his death, says he was not a student, that he knew nothing of economics and that he admitted he had never read a book on the subject.[24] Edward J. Flynn, his campaign manager in the 1940 election and closely associated with him as a friend and as Secretary of State of New York while he was governor, says he never saw him reading a book.[25] Three men who worked closely with him in the White House and one of them previously in Albany, also say they never saw him interested in a book, save an occasional detective story. The only books that really interested him were books on the Navy, particularly old books such as appeal to a collector. He did amass a considerable library in this field. It is to be assumed he read many of them. But the history of the Navy and its battles is not the history of the United States or of Europe or of their tremendous and complex political and social movements.

His career as a lawyer was extremely sketchy. He began as a law clerk with Carter, Ledyard and Milburn. Later a junior in that firm found an old memo addressed to the office manager and signed by Mr. Ledyard directing him "under no circumstances to put any serious piece of litigation" in the hands of "young Mr. Roosevelt."

In 1910 he was elected to the State Senate from Dutchess County. He had taken no part in politics and was scarcely known there. The Democrats usually named a candidate for the Senate from among the county families and got a good contribution. They never elected anybody. They offered the nomination to young Roosevelt and he took it reluctantly. But this was an auspicious year for the New York Democrats. Theodore Roosevelt and President Taft were at war. Charlie Murphy made his famous deal with big Bill Barnes, State Republican boss who wanted to defeat Theodore Roosevelt. Thus the Democrats elected their candidate for governor, John A. Dix, and swept in the Dutchess County Democrats with him, including young Roosevelt.

Charlie Murphy tried to force the legislature to name William Sheehan for the United States Senate. As the stories now go the youthful Roosevelt rose in revolt against the selection of the notorious "Blue-eyed" Billy Sheehan and led a movement of insurgent Democrats to thwart the will of the great Tammany boss. Actually there was a revolt even inside Tammany against the nomination. Edward M. Sheppard, a distinguished lawyer, Thomas Mott Osborne and William Church Osborne led the Democratic revolt with Sheppard as the candidate for the Senate. One of Murphy's closest friends, J. Sargeant Cram, openly denounced the Sheehan candidacy. The young senator from Dutchess County, bearing the illustrious name of Roosevelt, was interested in the fight because the party leaders from that county, led by Lewis Stuyvesant Chandler, were against Sheehan. There was, of course, good newspaper copy in the presence of the young Democratic Roosevelt, rich, handsome, lined up in the successful fight against the Boss. His name was thrust more and more to the front. He took an active and quite honorable part in the fight, but the legend as it is told is quite far from the facts.

In 1912, with the Republicans split in the great Taft-Roosevelt feud, the Democrats swept the country and Roosevelt, though in bed throughout the campaign with typhoid, was reelected State Senator. When Wilson entered the White House and someone suggested it would be a good idea to have a Democratic Roosevelt in the administration, Franklin Roosevelt was offered the post of Assistant Secretary of the Navy, a distinction on which he had no claim save that he bore the name of Roosevelt. He was then 31 years old. He had done nothing, had failed in his law examinations and had failed in practice. When the First World War ended he was 36. Apparently his service in the Department was satisfactory, though I have never seen anywhere any authentic evidence about it one way or the other. He did boast later that during the war he "threw money around like water" which may well be believed.

But his name had earned for him a great deal of publicity. He had announced himself a candidate for the nomination for the United States Senate in New York in the Democratic primary in 1914 but was badly defeated by James W. Gerard who in turn was defeated by the Republicans. In 1920, when James M. Cox was nominated for the Presidency and when a Republican victory loomed ahead as a certainty, Roosevelt was nominated for Vice-President. Actually he was not very well-known and had absolutely no record of his own to justify the nomination. But luck dogged his heels. Governor Cox chose Roosevelt for his running mate, banking on the value of the name. He told Charlie Murphy, Tammany leader, he wanted Roosevelt. No one expected Murphy to agree. But he said: "Cox is the first presidential candidate to do me the courtesy to consult me on anything, and so I am going to agree."

The Republicans swept New York State and the country and Mr. Roosevelt went back to New York. His friend Van Lear Black, a yachting companion, was president of the Fidelity and Deposit Company. He offered Roosevelt a job as a vice-president at $25,000 a year, again to use the name as a means of attracting business. Then in August, 1921 Roosevelt was stricken with infantile paralysis, which put an end to his career in politics for the next seven years.

At this point Roosevelt could not be tagged as a man with any indispensable qualifications in any field of life. He was 40 years old. He had the reputation of being a snob. In the legislature, says his devoted follower Frances Perkins "he didn't like people very much ... he had a youthful lack of humility, a streak of self-righteousness and deafness to the hopes, fears and aspirations which are the common lot." Democrats like Bob Wagner and Al Smith and others "thought him impossible and said so."[26] He had traveled very little around the United States until he went to the Navy Department when he made little trips to inspect ship launchings amid crowds. He had never really seen America. While he was in Washington he hobnobbed with a very small and exclusive set of the "right" people. He had never made a speech or uttered a word that anyone remembered.

During his Harvard days, shortly after his marriage, he and his bride took a trip to Europe—a regular tourist's wandering from city to city. He had not been in Europe since save twice when he went as Assistant Secretary during the war on a naval inspection tour for about a month, and at the end of the war on another tour in connection with the demobilization of naval forces in Europe. He was not in Europe, save briefly in 1931, until he went to Casablanca, 23 years later. Yet somehow his promotion managers whipped up the myth that he possessed some kind of intimate and close knowledge of the American people and that he also had, by reason of his childhood trips to Europe, his visit with his bride and his two trips during the war, some vast and comprehensive and deep insight into the lives and ideologies and ways of the people of the world. It is a simple fact beyond denial that when Roosevelt went to Washington in 1933 there were few men in the Senate who did not have a larger knowledge of European economic and political issues than the new President. Certainly alongside Herbert Hoover he was a child in arms. Roosevelt was a stamp collector all his life and like all stamp collectors he got to know the location on the map of all the countries whose stamps he owned. He loved to display this special knowledge. But this simple and rudimentary subject of geography is not to be confused with the far more formidable subject of European and Asiatic economic, social and political movements.

In setting all this down, I am not accusing Roosevelt of being a wicked man because he was not a good student, did not read books on economic or social science or law or politics and knew less about foreign affairs than William Borah or Herbert Hoover or Key Pittman or Carter Glass. I merely seek to set the picture straight and to frame Mr. Roosevelt within the more or less narrow limits which bound his intellectual energies and interests.

However, he did believe that he knew a great deal about these subjects, although occasionally he admitted he did not understand financial and economic questions too well. But he had a way of doing a little bragging about his intellectual equipment, about which he was secretly a little sensitive. For instance, he wore the purely honorary Phi Beta Kappa key given him while he was governor by William Smith-Hobart College, a girls' school in New York State, leaving visitors to suppose he had got it at Harvard. He used to tell a story about how he humiliated a legal antagonist before a jury. The weakness in the story was that it was an old courtroom joke told about lawyers time out of mind, that he took credit for it personally and that he had never tried a jury case in his life. Another time he explained to Emil Ludwig some course he had just taken by saying he had learned that technique "when he was a teacher" and his superior had taught him how to handle pupils. Of course he had never been a teacher. When he was President he told a room full of senators, all of whom had gone through World War I while he was in civilian clothes, that he had "seen more of war than any man in the room."

And in one of his speeches when he was assuring the audience of his horror of war, he explained it by the terrible things he had seen on the battlefield, describing the regiment he had seen wiped out, the thousands of young soldiers he had seen choked with blood in the mud of France, although he had never been in a battle in his life. And though he had never served in the Army or Navy, he got some local post to make him a member of the American Legion, after which he went around on occasion wearing a Legion cap.

Roosevelt, long before he became governor, had occasion to exhibit to Robert Moses a side of his character which caused the New York State park commissioner to administer to him a reprimand he never forgot or forgave. Governor Smith appointed Roosevelt a member of the Taconic Park Commission, an honorary post. The Commission, however, is entitled to an executive secretary at $5000 a year. Roosevelt asked Moses to appoint Louis Howe, Roosevelt's personal secretary, to that job. Moses was willing until Howe told him that Roosevelt's personal affairs took all of his time and he could not give more than a few hours a week to the job. This incensed Moses, who wrote Roosevelt sharply reproving him for attempting to put his own secretary on the state's payroll. This sort of thing is not uncommon in the down-on-the-ground level of practical politics. It is a kind of permissive graft, if kept quiet. It is not the kind of thing one looks for in the conduct of a wealthy man who poses as a dweller in the upper stories of political morality.

However, a change had taken place in Roosevelt. His affliction had done something to him and for him. The bitter experience he had endured in the long period of recovery from his attack of infantile paralysis had certainly softened and warmed and mellowed his personality. In his efforts at recovery he had gone to Warm Springs, Ga., and spent several years there. There he found himself sitting about talking to many other sufferers like himself, including many children. He swam in the pool with his fellow patients, sat around talking with them and getting for the first time in his life a look into the minds and hearts of other human beings in distress. He experienced this sort of human comradeship upon a level he had never touched before. Life up to this had been a long succession of gifts from Lady Luck, whose attendance he had come to think of as a settled and dependable affair. And she had failed him. The visitation of the terrible sickness had perhaps effaced from his character the assumption of superior fortune that made him hold his head so high—actually physically high so that people commented on it. His head had been brought down and, if the disease crippled his limbs, it set something free in his spirit. For the first time in his life he felt an urge to do something in the field of purely human effort for other human beings.

But Warm Springs became the subject of one of the most curious deals in the nomination of a man to high office. When Al Smith was nominated for the Presidency in 1928 he was anxious to get a candidate for governor in New York who could be elected. There were three or four men qualified. But the upstate and Tammany leaders could not agree on any of them for purely political reasons. Smith insisted that under the circumstances Roosevelt would be the best candidate, solving the problem because he was the only one the leaders could agree on. It was generally believed that Smith's amazing record as governor would make it possible for any Democrat to carry the state ticket provided the party was united on him. The Tammany leaders objected strenuously to Roosevelt. They said he was unreliable, flighty, and without any experience as a political administrator. Smith, however, convinced them that, despite these shortcomings, he had the indispensable qualification of having no enemies and hence of avoiding a split in the party. He had no enemies because since 1920 he had had no political career.

During the summer months, Smith asked Ed Flynn to put the matter up to Roosevelt. Roosevelt and Smith were friendly, but only in politics. There was little other relationship between them. The much publicized story of the "beautiful friendship between the Hudson River aristocrat and the boy from the sidewalks of New York" was a pure newspaper fable.[27] Roosevelt admired Smith. He had nominated him for the Presidency in the 1924 Democratic convention in a speech that still was quoted, in which he had called Smith the "Happy Warrior." Because of that speech, Smith knew that Roosevelt had political ambitions. Roosevelt had gone to Smith and asked to be permitted to make the nominating speech.[28] He wanted to begin his return to politics and he felt that would give him a place in the spotlight. Smith was not eager to yield but he did so, and Roosevelt made the speech which had been written for someone else to deliver, including the "Happy Warrior" phrase for which Roosevelt got a good deal of notice.

Smith told Flynn that as he was a mere political friend, while Flynn was a close personal friend, he, Flynn, would probably have more effect in persuading Roosevelt to run for governor. Flynn pressed the nomination on Roosevelt in a number of telephone talks to Warm Springs. At first he was adamant against it. But after several talks Flynn began to feel that Roosevelt was weakening. Roosevelt gave as his reason his need to continue for at least another year the Warm Springs treatments to regain the use of his legs. However, in one conversation he said "one of the reasons he could not stand for governor was because he had put a great deal of his personal fortune into Warm Springs, and he felt he should stay and manage the enterprise so that *it would eventually become a paying proposition.*"[29] (Italics supplied.)

The Democratic State Convention was to meet in Rochester on October 1. On September 26, from Milwaukee, Smith telephoned Roosevelt at Warm Springs to emphasize the importance of his candidacy. Smith argued with him. He got the impression Roosevelt was weakening. Finally he said: "If the convention nominates you, will you refuse to run?" Whatever answer Roosevelt made, Smith was convinced he would accept if nominated. When Smith got to Rochester he told the leaders Roosevelt would run.[30] Roosevelt must have had a feeling that he had not been definite about "not accepting" if nominated, because he later sent Smith a wire to Rochester. This Smith got after he reached Rochester and the convention had assembled. It read: "Confirming my telephone message I wish much that I might consider the possibility of running for governor." Roosevelt then gave two reasons why he could not: (1) "Your own record in New York is so clear that you will carry the state no matter who is nominated" and (2) "My doctors are definite that the continued improvement in my condition is dependent on avoidance of a cold climate" and "daily exercise in Warm Springs during the winter months." He added: "As I am only 46 years old I owe it to my family and myself to give the present constant improvement a chance to continue … I must therefore with great regret confirm my decision not to accept the nomination."[31]

Mrs. Roosevelt was in Rochester as a member of the Women's Committee for Al Smith. So were Ed Flynn and John J. Raskob, recently named chairman of the National Democratic Committee to manage Al Smith's campaign for the presidency. The situation was very bad. Roosevelt's wire definitely saying he would not accept restored the bitter split between Tammany and the upstate leaders, who could agree on no other candidate. His telegram seemed final. But Flynn told Smith that he believed Roosevelt could be induced to accept, that his health treatments were not the real reason for his refusal, that the real reason was the financial obligations he had outstanding at Warm Springs, that he was facing a heavy personal loss but that if this could be gotten out of the way he might yield. Smith told Flynn to tell Roosevelt they would take care of his financial problem. "I don't know how the hell we can do it, but we'll do it some way," he said.[32] Flynn suggested that the problem be put up to Raskob. This was done. Smith asked Raskob to telephone Roosevelt. Raskob thought it over but decided to talk to Mrs. Roosevelt about it.

He went to her sitting room in the hotel and told her that Governor Smith wanted him to telephone her husband. He said he felt greatly disturbed about it. Roosevelt had up to now been giving as his reason for refusing the nomination the condition of his health. Now, however, Smith had been told that it was because of the obligations he had at Warm Springs which was in the red and into which he had sunk a good part of his fortune. Raskob told Mrs. Roosevelt that he could not escape the feeling that these financial troubles were not the real reason, that the real reason after all was the advice of his doctors. If that were so Raskob felt he ought not to press her husband to run. If anything were to happen to Roosevelt as a result of a strenuous campaign or the labors of the governorship, perhaps endangering his life, he, Raskob, would feel he was responsible. But if the financial problem was the real reason then he would telephone Roosevelt. He asked Mrs. Roosevelt for her frank opinion. She replied that if her husband were to say his health would permit him to run then Raskob could rely on it and that the real reason was the financial problem at Warm Springs. Everybody got the impression that Mrs. Roosevelt wanted her husband to run.

At Raskob's request, Mrs. Roosevelt then tried to get in touch with her husband. Roosevelt suspected what it was about and tried to duck the call. It was late at night and he was at a picnic at Manchester, not far from Warm Springs, making an address. He went to the telephone only after he got back to Warm Springs. Mrs. Roosevelt put Raskob on the wire. The evidence seems to agree that Smith was there also. Roosevelt explained to Raskob that he had certain obligations in connection with Warm Springs, that they amounted to a great deal of money and that he was planning to launch a drive to raise funds to cover them and that he had to remain on the job at Warm Springs for that purpose. After some discussion, Raskob asked "if these obligations were out of the way" would he feel the road would be clear for him to accept the nomination. Roosevelt answered that he would but that he did not know how they could be taken out of the way. Raskob then asked him to say frankly what they amounted to. Roosevelt replied: "Two hundred and fifty thousand dollars." Raskob then brought the whole matter to a head by saying: "All right. Your nomination is important in New York State. I am in this fight to get rid of Prohibition which I believe to be a terrible social curse and I think the only way to do it is to elect Al Smith. I am willing therefore to underwrite the whole sum of $250,000. You can take the nomination and forget about these obligations. You can have a fund-raising effort and if it falls short of the total I will make up the difference." Roosevelt was a little flabbergasted at this offer. He said he felt it was very generous. Raskob then asked: "Now does this take care of the financial objection and will you run?" Roosevelt replied laughing: "Well, that offer knocks all the props from under me. You can say I will accept the nomination."

That night, immediately after this conversation, Raskob sat down in Al Smith's rooms, wrote out a personal check for $250,000 and mailed it to Roosevelt. The next day, October 2, Roosevelt was nominated for governor and Herbert Lehman for lieutenant-governor. Raskob got no reply to his letter until a week or more later when Roosevelt arrived in New York to arrange for his campaign. Then he met Raskob. After a cordial greeting he took Raskob's check from his pocket and put it on the table in front of Raskob. He said: "I can't take this check, John. You didn't promise to give me the money. All you did was promise to underwrite it and I am satisfied with that."

Shortly after this a committee was formed to raise the fund promised. Will Woodin was made chairman. A meeting of some men of
wealth was called and the whole purpose explained. Raskob subscribed $50,000. Others made subscriptions but the contributions
fell far short of the mark. Subsequently, however, Raskob subscribed
another $50,000, and other wealthy men made large contributions.
The $250,000 was raised and handed over to Roosevelt.[33]

A little history is necessary to complete the full significance of this
story. Merriwether Inn was a large, rambling summer hotel at Warm
Springs, Ga. George Foster Peabody, the philanthropist, had heard
that the warm waters of its springs had a peculiarly beneficial effect
upon infantile paralysis patients. He bought the Springs and later
told Roosevelt he ought to try them. Roosevelt, then eagerly seeking
recovery, visited Warm Springs in 1924. He spent some time there
and repeated his visits for several years and convinced himself that by
swimming in the warm waters of the pool, polio patients had been
aided greatly in regaining at least partial use of their limbs. He
sought some professional advice and then bought the Inn and 1,200
acres from Peabody and converted it into a hospital for polio patients. He believed that polio sufferers would be willing to pay for
these benefits and that the institution could be built up into a paying
proposition. He assumed general direction of the enterprise and in
the course of several years ran it at a heavy loss. He said later he had
sunk a large part of his fortune in it. He may have sunk some, but actually he had incurred heavy debts for which he was responsible. To
whom this money was owed cannot be said with definiteness. But
the obligation was pressing. He was thinking of starting a fund-
raising drive to cover this debt. But as it was really a drive to raise
money to pay himself off, to get him personally out of a hole, it was
not a very easy one to manage. This is why he could not accept the
nomination in New York. Raskob's offer not only made it possible
for him to run, but it bailed him out of a very difficult hole. The
meaning of it all is that Roosevelt did not agree to run for governor
until Raskob guaranteed $250,000 in order to get him out of debt.

After Roosevelt was elected governor many improvements were
made at Warm Springs. But they sprang from the generosity of various private donors. Mr. and Mrs. Edsel Ford built a beautiful glass-
enclosed pool. In 1930 patients raised $40,000 to build a small

infirmary and in 1935 Georgia Hall, the administration building, was erected by contributions from citizens of Georgia. In 1935 two dormitories were built with funds contributed by Samuel Rush and Claude Kress and another hall with funds donated by friends of the builders, Hageman and Harris.[34] The funds raised and turned over to Roosevelt were not used for any of these improvements. Roosevelt never publicly acknowledged the funds given him by Raskob and his associates. Compton Mackenzie and Emil Ludwig, both of whom wrote florid and adulatory biographies of Roosevelt and got most of their material from him, tell of the great Warm Springs enterprise in human welfare but never mention the fact that it was a group of rich men interested in Al Smith who put up the money to pay the debts incurred by Roosevelt in the enterprise.

We may now return to the money-making adventures of the family promoted from the White House. We have seen how Roosevelt lent his aid when Elliott was attempting to get a big loan from two Texas oil men at the moment when the hot oil indictments were pending in Texas. There is, however, a more direct connection between the President and some of Elliott's and Jimmy's commercial designs. In 1939, the late Congressman William I. Sirovich, of New York, telephoned Mr. Carruthers Ewing, the general counsel of the Atlantic and Pacific Tea Company and told him that the President had asked him to help his son Elliott borrow $200,000. At Sirovich's request, Ewing introduced Elliott to John Hartford, head of the A & P Company and Elliott explained to Hartford that he wanted to borrow $200,000 to purchase a new radio station for his Texas network and that the station would soon be worth a million dollars. Hartford was a little disturbed. He told Elliott such a transaction might embarrass his father, the President. At the time, New Deal Congressman Wright Patman was making war on the chain stores and had a plan to tax them in such a way as to hit the A & P a crushing blow. Hartford was just about to launch a big national advertising campaign in an effort to beat these plans. Under the circumstances, therefore, the presence of the President's son had a suspicious aspect.

Elliott took the most direct method of answering Hartford's objection. He picked up the telephone and called his father at the White House and introduced Hartford to him over the phone.

Hartford asked the president if he was familiar with his son's request. The President replied that he knew all about it and that the proposition was a perfectly sound one and that he would appreciate very much whatever Mr. Hartford might do to favor his son. Hartford was very much surprised to be addressed by the President as "John" and to be invited to visit him at the White House, since he had had no personal acquaintance with him before. Hartford sent the check for $200,000 to Elliott next day and got the Texas network stock as collateral. This was certainly an extraordinary performance up to this point—the President intervening to get a loan of $200,000 for his son, whose irregular behavior he was familiar with, from a man neither of them knew and whose firm was under attack by a New Deal congressman at the time. However, the most astonishing part is yet to come.

This loan was made in 1939. By 1942, Hartford had heard nothing from Elliott by way of payment on either principal or interest. He did not expect to, in fact. He figured, as he told a congressional committee, that by making the loan he "was being taken off the hook." However, in 1942 the President sent for Jesse Jones and asked him to try to straighten out Elliott's financial problems. Jones called on Hartford, told him he was acting on behalf of the Roosevelt family and suggested that Hartford accept $4000 in settlement of Elliott's $200,000 note—and of course return the stock. This stock, Jones assured Hartford, was worthless. This is what Jones had been told by the Roosevelts. Hartford accepted the proposal and on receipt of Jones' check for $4000 he returned the Texas network stock. His loss of $196,000 he wrote off in his income tax returns, so that the United States Treasury took the greater part of that loss. It was learned later that the stock was worth around a million dollars. Jones turned it over to the President and he sent it to Elliott's divorced second wife, half for her and half in trust for the children. It is probable that in all the history of the government this was the first time such a trick was turned by an American president and by one who exhibited himself before the people as the most righteous paragon of moral and political excellence that had ever occupied that office.[35]

There was much more to this story. Elliott, piloted by the late Hall Roosevelt, Mrs. Roosevelt's brother, made a loan of $25,000 from Charles Harwood, a New Deal faithful in New York who was ambitious to become a federal judge. He, too, got Texas network stock as collateral. He didn't get the judgeship but he was appointed governor of the Virgin Islands. But unlike Hartford, when Jones offered him $1000 for his note and the stock held as collateral, he observed that it made no difference whether he gambled on a 100 per cent loss or a 96 per cent loss and he held his stock and saved his money. There were three or four other loans which were settled at varying percentages of their face value by Jones at the same time. Altogether, Elliott had some $800,000 of this kind of paper out. The record is long and sordid. Business men were invited to the White House, from which issued so many angry blasts against the corrupt business man. Their names have been published. They were invited to make loans to or take insurance in the enterprises of the President's sons. Some of them had the good sense to refuse.*

---

* The business adventures of the Roosevelt family have been explored with the greatest thoroughness by Westbrook Pegler and the results have appeared in numerous of his syndicated columns. Roosevelt's apologists have tried to dismiss Pegler's charges, not by refuting the facts, but by calling him a Roosevelt-hater. But Pegler cannot be dismissed that way. Those who attempted to do so know little of Pegler or his methods. They are wholly unaware that he is one of the most painstaking and scrupulous reporters writing for American newspapers. No effort is too laborious to discourage his tireless pursuit of facts. He is as far removed from that type of gossip columnist so much courted and extolled by New Deal propagandists as are the two poles. The imputation in the criticism is that Pegler prints these charges against Roosevelt because he hates him. The notion that he hates the Roosevelt clan because he has made these unpleasant discoveries about them does not seem to occur to Pegler's critics. As a matter of fact, Pegler started out in 1932 as a very generous supporter and admirer of the Roosevelts and was often a partaker of Mrs. Roosevelt's hamburger fries at Hyde Park. He was also an earnest supporter of the whole program to aid the Allies. But Pegler, like a good many other men, experienced first a pained sensation of surprise, then of impatience and finally of anger when he discovered that people he had respected had deceived him. No one permits himself such a luxurious sensation of righteous wrath as a New Dealer who discovers a minor city employee or a little business man in some grafting adventure. Pegler thinks himself as much entitled to grow angry at graft when he finds it in the White House as they do when they find it in a courthouse or a city hall. Pegler's charges are endlessly documented with facts—names, dates, sums of money, names of witnesses, official testimony, etc. Pegler would have been in jail or bankrupt long ago if his victims had the slightest reason to suppose they could make good a libel charge in court. Most of the

There was a wide streak of egotism in Roosevelt which made it impossible for him in some circumstances to perceive the fine line that divides correct from improper conduct in public office—particularly in so exalted an office as the presidency. For instance, Roosevelt had been all his life an ardent stamp collector. He had never indulged himself in the more expensive fields of this hobby. An intimate says that he seldom paid more than $10 for a stamp. However, he knew all about the hobby and its business side. When he became President he found himself the actual head of the Post Office and of the Bureau of Printing and Engraving. Very early in the game he got Jim Farley, his Postmaster-General, who knew nothing of this seemingly harmless pastime, to get for him the imperforate first sheets (that is, sheets minus the usual perforations) of a number of new stamp issues. Farley got the sheets, paid face value for them, gave one sheet of each issue to the President, one to Mrs. Roosevelt, one to Louis Howe and a few others.

Shortly after, an authority in the field called on Farley and explained to him that these imperforate sheets were great rarities, because so difficult to get, that they would have immense commercial value and this was an act of dubious ethical value. Farley assured him that the sheets would not get into commerce, that they were merely given to the President for his personal collection, etc. Shortly after a sheet turned up in Virginia. The man who had warned Farley wrote to the owner and asked a price on it. He wanted $20,000. The story leaked into Congress and Huey Long was about to blast Roosevelt when the Post Office Department ordered a large number of the imperforate sheets run off and distributed in order to destroy the scarcity value of the one which had gotten out into trade.

However, the President had enriched his personal collection of stamps upon a very large scale. But this is not all. When a new stamp is made the first proof from the original die has an especially great market value, merely because it is so scarce. After a stamp is issued

---

material printed with reference to Elliott's operations are based on Pegler's extensively documented and particularized reports. Such as I have used I have, for the most part, checked, save such as were so completely proved or admitted to require no further proof.

the design is revised from time to time—a change in the lettering, the insertion of a little flag, a decorative curlycue here or there. The original die proof thus becomes more and more valuable, and in stamp collecting it is the scarcity feature of an article that makes the market value. It was a custom at one time when a new commemorative stamp was issued to permit some person—perhaps the senator or governor of the state involved in the commemoration or some other person connected with it—to have the die proof. But there were some abuses in which others got them. They became very choice articles on the stamp market, worth a great deal of money. Hence when Theodore Roosevelt was President he issued an order forbidding the delivery of these die proofs to any person. When Franklin Roosevelt became President, knowing of the value of these items and being the boss of the Bureau of Printing and Engraving, he issued an order to have delivered to him a large number of die proofs going all the way back to 1896. Under this new rule they could be delivered only to him. These he put into his personal stamp collection. When he died these die proofs alone, the result of this mass raid by the President, sold for $59,000 which went into his estate. The whole stamp collection, including the die proofs and the imperforate sheets, plus his otherwise modest collection, sold for $275,000.[36]

There remains an incident unique in national political history. It is the singular story of the Roosevelt estate and the schemes he personally managed to create a shrine for himself with government money and funds extorted from federal officeholders. So far as I know our political annals reveal no comparable example of personal vanity completely unrestrained by any sense of shame.

Statues are built by the hundreds to all grades of celebrities. But shrines are reserved for those few whose records, strained through the sieve of history, provide the evidences of greatness which merit this extraordinary tribute. In good time the candidate for such honors will have his claim recognized. The greatest of our shrines—Washington's home at Mount Vernon—was restored and is maintained by a private group, the Mt. Vernon Ladies Association. After Jefferson's death, his estate was saved for his heirs by some friends and his home—Monticello—is operated by the Thomas Jefferson Memorial Foundation, a private organization. The State of Illinois provides the funds—about $15,000 a year—for the care of Lincoln's tomb in Springfield. The imposing tomb of Grant was built by popular subscription and is controlled by the Grant Monument Association. The annual expenses are about $15,000 a year—$6000 of which is paid by the City of New York and the balance from the Grant Endowment Fund. Franklin D. Roosevelt took no chances on being neglected. He personally conceived the idea of a shrine for himself, organized and promoted the movement himself and personally pushed it through. And he did this long before the war—before he had been enlarged by events and propaganda for good or evil into a world figure.

The idea took form in Roosevelt's mind in 1938. By this time the depression had returned to his doorstep. Over 11,000,000 people were unemployed. He had just told Henry Morgenthau that the best course for them was to rock along for the next two years on a two or three billion dollar a year deficit and then go out of office, turn the mess over to the Republicans and wait for the people to call them back to power in 1944. It is incredible but true that it was at this moment of frustration he should have cooked up this plan for a national shrine for himself. In its inception it was mixed up with another more pragmatic objective. Roosevelt planned, when he went out of office, to turn to account his name and position to make some money as an author. Roosevelt's idea of authorship was a comfortable one. A staff to do research and a facile penman at his side to do the writing, while his name supplied the money value to what was turned out. We know that shortly after this he began negotiations with *Collier's* Magazine for a $75,000-a-year post writing or sponsoring a weekly column. He now conceived the plan of having built on his Hyde Park estate a library and workshop which he would use as his place of business when he left the White House. The next stage in this scheme was to make it a "memorial library," the funds for which would be put up by the thousands of party workers who held office in his administration. And so it turned out in this first stage—a Franklin D. Roosevelt Memorial Library. He would give the land out of his mother's estate. The Democratic officeholders would pay the bills to build and furnish it. As a "memorial library" it would be exempt from taxation. And there he and his staff would work, as later proposed, for *Collier's* at $75,000 for himself, plus three of four of his staff on the *Collier* payroll. All this was managed by a committee to raise the money and complete the project consisting of his law partner, Basil O'Connor, Joseph Schenck, later sent to jail by the government, Ben Smith, a Wall Street operator and several others. They raised $400,000 from those elements of the "common man" who held Democratic jobs. They spent $300,000 on the building, $15,000 for furniture, $10,000 for cases, $15,000 for administrative expenses.

By the time it was finished the idea had expanded. In July, 1939, Roosevelt deeded 16 acres of the Hyde Park estate on which the Library stood to the government. The United States, through the National Archives, became the owner and *maintainer* of the "library," thus taking that burden off his hands. The "library" was to house his papers and collection of ship models, etc., as well as provide him with a completely free workshop for the rest of his life and become a monument after his death.

If Roosevelt in retreat, harried by the return of the depression in 1938, repudiated by the country on the Court fight and by his party in the purge fight and faced with a grave revolt and split in his party, could envisage himself as the only American president to have a government-built and supported shrine, to what dimensions would the emanations of his ego swell after America got into the war, when, like a Roman emperor, he was throwing around unimaginable billions all over the world, when ministers, kings, dictators and emperors from everywhere were covering him with flattery as they begged millions at his hands? By the end of 1943, flattery, applause, sycophancy had literally rotted the nature of Franklin Roosevelt. In December of that year he decided, like an Egyptian Pharaoh, to transform his home into a great historic shrine—a Yankee pyramid—where his family might live in a kind of imperial dignity, where he might retire if he survived the war as a kind of World Elder Statesman and Dictator Emeritus, and where he would be entombed. In December, 1943, he deeded to the government "as a national historic site" his Hyde Park estate, with the proviso that he and the members of his family would have the right to live in it as long as they lived, provided they paid the state and local taxes while in residence. Secretary Ickes asked Congress for $50,000 a year for maintenance of the estate. An admission fee is now charged and it is estimated that the maintenance cost will be around $100,000 a year.

Thus Roosevelt is not merely the only president whose home and grave are maintained by the government as a national shrine, but the government was doing this even before he passed away and all in accordance with a project he thought up all by himself and put over before he died.

I know the inveterate New Dealer will say: what is the point in raking up all this unpleasant stuff about Roosevelt? What was the point in raking up all that unpleasant stuff about Sheriff Farley, a mere Tammany sheriff, whose modest tin box was used by Roosevelt to preach a sermon on official virtue? Can it be that the performances such as we have beheld in Roosevelt and his family are to be denounced in a mere $60-a-week policeman or an obscure city official but that they are not even to be mentioned with respect to an American President? Can it be that there is a ceiling on public and personal morals and that a president may be permitted to flourish above that ceiling where different rules control? Is there anyone who really believes this? Is there anyone who will insist that there is a point in the salary scale in public life at which the Ten Commandments cease to follow the rising personage; that the Fifth, Sixth and Seventh Commandments drop out of the picture as the officeholder moves let us say from the $10,000 bracket into the $12,000 bracket, or as he moves up through the Cabinet, the Supreme Court and finally to the Presidency. Or can it be that the moral law applies to all presidents save those who love the Common Man or Left-Wing Presidents, while Right-Wing Presidents are still held to old rules.

Roosevelt was built by propaganda, before the war on a small scale and after the war upon an incredible scale, into a wholly fictitious character—a great magnanimous lover of the world, a mighty statesman before whom lesser rulers bowed in humility, a great thinker, a great orator—one of the greatest in history—an enemy of evil in all its forms. In his first administration someone was responsible for a very effective job of selling Roosevelt to the public. His good looks, his purely physical vitality coupled with his physical misfortune, his buoyant spirits which he exhibited profusely, the role he instantly assumed as warm-hearted brother of the needy, the rich enemy of the "malefactors of great wealth" and of course the dispenser of those fabulous billions which Congress had put into his hands—all this, combined with the dramatic performance he put on in the first term, exhibited him before the people in an exceptionally favorable light. People who supposed he wrote his own speeches acclaimed him as a great orator. People who knew nothing of finance and economics extolled him as a great economic statesman. But over and above this some cunning techniques were industriously used to enhance the picture. For instance, Mrs. Roosevelt took over the job of buttering the press and radio reporters and commentators. They were hailed up to Hyde Park for hamburger and hot dog picnics. They went swimming in the pool with the Great Man. They were invited to the White House. And, not to be overlooked, it was the simplest thing in the world for them to find jobs in the New Deal for the members of their families.

After the war in Europe got under way and Roosevelt began to assume the role of friend not merely of the common man but of the whole human race, after he began to finger tens of billions, after he finally put on the shining armor of the plumed knight and lifted his great sword against the forces of evil on the whole planet—then the propaganda took on formidable proportions. The most powerful propaganda agencies yet conceived by mankind are the radio and the moving pictures. Practically all of the radio networks and all of the moving picture companies moved into the great task of pouring upon the minds of the American people daily—indeed hourly, ceaselessly—the story of the greatest American who ever lived, breathing fire and destruction against his critics who were effectually silenced, while filling the pockets of the people with billions of dollars of war money. The radio was busy not only with commentators and news reporters, but with crooners, actors, screen stars, soap opera, black-faced comedians, fan dancers, monologists, putting over on the American mind not only the greatness of our Leader but the infamy of his critics, the nobility of his glamorous objectives and the sinister nature of the scurvy plots of his political enemies. The people were sold first the proposition that Franklin D. Roosevelt was the only man who could keep us out of war; second that he was the only man who could fight successfully the war which he alone could keep us out of; and finally that he was the only man who was capable of facing such leaders as Churchill and Stalin on equal terms and above all the only man who could cope successfully with the ruthless Stalin in the arrangements for the post-war world.

The ordinary man did not realize that Hitler and Mussolini were made to seem as brave, as strong, as wise and noble to the people of Germany and Italy as Roosevelt was seen here. Hitler was not pictured to the people of Germany as he was presented here. He was exhibited in noble proportions and with most of those heroic virtues which were attributed to Roosevelt here and to Mussolini in Italy and, of course, to Stalin in Russia. I do not compare Roosevelt to Hitler. I merely insist that the picture of Roosevelt sold to our people and which still lingers upon the screen of their imaginations was an utterly false picture, was the work of false propaganda and that, among the evils against which America must protect herself one of the most destructive is the evil of modern propaganda techniques applied to the problem of government.

2.

What manner of man, therefore, was this highly advertised and promoted President? To put all the emphasis upon the aspects of his career which make up this chapter is, of course, to exhibit only one side of his character. It gives a picture quite as one-sided as that other picture that has been presented by his promoters. It has been necessary to introduce these other characteristics in order to complete the otherwise distorted portrait that has been given to the world.

Roosevelt, as the world saw him, was a man of unusual personal charm. He was large, broad-shouldered, handsome; he exuded physical vitality and there was a warm, genial, exuberant flow of spirits. There was the suggestion of personal force—a certain positive and resolute manner greatly enhanced by his physical appearance. People liked him quickly. The remote, somewhat lofty bearing of his earlier days had vanished. Amongst people he was easy, gracious, hearty and friendly.

The mind behind this had capacity of a high order. Roosevelt was no man's fool. But, like most men, his abilities were of a special kind and when he operated within the framework of those abilities he was a formidable antagonist. The mistake in appraising him is to picture him as a thinker and student. He was not, for instance, a student of social problems or of economic structure. He was not, as were Madison and Jefferson and Woodrow Wilson, a political philosopher. He had not, like these men, pondered the great problems of social organization and arrived at definite opinions touching their roots or the principles of life and growth in various systems of social government. The principles he had before his election on these subjects were the ones that went along with the faction of the party into which he was born. He accepted them. He did not think about them. And they had no hold upon his mind. If one political policy failed he could cast it off and move over to another without meeting resistance from any underlying philosophy to which he was attached. This is the explanation of the ease with which he could announce a whole collection of policies and plans in his first campaign for the presidency and, immediately after inauguration, toss practically all of it overboard and adopt another set of policies based upon a wholly different theory of government. And when in turn by 1938 all of these had been blown to bits by the inexorable logic of events, he could toss them over and open his mind to that weird collection of theories which the Tugwells and Hansens and Wallaces sold to him. Yet in making these shifts he was doing no violence to any real conviction. He was not being disloyal to any settled belief. He was in fact behaving with complete logical conformance to the one political conviction he held. A policy to Roosevelt was good or bad depending on whether or not it commanded valuable political support among voters. If it brought to his side any numerous group of voters it was a wise policy. If it failed to do this he could reject it or throw it over without doing violence to any controlling central political philosophy.

His abilities lay not in the field of the political philosopher but in the field of the political manager. When, therefore, Roosevelt approached a political policy he did not examine it as a student of the social order, but as a politician bent on winning power. For this reason he could adopt some shallow scheme like the gold purchase plan or the undistributed profits tax or the social security old-age reserve idea after a few moments' inspection. His mind just did not go to work upon the basic soundness of these ideas. But when he was presented with a problem of political management or maneuver his mind would attack it readily and actively. The mind goes into activity readily upon subjects to which it is hospitable, for which it has an affinity and an appetite. High proficiency in any field of human activity depends upon the inherent industry of the mind when dealing with its subject. Roosevelt's mind was busy night and day, incessantly, and profitably, upon one subject—and that was the correct political maneuver in any given situation.

He acquired the reputation of being a great orator. Even his enemies came to believe that Roosevelt could go on the radio and talk the props from under the opposition. That Roosevelt was a tremendously effective radio orator cannot be questioned. However, this must be analyzed. A speech consists in words the orator utters and the uttering of them. The general verdict was that he possessed a golden voice and a seductive and challenging radio technique. The voice, the manner, the delivery were Roosevelt's. But the words were supplied by others. The voice was the voice of Roosevelt; the words were the words of his ghost writers.

Up to the time he ran for the presidency—when he was 50 years old—he had made innumerable speeches. No one ever noticed he was a great speaker and no one remembers a single sentence he uttered save the title of "Happy Warrior" which he bestowed on Smith in a speech written for him by a very brilliant New York judge. However, when he launched his campaign for President he became suddenly a wondrous orator. The explanation, of course, is that he had acquired a group of ghost writers who supplied the ideas, the phrases, wisecracks, fancies and metaphors and he had two or three collaborators who were able to put these into notable English. For his acceptance speech in 1932 at the Chicago convention one speech was written by Ray Moley and one by Louis Howe. Louis was frantically anxious to have his delivered. He had written scores of speeches for Roosevelt. Here was to be his greatest anonymous achievement. When Roosevelt ascended the platform to speak no one knew which draft he would use. In characteristic Rooseveltian manner, he read the first page of Louis Howe's speech and the balance of Ray Moley's. His inaugural address—that really fine oration on the antique model—he delivered with skill and gusto. But he did not write it, in spite of the testimony of Charlie Michaelson that he did. Contributions were made from various hands, but the actual production was the work of Ray Moley, who wrote so many of his other speeches.

Roosevelt had a comfortable ability, after such a performance, of getting around to the belief that he had written these speeches himself. He was particularly fond of "quoting himself" and he went back innumerable times to repeat "what I have said before," namely "that the only thing we have to fear is fear itself." Roosevelt imagined that he had coined that phrase. Who put it in the speech I do not know. It had been said before in those precise words by Thoreau and one of Roosevelt's faithful servitors—Sam Rosenman—had first learned of them in an English class at Columbia conducted by John Erskine. Rosenman was one of the group which helped with that speech.

When Moley broke with Roosevelt he was nursed along for several years after he left the Brain Trust which he had created because he was indispensable in preparing Roosevelt's speeches. Roosevelt did not cut Moley off completely until he felt he had in Tommy Corcoran an able ghost to grind out his immortal utterances. And when, in time, Tommy found himself moving out of the charmed circle, he was kept dangling until Roosevelt found in Robert Sherwood a capable successor ghost.

This subject of the ghostly origin of Roosevelt's great efforts began to disturb him. He grew sensitive about it. And during his second term he began to use a different technique. He would ask a number of men—Tommy Corcoran, Stanley High, Sam Rosenman and others—to submit drafts of speeches or sections dealing with special topics and he would put them all together, inserting a phrase or two here and there. These phrases may be picked out in many speeches and the differing styles may be detected. Roosevelt could, of course, write a speech but it would always be a commonplace performance. He could stand before an audience and make a speech, but it would be a distinctly unimpressive affair. His speeches have been edited and published in eight large volumes, with elaborate footnotes supposed to have been written by him but actually written by someone else—another ghost. One may run through these volumes and pick out the speeches for which Roosevelt himself was responsible. One of the most trustworthy of the stigmata is the number of times the paragraphs begin with the letter I. Incidentally, he was paid $38,000 by a newspaper for serializing the first batch of his public papers and addresses—something quite new in presidents—after which they were published in book form—five volumes—at $15 a set.

This whole business of ghost-writing speeches is one for which perhaps, some sort of political professional code should be enforced. Many public men who are capable of writing speeches of a high order sometimes are compelled by the press of events to have some competent ghost writer put into form his ideas simply because he cannot get the time to do it himself. This, however, is very different from the practice of a man like Roosevelt who habitually had his speeches prepared for him by a corps of ghosts led by some capable master ghost who puts it in its final order, after which Roosevelt passed it off on the world as his own and as an example of his own great prowess in the field of oratory. One cannot imagine Webster or Clay, Jefferson or Madison or Monroe, Lincoln or Cleveland or Bryan or Theodore Roosevelt or Taft or Woodrow Wilson or Herbert Hoover having their speeches written for them and masquerading in another man's eloquence as a great orator.

The most difficult feature of the Roosevelt character to fit into the picture is his loose code in respect to the financial affairs of himself and his family. There is nothing like it in the history of the White House. There had been some lamentable looseness under Grant but he and his family were not involved and he was completely the victim of these transactions. There was some under Harding, but here again it did not touch the White House or its family occupants. It is a strange fact that this rash of financial exploitation of the White House by the President and his family appeared in the administration of one of its richest tenants and one who had been most extensively advertised as one of its noblest tenants.

It was this peculiar strain in the man which led some of his intimates to say he was a complex character. There was really nothing complex about Roosevelt. He was of a well-known type found in every city and state in political life. He is the well-born, rich gentleman with a taste for public life, its importance and honors, who finds for himself a post in the most corrupt political machines, utters in campaigns and interviews the most pious platitudes about public virtue while getting his own dividends out of public corruption one way or another. In any case, they are a type in which the loftiest sentiments and pretensions are combined with a rather low-grade political conscience.

In the case of Roosevelt, with his somewhat easy approach to official virtue, his weakness for snap judgments, his impulsive starts in unconsidered directions, his vanity, his lack of a settled political philosophy, his appetite for political power and his great capacity as a mere politician, the Presidency became in his hands an instrument of appalling consequences. The combination of qualities named above exposed him, when vast power came into his hands, to the corrosive influence of that power. An act of which he did not approve at first, that put three billion dollars into his hands to be expended at his sweet will, brought from every town and county hosts of suitors for his bounty, bowing and scraping before him, applauding and cheering him until it all went to his head. Little by little a nature not greatly unlike many well-considered public men of his type, disintegrated, until power corrupted him. In the end it corrupted him utterly. His career proved again what history had already abundantly taught us and what our forefathers knew so well when they fashioned this government, that power seldom expands and purifies the nobler parts of a man's nature but that it acts like a powerful drug upon the baser elements.

Chapter 4: Toward the Precipice

I.

As the year 1941 dawned, the experiments of Roosevelt had been under observation for eight years. There can be no dispute as to the commission he held from the people. He was not elected to substitute a new system of government and economy, to set up a socialist or fascist or communist system or any form of state-planned capitalism. His promise was to restore conditions under which the American system of free representative government and the free system of private enterprise could function at its highest efficiency.

The word "business" is well understood by our people. It refers to that collection of great and small enterprises which produce goods and services for the population. It does two things. It produces our food, our clothes, our luxuries and necessities; it provides, also, the jobs by which the people earn the income with which they can purchase these things. As Roosevelt came into power one might have supposed that business was some gigantic criminal conspiracy against the welfare of the nation. He began with a sweeping attack upon business and he kept it up until the war. Even during the war, in such moments as he could give to the subject, he was making plans for further assaults upon business.

What the nation needed when he took office was more jobs—jobs at machines, in shops, in mines and stores creating and distributing goods that were needed and providing wages and profits with which these goods could be purchased. If there are to be jobs for all they must be jobs producing something—materials or services.

The clear call of duty to him was to lend the powers of government by all means to improving conditions favorable to business. Those familiar with the subject of the economic organism at that time understood what everyone seems to understand now, that business cannot function at full measure unless there is a steady flow of savings into new investment. New investment means the flow of money into the establishment of new industries and the expansion of old ones. It means putting up houses and buildings, producing and installing new machines and tools. It means organizing new companies or partnerships, subscribing to new corporate shares and for this purpose borrowing funds from investors or from investing institutions like banks and trust companies. All this had slowed up around 1929, causing the depression. It was a typical capitalist-system depression, but one which was deepened (1) by the existence of so many shaky banks whose failure contributed to the general fear, (2) by the incidence of depression all over Europe which cut deeply into our foreign trade. Another factor arose out of a situation where President Hoover in 1930 was confronted by a Democratic House that was more interested in discrediting him than in cooperating with him to end the depression.

As we have seen, Roosevelt instead of aiding in checking the great banking crisis was determined to see it roll on to the lowest point with all the banks closed. We have seen that after that he took no interest in any sort of banking reform and that whatever was done was done without his aid or against his opposition. It was essential that he do everything in his power to reestablish confidence in our economic system. Instead he carried on a ceaseless bombardment of it, continued to browbeat it, to denounce it, to warn people against it, and to subject it to a dozen crack-brained, semi-revolutionary schemes, including deficit financing, inflation, utopian panaceas and the everlasting preachment that profit was evil, investors parasites and business men scoundrels.

The simple truth is that private business never did recover—and that must be the supreme test. Public spending and rising public debt kept the frightened and harried business machine going at a halting gait. But it never went back into full production and by 1938, despite all the spending, faltered again and sank back into a full depression. Roosevelt had launched a dozen theatrical projects like the NRA, the AAA, the CCC, the PWA, the WPA and other gaudy and giddy adventures in boondoggling without ever touching the real trouble and in the end, by 1938, he was back almost from where he started, plus a federal debt that had doubled.

Through all this, however, one pattern ran, because it fell in perfectly with the natural bent of the President's mind. This consisted in persistent pressure for changing the structure of the government by enlarging the powers of the President. It consisted in the gradual use of one technique after another to increase the powers of the federal government at the expense of the states and, in the federal government itself, of enlarging the powers of the presidency at the expense of the Congress and the courts.

The first of these devices was the use of blank-check appropriations and blank-check legislation. Under our system, Congress holds the purse strings. If the President wanted to spend money he had to ask Congress for it specifically. If a congressman or senator wanted something for his district or state he had to introduce a bill to authorize it and appropriate the money to pay the bills. But early in Roosevelt's first term the NRA Act provided an appropriation of $3,300,000,000 which the President was given to be spent for relief and recovery at his own discretion. He now had in his hands a sum of money equal to as much as the government had spent in ten years outside the ordinary expenses of government. He decided how it should be spent and where. If a congressman or senator wanted an appropriation for his district, instead of introducing a bill in Congress, he went up to the White House with his hat in his hands and asked the President for it. All over the country, states, cities, counties, business organizations, institutions of all sorts wanted projects of all kinds. Instead of going to Congress they went to the President. After that congressmen had to play along with the President or they got very little or nothing for their districts. This was the secret of the President's power, but it was also a tremendous blow at a very fundamental principle of our government which is designed to preserve the independence of the Congress from the Executive.

In the same way, blank-check legislation led to the subservience of Congress and the rise of the bureaucracy. Under our traditional system, Congress alone could pass laws. The executive bureau merely enforced the law. But now Congress began to pass laws that created large bureaus and empowered those bureaus to make "regulations" or "directives" within a wide area of authority. Under a law like that the bureau became a quasi-legislative body authorized by Congress to make regulations which had the effect of law. This practice grew until Washington was filled with a vast array of bureaus that were making laws, enforcing them and actually interpreting them through courts set up within the bureaus, literally abolishing on a large scale within that area the distinction between executive, legislative and judicial processes.

As the war effort got under way these bureaus grew in number until they sprawled all over Washington and into adjacent cities. Washington could not hold the bureaus or house the bureaucrats.*

---

*The following is a partial list of New Deal bureaus compiled by Mr. E. M. Biggers of Houston, Texas:

FWA	Federal Works Agency	FDIC	Federal Deposit Insurance Corporation
NRA	National Recovery Administration	FSA	Federal Securities Administration
USMC	United States Maritime Commission	NLRB	National Labor Relations Board
HOLC	Home Owners Loan Corporation	NHPC	National Historical Publications Commission
AAA	Agricultural Adjustment Administration	NMB	National Mediation Board
CCC	Civilian Conservation Corps	USHA	United States Housing Authority
NYA	National Youth Administration	USES	United States Employment Service
SSB	Social Security Board	FIC	Federal Insurance Corporation
BWC	Board of War Communications	CWA	Civil Works Administration
		RA	Resettlement Administration

FPHA	Federal Public Housing Authority	CEA	Commodity Exchange Administration
FHA	Federal Housing Administration	SMA	Surplus Marketing Administration
CCC	Commodity Credit Corporation	FSCC	Federal Surplus Commodity Corporation
FCIC	Federal Crop Insurance Corporation	FFC	Foreign Funds Control
FSA	Farm Security Administration	PRP	Production Requirements Plan
SCS	Soil Conservation Service	CRMB	Combined Raw Materials Board
AMA	Agricultural Marketing Administration	CMB	Combined Munitions Board
FREB	Federal Real Estate Board	CSAB	Combined Shipping Adjustment Board
CES	Committee on Economic Security	CPRB	Combined Production and Resources Board
WPA	Works Progress Administration	CCS	Combined Chiefs of Staff
FCC	Federal Communications Commission	PWA	Public Works Administration
OBCCC	Office of Bituminous Coal Consumers Council	AOA	Administration of Operation Activities
RRB	Railroad Retirement Board	EIBW	Export-Import Bank of Washington
SEC	Securities and Exchange Commission	EHFA	Electric Home and Farm Authority
TVA	Tennessee Valley Authority		
BIR-T	Board of Investigation and Research-Transportation	CPA	Council of Personnel Administration
CAA	Civil Aeronautics Authority	PRA	Public Roads Administration
NIC	National Investors Council		
DPC	Defense Plant Corporation	EPCA	Emergency Price Control Act
RRC	Rubber Reserve Company		
MRC	Metals Reserve Company	FPA	Food Production Administration
DSC	Defense Supplies Corporation	OES	Office of Economic Stabilization
WDC	War Damage Corporation		
DLC	Disaster Loan Corporation	PAW	Petroleum Administration for War
FNMA	Federal National Mortgage Association	SWPC	Small War Plants Corporation
RACC	Regional Agricultural Credit Corporation	PIWC	Petroleum Industry War Council
CFB	Combined Food Board	NRPB	National Resources Planning Board
UNRRA	United Nations Relief & Rehabilitation Administration	LOPM	Liaison Office for Personnel Management

OEM	Office of Emergency Management	NHA	National Housing Authority
SSS	Selective Service System	FCA	Farm Credit Administration
NWLB	National War Labor Board		
OCD	Office of Civilian Defense	REA	Rural Electrification Administration
OCIAA	Office of Coordinator of Inter-American Affairs	SA	Sugar Agency
ODHWS	Office of Defense and Health Welfare Services	PCD	Petroleum Conservation Division
ODT	Office of Defense Transportation	OPCW	Office of Petroleum Coordinator for War
OLLA	Office of Lend-Lease Administration	WEPL	War Emergency Pipe Lines, Inc.
OSRD	Office of Scientific Research and Development	BCD	Bituminous Coal Division
		PRRA	Puerto Rico Reconstruction Administration
OWI	Office of War Information		
WMC	War Manpower Commission	BPA	Bonneville Power Administration
WPB	War Production Board	NPPC	National Power Policy Committee
WRA	War Relocation Authority		
WSA	War Shipping Administration	OC	Office of Censorship
		FRC	Facilities Review Committee
OPA	Office of Price Administration	PWRCB	President's War Relief Control Board
BEW	Board of Economic Warfare		

Many of these bureaus were never even authorized by Congress. Even the Comptroller-General of the United States, who audits the government's accounts, declared he had never heard of some of them. They were created by a new method which Roosevelt exploited. Instead of asking Congress to pass a law, set up a bureau and appropriate money, the President merely named a group of men who were authorized by him to organize a corporation under the laws of the states. This done, there was a government corporation instead of a bureau and a group of corporation directors instead of commissioners. The Reconstruction Finance Corporation was given a blanket appropriation by Congress and authority to borrow money. It borrowed twenty or more billions. The RFC would buy the stock of a new corporation and lend it money—ten, fifty or a hundred million, billions in some cases. Thus the President bypassed Congress and the Constitution and engaged in activities as completely unconstitutional as the imagination can conceive, such as operating business enterprises in Mexico and Canada. By means of the blank-check appropriations, the blank-check legislation and the government corporation, there is no power forbidden to the government by the Constitution which it cannot successfully seize. And if these techniques are permitted to continue the Constitution will be destroyed and our system of government changed utterly without a vote of the people or any amendment to the Constitution. Roosevelt, by his various hit or miss experiments all designed to get power into his hands, prepared a perfect blueprint for some future dictator of the modern school to usurp without very much difficulty all the powers he needs to operate a first-class despotism in America.

However, the crash of war in Europe changed the President's whole outlook. As he confronted his own depression in 1938 he had but one weapon to use against it—to increase the volume of public spending. But as he confessed, the great problem was to find projects upon which the federal government could spend. Hitler's attack on Czechoslovakia provided the President with an easy means of spending with general consent—national defense. And the attack on Poland in September, 1939 and the blazing up of a full-scale European war between Hitler and Russia on one side and all western Europe on the other put in the President's hands all the objects of spending he needed.

But the war did more than this. It took possession of his mind and his imagination. He who had set up as the indispensable savior of America, now saw before him a new and greater role. In spite of his tragic failure in America he now took upon himself the role of savior of the world. Gone were the woes of America and her problems. War spending would take care of that. Out of his mind flew all those mean and petty problems of the farm and the shop and of taxes and debt. Before him opened the glorious vista of war. Here was not merely escape, but glorious, magnificent escape from all the insoluble problems of America and he strode forward not like a man running away from the falling fragments of his shattered temple but as one going to a festival.

2.

Should America have embroiled herself in the European war? There were many men eminent in public life who believed that the United States should go swiftly to the aid of the allied nations, even at the risk of being drawn into the war. There were others who felt we should aid the allies but very definitely "short of war." There were others who opposed aiding the allies "short of war" because they believed that would lead us into the war. These, generally, were the three great groupings of the population when Germany struck at Poland. Into this problem I will not enter here. I will assume that all the groups were moved by perfectly honest motives and sentiments. And I shall not undertake to say which group was right. That in itself becomes a question of enormous proportions and cannot be dealt with here.

But the behavior of Roosevelt in this crisis and the manner in which he dealt with the American people is a proper subject. It is a fact that in September, 1939, the nation was overwhelmingly for staying out of the war. Here was the situation that Roosevelt had described in his speech at Chautauqua in 1936. He had talked about the Americans who "seeking immediate riches, fool's gold" would attempt to break down our neutrality. He warned it would be hard for Americans to look beyond "to the inevitable day of penalties." And he warned that peace would depend on the day-to-day decisions of the President and the Secretary of State. "We can keep out of war," he said, "if those who watch and desire have a sufficiently detailed understanding of international affairs to make certain that the small decisions of today do not lead toward war."

The President knew the people did not wish to go into the war. He therefore took his position as the leader of those who wanted to stay out of the war—and the Gallup Poll showed 83 per cent felt that way. But as the leader of those who wished to stay out, he asked Congress "to break down the Neutrality Act" by authorizing arms traffic with Britain and France. The President told the people if they would follow his lead we would stay out of war. Early in 1940 he made the next decision—to give to Britain over a million rifles from the supplies of the American army. Then he spoke of aid "short of war." The third step was conscription. The army asked for 500,000 men. The President insisted on 1,500,000. Army authorities said the only use for an army of that size was for overseas operations.

Next the President began to give out statements from the White House about submarines being found off our coasts. In a speech he told how German bombers could fly to Greenland and from there bomb Omaha. He declared that if Hitler defeated England we would lose our independence and our liberties. He declared that "we were next on Hitler's list."

Having changed the Neutrality Act, given a million army rifles to England and increased the army to 1,500,000, the President took the next step—he handed over to Britain 50 destroyers belonging to the American navy without authority of Congress. Those men and women who formed the various committees to induce this country to go into the war approved these moves. They were honest about it and logical, because they were saying openly we should give every aid, even at the risk of war. But the President was saying he was opposed to going to war and that he was doing these things to stay out of war. I do not here criticize his doing these things. I criticize the reason he gave, which was the very opposite of the truth. At the time he did these things, 83 per cent of the people month after month were registering their opposition to getting in the war.

After the 1940 election, in fact early in 1941, the President's next decision was the Lend-Lease proposal. Senator Burton K. Wheeler declared that this was a measure to enable the President to fight an undeclared war on Germany. The President angrily denied that. After the bill passed, Mr. Herbert Agar, one of the leaders of the Committee to Defend America by Aiding the Allies, made a speech at Boston. Mr. Agar was then very close to the President. But he did not like the line the President was taking before the American people. He said: "There has been too much lying by the supporters of the Lend-Lease bill in the United States Senate and the press. As one who has taken a leading part in supporting the bill I prefer Senator Wheeler's analysis of it." Senator Wheeler had denounced the measure as one not to keep America out of the war but "a bill to enable the President to fight an undeclared war on Germany." "That," said Mr. Agar, "is precisely what it is ... Our side kept saying that this is a bill to keep America out of war. That's bunk."[37]

The question arose during the debate: How will we get the arms to Britain? Critics of the President said the next step would have to be convoys to see the arms delivered safely. The President denounced this and said he was opposed to convoys. "Convoys," he had declared, "mean shooting and shooting means war." Yet at that very moment, almost while these words were on his lips, he began convoying.

The truth is that the President had made up his mind to go into the war as early as October, 1940. To believe differently is to write him, our naval chiefs of staff and all our high military and naval officers down as fools. In the First World War it took a gigantic effort to defeat Germany. Then Britain had a million men in France. France had three million in arms. Italy and Russia were our allies. So was Japan. Italy had a million men against Germany, and Russia had four million. Yet with all this Germany was never driven out of France. She surrendered while in possession of most of what she had conquered. Does anyone believe that Roosevelt or General Marshall or any other high military leader thought that England fighting alone could drive Hitler's armies out of France? England did not have a soldier in France. France was prostrate. Her arms factories were in Hitler's possession. Italy was against us rather than for us. So was Japan. The President knew that to drive Hitler out of France it would be necessary to send American armies to France and to send the American navy full blast into the war. And he knew this in October, 1940.

The first evidence that he intended to go into the war came on October 10, when Secretary Knox sent for Admiral J. O. Richardson, commander-in-chief of the American Fleet in the Pacific. Knox told Richardson that the President wanted him to establish a patrol of the Pacific—a wall of American naval vessels stretched across the western Pacific in such a way as to make it impossible for Japan to reach any of her sources of supply; a blockade of Japan to prevent by force her use of any part of the Pacific Ocean. Richardson protested vigorously. He said that would be an act of war and besides we would lose our navy.[38] Of course Roosevelt had to abandon it. The President wanted that done as early as October 10, though of course the public knew nothing of this. Yet three weeks later he said in a speech at Boston: "I say to you fathers and mothers and I will say it again and again and again. Your boys will not be sent into foreign wars."

As soon as the Lend-Lease bill was passed he began, without admitting it, to convoy British and American ships loaded with arms to England. And as he had said "Convoys mean shooting and shooting means war," the shooting began and we were to all intents and purposes at war, American vessels actually going with British vessels in pursuit of German submarines.[39]

In January, 1941, while the Lend-Lease bill was being debated, a commission of high American and British army and naval officers representing the respective chiefs of staffs were secretly in session in Washington preparing a document which declared its purpose to be: "To determine the best methods by which the armed forces of the United States and the British Commonwealth with their allies could defeat Germany and her allies, should the United States be compelled to resort to war." Then followed the whole plan of war. This was signed March 29, 1941. Immediately a similar group of American and British naval and army officers met at Singapore to fill in the details of the joint war in the Pacific. The object of this plan is stated on the document "To defeat Germany and her ally Japan in the Far East." The part for the navy in this war plan was set out in full and was called the Rainbow Plan. This is the plan which Admiral Kimmel was ordered to put into effect in the event war started. All this was from a year to eight months before Pearl Harbor.[40]

The whole point I am trying to make clear here is not a criticism of those who believed this country should go into the war. They affirmed this openly and frankly. The President, however, declared he was for those who wanted to stay out of the war while he secretly decided to go into the war, and his public avowals were the precise opposite of his secret intentions. He did not tell the truth to the American people and from the beginning to the end pursued a course of deliberate deception of them about his plans.

When these criticisms of him were made at the time, those who made them were denounced as fascists and Hitler-lovers. But now a new kind of apology appears. Professor Thomas A. Bailey, in his recent book "The Man in the Street," writes:

> "Roosevelt repeatedly deceived the American people during the period before Pearl Harbor ... He was faced with a terrible dilemma. If he let the people slumber in a fog of isolation, they might well fall prey to Hitler. If he came out unequivocally for intervention, he would be defeated in 1940."[41]

This is written not by a critic of Mr. Roosevelt but by a defender. And Mr. Arthur M. Schlesinger, Jr., professor of history at Harvard, a most industrious champion of Mr. Roosevelt, approves this statement and adds as a comment that "If he (Roosevelt) was going to induce the people to move at all, Professor Bailey concludes, he

(Roosevelt) had no choice but to trick them into acting for what he conceived to be their best interests."[42] I am sure that Machiavelli could do no better than this. It is this teaching of the Florentine philosopher that caught the fancy of Mussolini and brought him to the feet of Machiavelli as to an altar. At least this leaves no further question about Roosevelt's settled policy of mendacity. Whoever wishes now to say, as Herbert Agar said, that Roosevelt lied to the people about the maneuvers he was employing to lead them into war may do so without contradiction. The answer must be that Roosevelt lied to the people for their own good. And if Roosevelt had the right to do this, to whom is the right denied? At what point are we to cease to demand that our leaders deal honestly and truthfully with us?

If there be anything to this view it is high time someone set about reducing to form what might be called the moral basis of political lying. If we are to believe the memoirs of some of Mr. Roosevelt's colleagues, he did not feel limited in the use of this "moral" lie merely when dealing with the people. He felt justified in employing this useful weapon in dealing with his cabinet officers, as well as with his own Democratic organization. Upon other occasions he turned to this same new ethical device when seeking to extract $200,000 out of John Hartford for his son Elliott and later in getting back from him for a mere $4000 the stock on which he had loaned $200,000. There must be a thorough philosophical inquiry into the limits within which this convenient discursive weapon can be used. It has been generally supposed that our diplomats are free to lie to foreign diplomats, also that in war and on the way into war we are free to lie *ad libitum* to the enemy. The right of the President—and maybe certain lesser dignitaries—to lie to our own people and, perhaps, in certain defined situations, to each other ought to be explored and settled. Thus it may be used impartially by the representatives of all parties. It does not seem fair to limit the right of lying only to good and truthful men.

Chapter 5: The Atlantic Charter

The next chapter of this story of America's march into war came on the morning of August 15, 1941. The headlines in the morning newspapers told that Roosevelt and Churchill had met at sea in Placentia Bay off the coast of Newfoundland—the President on the *Augusta*, the Prime Minister on the *Prince of Wales*, surrounded on deck by a numerous entourage of the highest ranking military and naval dignitaries of both countries and in the sea by an imposing fleet and with a sky full of protecting war planes. When it ended the President and the Prime Minister issued what they called a Joint Declaration. The most important parts of that document were the first three paragraphs:

"First, their countries seek no aggrandizement, territorial or otherwise.

"Second, they desire to see no territorial changes that do not accord with the freely expressed desires of the peoples concerned.

"Third, they respect the right of all peoples to choose the form of government under which they will live and they wish to see sovereign rights and self-government restored to those who have been forcibly deprived of them."

There were other clauses—to open to all, victor and vanquished alike, access to the raw materials and trade of the world, to promote the fullest collaboration of all peoples for improved economic conditions; a peace in which all men may dwell in safety; the freedom of the seas to all and the abandonment of the use of force as an instrument of national defense.

The theatrical setting of this conference had been a pet idea of Roosevelt's for some time. At different times he had considered different persons as part of the cast. His first candidate for a great sea conference, before the European war began, was Hitler. There was no reason for meeting at sea save the purely spectacular features which Roosevelt always loved. The dramatic effect of the meeting was very great. It made a thunderous radio story and massive headlines. But, as was so characteristic of Roosevelt, the great declaration of principles was a mere incident of the meeting. The purpose was wholly military. Having made up his mind to take America into the war when that was possible, having formulated with the British military and naval chiefs a full program of action when the moment arrived to strike, there remained some grave matters to be settled. We now know from Mr. Sumner Welles' memoranda, which are part of an official record, what happened. Churchill did not think the Singapore agreements went far enough. When the two men met Churchill brought up three matters.

First, he confided to Roosevelt a startling piece of news, namely that England's position at Gibraltar was becoming precarious. The British staff expected Hitler to occupy Spain within 30 days. If that happened the British would have to evacuate Gibraltar. They would, therefore, have to take over the Canary Islands to protect their gateway to the Mediterranean. These belonged to Spain and the British navy believed the operation would call for an immense force. This would make it impossible for England any longer to guarantee to Portugal the protection of the Azores Islands. Churchill had therefore suggested to the Portuguese Premier that he request Roosevelt to take over England's commitment to protect the Azores. And a letter from the Portuguese Minister, Dr. Salazar, was already in Roosevelt's hands. The Azores are off the coast of Spain. Roosevelt very promptly agreed to undertake this commitment.

Churchill next discussed the situation in the Pacific. Japan had seized Indo-China; Churchill did not want her to advance further lest she menace Singapore and he asked the President to issue a warning to Japan. Roosevelt agreed to do so in the following words:

> "If the Japanese government undertakes any further steps in pursuance of the policy of military domination through force or conquest in the Pacific region upon which it has apparently embarked, the Government of the United States will be forced to take immediately any and all steps of whatsoever character it deems necessary in its own security, notwithstanding the possibility that such further steps may result in conflict between the two countries."

Cordell Hull, in his memoirs, said this amounted to an ultimatum to Japan and that he was shocked when he saw it. The President, on his return to Washington, immediately delivered the warning to the Japanese ambassador, but at Hull's insistence it was somewhat watered down in diplomatic language—but, according to Sumner Welles, the meaning was unchanged.

Churchill then brought up the final problem: they would have to give the press an explanation of what they had been conferring about. The President suggested that he could not reveal the commitments he had made. Churchill objected strongly to this. He wanted to stimulate the courage of the British and of the peoples of the occupied countries, who would be profoundly depressed if told that America had made no commitments.

It was finally agreed that they would make no mention of the commitments; instead, they would merely say that they had discussed aid as authorized under the Lend-Lease Act to the nations resisting aggression and follow this with an announcement of principles on which they based their hopes for a better world. This pleased Roosevelt. When he got home and was asked point-blank at a conference with his own Congressional leaders whether or not he had made any commitments he replied "No." He dared not admit that he had made two grave commitments, one to send American troops into a European island where an attack was expected and the other to issue to Japan what the Secretary of State characterized as an ultimatum. This denial was to his own leaders. On the other hand, Churchill felt at liberty when he got home to create the impression that they had done plenty at that meeting. He made that magnificent speech in the Commons, in the finest manner of that historic body, in which he carefully created the expectation that the vast power of America was at last about to be used—though he did not say so outright.[43]

When the statement was published it was headed "A Joint Declaration." Next day in the New York *Times* it was referred to in a headline as "America's Mein Kampf." But after a few more days the name "Atlantic Charter" was given to it in the newspapers. And when the United States entered the war the noble principles enunciated were accepted as a guarantee of the allies' conduct to all the occupied countries. On the day of Pearl Harbor, the countries occupied by Germany or the Axis powers were France, Belgium, Holland, Norway, the Baltic states, Poland, Czechoslovakia and the Balkan states (Rumania, Bulgaria, Yugoslavia, Hungary and Greece) and, of course, China.

Three weeks after Pearl Harbor, Roosevelt sent for all the representatives in America of these occupied countries and said to them:

"Be assured, gentlemen, that the restoration of the countries occupied by Germany and suffering under the Axis yoke is my greatest concern, which is shared in like degree by Mr. Churchill. We promise that all will be done to insure the independence of these countries."

Churchill was present. He turned to the Polish Ambassador and said:

"We will never forget what glorious Poland has done and is doing nor what heroic Greece and Holland have done in this war. I hope I need not add that Great Britain has set herself the aim of restoring full independence and freedom to the nations that have been overrun by Hitler."[44]

These reassurances were to be repeated many times with varying oratorical flourishes. And as for the "Atlantic Charter," which was nothing more than a screen to hide what had actually been done at Placentia Bay, a handsome copy of it was made, bearing the names of Churchill and Roosevelt, and placed on exhibition in the National Museum in Washington, where crowds viewed it with reverence as one of the great documents of history.

The final chapter in the history of this "document" would come three years later.

Chapter 6: A Boondoggler's Dream

This country went formally into the war on December 7, 1941 when the Japanese struck at Pearl Harbor. The President could not, without Congress, launch an attack. He knew that if he asked Congress for a declaration of war he would not get it. The week before Pearl Harbor, the polls still showed 75 per cent of the people against going into the war. But the President was committed to war. And he had been carrying on an undeclared war for many months. The events leading to Pearl Harbor have been extensively investigated, though there is yet much to be obtained. This much has been established completely and that is that the President and his war cabinet knew an attack was coming. That they knew the attack was coming at Pearl Harbor has since been amply proved by Admiral

Robert A. Theobald and others. The President had told the Japanese that if they made any further move in the Pacific the United States would have to act. The move expected was against the Kra Peninsula or perhaps Singapore itself, the Dutch East Indies or the Philippines. On November 27, just ten days before the attack, the President told Secretary Stimson, who wrote it in his diary, that our course was to maneuver the Japanese into attacking us. This would put us into the war and solve his problem. The attack did put us into the war. It did solve Roosevelt's problem. It was a costly solution. But it got him out of a difficult hole and into the one he maneuvered to get into—the war.

Of course, after the attack the nation was united behind the government. The conduct of the war covered a number of separate areas. There was the war at sea and the war on land. The whole story of how this was managed cannot be told in detail yet and when all the official data is available the task will be an immense one and wholly outside the competence of this writer. I shall not, therefore, deal with any portion of it.

Another sector included the direction of the great task of producing the arms and all the auxiliary material needed by our own forces and our allies. This is another subject which remains only partially told. Adequate material to tell it authentically will not be available until the records of the government are opened on a far more complete basis. I do not feel the time has yet come for this task.

There are, however, two other sectors of the war which can be told with reasonable fullness. One has to do with the management of the civilian population and certain other economic factors not directly connected with the fighting or the production line. The other has to do with the settlements that came out of the war so far as our allies and the peace of the world are concerned. These are subjects which fell under the hand of the civilian managers and were influenced more directly by the President. The first of these to claim our attention came under the supervision of the Vice-President of the United States, Mr. Henry Wallace.

The problem of raw materials was a grave one. We had to conserve those we had here and we had to be sure to get our share and more of those from other parts of the world where Germany and Japan were also competing for them. The Board of Economic Warfare was created to control the export of all materials seeking private export and to look after the procurement of all materials essential to the war effort, except arms and munitions. Vice-President Wallace was named chairman of the Board of Economic Warfare (BEW). Several cabinet members were also members, but Mr. Wallace ran it with little interference from them.

There was an element of "cloak-and-dagger" in this institution. It was at war with Hitler and Hirohito in the markets of the world. It bought things we needed. But it also bought, where necessary, things we did not need in order to preclude the enemy getting them. This was called "preclusive" buying. It issued thousands of export licenses every day. It was quite a bureau and it bulged with bureaucrats. At the top, next to Wallace, was a somewhat cheaper edition of Wallace—an authentic New Deal bureaucrat, if there ever was one. He was Milo Perkins, executive director.

Perkins was born in the West but went to Houston, Texas when his father inherited a ranch there and failed to make a go of it. Young Milo skipped college and became a burlap bag salesman. Bags were a scarce article in World War I and Milo made $100 a day selling them. After the war he established his own burlap bag business with a partner. It nearly foundered during the depression but pulled through and Perkins claimed he was making $20,000 a year when Wallace became Secretary of Agriculture. Perkins was a man with a soul—one of those souls that keeps making a lot of noise inside his body. He went in for art and music and finally Theosophy. The *New Republic* said of him that "for nine years at nine every Sunday morning, he donned his priestly robes, took along his sons as acolytes and preached to a congregation of fifty people."[45] Of course he was a vegetarian, abjured alcohol and hated tobacco.

In 1934 he broke into print in the *Nation*. He uttered a clarion cry: "Grab the Torch! Men of Means, Grab the Torch!" He wanted them to grab a plan for a 30-hour week and 25 per cent wage boost. Then he wrote to Wallace. He told Wallace that "from childhood I have wanted to live in a world I could lift." As Wallace was always in the market for planetary jugglers this was his man and in very short order he found himself in Wallace's department lifting $5600 a year salary—not much, however, for a $20,000-a-year bag salesman—and before long he got a $3,000,000 loan for one of Tugwell's whacky

Resettlement homesteads to build a hosiery mill where the tenants could work in the Factories of the Lord, "splitting the profits from the mills between the people and the management." Only they never got around to splitting anything. He moved into various Wallacian activities and finally into the BEW carrying on "the war behind the war" where, according to the *New Republic*, he would find "the elbow room he needed to put his ideas into practice." Little things like "full-blast production" and "abundance for everybody" and "jobs for all" were simple matters to Perkins. The *New Republic* quotes him as saying: "Some people ask how are you going to do all this?" But, says Perkins: "Actually only the timid ask the question. The only problem is 'Which method to use.'" Perkins knew a lot of ways of doing it. He said: "The 'How' people are afraid of the future. The 'Which' people welcome it." Perkins was a real Which man.

By 1943 the BEW had 200 economic commandoes in the field fighting Hitler in the market places of the world and around 3,000 in Washington directing their weird operations. "Which" men or "Which" doctors like Perkins, as he says, have a choice of many ways of producing abundance, but they do their best work with billions. Much of the BEW's work was in South America and a lot of its purchases there were made to provide those countries with abundance and thus keep them from deserting us and going over to the Axis.

Although this outfit spent $1,200,000,000, no law ever authorized it, and the Senate never confirmed the appointment of Wallace or Perkins. The President "grabbed the torch" and created it by edict. The President told the RFC to give the BEW whatever funds it asked for. Jesse Jones testified that if either Wallace or Perkins asked for money he had no choice but to give it, and they asked for and got a billion and a quarter.[46]

Of course, a great legion of economic soldiers had to have a chief economist. How they picked him I do not know. But these two great geopolitical warriors—Wallace and Perkins—came up with a gentleman named Dr. Maurice Parmalee, born in Constantinople. He had spent many years drinking deep of the "new learning" in Europe and wrote a book called "Farewell to Poverty." Wallace and Perkins and Parmalee made a marvelous trio of musketeers as they figuratively strutted over this hemisphere arm-in-arm singing "Hello Plenty! Here We Come!" Parmalee wrote another book labeled

"Bolshevism, Fascism and the Liberal Democratic State." In this he said: "The high technological development in the United States renders it feasible to introduce a planned social economy much more rapidly than has been the case in the U.S.S.R. ... *The superficial paraphernalia of capitalism can be dispensed with more quickly than in the Soviet Union.*" But the doctor had strayed into much lighter fields of literature. He had also written a book called "Nudism in Modern Life" which is secluded in the obscene section of the Library of Congress. In it the doctor revealed his interest in a science called Gymnosophy, a cult of the old gymnosophists who it seems were ancient Hindu hermit philosophers who went around with little or no clothing. Dr. Parmalee felt that nudism ought not to be limited to hermits. He urged its widespread use "wherever feasible in office, workshop or factory." He wrote: "Convent and monastery, harem and military barrack, clubs and schools exclusively for each sex will disappear and the sexes will live a more normal and happier life." There is certainly something of a practical nature in the amalgamation of the harem and the barracks in a happy, carefree nudist life as a substitute for conscription in keeping the army up to quota.

The doctor, who seems to have gone in for what might be called G-string economics, was not too hopeful of results in our capitalist civilization. He perhaps saw pressure groups like Sidney Hillman's Amalgamated Clothing Workers, for all its pink idealism, insisting on its products. He felt that while gymnosophists are not necessarily Communists, "these gymnosophist nudist colonies furnish excellent opportunities for experiments along socialist lines ... Customary nudity is impossible under existing undemocratic, social and economic and political organization." There was actually outside Washington a delightful club—the Washington Outdoor Club—composed of a number of bureaucrats and others which had a lovely sylvan hideaway in an isolated glen where the savants, weary of their fatiguing billions, could toss away their undies and play tennis, volley ball and leap frog.

These facts were brought to Wallace's attention by Martin Dies. Mr. Wallace suggested that it would be better for what he called the "morale" of his department if Mr. Dies were on Hitler's payroll. Nevertheless, Dr. Parmalee was eased out of BEW—but into another bureau. A new chief economist was brought in—Dr. John

Bovingdon. Bovingdon was no fool. He went to Harvard and graduated with honors, which is more than Mr. Roosevelt did. But he, too, was one of those free spirits of the wandering winds who had managed to live for a while in the Orient, three years in Europe and England, two years in Russia and for smaller terms in 22 other countries. His Harvard class reunion book said he "engaged in art activities, painting on fabrics, poetry, dancing, acting, consultant on the Moscow Art Theater, one-man commercial monodrama programs, weaving, sandal-making" and so on. In 1931 the police in Los Angeles raided a Red pageant for a Lenin Memorial which Bovingdon was staging. The experience shook Mr. Bovingdon terribly and he went to Russia. He got a job in Moscow as a director of the International Theatre. He worked as a journalist in the world of free Russian speech, wrote radio scripts and plays. He decided to return to the United States to make us understand Russia. The *Western Worker*, a Communist organ, wrote February 7, 1935: "John Bovingdon, former director of the International Theatre in Moscow and well-known as a dancer, having recently returned from the Soviet Union, will give a lecture and dance program in Jenny Lind Hall ... The affair is being arranged by the Friends of Soviet Russia under whose auspices Bovingdon is touring this country." In January, 1938, he appeared in Long Beach, California, at the town's first "Communist Party celebration of the 14th anniversary of Lenin's death."

He made an application for a government job in 1943, omitting the items noted here, of course. The only thing which seemed to qualify this adagio economist for work in that specialty was his employment 23 years before by the American Woolen Corporation, long before he felt the mystic spirit of bolshy economics stirring in his tootsies. By what curious movement of the stars did these weird ideological brothers turn up in posts of the greatest importance in the councils of the New Deal? As fast as one was pushed out another moved in. It could not be by chance, since this happened in practically every important bureau. What aid could Bovingdon give to Mr. Perkins and Mr. Wallace, struggling with some baffling problem of world boondoggling? A clap of Mr. Wallace's hands and in before the two great "Which" men, amidst a crash of Hans Eisler music, comes Mr. Bovingdon in a series of leaps and whirls, kicks and postures. How else could he solve their problems?[47]

These two strange birds were not isolated cases. The Un-American Activities Committee gave Wallace a list of 35 Communists in the BEW. That information was merely brushed aside with some insulting smear against the Committee.

By the fall of 1943 the squabbles between Roosevelt's bureau chiefs became so general as to amount to a scandal. The President issued a decree to them to refrain from airing their differences in public. During the next ten months, behind the scenes, there was a continual row between Vice-President Wallace and RFC head Jesse Jones. On June 29, 1944, Wallace issued a public statement accusing Jones of "obstructing the war effort." It made a week's dog-fight in the newspapers. In the end Roosevelt publicly scolded both men but issued a directive ending the life of the BEW and creating a wholly new agency with a different set of letters, and with Leo T. Crowley as its head. One of the first things Crowley noticed was the data respecting Bovingdon. Crowley asked for his resignation, which he refused, whereupon he was fired.

Thereafter the country had to depend on the management of a mere business man to handle an obviously business problem—getting strategically scarce materials for our factories.

It mattered not what the New Dealer touched, it became a torch to be grabbed, it became an instrument for use in his adventures in social engineering, and after June, 1941 when Hitler turned on his partner Stalin, these bureaus became roosting places for droves of Communist termites who utilized their positions as far as they dared to advance the interests of Soviet Russia and to help "dispense with the superficial paraphernalia of capitalism" in this country under cover of the war.

CHAPTER 7: THE HAPPIEST YEARS OF THEIR LIVES

Even before the war, the country had become a bureaucrat's paradise. But with the launching of the war effort the bureaus proliferated and the bureaucrats swarmed over the land like a plague of locusts. In 1940, Roosevelt named a National Defense

Commission with three horns. Edward Stettinius, of United States Steel, managed one horn on industrial materials, Sidney Hillman another on labor and Leon Henderson a third on price stabilization. It didn't work. In January, 1941, it became the ill-fated Office of Production Management (OPM) under William S. Knudsen and Sidney Hillman. By August it was snarled in feuds. Roosevelt named a super-bureau over it called the Supply Priorities and Allocation Board (SPAB) with Henry Wallace at its head. That blew up, of course, before it got well started and after Pearl Harbor was attacked the WPB—War Production Board—under Donald Nelson took over. At some point, Leon Henderson and his Price Stabilization Division got lost until April, 1941 when it was made a separate bureau and called the Office of Price Administration with Henderson at its head. After that it proceeded to go to town. The odor it created still lingers amongst us and it will remain for all time a classic for students in what not to do and how not to do it.

Henderson was perhaps the worst possible selection for this post. In a position requiring infinite tact and understanding, he had as much tact as a runaway elephant. By no means a basically bad person, he was congenitally incapable of resisting the destructive personal effects of power. Power went not merely to his head, as in the case of others; it went to his muscles besides. Five feet six, weighing 210 pounds, he began to throw his pudgy body around, to yell and shout orders, to threaten to throw people out of windows and to exhibit himself before the populace as a sort of burly ideological comedian. He had himself photographed riding a victory bicycle in front of the Capitol; he rode ostentatiously around town in a dilapidated automobile; he appeared, like Churchill, with a huge six-inch cigar, and generally displayed himself as a man of imposing and terrifying power. He did the light fantastic at the night clubs and presently his home became the rendezvous of the intelligentsia where at numerously attended cocktail parties the mighty thinkers gathered to rest their massive brains.

He antagonized everybody, he made everybody mad. But he had a wonderful time. The poor housewives cursed him. The harried business man, driven almost mad by his foggy and multitudinous directives, asked only for his blood. But to Leon, it was all just good fun. Writing about it all after he himself had been heaved out, he said:

"When I think now it's already the good old days. It's like reminiscing with my old cronies of the Millville baseball team—I can't remember ever losing a game or making more than one error. Nature is kind that way." He recalled that he had almost missed the bus—it all came out of a chance talk with Harry Hopkins which led him to a job in the TNEC. Then it was just a romp from one bureau to another—the TNEC, SEC, NDAC, SPAB, OPM, WPB, OES, OPACS and, of course, OPA. "And," he said, "it was fun all the time, even when I was mad." For the rest of us, of course, it was no fun at all—just being mad. But for Leon—poor Leon, who before his accidental appearance in Washington had never had a real first-class job—it was a world of fun pushing 130 million people around.

He went to work upon a wholly crazy basic principle—that inflation is caused by high prices and that the inflation could be prevented by holding prices down. It is really the other way around. Inflation is not caused by high prices. High prices are caused by inflation. The inflation is the expansion of the quantity of purchasing power available to buy things in excess of the goods available for purchase. Increase the number of dollars in the pockets of the people without increasing the volume of goods on the shelves for sale and you have inflation. The inflation came from the method by which the government financed the war. First of all, it threw itself with something approaching utter intoxication into the job. This started at the top. Money was no object. Throw it around with complete abandon! While the prices that merchants charged for goods were watched by Henderson's price police, the prices paid by the government for war materials and war production and war wages were no object. Money was poured out freely. And the money was obtained chiefly from loans made at the banks, the most inflationary kind of money. A nation whose people had been collecting from their wages and profits about 70 billion dollars a year were suddenly collecting 100 billion and then 150 billion and then 200 billion a year, but the number of automobiles and refrigerators and radios and electric irons and the amount of meat and butter and flour and eggs and clothing was less and less. That is what produced the inflation. Of course, prices had to be kept down within reason because runaway prices tend to aggravate the central cause of the inflation and, more than that, result in the necessities of life going to those with the most money to spend. But whatever was done about this there had to be some rational relationship between the prices and the costs of production and this law the OPA snapped its fingers at.

And of course it did not keep prices down. It put out press releases boasting of the price scales that were maintained. But the scarcer goods went into the black markets where prices in the end were far higher than they would have been if the regulation had been first of all realistic, and second, managed by an agency that understood the popular mind and that would have treated the people with some degree of understanding.

It began with controls on coffee and sugar. And it began as it ended by supposing that it could reach into every office, every warehouse, every shop and every home and watch and regulate every transaction. It is impossible in a small space to describe the colossal folly of the experiments in sugar and coffee, the first result of which was to paralyze almost completely the whole trade. The same thing was done with meat. Meat begins, as to most of its supply, far out on the ranches among the big herds. Next the young steers and cows move East to the feeding lots where the farmers dispose of their grain by feeding it to the cattle for a season and then selling the cattle to the slaughtering houses. Then it goes to the wholesalers and then to the retail butchers. But in between are warehouses, railroads, truckers, commission agents and processors of all sorts.

This vast complexity of men and trades and utilities has grown up through the years through that hit or miss method that characterizes our system, one man trying an experiment that works and then being imitated by all the others in his trade. The cattle thus move from the ranch to the retail butcher shop through a long series of transactions and processes which the men in this vast business understand. Now whether this was the best system in the world or not, it was the system in existence—the system that has always been able to produce all the meat required upon a scale exceeded by no other country. OPA was not created to change this system. As a matter of practical horse sense any attempt to change it could only result in enormous delays while some other system was put into operation. It is too immense and complicated a thing for such change. And what is more, any attempt to change it would meet resistance, bitter and even violent, all along the line. The problem before OPA was to prevent prices from going to unreasonable heights, while at the same time getting as much production as possible and ensuring a fair distribution of the supply to all the people. The only way to do this was to aim at making the existing system function at its highest efficiency and this would require the cooperation of all the various groups engaged in it.

OPA was in the hands of men who knew little or nothing of the meat industry. They could, of course, have got expert aid, but they were determined to make the meat industry over. Fate had put the vast productive and distributive system of America into their power. Here was the golden chance to change it—to show these dumb business men how so much of this costly and ignorant mechanism could be dispensed with. They believed that Fate had presented them with the precious opportunity of making America over. They proceeded to administer to the meat industry a wallop which staggered it and in the end almost ruined it. For instance, their first target was the commission man—that hated middleman, that wretched interloper who has been the object of the scorn of the economic dilettante for decades.

They did not realize that when they tried to liquidate the commission man they made no provision for handling the function he performed. Also, if ceilings are put on prices, the ceiling must govern all along the line as the cattle pass from one stage of distribution to another. OPA put ceilings on prices at various points but not on the rancher, which was about as stupid a performance as the human mind could invent. Meat on a cow is produced by eating—eating fattening foods, chiefly corn. The corn farmer can sell his corn directly in the corn market or he can buy a cow and feed the corn to her. He decides what he will do by the price of corn. If he can get a better price for his corn selling it in the market he will not feed it to cattle. If the meat prices are more attractive he will turn his corn into meat. Our highly intelligent bureaucrats allowed the price of corn to soar while holding down the ceiling on meat. The corn farmer sold his corn in the corn market. He refused to buy cattle to fatten and the young animals, minus two or three hundred pounds of meat, went directly to the slaughterers. Countless millions of pounds of meat were lost. The whole story of meat is full of these costly blunders. Wages were held down in slaughter houses. The workers quit the legitimate slaughterers and went to work for black-market slaughterers at twice the legal wages, or went into munitions plants, and scores of slaughter houses were put out of business. The unfortunate slaughterer or meat dealer or packer who complained was called a fascist.

This stemmed from the kind of men who were brought into OPA. At first it began with the redoubtable Leon Henderson and 84 office assistants. In August, 1941 a new bill, reorganizing OPA, was being considered by Congress. A member asked if the plan would not require a staff of 100,000. Henderson replied: "Oh, no. This bill will be practically self-enforcing." The next year—May, 1942—Henderson asked for 110 million dollars and said he needed a staff of 90,000. The next year it cost 153 million and the following year it had a staff of 53,500 paid workers and 204,000 volunteers.

From the four corners of the land, as well as from the pink and Red purlieus of New York and Chicago and every big city, came the molders of the Brave New World. At the top, as economic adviser, was Richard V. Gilbert, one of those young professors who in 1938 marched on Washington and sold Roosevelt the theory that government debt is practically meaningless, that it is not a burden, that we owe it to ourselves and that Roosevelt could go right on borrowing indefinitely without ever wrinkling his god-like brow in worry. The place swarmed with little professors fresh from their $2500-a-year jobs now stimulated by five, six and seven-thousand-dollar salaries and whole big chunks of the American economy resting in their laps. Tugwell in college had sung: "I am young. I am strong. I will make America over." And here was the God-given chance. They put their busy fingers into everything. They dictated women's styles, the shapes of women's stockings; they told butchers how to carve a roast; they limited the length of Santa Claus' whiskers in department stores.

Back in the days of the TNEC—one of Henderson's early adventures—a gentleman named A. C. Hoffman made studies in merchandising. He wrote: "One of the aspects of food distribution which the writer finds much to his dislike is the growing expenditure of money on brand advertising for food products." Under OPA manufacturers began to be aware that OPA was trying to do away with all brands and quality differentials. This was also one of Tugwell's pet theories—no brand names on goods, no quality differentials, just a label telling what was in the can. And sure enough, it was A. C. Hoffman, from Henderson's old TNEC days, who was ranking officer in the OPA Food Price Section working to put over his pet theory. He was forced out and went back to the Agricultural Department.

From the London School of Economics came an organization to advance Political and Economic Planning—PEP. This was a scheme for fascist planning through a "national Council of Agriculture, a National Council for Industry, a National Council for Transport, all to be statutory bodies with powers to govern their special provinces of business." The chairman of this group was Israel Moses Sieff. He turned up as a special consultant to OPA in 1941. The place was full of these boys.

At one time there was an almost complete breakdown of food distribution throughout the United States. The paper work required of an ordinary small merchant was so extensive that it was practically impossible to comply with. A Michigan grocer who had run a successful business for 40 years testified that "For the last six months I have been behind the counter ten hours a day, then up half the night filling out government forms. Sunday is needed for inventory reports, ration accounts or applications for coffee, sugar and canned goods. I couldn't keep up with it, so I closed my doors." Small food distributors were going out of business by the tens of thousands a month. Whole states were insufficiently supplied with meat, butter, lard or potatoes for two months at a time. OPA fixed the price of Louisiana potatoes at $2.50 per cwt., and the price of Texas potatoes at $3.75 per cwt. Louisiana potatoes were just trucked across the line and sold as Texas potatoes. Uniform prices on farm products for all markets very nearly starved out many large cities. Shippers sent their supplies to the nearby markets and abandoned the high-freight markets. OPA put a ceiling price on lard of $14.55 a hundred pounds, but they allowed a price of $26.50 on dressed hogs including fat. A packer could get 26 cents a pound for the fat on the hog but only 15 cents for the same fat as lard. This was done at a time when this country and the world were starving for fats. Approximately a billion pounds of lard went to the food stores on the hogs at 26 cents a pound; then we had to have a salvage campaign to get back from housewives the drippings which should never have gone into their kitchens.[48]

The rules and regulations, the directives issued were frequently beyond the power of the human mind to understand. Here is a sample:

> "The maximum price which a manufacturer may charge to any class of purchasers for any packaged cosmetic priced under the general maximum price regulation shall be the maximum price established under the general maximum price regulation for sales of such packaged cosmetics by him to a purchaser of the same class."

These rules and regulations became so irksome that people ignored them. Then the OPA set up a nation-wide network of courts before which citizens could be hauled up and tried for breaking laws enacted by OPA bureaucrats. If convicted, they could, under OPA rulings, have their ration cards taken away from them—sentenced to starve. But the OPA heads themselves were not too meticulous about observing the government rules. All buildings were ordered to keep their heat no higher than 65 degrees. A reporter took a thermometer to Leon Henderson's office at this time, where it registered 80 degrees.

The record of OPA's follies and blunders is incredible. I can give merely those types of examples that can be quickly explained without going into the intricacies of trade practices. The trouble stemmed fundamentally from the type of men who were put in control, men of the stamp of Leon Henderson who had been, as I have already pointed out, a technocrat and one of the sponsors of Howard Scott and later a director of Technocracy, Inc. It was during this OPA circus that Henderson was charged with being part of the Technocracy movement. Henderson denied it and said if it could be proved he would eat a Washington telephone book on the steps of the Capitol. As we have seen, Leon's name is signed to a document published in the New York *Times* when he and some others resigned from Technocracy, Inc., not because they disagreed with Scott's fundamental theories, as they explained, but did not like his methods. And what happened in OPA happened wherever these New Deal minds were put in control. In December, 1942, things got so bad that Henderson had to be eased out. A former senator, Prentiss Brown, succeeded him with no better results, after which Chester Bowles was made head of that bureau. He did a better job, but by that time it was impossible for anyone to do very much better.

This mere peep behind the curtain of the hippodrome will serve to afford a glimpse of that stupendous fiscal extravaganza put on in Washington. On the economic side of the war there was the formidable task of producing the mountains of materials which the generals and admirals demanded. That was done by the American productive machine. This was a machine of epic proportions that had been created and developed long before the New Deal was heard of. And it was, in fact, that very machine upon which all the engines of scorn and calumny of the New Deal had been trained and which the Tugwells and Wallaces and their subalterns wanted to liquidate. This machine was operated by that immense army of engineers, technicians, financiers and administrative leaders who had developed the great resources of the nation, who had invented and perfected the amazing technical processes and who had built that fabulous mass of plants and machines which turned out guns, planes, tanks, cars, ships, arms, munitions, food and all the accoutrements and necessities of war. They were told what was wanted and they supplied it. The Tugwells, the Hopkinses, the Hendersons and Wallaces had nothing to do with this. This was the work of the hated business man.

In the hurry and jostling of the war there were miscalculations and even misdeeds. But a good deal of that will be found in the wide ranks of that horde of suddenly aroused and hungry gentry who from the corners of the land swarmed into Washington to get a little piece of the monstrous melon and who took their ill-gotten gains into that economic jungle called the black market. One may talk about the profits of the war, but there were in truth little profits for honest men because the government—and rightly—during the war drained away in drastic taxes most of the profits.

But there was another sector on this economic front—the embattled legions of the bureaucrats mobilized to police the real producers and to supervise for the State the actual task of production. And at their side was that other battalion of New Deal fiscal philosophers—the bright evangelists of national debt, who were now permitted to gorge themselves on their pet theories. At the top, in the driver's seat, sat a man who despised all the traffic rules and the warning signals, the red lights and the hazards along the road. He threw the monstrous machine into high, stepped on the gas, closed his eyes and turned it loose. Had some commission of hostile angels been named to devise a scheme for making production costly they could not have done a better job. The tens of thousands of bureaucrats from a score of bureaus crawled over the producing plants. They inserted themselves into the processes at each new step, to slow it up, to increase its costs and to drive to distraction the practical men who were running the machine. The feeling that cost meant nothing, that the only thing that mattered was "hurry," the theory that a hurrying engine need not be careful, introduced so many distractions and halts and changes and bickerings into the whole process that both economy and speed were sacrificed. Worst of all, sane and sober men surrendered after a while to the contagion and, equally with their bureaucratic persecutors, threw arithmetic to the winds.

In the financing and supervision of the war effort from Washington practically every fiscal crime was committed. And the plain evidence of that is before us in the bill for the war. Few realize how vast it was. For the mind, even of the trained financier, begins to lose its capacity for proportion after the figures pass beyond the limit of understandable billions. The war cost I reckon at 363 billion dollars. To form some estimate of this figure it may help to recall that during the 144 years which cover the administrations of all the presidents from Washington to the first inauguration of Franklin Roosevelt, the total expenditures of the federal government equaled 117 billion dollars. Yet in the seven years from 1941 to 1947, the cost of supporting the war and its consequences alone was 363 billion—three times as much in seven years as in 144 years of our history. The total amount expended in these seven years was 463 billion. I have subtracted a hundred billion to cover the sums which our extravagant government would have spent had we not entered the war. To complete this picture we must not overlook the solemn fact that we have paid to date only one-third of this prodigious bill. The remaining two-thirds stands against us as the national debt, the interest on which alone, when the debt is all funded, will be nearly twice the cost of government before Mr. Roosevelt came to power.

The story of how this vast account and this staggering debt was accumulated is a long and an intricate one. The follies, the recklessness, the appalling ineptness and incompetence, the deep and dark corruption remain yet to be told. It would be futile to attempt it until the government has passed into responsible hands charged with the task of subjecting the whole terrible performance to the fullest investigation.

There is no doubt that this intolerable burden, which will bear down upon the shoulders of this generation and the next, is the direct result of President Roosevelt's utter incapacity for administration. Here, again, we may turn to a cabinet officer for the testimony. Secretary of War Stimson is lavish in his praise of Mr. Roosevelt and is prepared to forgive him the most costly defects of character in his admiration for Roosevelt's great stroke of genius in naming Stimson to his cabinet. However, he wrote in his diary in March, 1943: "The President is the poorest administrator I have ever worked under in respect to the orderly procedure and routine of his performance. He is not a good chooser of men and does not know how to use them in coordination."[49]

The positive task of stimulating and directing war production, as distinguished from policing it, was given to Donald Nelson, a business man competent in the limited field in which he worked but of no special distinction. He was made head of the War Production Board in January, 1942, after a whole series of break-downs. Nelson proved inadequate to the task committed to him. In February, 1943, the Secretary of War and other administrative leaders joined in asking the President to replace Nelson with Bernard Baruch. But, says Stimson, no action was taken for 18 months. Stimson sums up the story by saying that after tinkering for two years with a variety of boards and commissions, the President finally put power into the hands of one man and then named the wrong one, and when that man got into trouble he neither backed him nor fired him.[50]

Yet we are asked to accept Roosevelt as the great administrator, the great military leader, the great naval leader, the great civil statesman and finally the great master in the field of foreign affairs. We shall presently see that in the last he chalked up for himself the most unbelievable record of failure in the annals of foreign relations in the history of this country.

Chapter 8: The Thought Police

I.

If there is one department of human struggle which the radical revolutionist understands and loves it is the war that is waged on the mass mind; the war that is carried on with poisons distilled in the mind to produce bias and hatred. It would be strange indeed if we did not find some of the practitioners of this dark art from New York and some of the off-scourings of Europe's battered revolutionary emigres numerously entrenched in that thoroughly un-American institution during the war which was known as the OWI—the Office of War Information.

It began with a thing called the Office of Facts and Figures. At the head of this Roosevelt put one of his dainty intellectual pets, Archibald MacLeish. MacLeish was the scion of a wealthy American family who in 1923 decided he would give his life to poetry and so "chucked it all," took his wife and children and went to France. He remained there until 1930 where he worked upon the ornate edges of journalism and wrote poetry. Here is a sample from what he considers his best poem—"America Was Promises":

> "Who is the voyager on these coasts?
> Who is the traveler in these waters
> Expects the future as a shore; foresees
> Like Indies to the west the ending—he
> The rumor of the surf intends."

A man who writes poetry like that inevitably becomes a New Dealer, if not worse. In 1939 Roosevelt made him Librarian of Congress, where he proceeded to use the facilities of the Library for New Deal propaganda. In 1941 the Library "loaned" MacLeish back to the President to head the Office of Facts and Figures. He brought together a drove of writers and journalists whose souls were enlisted in the great crusade to bring on the Brave New World of the Future. It was in fact an agency for selling Roosevelt's Third New Deal and Roosevelt himself to the people under the guise of "maintaining public morale" and conducting "psychological warfare." It was costing $600,000 a year and managed to keep itself in hot water as it stumbled from blunder to blunder until it became a national nuisance and

Roosevelt was forced to end it. He created as its successor the Office of War Information with Elmer Davis at its head. In the next two years, OWI spent $68,000,000 and had 5,561 agents scattered all over the world. In the First World War, George Creel had done the job—and an excellent one at that—with a staff of 500 and an appropriation of $2,500,000 a year.

One job of OWI was to sell America to various foreign peoples. Among its first adventures in this field was selling us to the people of North Africa. Its agents dropped things from planes on the North Africans, the purpose being to make those simple people love us. Among the winged messages of good will were a cake of soap inscribed "From your Friends, the Americans," a children's coloring book, a rubber stamp with ink pad attached, a picture book called "The Life of Franklin D. Roosevelt," a small package of seeds. The prize package was a pin button. On one side was an American flag. On the other side was a picture of Roosevelt—but not the Nordic FDR we knew. The picture was colored to make him look like an Arab. All this junk rained down in countless thousands on North Africa. Picking up the soap, the rubber stamp, the Life of Roosevelt and the pin with the Arabian Roosevelt, Arabs, Berbers and Senegalese were expected to take a wholly different view of war politics.

But OWI had other tasks than selling America to the Arabs. It was also busy selling Russia to the Americans. The chief of the Foreign Language Section of OWI was a young gentleman 28 years old who had spent his entire life on New York's East Side, who spoke no foreign language and yet had the decision on whether news should be released to Europe or not. Anybody who disagreed with his high admiration for our Soviet ally was labeled a fascist. There was another child wonder—23 years old—who was the Russian expert of the OWI and who saw to it that nothing went out that was displeasing to the objectives of our noble ally—including grabbing Yugoslavia. OWI's broadcasts to Poland ended not with the Polish national anthem but with a song adopted by the Polish emigres in Moscow who were known as Stalin's "Committee of Liberation." The expert in charge of the Polish section was actually born in Poland, but left there and spent the rest of his life in France where he was notorious as a Communist. He fraternized with the Vichy government while Hitler and Stalin were pals, but when Hitler invaded Russia he came to America and quickly became OWI's expert in explaining American democracy to the people of Poland.[51]

The deputy director of the Pacific and Far Eastern Area was a British subject until he got a government job in Washington in 1942. While running this important bureau for OWI, he wrote a play which was produced at Hunter College. Burton Rascoe, reviewing it, said: "Its most conspicuous purpose is to idealize the Red Army in China, to defame the Chungking government under Chiang Kaishek and to ridicule the political, social and educational ideas of the vast majority of the American people."[52]

The OWI made blunder after blunder, many of them very costly. While our State and War Departments were trying to get defeated Italy out of the war, OWI beamed a broadcast to Italy smearing Badoglio and calling King Victor Emmanuel the "moronic little king." The State Department was indignant. Roosevelt had to administer a public reprimand to Elmer Davis.

The men, material, cable and wireless time used up by OWI were immense. It ran 350 daily radio programs and had a daily cable-wireless output of 100,000 words. It was the world's largest pamphlet and magazine publisher and a big movie producer, sending shorts to every country in the world. It sent out 3,500 transcribed recordings a month and turned out 50 movie shorts a year. The content of most of this material was pure drivel. An American reporter made a study of the stuff sent to Australia. It was so voluminous that on a single day it tied up the army's signals for four hours at MacArthur's headquarters in the Pacific. In one day, for instance, it sent 37 separate items. One was a 625-word summary of a magazine article on "Three Conceptions of Modern Civilization," another on the meaning of the words "left" and "right" in American politics, another from a magazine article on "How To Obtain Lasting Peace," another about the opening of the New York City Symphony concerts. These were all sent to MacArthur's headquarters, then mimeographed and sent to 70 daily newspapers and about 400 weeklies in Australia. A check with the larger dailies showed that not a line of this stuff was used. Paper was too scarce to carry such flimsy padding.[53]

All of this work was not just naive. OWI printed 2,500,000 pamphlets called "The Negro in the War,"[54] with pictures of Mr. and Mrs. Roosevelt, the Negroes' friends, in preparation for the fourth-term campaign. It printed a handsome volume called "Handbook of the United States"[55] and gave a British firm the right to publish it. This gave a history of America, with the story from Leif Ericson's discovery up to 1932 in four and one-half pages. The rest of the history was devoted to Roosevelt and his New Deal. This was in 1944 and a national election was coming and England was jammed with American soldiers who could vote.

It had a department that supplied the pulp paper magazines with directions and suggestions on how to slant mystery and love stories. Western story writers were told how to emphasize the heroism of our allies—you know which one. Writers were told to cast their soap operas with silent, dogged Britons, faithful Chinese and honest Latins. They must portray Japanese as having set out to seize our Western seaboard and the sly and treacherous characteristics of the Jap must be contrasted with the faithfulness of the Chinese. They suggested that Sax Rohmer's Fu Manchu be turned into a Jap instead of a Chinese.

They supplied the plots to the pulps. What was at the bottom of this one I do not know, but it is a sample:

> "A seduced girl throws herself into some type of work, say physiotherapy, to forget. Working side by side with a crippled doctor, she learns to love him. After crisis in their task which she helps him meet, she discovers that although he knows all about her past, he loves her. Clinch and fade-out."[56]

Actually, we had in this incredible institution a mixture of inconsequential nonsense, New Deal politics and Communist infiltration. Of course, Elmer Davis, Gardner Cowles and Robert Sherwood were not Communists. I do not know quite how much they were even New Dealers. Elmer Davis, at least, gave up a very profitable radio contract to work at one-fourth the pay, which could be said of few of his collaborators who were making more money than they had ever known in their lives, besides escaping military service. But as America moved toward the war there blossomed the most fantastic comradeship between flaming Red revolutionaries, foggy-eyed New Dealers and deep purple conservatives. The war brought them together in an incongruous brotherhood. They were united in the drive for American entry into the war, but for a variety of different and contradictory reasons. But among these hostile elements the one group that was not foggy was the Communist group. Of them at least we can say they knew what they wanted. The mere New Dealers, as that term came to be understood, comprised those wandering, vague dreamers who held to a shadowy conviction that somehow the safety of humankind depended upon the creation of some sort of ill-defined but benevolent state that would end poverty, give everybody a job and an easy old age, and who supposed that this could be done because they had discovered that money grew in government buildings. The others were largely devoted lovers of or worshipers at the ancient altars of Anglo-Saxon world hegemony. But they could all unite in a weird conventicle—Anglo-Saxon imperialists, groping New Dealers and dogmatic Red bigots—under banners like those of the OWI, the OPA and the BEW. And here and there was a fellow acutely conscious of the German blood in his veins and eager to purge himself of the stain.

2.

When the war began the government, recognizing the need for protecting our military operations from leaks through careless or un-informed press reporting, organized the Office of Censorship headed by Byron Price, an able official of the Associated Press. To this bureau was given the power to monitor all communications. It set up a censorship organization which all publishers and broadcasters voluntarily cooperated with. It worked admirably and Mr. Price won the unstinted approval of the press for his capable and tactful, yet firm, handling of this difficult problem. No other government agency had any authority whatever to engage in this activity. And it was never intended that anybody should have the power to attempt to interfere with the rights of citizens to discuss with freedom all political questions, subject only to the obligation not to divulge information that would aid the enemy or defeat our military operations.

Nevertheless, the OWI and Federal Communications Commission (FCC) took upon themselves the power to carry on the most extensive propaganda among and the most dangerous interference with the foreign-language broadcasting stations. Of course the ordinary American official was hardly aware of the opportunities this kind of thing gave to those who had political or ideological axes to grind.

The FCC set up a bureau which it called the War Problems Division. There were probably 125 or more radio broadcasting stations which specialized in foreign-language programs to our foreign-born populations. They reached many millions of people. Of course, a war in Europe immediately creates very serious and delicate repercussions among those people here whose homelands are involved. Their position is generally very uncomfortable and often painful. The radio stations are bound to notice the war and the problems of the war here. It was important, of course, that these stations be closely watched to see that nothing subversive and nothing that would adversely affect the war effort was used. And for this purpose the Office of Censorship was admirably equipped and managed. But the FCC decided that it would take a hand, not merely in monitoring the stations but in literally directing and controlling them. The OWI similarly arrived at the same conclusion. It also set up a division for dealing with the problems of the foreign-born through radio.

The FCC's War Problems Division operated throughout the country but we will understand what they were doing if we limit the story to just a few stations. The Division took over control of the Commission office in New York, putting a young lawyer with very little experience in charge. This office, in collaboration with a bureau of the OWI, proceeded to go to work upon the New York stations. The OWI was represented by a gentleman named Lee Falk.

One of these stations in the metropolitan district was WHOM. It was owned by a gentleman obviously of complete loyalty and devotion to this country and its principles. Nevertheless the FCC and OWI guardians of "democracy" swarmed over his station. A broadcasting station operates under the direction and observation of a certain type of staff. There is a station manager, a program director, a censor, a monitor, announcers and commentators. If you can get control of most or all of these you are sitting pretty so far as controlling the content of the broadcasts is concerned. Into this station, as program director, was introduced Mr. Giuseppe Lupis. Mr. Lupis first entered the United States in 1926 but left and did not return as a resident until 1937. He went to work for the OWI in 1942. He established a monthly magazine called *Il Mondo* for circulation among Italians. He made Mr. Carlo a Prato its editor. Mr. a Prato's first point of operation before coming here was Switzerland. He was put out of Switzerland for life because he was accused of being an agent of Maxim Litvinov. He got out of Marseilles on a Czech passport under the name of Milan Javota and arrived here in 1941. He quickly found himself editing an Italian propaganda paper and with a job in the OWI as chief Italian script writer.

How did these people get employment in the OWI and FCC so swiftly? There was a private organization called Short Wave Research, Inc. Its purpose was to corral refugees as they arrived and get them employment with the OWI and FCC. It was a non-profit organization, but that it did a large business in this traffic is evident from the fact that when it was liquidated it had $15,000 or $20,000 cash in its treasury, all made from charging fees of 10 per cent to all aliens placed in these government agencies. The money was divided up among various war charities when it closed down. Lupis worked as a script writer for Short Wave Research for a while.

One Italian whose trade was bricklayer was hired as censor and monitor. Another Italian walked into the station five weeks after he got here without letters of recommendation and became a censor and at Christmas and Easter imposed his own peculiar notions in censoring religious programs.

While infiltrating the stations with these recently arrived refugees, others who did not meet the specifications of the guardians of our liberties were forced out. In one case an announcer named Stefano Luotto, an American citizen of good standing and unimpeachable loyalty, was forced off the station. He was charged with being a fascist by that singular process by which one who was anti-Communist was also a pro-fascist because he was against an anti-fascist Communist. Lupis urged his dismissal and a little Italian paper, *La Parola*, edited by a fellow named Valenti, peddled the smear. Luotto had Valenti arrested for criminal libel and after a long struggle the FCC had to admit there was not a scintilla of evidence against Luotto. This case was only one of a brace of instances which amounted to outright persecution.

Mr. Eugene L. Garey, chief counsel of the Congressional Select Committee Investigating the FCC, speaking of these conditions, said:

> "From the record thus far made it appears that, in one foreign language broadcasting station in New York City, the program director,

the announcer, the script writer, the censor, and the monitor of the Italian-language programs are all aliens or persons owing their positions to the Office of War Information, with the approval of the FCC.

"The situation thus portrayed is not peculiar to this single station, or to this one city. Information in our possession indicates that the same situation prevails generally in the foreign language stations throughout the country. Every such key position in each of the three radio stations presently under investigation are found to be similarly staffed. These staffs select the news, edit the script, and announce the program. The program, in turn, is censored by them, monitored by them, and is presented under the direction of a program director of similar character.

"From these apparently unrelated facts the picture must be further developed.

"OWI had the men and the material. It had the proper dye to color the news. It also had the desire to select and censor the news. What it lacked was the power, or perhaps more accurately stated, even the color of power, to carry their designs into effect. Hence the need to enlist the Federal Communications Commission in its purpose.

"True it is that the Federal Communications Commission had no such lawful power, but the Federal Communications Commission did have the power to license and hence the power to compel obedience to its directions. The record now shows their unlawful use of this power.

"Working together in a common purpose, the Federal Communications Commission and the Office of War Information have accomplished a result that compels pause—and presents the solemn question of 'Whither are we going?'

"A division called the War Problems Division was created by the Federal Communications Commission, and a staff of attorneys began to function.

"This division was not a regulatory body. It was not formed to instruct, or supervise, or to correct. It was formed for the avowed purpose of unlawfully liquidating all of the radio personnel in the foreign-language field that did not meet with its favor. A real gestapo was created and a lawless enterprise was launched.

"It is suggested that we accept this unlawful situation as a benevolent expedient of the moment, but no such purpose as we find here disclosed, however benevolently cloaked, can justify the practices we find. All tyranny begins under the guise of benevolence.

"In time of war we are asked to place trust in lately arrived aliens whose sole claim to trustworthiness is the assumption that because they have been unfaithful to past vows they will be faithful to their new ones.

"The voices of these aliens go into our homes, and the unwary are led to believe that they speak with authority and official approval. They even censor our Christmas and Easter religious programs, and tell us what music we may hear. The FCC is alarmed about whether we will react properly to news furnished by our national news agencies. Apparently we can still read the news in our press, but we can only hear what these aliens permit us to. What next medium of communication will receive the benevolent attention of these misguided zealots? Obviously, the press.

"These interpreters of our national policy—these slanters of our news—these destroyers of free speech—are alien in birth, alien in education, alien in training and in thought.

"And still these are the people who are permitted to mold our thoughts—to tell us what America's war aims and purposes are. These people are in position to color, to delete, or to slant, as they see fit, in accordance with their own peculiar alien views and ideologies.

"Persons are being accused of being pro-fascist, and that without proof and without trial. Persons suspected of being pro-fascist, and without proof, have been removed from the air and replaced by wearers of the Black Shirt ...

"If the radio can thus be controlled in August, 1943, there is nothing to prevent the same control from slanting our political news and nothing to prevent the coloring of our war aims and purposes when peace comes."[57]

These lawless snoopers queried station staff members about their religious views and in one case wanted to know where they thought the Polish-Russian border should be fixed. Falk took the position that station owners should not do business with certain advertising agencies which he named. He carried a blacklist and attempted to enforce it. They investigated anybody and everybody connected with the stations and, of course, inevitably went to various smear organizations to traduce and destroy loyal Americans who did not suit their purposes.

3.

In the presence of a government which had enlarged its power over the lives and the thoughts and opinions of citizens and which did not hesitate to use that power, the whole citizenry was intimidated.

Editors, writers, commentators were intimidated. Men whose opinions did not conform to the reigning philosophy were driven from the air, from magazines and newspapers. While American citizens who were moved by a deep and unselfish devotion to the ideals of this Republic—however wrong-headed that may be in the light of the new modes of "freedom"—were forced into silence, the most blatant and disruptive revolutionary lovers of the systems of both fascism and Communism and that illegitimate offspring of both—Red fascism—were lording it over our minds.

All this was possible for one reason and one reason only—because the President of the United States countenanced these things, encouraged them and in many cases sponsored them, not because he was a Communist or fascist or held definitely to any political system, but because at the moment they contributed to his own ambitions.

Chapter 9: The Great Conferences

When a nation is at war, its leaders are compelled by the necessities of practical administration to use every means at hand to sell the war to the people who must fight it and pay for it. As part of that job it is usual to include the leader himself in the package. He is therefore portrayed in heroic proportions and colors in order to command for his leadership the fullest measure of unity. War, as we have seen, puts into the hands of a leader control over the instruments of propaganda and opinion on an ever-increasing scale. In our day the press, the radio, the movies, even the schoolroom and the pulpit are mobilized to justify the war, to magnify the leader and to intimidate his critics. The citizen who is hardy enough to question the official version of the leader and his policies may find himself labeled as a public enemy or even as a traitor. Hence as the war proceeds, amidst all the trappings which the art of theater can contribute, it is possible to build up a vast fraud, with an ever-mounting torrent of false news, false pictures, false eulogies and false history. After every war many years are required to reduce its great figures to their just proportions and to bring the whole pretentious legend back into focus with truth.

Perhaps no other American war leader was ever exhibited, during a war, upon so heroic a scale as Franklin D. Roosevelt. Why this was so and how it was done forms a separate story. But here we are concerned with presenting the record of his achievements in the field of war-time statescraft, rescued from the deformities of propaganda and corrected to correspond with the facts.

The story of Mr. Roosevelt's management of our relations with our allies and our enemies was unfolded to us during the war in a series of great conferences arranged with the most minute attention to their theatrical effects. Like the historic meetings of Henry VIII and Francis on the field of the Cloth of Gold or of Napoleon and Czar Alexander on a barge at Tilsit in the Niemen River or the massing of the monarchs and their ministers at Paris after Waterloo or the Big Four at Versailles, the public was treated to the royal spectacles off the coast of Newfoundland aboard the *Augusta*, at Quebec, Casablanca, Moscow, Cairo, Teheran and finally at Yalta. Eloquent communiques pretended to inform the people of what had been agreed on. And after each such meeting the press and radio rang with the story of the great triumphs of the President, who brought victory after victory back to his people as the reward of the great battles that were being fought in various parts of the world.

We now know that these communiques told us little of what had happened; that the whole story lay, for long, behind a great curtain of secrecy; that much—though not all—has now been painfully brought to light and that what stands revealed is a story very different from that heroic chronicle of triumphs with which we were regaled at the time.

It was while France, Norway and the Low Countries were occupied, while Britain was under attack from the air and Hitler was driving through Russia in 1941 that we formally entered the war with the Japanese attack on Pearl Harbor. What, then, were our objectives? The first objective was to defeat the enemy in the field. But victory in war is not like victory in a prize fight. It does not consist in merely flooring your antagonist for the count. After the enemy is forced to surrender there comes the always difficult task of translating the knock-out of the enemy into the achievement of those objectives for which we wished to knock him down.

In this case we were not alone in the struggle. We had allies. Each of these allies had his own special ambitions. A complete victory over the enemies would mean the liberation of all the occupied countries. And those countries too had their special ambitions, while our own allies had very special designs of their own with respect to the liberated victims. We had our own great objectives. We fought to drive the aggressors from the lands of these victims; but also for an arrangement of the post-war world that would ensure a peaceful world and, of course, a world safe for democratic peoples to live in. In World War I the victory was poisoned by the fact that, having defeated the aggressions of the Kaiser's Germany, the victors proceeded to satisfy their own aggressive ambitions in a manner to reduce to nothing the lofty proclamations before victory. Thus Mr. Roosevelt had on his hands not merely a war of weapons with our enemies in the field, but a contest in diplomacy with our allies about the fruits of victory. We shall now see him as he moved from "triumph to triumph" in his bouts with our allies.

We have already seen how at the meeting in Placentia Bay the President and Mr. Churchill agreed upon a set of principles to govern the peace and which came to be known as the Atlantic Charter. These assurances to the world were:

First, their countries seek no aggrandizement, territorial or otherwise.

Second, they desire to see no territorial changes that do not accord with the freely expressed desires of the peoples concerned.

Third, they respect the right of all peoples to choose the form of government under which they will live; and they wish to see sovereign rights and self-government restored to those who have been forcibly deprived of them.

Both the President and Mr. Churchill subsequently repeated these assurances in various private audiences with the representatives of those nations, as well as in glowing oratorical pronouncements on their grandiose aims for the world. After America's participation in the war had been under way for some time the question of the collaboration of our allies in these great plans for the future had to be dealt with and accordingly the first of that succession of conferences was arranged.

1. MOMENTOUS DECISION

On June 19, 1942, Winston Churchill arrived in Washington for a momentous conference with the President. What happened at that conference remained a secret until revealed recently by various persons involved in it.

The top-ranking military and naval leaders in America favored from the beginning of their planning a cross-channel invasion of France at the earliest moment. The President, however, was "charmed" by a Mediterranean adventure. So was Churchill, but of a very different type. Secretary Stimson says that the Army's plan was for an operation called BOLERO—an invasion of France in 1943, with a proviso that in the event pressure on Russia became critical, a beachhead invasion of France in 1942 (called SLEDGEHAMMER) be undertaken. By April, 1942, Roosevelt approved the BOLERO plan for 1943 and sent Hopkins and Marshall to London to sell it to Churchill, which they did.

On June 3, 1942, Lord Louis Mountbatten appeared as a White House guest. He spent much time with the President throwing cold water on BOLERO. Suddenly on June 17, the President summoned Stimson and Marshall. Roosevelt wanted to reopen his plan for an invasion of North Africa called GYMNAST. Marshall was primed with elaborate data and seemed to talk the President out of it for the moment. On June 19, Churchill arrived, informed as he was by Mountbatten, that Roosevelt was weakening on BOLERO. On June 21, there was what Stimson described as a "big pow-wow and fuss" at the White House. Churchill was there. Roosevelt hastily summoned Stimson, Marshall and other top ranking military and naval men. Churchill agreed there must be an attack in 1943 but insisted on a Mediterranean and Balkan plan. Churchill, says Stimson, insisted Germany could be defeated by a series of attritions in Northern Italy, the Eastern Mediterranean, Greece, Balkans, Rumania and other satellite countries—then satellites of Hitler, now satellites of Stalin. Marshall took with him Colonel Al Wedemeyer of the War Plans Division, who was working on plans for the 1943 invasion. Wedemeyer presented the case against the Balkan invasion in 1943 so powerfully he convinced everyone, including Churchill, it was too hazardous. Operation BOLERO (1943 invasion of France), Operation GYMNAST (invasion of North Africa) and Churchill's plans were reviewed. Roosevelt stood by BOLERO, Churchill assented, the conference ended and Churchill went home.

Less than a month later, Stimson and Marshall learned that the British again were questioning BOLERO. Marshall was so outraged that he proposed to Stimson that the English be told flatly that as they "won't go through with what they agreed to, we will turn our backs on them and take up the war with Japan." Stimson agreed but merely as a bluff to bring the English around. The President assured them he "was sound on BOLERO." But Stimson felt he was still nursing a lingering preference for the North African operation. Marshall, King and Hopkins were sent to London to decide on the strategy for 1943. The upshot of that was that Roosevelt's pet plan, GYMNAST (a North African invasion) was adopted. It was rechristened TORCH. It meant the end of BOLERO (a 1943 cross-channel invasion). The North African project would consume so much materiel that a French invasion in 1943 would be impossible. The 1943 French invasion was the "baby of the American War Department, approved by all its top-ranking generals and planners." Actually the British professional military staff in Washington also agreed to it. In turning to his own pet scheme—the North African invasion—and thus making the 1943 invasion of France impossible, Roosevelt acted against the advice of all his military and naval leaders. The invasion of Europe was put off for another year—until 1944.[58] Had it been carried through in 1943 as the military men demanded, the British and American forces would have had a full year longer to batter their way across France, into Germany and all Western Europe, including the satellite states—to take large areas Stalin was later to take. There would have been no divided Germany, no divided Poland. Czechoslovakia, Austria, Hungary and perhaps large parts of the Balkans would never have fallen into the clutches of Russia. The one chance of avoiding all those terrible conditions in Eastern Europe which later bedeviled us was thrown away. Either Churchill's Balkan proposals or Marshall's and Stimson's 1943 project might have accomplished this. Roosevelt's pet scheme of GYMNAST, which Churchill seized on as a means of defeating the 1943 invasion, ended any hope of seeing a victory map of Europe favorable to the ideas we were fighting for. Any statesman looking realistically into the future would have known what Russia's intentions were. The evidence was overwhelming. It was presented frequently by men who were rewarded for their pains with the smear of being fascists and Hitlerites. But Roosevelt had taken that incredible line of opinion and policy about Stalin which resulted in ruling out of his calculations the tremendous political consequences of a Russian victory before the Allies could liberate the conquered countries.

2. ROOSEVELT'S GREAT DESIGN AND CASABLANCA

It was January, 1943—at Casablanca—before the first great conference of the Big Three was set. Then it turned out to be a conference of the Big Two. Stalin refused to appear. And behind this lies a story which explains in a general way all that follows.

On September 24, 1941, a month after the Atlantic Charter was proclaimed, an inter-allied meeting was held in St. James Palace. Mr. Maisky, the Soviet Ambassador to Great Britain, said:

> "The Soviet was and is guided in its foreign policy by the principle of the self-determination of nations. Accordingly the Soviet defends the right of every nation to the independence and territorial integrity of its country and its right to establish such a social order as it deems opportune and necessary for the promotion of its economic and cultural prosperity."[59]

He then proclaimed Russia's agreement with the declaration of the Atlantic Charter.

Could anything be plainer? Yet surely Roosevelt must have reflected that in September, 1939, Stalin made a pact with Hitler under which he was given eastern Poland as the price of his perfidy. Our State Department knew that Soviet Russia had never ceased to assert her claim to these countries. Not long before the signing of the pact in London adhering to the Atlantic Charter, Anthony Eden had been in Moscow where he was confronted with a proposed Soviet-British-American agreement *recognizing Russia's claims to the Baltic states, Finland and the eastern half of Poland.* Assistant Secretary of State Berle knew of it and suggested it would be difficult for the small states to withstand the inevitable expansion of a great power after the war. The President himself admitted that the British government had approached him on the subject of Russia's claims on the Baltic states. Ambassador Halifax suggested to the Polish Ambassador in Washington that Russia "was not bluffing" and posed some arguments in support of her claims. Our Ambassador in London, Winant, was impressed with the reasonableness of the Russian claims. Actually the British and Russians signed a treaty in May, 1942, and Secretary of State Hull told the Polish Ambassador, Jan Ciechanowski, that up to the last minute the concessions to Russia were included but were taken out at his insistence.[60]

The Polish Premier, Sikorski, visited America and talked with Roosevelt. He told the President he feared the British would yield to Russia. Roosevelt said to him: *"I want you to understand, General, that the American government has not forgotten the Atlantic Charter."* [61] The situation was saved for the moment. But the point I am trying to make clear is that Roosevelt was fully informed of the ambitions that Russia was pressing so vigorously before the ink was dry on her explicit adoption of the Atlantic Charter.

Roosevelt must have known that Russia continued to plan to carry out her intentions. Already she had organized in Russia a collection of Red Polish expatriates as the foundation of that phony Lublin government which she ultimately set up over Poland. And in February, 1942, a score of American writers had published a statement supporting the claims Russia was making to these menaced countries.

The truth is that what Russia wanted was as plain as the mustache on Stalin's face. More than one American observer pointed out these aims. Early in the Spring of 1943, Demaree Bess, in the *Saturday Evening Post*,[62] wrote a very clear prospectus of what Russia wanted. There had been a lot of foggy talk about the "great Russian mystery" and "Stalin, the Great Enigma." Bess pointed out what was perfectly obvious, that there was no enigma about Stalin and Russia. He confirmed the story that soon after being attacked the Russians revealed to the British their claims upon Poland and parts of Rumania. Sir Stafford Cripps and the conservative London *Times* both advocated their acceptance. And while, under pressure from Hull, the grant of these claims was omitted from the 1942 treaty between Britain and Russia, Russia never abandoned these claims.

Bess wrote: "Since they (the Russians) have made their desires so clear in negotiations with the Germans and later with the British,

*nobody has any right to be surprised if the Russians move again into all the
territories they occupied in 1939 and 1940 and incorporate them into the
Soviet Union.*"

As to the war in the Pacific, Bess wrote: "It is clear that war in
Europe will end before war in the Pacific. Russia will be at peace
while we are still fighting. Is it likely she will enter the Pacific war?
Why should she? Russia wants the defeat of Japan. But the United
States will do that job. Stalin has shown that he does not involve his
country in unnecessary wars. If they want any territories in the Far
East they can come into the war whenever they like and take over any
territories they desire as their share of the spoils." Russia, he said,
"makes no pledges, demands a free hand in the post-war settlements
in territories adjoining her borders and a full and equal partnership in
world affairs when peace comes." A man took the risk of being called
a fascist for making such statements in 1943.

Against all this what was Roosevelt's plan? We need be in no doubt
about that. First of all, he had set up in his mind an objective which
he called his "Great Design." Forrest Davis, writing in the *Saturday
Evening Post*[63] an obviously White House-inspired article, described
it. This Great Design was a union of the nations of the world in a
great organization for peace at the end of the war. He would bring
into being a United Nations. It would be modeled on our own inter-
American system—a loose and flexible association without any surrender of sovereignty. It would have no police force of its own to enforce its authority but would depend on the air forces of its powerful
partners. It would have to include Russia, and, to bring Russia in, she
and all countries would have to submerge their ideological differences, subdue their racial grievances, their ancient ambitions and
collaborate loyally with all other nations in the reorganization of
Europe. And of course at the bottom of this association would be the
principles of the Atlantic Charter. And at the very center of this
"Great Design" was Roosevelt's belief that he could bring Stalin in as
a sincere and willing collaborator in the post-war settlements.

As he saw it, Stalin was his great target. He began by completely
deceiving himself about Stalin. First of all, he decided he must cultivate Stalin's good will and to do this he convinced himself he must
sell Stalin to our people. Accordingly the instruments of propaganda

which he could influence—the radio and the movies and to a considerable degree, the press—were set to work upon the great task.

Under the influence of this benevolent atmosphere the Reds in New York and their compliant dupes, the fellow-travelers, swarmed into Washington and presently were sitting in positions of power or influence in the policy-making sections of the government. Joe Davies had been induced to go to Moscow and wrote his notorious "Mission to Moscow," a jumble of obvious fictions which were later transferred to the screen several times exaggerated and shot into millions of minds in movie houses. Commentators on the air—some outright Reds, some Reds at heart, some shallow tools of the Reds—poured out the propaganda for Red objectives seven days a week, 24 hours a day while the time on the air plus their own princely salaries were paid by the most conservative business houses of America—often induced to hire these Russian tools to please a government that exercised tremendous power over their affairs.

Let me repeat that, under the influence of the propaganda he had promoted, and reinforced by his own eagerness to please Stalin, no one in the country was more thoroughly deceived by it than Roosevelt himself. As soon as Russia was invaded Roosevelt sent Harry Hopkins to visit Stalin and to learn what he wanted. Averill Harriman, an agreeable but not too sagacious emissary, was sent to Stalin as American Ambassador. Hopkins made several visits. Roosevelt boasted that "Harry and Uncle Joe got on like a house afire. They have become buddies." Hopkins said it was ridiculous to think of Stalin as a Communist. He was a Russian nationalist. Harriman told various persons that Stalin was not at all a revolutionary Communist but just a Russian nationalist. He told the Polish Ambassador that not once in his conversations with Stalin did he indicate that the old Leninist policy of world revolution was still the aim of Stalinist Russia.[64] Both of them, Hopkins and Harriman, plus Joe Davies, were completely taken in and they in turn passed on their deceptions to Roosevelt, who swallowed them without salt. He, too, assured visitors that Stalin was not a Communist at all but just a real Russian patriot.

Having satisfied himself on this point, Roosevelt decided he would force a meeting with Stalin, convince him of his own friendship, turn upon Stalin his disarming smile and break down with his famous charm the cold realism of that hard-bitten old tyrant. The notion that he could talk Stalin out of the age-old aims of the Russian government by turning on him his charming manner seems now, to say the least, a little naive.

The moment came, however, when he hoped he would get Stalin to expose himself to his seductions. In January, Roosevelt and Churchill agreed to meet with their respective military advisers at Casablanca. Not until just before they got to Casablanca were they sure Stalin would not appear. When Elliott Roosevelt arrived the first question to his father was: "Is he coming?" Later Roosevelt said: "I have tried five times to see that man and he has always eluded me."[65]

Stalin did not elude Roosevelt because he feared to face his charm. It was his inflexible purpose not to make any commitments to anyone. He pursued a relentless line of demands upon Roosevelt and Churchill. He wanted that second front. He said he was fighting Hitler alone, Russia was throwing millions into the battles; the Allies were merely promising. When would they make good? He wanted allied armies in France and he wanted Lend-Lease and more Lend-Lease. He kept the American military mission in a state of continuous apology and explanation. When Molotov or any other Russian was questioned about Poland and the Baltic states and the war, he simply said he had no authority to talk about them. And Uncle Joe, as Roosevelt always referred to him, refused to show up. Meanwhile time was running against Roosevelt. He deferred every other effort in favor of his hope to meet Stalin personally and talk him into his "Great Design"—his One World with its arrangement for perpetual peace. It was January, 1943, when Churchill and Roosevelt met at Casablanca. Two full years had been wasted, instead of applying to Stalin the only pressure he could understand. All he could hope for in arms and material aid he got as fast as we could get them to him without laying down a single condition. Now the Russian armies were pushing the invaders back. Roosevelt's hands were weakened and Stalin's were strengthened. So at Casablanca, Roosevelt and Churchill discussed getting more goods and aid to Russia without any conditions. They discussed the rift between DeGaulle and General Giraud and settled it by getting them to shake hands before the camera. There was a great theatrical display and when the conference ended the President sailed for Dakar in Africa and then to Brazil where he and Vargas put on a Roman display to the huzzas of the people.

3. FIRST QUEBEC CONFERENCE

Once again the leaders met to confer. This time it was August 17, 1943 at Quebec and once again it was the Big Two and not the Big Three. Once again the great war spectacle went into action—clouds of planes, fleets of ships, a huge cast of brass. Churchill and Roosevelt and their foreign ministers, Eden and Hull, were there. So was Harry Hopkins.

This conference had been originally scheduled to meet at Manitoulin Island in Lake Huron with Stalin in the party. But Stalin was too busy managing his war. Besides, as Churchill observed, Stalin had nothing to say to these men but one thing—second front! There was the big front in Italy and the tremendous war from the air on Germany. But Stalin did not admit that the bombing of Germany from London or the Italian drive were second fronts. Some of his under-strappers became actually offensive. And as for conferences, he was too busy managing his great armies in Russia. Moreover the tide was running his way. The Russians were driving the Germans before them now. And all that Stalin wanted was allied soldiers in France, and guns, tanks, planes, munitions for his own armies. The latter he got in vast quantities *without any conditions being annexed to the grants.*

At this time Italy was prostrate. Mussolini had quit and fled to the North. Badoglio was made chief of the ramshackle remnants of the Italian state. Crowds in the streets of Rome were crying for peace. Italian surrender would have come sooner but for the policy of "unconditional surrender" adopted by Roosevelt and Churchill. The beaten and terrified Italian leaders feared to surrender unconditionally not knowing what their own fate would be because of the dire prophecies of punishment for all the guilty collaborators in the Nazi aggression. Thus the Italian war dragged on, adding to the death toll of Italian and American soldiers every day surrender was postponed. Italy did actually surrender on September 8.

The Italian debacle had altered materially the face of things in Europe. Now that Italy was beaten, Churchill came forward again with his plans for a Balkan invasion. The military obstacles that were truly great while Italy was in the war were now immensely reduced. Churchill believed an allied invasion could be made through Yugoslavia. But Stalin was as much as ever opposed to such an adventure and he had been making this opposition known vehemently. Roosevelt was determined to do nothing to displease Stalin. The moment was near at hand, he hoped, to bring that gentleman across the table from him and to induce him to discard his ruthless ambitions in east Europe and to come peacefully into the "Great Design." It has been reported that Churchill at Quebec sought to convince Roosevelt to take a more realistic line with Stalin, but without effect. Indeed by this time, as we shall see, the mere project of a meeting with Stalin had become a kind of objective in itself, for which Roosevelt seemed willing to risk the most important considerations. He had now persuaded the Russian leader to agree to a conference of the foreign ministers. In fact, Hull and Eden, while at Quebec, were making arrangements to go to Moscow to meet Molotov. Roosevelt was expecting great things from this prologue to the ultimate grand conclave of the Big Three where he would pin Stalin down.

4. HULL'S GREAT TRIUMPH AT MOSCOW

The next act in this great tragi-comedy was Mr. Hull's conference in Moscow. Hull, Molotov and Eden sat down together and talked about some pressing matters. Nothing was known of what occurred until Mr. Hull returned. And when on November 10, 1943 he came back to Washington, it was as a conquering hero. The newspapers broke out in a lurid rash of headlines proclaiming his magnificent success. "HULL RETURNING IN TRIUMPH FINDS PRESIDENT AT AIR-PORT" was the New York *Times* headline. "The whole welcome had the air of a triumphal return which indeed it was," ran the *Times'* story. Senator Byrd said "Secretary Hull has achieved a diplomatic triumph almost beyond belief."

On November 18, 1943, amid an elaborately arranged appearance before a joint session of the Congress, the Secretary told of his meeting with Molotov and Eden. Russia, Britain and the United States had pledged themselves to prosecute the war to a successful conclusion. They recognized the necessity of establishing an international organization. They agreed to consult with each other until this was done. They agreed further that after hostilities they would not use their military forces in other states except after joint consultation.

All this, as we now know, was pure show. There had been no triumph. It was a deliberate deception of the American people and they, along with Congress, were thoroughly taken in by it. No mention had been made of the only really controversial question that had intruded itself on this unequal contest of men in Moscow. That was the question concerning those countries in eastern Europe, particularly Poland, whose fate, should Russia occupy them, was a subject of grave concern.

It was also a subject of grave political concern to Mr. Roosevelt who by this time was thinking in terms of 1944 and his ambition to be elected for a fourth term. The votes of American citizens of Polish birth and descent, to say nothing of great numbers of Lithuanians, Greeks and peoples of other Balkan ancestries who had supported him were a matter of very immediate importance. As we have seen, these votes are powerful altogether out of proportion to their numbers because they are centered in a number of great industrial areas where they can, in certain circumstances, hold the balance of power when they act in unity. By this time the Russian armies had forced the Germans back to the banks of the Dnieper. Hitler was still in possession of the Baltic states, all of the Balkans and of Poland. But it was evident that the time was not far distant when Stalin's generals would approach the Baltic and Polish borders. American Poles and Baltic peoples were nervous about Stalin's intentions in these menaced lands.

The day before Hull had left for Moscow he had sent for Mr. Ciechanowski, the Polish Ambassador. He wanted an exchange of views with the Ambassador. The Ambassador told him the Polish government wanted some arrangement that would protect Poland against the danger when Russian armies should occupy their country. It felt that as soon as the Russians entered Poland, the Polish government-in-exile in London should be brought back to Warsaw. The Polish army and government should occupy Poland and continue to collaborate with the Russians. Mr. Ciechanowski appealed to Mr. Hull for a guarantee by the United States and Britain of Polish territorial integrity and independence.

Hull agreed with this. He shared the Ambassador's apprehensions about Russia's plans. The Ambassador warned him against the wiles of Russian diplomacy. But the aged Secretary smiled and said he was not likely to be taken in by such methods. In bidding the Ambassador good-bye, Hull assured him *"he was decided to defend the cause of Poland as he would defend the cause of his own country."* Actually, Hull was a sick man. He told friends that, in the last analysis, despite his poor health and the difficulties of the voyage, it was the Polish question which had decided him to make the trip. He declared he felt "he had to defend Poland to the death."

When Hull returned to Washington it was natural that the Polish Ambassador should be eager to know what had happened. Presently whisperings were heard around the State Department that Hull had to make some serious sacrifices at Moscow. Some White House officials told the Ambassador that the account of Mr. Hull's triumph was much exaggerated. He learned that Harry Hopkins had said to a friend that "we are prostrate about the Moscow conference." Ciechanowski sought him out and Hopkins confirmed it. Then why all the enthusiasm about the conference? Ciechanowski put that question to Hopkins. "Perhaps," he answered, "we want to show the Soviets we harbor no suspicions of their conduct." There were other rumors that Poland and the Baltic states had been sacrificed at Moscow.

But Hull kept himself incommunicado until he addressed Congress. The next day he received the Polish Ambassador. Then he talked with the air of a man who felt explanations were needed. He said he found himself in an unfamiliar setting. He had to discuss a lot of problems with a partner—Molotov—who was, to say the least, difficult. Besides he did not know him very well. He felt he had to create a favorable atmosphere and he had done that. He had gone to Moscow feeling that his "main aim was to bring about the establishment of Soviet-Polish relations." In talking with Molotov he had tried to impress that on him. He admitted that he got nowhere with Molotov, who would not even discuss the matter unless the Poles were ready to acknowledge territorial changes. The Soviets were taking advantage of their military position and regarded the subject as solved in their favor. Then came the truth. *He had not even discussed the subject. The Russians wouldn't even talk about it.* Mr.

Ciechanowski reported that Hull "faced with the choice of forcing the discussion or putting it off to future meetings, he thought it more judicious to take the latter course." Such was his triumph.

Mr. Ciechanowski asked the Secretary point-blank if the optimism that had been spread in Washington was justified. Hull replied that his effort at initiating a good understanding had been successful but "he certainly didn't think anyone could draw optimistic conclusions from it." And then this aged, tired and ailing old man who had been exploited perhaps without his full consent as the hero of a great diplomatic victory, said pathetically that "he had tried to take the Soviets by the hand and lead them along the way to understanding."[66]

What did Stalin think when Molotov had sent Hull away empty-handed and then witnessed the American President and Congress celebrating the incident as a great triumph? He knew now he was dealing with weak partners who could be pushed around at will.

The conference concerned itself with military matters also and Major General John R. Deane,[67] head of the American military mission, was there with a staff. Fortunately, General Deane is undoubtedly a man with a sense of humor and we owe to him much of what we know about the caviar and vodka aspects of the great Russian conferences. This one opened with a luncheon. Around the board sat the gentlemen who were, when the feast ended, to sit around another board to discuss some of the gravest issues affecting the destiny of the world. On the vast table were bottles of vodka, wines, liqueurs in profusion. Then came a succession of courses, borsch, fish, roasts and so on. Before the borsch was down, Molotov was up with his glass and a toast. Then followed a succession of toasts in which the eminent statesmen toasted Stalin, Churchill and Roosevelt and then each other and then almost everyone at the table, together with such abstract ideas as Peace and Justice and Victory. They drank bottoms up. The liqueurs flowed, the good cheer rose, the eloquence glowed. General Deane frankly confesses in his entertaining book that at the end he was goggle-eyed and that old Mother Russia, as he beheld her through vodka-tinted glasses, presented a very rosy picture.

From this feast, loaded with victuals and vodka, the remodelers of the new world rose around four in the afternoon and walked across the hall to the conference room, where around another board they assembled to begin their deliberations. Hull and Eden and Molotov were there, plus Vishinsky, the famous purge prosecutor, Marshal Voroshiloff and the numerous staffs of all the ministers. Hull, however, being ill, did not attend any of the feasts. Russia had one question—second front. General Deane, gradually emerging from the warm fumes of the vodka, armed with maps and charts, answered the question. The second front would be, as Stalin wished it, through France. It had been fixed for a somewhat earlier day but had had to be put off. He described in realistic terms the effects of the strafing of Germany. The whole discussion, he writes, began in an atmosphere of suspicion, but he had photographs to prove his points and the Russians were satisfied. But when is the second front coming? In the Spring. Yes, but when in the Spring? Finally the General said in May. This finally suited the Russians.

When the whole conference ended there was a banquet given by Stalin—a gargantuan feast that made the first luncheon look like a slight barroom snack. There was one incident which must not be overlooked. At one point General Deane was called to rise, drink bottoms up and deliver his toast. He did. To his amazement, Stalin left his chair, walked around the diners to the General who, glowing with vodka, beheld himself standing face to face with the most famous man in the world, clinking glasses with him and receiving his approval in a rumble of Slavic gutturals. The General, speaking of the whole affair later, had to allow that Uncle Joe was a very nice fellow. As we work through the numerous eye-witness accounts of these Russian affairs we will find that one after another of our American agents who went to Moscow went through the same exhilarating experience as the General. They beheld themselves standing clinking glasses with the mighty Dictator of all the Russians. He even put his arm around some of them. It was too much for them. With the steam of the vodka in their brains and the hand of the dictator on their shoulder, they one and all had to confess that Uncle Joe was a swell guy.

As Hull set out for home, Roosevelt was making ready for his journey to the next conference, which was scheduled for Cairo between himself, Churchill and Chiang Kai-shek. When Hull got home he had one thing to report to Roosevelt which the President looked upon as a real victory. Hull had made an appointment—at least a tentative one—for Stalin to meet Roosevelt and Churchill at

Teheran in Iran, following the Cairo meeting. This was great news to the President. He would get the Russian dictator across the table from him at last.

5. CAIRO AND TEHERAN

A.—CAIRO

President Roosevelt left for Cairo in November, 1943. He was still not sure he would meet Stalin. He told his Secret Service guard, Mike Reilly,[68] that he was going to Cairo and "hoped" to meet Stalin at Teheran. He left on the battleship *Iowa* for Oran and went from there to Cairo by plane. He was accompanied by General Eisenhower, Admiral Leahy, Admiral McIntire, Harry Hopkins and a considerable staff. At Cairo the numerous British and American staffs were quartered in various hotels and villas outside Cairo around the site of the Pyramids. Roosevelt took up his quarters in the villa of the American Ambassador. At the time allied armies were moving on Rome. Allied production of planes, ships, guns, tanks was reaching its peak. And Roosevelt was greatly relieved when Andrei Vishinsky called on him at Ambassador Kirk's to say that Marshal Stalin would leave his troops for a few days to be with Roosevelt and Churchill at Teheran.

At Cairo, Roosevelt and Churchill met General and Madame Chiang Kai-shek. As Stalin had an alliance with Japan and was not at war with her, he was not asked to Cairo. The conference between Roosevelt and Chiang lasted from November 22 to 26. When it ended the inevitable communique announced that they had agreed upon military plans against Japan with increasing pressure and without desire for territorial expansion, which was not news. More to the point was the announced agreement to strip Japan of all the territories and islands in the Pacific which she had conquered or occupied in World Wars I and II, to drive her out of the vast provinces she had stolen from China, to restore freedom and independence to Korea and to force Japan to unconditional surrender.

As always, the important things were not disclosed. Roosevelt told his son, Elliott, that Chiang had not been fighting the Japs seriously but instead was using his armies to fight the Chinese Communist army.[69] Here we must note that the real nature of the aggression of Japan in China was never made clear to the American people. It was in fact intentionally obscured. The Japs did not fight China in order to seize all China. They wanted Manchuria in the North. Manchuria is the great storehouse of natural resources in China. It was Chinese. Japan wanted those resources and her purpose was to set up there the kind of government Stalin would later set up in Yugoslavia and Poland. *It is important to keep in mind that there never was a time when China could not have made peace with Japan by agreeing to let Manchuria go, to be ruled by a Manchurian puppet of Japan.*

However, Russia also wanted Manchuria. She did not want to incorporate this rich province into Russia. She wanted to do what Japan wanted to do. She wanted a Communist puppet government there. She wanted to assist in its conquest by Chinese Communists just as Yugoslavia was conquered by Yugoslavian Communists under Tito, a puppet of Stalin. For a long time these Chinese Communist armies under Mao-Tse and Chu-Teh had been pushing their Red army toward Manchuria poised to enter and seize it the moment the Japanese were driven out. In fact, they wished to perform the service of driving them out and occupying Manchuria.

Chiang, of course, was as much opposed to this as he was to the Japanese aggression. And for an obvious reason. Chiang was using all his military power to defeat these Communist armies. What would he gain by driving the Japanese out of Manchuria merely to open it to the Communists? But what we denounced in Japan as a heinous aggression, our government was willing to condone in Russia.

At this time we were selling Russia on a grand scale to the American people. Russian agents and sympathizers, native and foreign, had inserted themselves into all of the instruments of propaganda, where they kept up a steady offensive against the minds of the American people. At this moment what they wanted was to compel Chiang to stop fighting the Communists and to take them in fact into his own government, where, with our aid and Russia's, they would soon perform on Chiang the same job that Tito performed on Mikhailovitch and that the Polish "Committee of Liberation" performed on Sikorski and Mikolajczyk. All this they compressed into one of those fatal sloganized arguments with which, during the war, they did such terrible work upon our minds. They called it "Unity in China." The glorious achievements of Mao-Tse and Chu-Teh were sounded daily in radio commentaries. Edgar Snow, in the *Saturday Evening Post*, praised the work of the Communist army which he presented under the euphemistic name of the Partisan army, which fell easier upon American ears. What Stalin wanted and what Mr. Snow and those of his school wanted in China was inadvertently given away in that article in the following sentences:

"The situation in China is *somewhat similar to that in Yugoslavia,* (italics added) with the Chinese Partisans led by General Chu-Teh and Mao-Tse-Tung corresponding to Marshal Tito and his following and the policy of Chungking being the same which Mikhailovitch and King Peter tried to enforce toward Yugoslav guerrillas.

"In Yugoslavia, we and the British now actively aid Tito, simply because his forces actively fight the Axis, but in Asia we have so far given no official recognition to the Chu-Mao armies, which offer the only armed opposition to the Japanese in North China."[70]

And so Roosevelt secretly demanded of Chiang Kai-shek that he take the Communists into his government, quit opposition to the Communist army which might then take Manchuria for the benefit of Stalin. In return, and behind Churchill's back, he pledged to Chiang that he would keep the British out of Hong Kong and other ports where they were formerly entrenched.[71]

B.—TEHERAN

Leaving Cairo, Roosevelt and his party flew 600 miles to Teheran, the capital of Iran, where at last he was to achieve his dream of meeting the Russian dictator. Churchill and his immediate staff were housed at the British embassy. But Roosevelt was taken to the Russian embassy. The Russian secret police had convinced Mike Reilly, Roosevelt's bodyguard, that this was essential to Roosevelt's safety in a neutral country swarming with Nazi spies.

The conference of the Big Three lasted from November 28 to December 1. When it ended the world learned what the communique told it. Once again "they had met, they had talked, they had resolved." Resolved what? They would work together. They had concerted plans that would guarantee victory. They would forge a peace after the war that would command the good will of the world and banish the scourge of war for generations. They had surveyed the future. They would seek the cooperation of all nations opposed to slavery and intolerance in the Family of Nations. Then a cryptic boast about what they would do to Germany on land, at sea and in the air. And of course they looked to the day when all peoples would live untouched by tyranny and according to their desires and consciences. "We came with hope and determination. We leave here friends in fact, in spirit and in purpose."

That is all the world knew about it and when the President returned to America it was amidst the usual demonstrations of triumph. All the publicity revealed him as the great figure dominating the conference, enforcing his plans, imposing his will upon his two powerful colleagues.

But little by little the curtain has been drawn aside and we have been allowed a peep into the councils of the great men who met and talked and proclaimed at Teheran. As they met Roosevelt was eager. He was going to charm Stalin by exhibiting at every turn a desire to agree with him, even at the expense of disagreeing with Churchill. In an obviously White House-inspired article, Forrest Davis[72] wrote that Roosevelt purposely pursued a soft policy toward Stalin, and that he avoided from the beginning giving the slightest offense to him. He complied with every wish of Stalin's as readily as possible. He believed that Russia could organize her vast powers and that, when victorious, she could be brought into the family of nations. He was convinced that the thing Russia needed most was peace. And he believed that Stalin was far more interested in Russia's national welfare than in Marxian socialism. Of course Stalin's desire for those eastern European countries which he seemed planning to seize under one pretext or another was based on a natural desire to ensure friendly and peaceful states on Russia's borders. But when the world organization would be formed with Stalin in it, Roosevelt thought Stalin would no longer have anything to fear from his neighbors in this brave new world organized for security and that he would freely release the peoples he was seeking to take over.

Roosevelt proposed to do a little educational work on Stalin. He gave him two long lectures—one on our federal system and one on our good neighbor policy. He stressed how we had such good neighbors because we had no aggressive ambitions against our Central and South American friends. Of course Stalin listened to all this with approval. He assured Roosevelt he had no desire to "own all Europe."

Russia, only half-populated, had plenty to do at home without interfering with her neighbors.

In order to avoid irritating disputes, Roosevelt arrived at the incredible conclusion that it was more important to have a reciprocal spirit among the Big Three than specific compacts. His purpose was to *build Uncle Joe into a good neighbor, a better democrat and a good fellow.*

Stalin, on the other hand, had a definite collection of objectives to attain. He would reach them either in definite compacts to secure those objectives or, where possible, without bothering with his allies. What he wanted was as clear as day. He wanted the Baltic states, East Poland, parts of Rumania and he wanted puppet governments in West Poland, Yugoslavia, Rumania, Bulgaria, Czechoslovakia, Hungary, Greece and, of course in Korea and Manchuria. His policy was to commit himself to nothing, to admit nothing and to demand and demand and demand—and to keep Roosevelt, particularly, in fear of his making a separate peace and in a state of continuous apology for not opening a second front. He wanted that front and he wanted it in France. His armies were approaching the very territories he proposed to take and when he entered them he intended to hold them and organize them to suit himself. Nobody but an infatuated man could fail to perceive all this. Stalin saw that in Roosevelt he was dealing with an easy mark and he played him to the top of his bent.

Churchill, a far more experienced diplomat than Roosevelt and also far more realistic, wanted to save from Stalin's grasp as much of the southern Balkans as possible. He was determined to prevent Stalin from realizing the old Russian dream of a Russian-controlled outlet on the Mediterranean. He was willing to sacrifice Poland for this. He wanted to see the allied armies go into the continent through the Balkans in order that they would be in possession of as much of those countries in the south—Greece, Yugoslavia, Hungary, Austria and whatever else they could take—before the Russians got in. Besides, it was now too late to beat the Russians into Poland and the Baltic. Churchill was not fooled by Stalin and Stalin knew it and that is why they were at each other's throats during the several conferences.

As these three men sat down to confer, two of them, Stalin and Churchill, were realists with their eyes fixed on definite objectives in the interest of their respective governments. They wanted specific and realizable things. Roosevelt deceived himself into believing that the mere meeting of himself and Stalin was "half his battle" as he told Elliott, and that, for the rest, he wanted to create a condition of mutual trust and understanding. *Specific agreements about the post-war world could wait, trusting to mutual good will to provide the desired solutions.*[73]

Major General Deane, who was at all the conferences as the head of the U. S. Military Mission, wrote:

> "Stalin appeared to know just what he wanted at the conference. This was also true of Churchill, *but not of Roosevelt* ... His apparent indecision was probably the result of our obscure foreign policy." (Italics added)[74]

General Deane points out that Roosevelt was thinking of winning the war but that Stalin and Churchill were thinking of *their relative positions when the war was won.* Stalin got everything he wanted—everything without any exceptions. Churchill did not, because Roosevelt, in pursuit of his vain policy, sided with Stalin against Churchill. Roosevelt got nothing, as we shall see. He got, of course, the United Nations. But this had already been settled on before he went to Teheran. And what is more this was no victory because Stalin got the United Nations precisely on his own terms and in a form that has enabled him to put his finger into every problem in the world and to completely frustrate the British and Americans in every effort to introduce order, peace and security. Roosevelt did not get what he believed to be his objective because he made it clear he had to have Stalin's free and wholehearted support in the United Nations or it would be a failure from the start. Forrest Davis commented that Stalin acted with dash, Roosevelt with tardy improvisation. Stalin keyed *his* "great design" to control those sectors of eastern Europe which he wanted in his orbit. Roosevelt put all his eggs in one basket—his world organization scheme for which apparently he was prepared to sacrifice everything else, including the very things a world organization was expected to ensure. Meantime Stalin and Molotov did not shrink from lying or indulging in double talk and Roosevelt was foolish enough to believe them. At home Roosevelt's Red and pink collaborators and his closest consultants were busy pouring out Soviet propaganda. Harry Hopkins never tired of plugging for his friend Stalin. Henry Wallace, then Vice-President, was talking about encouraging a people's revolution in Europe to advance the cause of the common man. Tito was being glorified in American magazines by Red and pink writers and others who were just plain dupes. Stalin himself and the Soviet government were offered to the American people in new and happy colors until, as James F. Byrnes[75] conceded, as the war neared its end Russia occupied a place in the good will of the American people exceeding that of any other ally. All this had been instigated and urged by Roosevelt himself. And no one knew it better than Stalin.

The President was eager to have Russia join in the war in the Pacific, according to General Deane. Stalin explained that Soviet forces in the East would have to be increased threefold before an offensive could be undertaken and this could not be done until Germany was defeated. "Then," he said, "by our common front we shall win." That is as much as Roosevelt got.

Once again Churchill brought up the question of shifting the invasion effort from the west coast of France to the Balkans. He wanted to hurry the Italian invasion by amphibious landings in the North and on the Northeast Adriatic aimed at the Danube Valley, an operation in the Aegean aimed at Rhodes or the Dodecanese and operations in and from Turkey if she would come into the war. General Deane says that Churchill wanted the Anglo-American forces in the Balkans as well as the Russians and he suggests that Churchill's foresight was later approved by our hindsight. There can be no doubt that the invasion of the French coast was a less formidable undertaking than an invasion of the Balkans when the subject was first considered. Our opportunity to get into France in 1943 had been thrown away by Roosevelt's agreement to yield to Churchill against all his military advisers. But the African invasion had gone more swiftly than was hoped for when launched, though the Italian operation had been troublous. Now, however, that Italy was successfully invaded and the guerrilla forces in Yugoslavia were so strong the question of the Balkan invasion took on added significance. Churchill urged it now with fresh vigor. But Stalin was adamant against it and this was enough reason for Roosevelt to object. Moreover, time was now running heavily against Roosevelt and Churchill. Stalin's armies were winging their way toward his territorial objectives.[76]

Roosevelt had made his first mistake when Hitler attacked Stalin in 1941. He rushed Hopkins and Harriman to Stalin, to ask Uncle Joe what he wanted. We agreed to send him $1,500,000,000 of Lend-Lease without any condition whatever. That precious moment when the Russian armies were being driven back like cattle before Hitler's onrushing legions, when Stalin lacked everything save men, was thrown away by Roosevelt. Then was the time to force the conditions. General Deane, who remained in Moscow and saw the whole show, says Harry Hopkins carried out his collaboration with Stalin with a zeal approaching fanaticism.[77] Now Stalin wanted no Anglo-American armies in the Balkans and he wanted that second front at once. The second front was agreed on to be launched in France about May, 1944.

Then came the question of Poland, the Baltic states and Finland. Stalin said he had not decided whether he would incorporate the Baltic states into the Soviet or make them into independent (puppet) states. But it was clear that *he* would make the decision and for his own reasons. On Poland, Roosevelt could get no direct answer. Finally Churchill switched the question to Poland's Russian boundaries and then suggested the Curzon line, which is practically the same as the Stalin-Ribbentrop line agreed on between those two worthies when they decided to partition Poland. This meant Poland was to be split in two. Actually this was agreed on. But what about the fate of what was left of Poland? There was silence on that. In fact the President had gotten a complete brush-off on Poland and had taken it with complete composure.[78]

Here, too, Yugoslavia was yielded up to Stalin. And Marshal Tito was given the favor of the Big Three as against Mikhailovitch—one of the most appalling tragedies of the war. Stalin did not have to move his finger to accomplish this. It was an inside job—a job done in London inside the Foreign Office and in America inside the White House. The German army in 1940 invaded Yugoslavia and swiftly reduced it to submission. Its occupation, however, was never complete. Yugoslavia is populated by three peoples—the Serbs, the Croats and the Slovenes. The Serbs are by far the most populous. Shortly after the invasion the world began to hear of a Chetnik underground army under heroic Colonel Draja Mikhailovitch, a brilliant officer in the then dispersed Yugoslavian forces. At a later date a new name appeared, that of Josef Broz Tito, a Croat who had spent much time in Russia and became a member of the Communist party there, returning to Yugoslavia and functioning as a leader of the small Communist party. The world is familiar with the struggle between these two underground native armies—Communist and non-Communist.[79]

In the United States and Great Britain powerful influences inside both governments, operating under the tolerance extended to the Reds, got the confidence of both Churchill and Roosevelt. Leading American newspapers and magazines, deceived by government propaganda, threw themselves on the side of the Communist Tito. The most active individual with his pen was Louis Adamic,[80] a more or less professional Yugoslavian in America. He had access to the ear of Mrs. Roosevelt. He was a dinner guest at the White House. He kept up an incessant pressure at every point he could reach. He got a chance to tell President and Mrs. Roosevelt about the fine and truly democratic movement led by Tito. He had a very intimate association with the Office of War Information which was crawling with Communists and their current stooges. At the same time Mikhailovitch was berated as a fraud, as an ineffectual interloper with so little backing that Hitler offered a reward of 100,000 marks for Tito's head but nothing for Mikhailovitch's, which was a lie.

These libels on Mikhailovitch and these exaltations of Tito were repeated in other magazines. Frank Gervasi in *Collier's* wrote how Tito led 250,000 men while Mikhailovitch had no more than 10,000. The Yugoslav government-in-exile in London supported Mikhailovitch. This embarrassed the British Foreign Office in its dealings with the implacable Stalin. Hence the British Broadcasting Company was closed to the Yugoslav government-in-exile and a little later put at the disposal of Tito and his Partisans. Churchill allowed himself to be swayed for Tito. Roosevelt in 1942 had paid tribute to Mikhailovitch and his daring men. But at Teheran, as part of the policy of appeasing Stalin, the two Western leaders deserted Mikhailovitch completely and yielded to Russia. Shortly after Teheran, Churchill in a speech (February, 1944) indicated that the allies were no longer sending supplies to Mikhailovitch. Two months later King Peter was forced to dismiss Premier Purich, which meant his whole cabinet in which Mikhailovitch was Minister of War. The

Communist Subasich was made Prime Minister. The complete victory of Tito with the aid of the subsequent Russian invasion and American supplies is well known. Well known—and with shame—is the tragic story of Mikhailovitch who was shot as a traitor by Tito.

Roosevelt got nothing. He agreed with Stalin on everything—the second front in France, no attack through the Balkans, the surrender of eastern Poland, the desertion of Mikhailovitch, the sacrifice of the Baltic states. Above all, he had revealed himself to Stalin as a compliant ally. Stalin must have wondered why Roosevelt was yielding to him on everything so swiftly.

There was still something more to be settled. Stalin had engineered Roosevelt into living in the Soviet embassy although the American embassy was available. He had done this by exploiting the danger to the President from German spies. Roosevelt was, of course, in no greater danger than the British Prime Minister. The success of Stalin's maneuver in this matter was soon to become clear. Later Roosevelt told his son Elliott that "in between times Uncle Joe and I had a few words, too—just the two of us." As Stalin's guest in the Russian embassy, Roosevelt was accessible for a secret talk or two without Churchill's knowledge. One of these dealt with the Chinese Communist issue. Roosevelt told Elliott we couldn't do much about that "while Winnie was around." He brought up the question of a common front against the British on the matter of Hong Kong, Shanghai and Canton. Chiang, Roosevelt told Stalin, was worried about what Russia would do in Manchuria. Roosevelt and Stalin agreed that Manchuria would remain with China and that Stalin and he would back Chiang against the British. Referring to this, Roosevelt confided to Elliott that "the biggest thing was in making clear to Stalin that the United States and Great Britain were not in one common block against the Soviet Union."[81] After that, the way must have seemed wide open to Stalin for all his plans. Here was Roosevelt suggesting a secret deal between himself and Stalin against Churchill, just as he had suggested a secret deal between himself and Chiang against Churchill and as he was later to make another secret deal between himself and Stalin against Chiang.

He was to have a golden opportunity to convince Stalin of this attitude before he quit Teheran. Roosevelt gave a dinner the first evening, Stalin the next and Churchill on the final evening at the British embassy. At Stalin's dinner the guests gave themselves over to the victuals and the vodka in a big way. Elliott Roosevelt tells how Stalin thrust a barbed shaft into Churchill's temper. In one of his numerous toasts he raised his glass and said: "To the swiftest possible justice for all Germany's war criminals—justice before a firing squad. I drink to our unity in dispatching them as fast as we catch them, all of them, and there must be at least 50,000 of them."

Churchill flushed, leaped to his feet. He declared that any such mass murder was contrary to the British sense of justice. He was opposed to anybody, Nazis or anyone else, going before a firing squad without a proper legal trial.

Certainly no American could take exception to that and no decent American could endorse the sentiments of Stalin. Churchill having taken up the challenge, Roosevelt might have been well advised to remain out of it or, if he intervened, to either support Churchill or, in any case, attempt to mollify both men. Instead he said in a jocular vein: "Clearly there must be some compromise … Perhaps we could say that instead of summarily executing 50,000 we should settle on a smaller number, say 49,500." The Americans and Russians laughed. The British remained silent "in the presence of Churchill's mounting fury." Stalin was delighted. He took up the cue and pressed the matter. He called on everyone present for an opinion. He got around to Elliott who was flushed with liquor, as he admits, and who rose "unsteadily to his feet." Elliott said "Our armies will settle the matter for most of those 50,000 and perhaps a hundred thousand more." Stalin, greatly pleased, walked around the table to Elliott, put his arm around his shoulder and drank to his health. Churchill, infuriated, rushed to Elliott, shaking his finger in his face and crying: "Are you interested in damaging relations between the allies? Do you know what you are saying? How can you dare to say such a thing?" Elliott says he had good reason to believe Churchill never forgot the incident but that his father was greatly amused by it.[82] It was a happy opportunity for him to add, by an amusing incident, to the proofs he was giving that he and Stalin, like Hopkins and Stalin, were buddies.

The following evening there was a dinner at the British embassy on the occasion of Churchill's birthday. The Prime Minister put the incident aside and appeared in his most joyous humor, actually entertaining the guests by doing a highland fling. Czechoslovakia's disappearance in 1939 into the darkness of Hitler's tyranny had called forth doleful eloquence from Mr. Churchill. Now the disappearance of Poland and the four little Baltic states behind the dark iron curtain of Stalin's tyranny was made to the flowing beakers of vodka and the merry shouts of the happy chieftains who were arranging the affairs of the brave new world.

C.—CAIRO AGAIN

The triumph at Teheran completed, Roosevelt returned to Cairo where a few loose ends in the tattered garments of the world were yet to be tied up. There was a further meeting with the combined chiefs of staff where General Marshall was directed to announce to General Eisenhower the President's decision to name him supreme commander in the West. Incidentally, Mr. Stimson later corrected Elliott Roosevelt's version of this. Elliott says his father wanted to name Marshall supreme commander but Churchill objected. Mr. Stimson says Churchill wanted Marshall but that Roosevelt himself made the choice of Eisenhower.[83] President Inonu of Turkey was delivered to Cairo for a two-hour conference with Roosevelt and Churchill. Stalin had wanted Turkey in the war. He wanted the provinces of Kars and Ardahan and he wanted the Straits opened and kept under his protection. This meant Russian troops on Turkish soil. Inonu was willing to come in but not on these terms. Churchill wanted Turkey in, but not on Russia's terms. In the end it was decided at Cairo that Turkey would not enter the war but that the decision should be hidden behind some double talk in the communique.

With this Roosevelt's great labors abroad were over. He told Elliott he was anxious to get home. But he did not go directly. He went to Malta and then to Sicily and was photographed there presenting a medal to General Clark. Then he flew to Dakar, boarded the *Iowa* and sailed for home and Christmas with his family at Hyde Park. His return was welcomed with the usual blast of glorification for the great victory at Teheran.

On January 4, Stalin's victorious legions swept into Poland. A tremor of doubt and fear went through the diplomatic representatives of Poland, Yugoslavia, Bulgaria and Greece. What agreement had Roosevelt been able to wring from Stalin before he could set foot upon the soil of the Balkan countries? They besieged Hull for some information. But he had to confess that Roosevelt tried to raise the question but met no encouragement from Stalin. It is doubtful if Hull really knew. However, on January 11, Stalin announced the incorporation of the eastern half of Poland into the Ribbentrop-Molotov line (now rechristened the Curzon line). But what would he do with the western half of Poland? Stalin praised his Red-sponsored Union of Polish Patriots made up of former Poles living in Russia. There was an ominous portent in that. On February 22, Churchill made a speech in the Commons in which he said that Poland must make territorial concessions to Russia. The Polish, Baltic and Balkan diplomats in Washington could not get to Roosevelt. He was either away from Washington, ill, or too busy with the coming second front. The Polish Ambassador tried to arrange a meeting for the new Polish premier Mikolajczyk. But he was put off for one reason or another. He did not succeed in arranging an audience for Mikolajczyk until June.

By this time the President's fourth-term nomination and approaching election were at hand. It was what he called his "political year." It will be recalled that Hopkins had said "they were prostrate about the Moscow conference." Why? Because Poland was endangered? Hopkins cared nothing about Poland. It was at this time, when Mr. Ciechanowski twitted Hopkins about his "indifference to the human angle," that Hopkins agreed with him and told him "I love only Roosevelt." This was Hopkins' career—serving Roosevelt from whom he derived his own power and the exquisite pleasure of moving the pawns in so prodigious and delirious a game as a planetary war. He was prostrate about the Moscow conference because of its effect on Roosevelt's coming bid for another term as President. He explained to the Polish envoy: "How can we expect him, now we are getting busy preparing him for his reelection, suddenly to get up and express his doubt of the possibility of Soviet-American collaboration?"[84]

When the Polish Prime Minister Mikolajczyk arrived for his visit with Roosevelt, everywhere he was cautioned about Roosevelt's "political year." The President talked to him about it. Stettinius, who was functioning as Acting Secretary of State in Hull's absence, told him about it several times. Hopkins talked about it. Stettinius told

Mikolajczyk that the President could not adopt a more decisive attitude with Stalin "in view of the elections." But why not? What could Stalin do about the American elections? Did Stalin control any votes here?

In fact the political problem presented to Roosevelt was very delicate. We know now from the election returns of 1944 that the Reds had in their hands enough support to have turned the tide against Roosevelt. In New York State, for instance, Roosevelt won its 47 electoral votes by a majority of 317,000. But he got 825,000 votes from the Red American Labor Party dominated by the Communists, which had also nominated him, and the American Liberal Party made up of the pinks, which also nominated him. Without these votes he would have lost the state. He dared not defy these two powerful groups. On the other hand, he was in a very deep hole with the votes of the Polish, Lithuanian, Serbian and other Baltic and Balkan peoples living in America who were citizens. He had betrayed the Poles, the Serbs and the Baltic peoples. But he had managed to keep it dark. Somehow he must avoid any publication of the truth until after the election. This was his last try for power. He needed the votes of these American minority groups for one more election.

He therefore avoided any whisper of dissatisfaction with his Moscow and Teheran conferences in order to hold his Red and pink vote in the big industrial centers. And he used every artifice to deceive the Poles and other "liberated" peoples for just one more election. Accordingly, after holding the Polish Premier off for as long as possible, he arranged for a visit in June. When Mikolajczyk arrived he was received with every distinction. Stettinius remained with him constantly. Roosevelt talked with him at least four times. He gave a state dinner for him. But Stalin was making the going difficult for his friend Roosevelt. In July he handed over the western part of Poland which remained "free" to the "Committee of Liberation" headed by a Soviet Quisling named Bierut, a former Pole long a Soviet citizen. This frightened the Palace Guard in the White House and the discerning men around Democratic headquarters. They confessed that the Polish vote was critically important in Illinois, Michigan, Pennsylvania and New Jersey and above all in New York.

But before the election the Polish leaders in Europe were to learn the whole dark truth. Mikolajczyk went to Moscow to meet Stalin and see what could be done. There was a conference between Stalin, Churchill, Mikolajczyk, Molotov, Eden, Harriman and others on October 13. Mikolajczyk argued against the seizure of Poland up to the Curzon line. Stalin demanded that the Soviet's absorption of eastern Poland up to the Curzon line be recognized and that the Red Committee of Liberation to whom he had delivered western Poland be also recognized.

Churchill supported Stalin. Mikolajczyk pressed his argument. Suddenly Molotov said it was necessary to remind those present that at Teheran *President Roosevelt had expressed his complete agreement with the Curzon line as the Polish-Soviet frontier* and that the President had merely added *that for the time being his agreement on this point should not be made public.* Then he challenged Churchill and Harriman to deny the statement if it was not true. "Because," he said, "it appears to me that Mr. Mikolajczyk is not aware of the fact." Molotov paused for a reply. No denial was forthcoming.[85] The truth was out at last. Later Churchill urged the Polish leader to yield. Churchill grew angry. He said he "was not going to wreck the peace of Europe because of a quarrel between Poles."[86]

There was but three weeks now to the American elections. That is why Roosevelt wanted his agreement kept secret "for the time being." The news of this revelation was kept away from the United States until after the election was over.

Chapter 10: Politics, Disease and History

When Roosevelt returned from Teheran and Cairo it was not a return from the old world to the new; it was as if he had opened a door and put his foot upon the first step of that dim flight that leads from this world into the next. He went, as was his custom, to Hyde Park for the Christmas holidays. There he contracted an illness the precise nature of which we do not yet know. Admiral Ross T. McIntire,[87] the President's physician, says it was an influenza which left an irritating bronchial inflammation causing coughing spells that racked him and that he showed a *definite loss of his usual ability to come back.* In the new year he returned to Washington, but this bronchial irritation hung on and by April it was necessary to take him South into the sunshine, from which he did not return until May 10.

In June the long-awaited invasion of the continent was launched. With this we will not concern ourselves. The other subject that occupied Roosevelt's mind was his plan to have himself renominated for a fourth time.

The President had lost his head, at least a little. Congress was slipping away from him. A growing section of his party, particularly in the Senate, was moving out of that collection of incongruous elements called the Third New Deal. It was crawling with Reds and their gullible allies who got themselves into key positions in all the bureaus and were talking with great assurance about what they were going to do with America and the world. The Communists had all become anti-fascists and everybody who was against the Communists was, therefore, a fascist. A group of organizations financed by undisclosed benefactors was riding roughshod through the country smearing everybody who questioned the grandiose plans of the Great Leader for remaking America and the world. Nobody was getting a hotter dose of this smearing than the American Congress. The radio and the frightened press and magazines kept up a barrage against the members of the President's own party in both houses.

As a result the breach between the President and Congress was widening. It came to a head in February when Congress rejected Roosevelt's demand for a $10,500,000,000 tax boost and cut it to $2,300,000,000. Roosevelt vetoed it. He sent a sizzling message impugning the good faith of Congress and saying this was a "bill not for relief of the needy but of the greedy." It was a Democratic bill and the blast that exploded in his face brought him up with a jerk. In the upper house, Senator Barkley, Democratic leader, Roosevelt's own representative there, rose to upbraid him. He said the message was "a calculated and deliberate assault upon the legislative integrity of every member of Congress." He cried: "I do not propose to take it lying down," as Democratic and Republican senators united in a roar of applause. He ended his philippic with an announcement that made big black headlines in every paper in the country. He declared that after seven years of carrying the New Deal banner for the President, he now resigned his post as Democratic majority leader and he called on every member of the Congress to preserve its self-respect and override the veto. The Senate overrode it 72 to 14 and the House 299 to 95. It brought Roosevelt tumbling off his high horse. He sent Steve Early running to Barkley's home that very night to beg him not to quit. Barkley yielded.

But something else was afoot. Roosevelt was giving what was left of his dwindling energies to the plan for a fourth nomination. In 1936, Garner[88] had said to his intimates: Roosevelt will run for a third term and a fourth term. He will never leave the White House unless he is removed by death or defeat. And he was at this very moment concerned with the problem of frustrating both these enemies. He was a sick man but still clutching for the power that had become a part of his being. The Empress Theodora, wife of Justinian, said: "We must all die some time, but it is a terrible thing to have been an Emperor and to give up Empire before one dies." Roosevelt had no intention of giving up his power. Yet before him lay some of the most imposing problems of the war and the peace, to be solved against the stubborn resistance of a man of iron. He proposed to solve them by matching his fading energies and his weary mind against the resolute and confident realist in the Kremlin, limited by no laws, restrained by no parliament, responsible to no master but himself, without pity and without remorse.

The full story of Roosevelt's physical condition must be frankly examined. He was beyond doubt a man of naturally robust constitution united to a buoyant temperament. His affliction had deprived him of the use of his limbs but beyond that had apparently no other effect upon his general health save the extent to which it deprived him of the means of the physical activity necessary to continuous good health. He was addicted to colds and his associates in Washington soon noticed that an ordinary cold had a way of flooring him quite, but that he could come back quickly. Jim Farley wrote in his diary as early as 1935 that "the President looked bad, suffering from a cold, face drawn and his reactions slow," and he felt that the strain of office was showing on him even at that early day. In 1937 he visited the President in his bedroom and was "shocked at the President's appearance"—his color bad, his face lined like a man worn out.[89]

Farley was so concerned that he went to Dr. Cary T. Grayson, who had been Wilson's physician and had recommended to the President

Dr. Ross T. McIntire as his physician. Grayson was already aware of Roosevelt's condition and said he was in daily contact with Jimmy Roosevelt about it. Farley got the impression from Grayson that there was something the matter with Roosevelt's heart and that it might become serious and urged that a good doctor be called into consultation. Grayson agreed, but felt it should be "one who would not talk."[90]

In 1940, Edward J. Flynn said it was obvious to him that "the President's health was beginning to suffer ... He was no longer young and he lacked some of the early resilience and power of quick reaction he once had."[91] This was the observation of a man who was close to him and saw him often. In 1940 when the President was discussing with Farley a possible vice-presidential candidate, he said to the Democratic chairman that the man named on the ticket with him would have to be in good health because there was no telling how long he could hold out. "You know," he said, "a man with paralysis can have a break-up any time." He said his vital organs were all right but that nothing in life was certain. And to point this up he opened his shirt and showed Farley a large growth of flesh and muscle under his arm caused by his affliction.[92] He was three years older when he went to Teheran—61 years of age—and the youngest of the three men who conferred there. Churchill was 69 and Stalin was 64. But Roosevelt was biologically in every way the oldest of the three and he looked it. He met Chiang Kai-shek and Madame Chiang at Cairo just before Teheran. Afterward she said "she was shocked by the President's looks during the Cairo conference. She thought he had fallen off considerably and looked quite ill."[93] Churchill too was reported to have said he noted signs of deterioration in the President. Admiral McIntire, the President's doctor, was annoyed by these reports. He completely disagreed with them.

Despite the doctor's complacence, Roosevelt was unable to throw off the bronchitis which followed the influenza attack at Hyde Park. He was up one day, says McIntire, and down the next. When he got back to Washington two specialists were called in. They found "a moderate degree of arteriosclerosis." McIntire says it was "no more than normal in a man his age."[94] They found some changes in the cardiographic tracings, cloudiness in the sinus and bronchial irritation. The President saw fewer people and for some reason rumors began to circulate. The press asked the Admiral about it. He said it was just a residual bronchitis; "he is feeling quite well." But apparently he was not, for very soon thereafter, on April 8, he left Washington for Bernard Baruch's plantation in South Carolina. He did not return until May 10. It was hoped seclusion from the pressures of his office and exposure to the Southern sun would bring him around. He did nothing but rest, sleep and fish in the sun. However, five doctors were called in to aid the sun. Admiral McIntire gives a sample report on the President's physical examination there. But he omits the blood pressure and nowhere do they say exactly what the President had at Hyde Park or how it all started.[95]

There were reports going about Washington that the President had had some sort of stroke—perhaps a mild one—after returning from Teheran. Dr. McIntire says this was not true. But in spite of his apparently blanket statements, his book leaves the subject still open. He unconsciously makes a grave revelation without intending to in his account of these days. McIntire was a naval doctor in 1932 and was recommended to Roosevelt as White House physician by Admiral Grayson. McIntire was an eye, ear and nose specialist. He got along famously with Roosevelt, was elevated by him to the grade of admiral and made head of the Naval Hospital Service. What his capabilities as a doctor may be I do not know, but he reveals himself in the volume which recounts his White House experiences as a complete servitor of Roosevelt, laughing at his jokes, swallowing his stories and accepting Roosevelt's own exalted opinion of himself at face value. Any suggestion that the President was not in excellent health he seemed to look upon as some sort of offense against the Republic.

In spite of the care he has exercised to give the President a good bill of health he unwittingly reveals what the President's real condition was. When rumors multiplied about the President's long ailment from Christmas to May—four months recovering from a case of bronchitis—McIntire, after bringing five specialists in to examine his patient, decided to bring in two more—Drs. James E. Paullin of Atlanta and Frank Lahey of Boston. But all he reports as to their findings is that they declared Roosevelt had recovered from infection of sinus and chest and was "well and active." Then Dr. Paullin talked to Roosevelt and reminded him he was like an old motor, that his heart and arteries were like the engine and the tires and that if he wanted to finish the journey he would have to slow down—he would have to live within his reserves. Then a regimen was outlined for the President—and this tells the whole story.

He was to have breakfast from 8:30 to 9:00; office hours from 11:00 to 1:00; from 1:00 to 2:00 luncheon, but no business guests; 2:00 to 3:00 rest lying down; 3:00 to 5:00 office hours; then 45 minutes massage and ultra-violet rays and rest lying down until 7:30; 7:30 to 8:00, dinner in quarters; no night work and sleep for 10 hours.[96] This was to be the President's schedule and the important part about it was that *he was to go on the* FOUR-HOUR DAY. His working hours were from 11:00 to 1:00 and from 3:00 to 5:00, the balance of the 24 hours were for resting, lying down, getting massaged, eating his meals and sleeping. This was the condition they gave him if he wanted to finish the journey. This was not a program for a period of convalescence. It was literally a program for "the rest of the journey." The doctors were telling him as plainly as words that the only way he could avert death was to go into a form of semi-retirement.

Thus once again the problem of disease entangled itself in the making of history. The vast war powers of the most powerful nation in the world were concentrated in the hands of one man. The decisions of that one man would affect our destiny, the security of our institutions and the peace of the world. These decisions were in the hands of a sick man, whose mind was trudging along in low gear, whose physical organisms were disintegrating under the impact of disease and whose mental and moral faculties were deteriorating under the impact of power. It had happened after the First World War when the President was stricken by a brain hemorrhage that paralyzed his body and impaired his mind and, worse than this, disturbed his normal mental balance. What might have been the course of history had Woodrow Wilson's mental and physical powers survived must be a matter of speculation. Those who may be interested in the subject of disease as a factor in human affairs may want to look into those two brilliantly written little volumes, "Post Mortem" and "Mere Mortals" by Dr. C. MacLaurin[97] in which he pursues these ravages of disease in monarchs and statesmen and the costs passed on to the populations they ruled.

What would have happened in Europe, for instance, if Henry VIII had not had syphilis? It was Henry's syphilis that made it impossible for Catherine of Aragon to bear him a living child, save the solemn Mary, and from whom, after seven or eight miscarriages he secured a divorce. This caused his break with Rome and a whole train of consequences which, says Dr. MacLaurin, a good modern surgeon might have avoided and thus changed the course of history. Arteriosclerosis and its somber effects upon the mind and nature of Charles V led him to retire at 52 in favor of his son Phillip, when perhaps the curative and moderating techniques of modern medicine might have preserved his genius as the ruling force in Spain and saved her from the disasters which overtook her under Phillip.

When we consider, says Dr. MacLaurin, "that the destinies of nations are commonly held in the hands of elderly gentlemen whose blood pressures tend to be too high owing to their fierce political activities, it is not too much to say that arteriosclerosis is one of the greatest tragedies that afflict the human race. Every politician should have his blood pressure tested and his urine examined about once in a quarter, and if it should show signs of rising he should undoubtedly take a long rest until it falls again; it is not fair that the lives of millions should depend upon the judgment of a man whose mind is warped by arteriosclerosis."

There were plenty of examinations of Roosevelt made during all this time, but the people of the United States did not know what they revealed—and do not know fully yet. The necessity of rest was imposed upon Roosevelt by the doctors called in to examine him. It was observed throughout the year 1944 that he spent 200 days outside the White House in rest or travel which, save in the brief campaign tours, was undertaken for his health. Dr. McIntire makes much of the many miles he traveled, as if this were some terrible strain upon him. Most of them were miles of leisure in the sun aboard luxurious vessels or trains. The doctor admits they always benefitted him. But the people were never told that they had in their service an executive whose doctors said he could not take more than four hours a day of work and who must spend most of the day and night lying down resting and sleeping.

After Roosevelt returned to the White House in the middle of May, the chief item of business was managing his nomination for a fourth term at the Democratic convention which would meet in two months. That was simple enough, but, like the third nomination, had to bear the marks of a command from the people. To understand that convention we must recall an incident of the greatest importance.

We have seen how the Communist party had successfully penetrated the unions organized by the Congress of Industrial Organizations—the CIO—and how John L. Lewis and David Dubinsky had got out of it for this reason, leaving Sidney Hillman in complete control. We have also seen how the war brought Hillman to the top in White House circles when he and William Knudsen became the directors of the economic war effort. Knudsen departed in good time, but Hillman remained close to the White House.

Meantime on a neighboring social front certain changes were taking place. By 1943, Earl Browder, Communist leader, had about completed the discovery that there was no hope for a proletarian revolution in America. The party got nowhere preaching Communism. The people just wouldn't listen. But it learned that it could get very far by using a different technique. After all, Communist revolutionaries know that before they can introduce Communism they must destroy the political and economic system of the country in which they conspire. Wreck the American system of free enterprise and kill the confidence of the people in their political system and it will collapse. Once this takes place in any country it is not difficult for the Communist to move in. He is willing to support and promote the rise of fascist states because he knows that fascism—the Planned Capitalist Economy—is merely a decadent phase of capitalism. For this reason the Communist party had been promoting with great success Red-front organizations and inducing the most important people, like Mrs. Roosevelt, Henry Wallace and scores of prominent leaders in education and public life, to work with them.

As 1944 opened, Browder decided to liquidate the Communist party. It would go out of politics. It would become a mere educational association. This was done, and Browder and Sidney Hillman teamed up to capture the American Labor Party. This had been formed originally in New York City to provide a political vehicle for Fiorello LaGuardia in his local politics. It had all sorts of people in it. There were a lot of Reds, a lot of socialists and a lot of parlor and campus pinks of all sorts, plus a lot of social reformers and welfare reformers. It had corralled a lot of votes—*enough to swing an election in*

New York State—by giving or withholding its vote from the Democrats. It supported Lehman in 1940 and elected him on the Democratic ticket. It refused to endorse the Democratic candidate, Bennett, for governor in 1942 and the Democratic vote, without it, was insufficient and thus Dewey became governor. Now Browder and Hillman joined forces and decided to take over the American Labor Party. They met resistance from the mixed collection of pinks who had control, but in a bitter battle Browder and Hillman took it over. Actually Browder dominated this team because it was Communist votes that did the trick.

In addition to this, Hillman had organized in 1943 a new political labor group called the CIO Political Action Committee. The CIO had violated the law by supporting candidates in various primary elections and to get around this Hillman formed this Political Action Committee and pressure was put on members of CIO unions to compel them to join. This organization was now being used as a club in the Democratic party to bludgeon Democratic congressmen and officials generally to play ball with Hillman, Wallace and their crowd, while Hillman and Browder did business as a team in New York State in the newly re-formed Communist American Labor Party.

The Democratic party could win if it could carry the Southern states and in addition New York, Massachusetts, Illinois, Michigan and New Jersey. These states could be carried with the support of Sidney Hillman's Political Action Committee and Browder's American Labor Party, but not without them and Roosevelt was the only possible candidate who could get this support. The Democrats had to nominate Roosevelt or lose the election. There were some Democrats who thought it was better to lose the election, but not enough of them. Accordingly when the convention assembled in Chicago on July 19, Sidney Hillman was there, not as a delegate—he was not even a member of the party—but to see that the subservient Democrats behaved to his satisfaction and to the satisfaction of his friend and partner, Browder. To this pass had Roosevelt's personal political ambitions brought the Democratic party of Jefferson, Cleveland and Wilson. Hillman had a headquarters there. He wasn't worried about Roosevelt's nomination. That was settled. He wasn't worried about the platform. That was written to his satisfaction before the convention assembled by Sam Rosenman. He had one more demand. He wanted Henry Wallace nominated again for Vice-President.

But the nomination for Vice-President, this time, was perhaps the great prize itself. Leaders in Washington had a feeling that Roosevelt's health was not all it should be. But the fact is that the truth about his health was concealed not merely from the people but from the Democratic leaders. It must be remembered that they had seen very little of him since his return from Teheran. He had been hidden away first at Hyde Park and at the White House where he had few visitors and finally at Baruch's place in South Carolina until two months before the convention. Every effort was made to prevent the facts from leaking out. The Democratic leaders had been accustomed to see Roosevelt become suddenly weary and ill and then bounce back quickly and look well after a few days in the sunlight. But this time he didn't bounce back. However, the public was told that he did after his sojourn in the South. Meantime the Democratic leaders had drifted along in an incredible state of negligence with respect to the problem before them. But those around the White House close to Roosevelt knew better. Harry Hopkins and Henry Wallace and, of course, Sidney Hillman knew. They knew that Roosevelt was doomed and that if they could name Henry Wallace Vice-President this time, the government would be in their hands.

Accordingly, Hillman and Wallace used the immense power they had by virtue of their control over large minorities in the big industrial states to push the movement for Wallace's renomination. After all, he was then already Vice-President. Wallace saw Roosevelt three times on the subject and Roosevelt agreed to give him a letter which they discussed and which Wallace felt would settle the matter at the convention. There was much newspaper speculation about the nature of this letter before the convention convened. And when the convention did convene, the vice-presidency and Roosevelt's expected letter were the big subjects in Chicago. Sidney Hillman had his headquarters in a penthouse on top of a Chicago hotel and from that point the drive for Wallace was managed.

Wallace's supporters, as the convention opened, said they knew exactly what the President would say in the expected letter and they were satisfied. Senator Joe Guffey said exultantly "Wait until you see the letter." There were other candidates for the post—former Senator James Byrnes, Senator Barkley, while the names of Justice William O. Douglas and Senator Harry Truman were being prominently mentioned. However, no one had any delegates but Wallace and he was known to have 300 at least. The others had their home states and little else. It was plain that if Roosevelt said he wanted Wallace no one else had a chance. Until Roosevelt's letter was received, therefore, the other candidates were handicapped. Roosevelt could not win without Sidney Hillman and Earl Browder and they wanted Wallace. Hillman said, "We have no second choice."

Former Justice James F. Byrnes, at that moment serving in a post that was called "Assistant President" with an office in the White House, was an active candidate, as was Senate Majority Leader Alben Barkley. Byrnes was easily the ablest man in the race. It was supposed by those in the know that had the convention been completely free he would have been nominated. Barkley believed that he could win in a free contest. Because of the close association of Byrnes with the President, few believed that he would be an active candidate without the President's approval.

But Chicago had a visitor about whom nothing was known until later. On the evening of July 14, Roosevelt left Washington with great secrecy on a special train. It reached Chicago on Saturday, the 15th. That same day, Robert E. Hannegan, Democratic national chairman, got to Chicago. Reporters awaited him at the station. But he slipped out through a rear door of his train and into Mayor Kelly's police-escorted automobile and vanished. Reporters frantically hunted him all over town. He remained out of sight until the next day. But in the meantime he had made a visit to Roosevelt's train, secretly parked on a remote railroad siding. There poor Wallace's goose was cooked. Hannegan, too, got a letter. It said the President would be happy to have either Harry Truman or William Douglas as his running mate. And as Hannegan was leaving the train, Roosevelt warned him "to clear everything with Sidney." The Presidential approval of Truman was no good until Sidney O.K.'ed it.

However, the letter for Wallace was not yet delivered. It was delivered Wednesday, the 19th. It was then conveyed from the President to Senator Jackson, temporary chairman of the convention, and read to the delegates. In the letter Roosevelt said he wanted to give his personal "thought in regard to the selection of a candidate for the Vice-Presidency." The letter continued:

> "I have been associated with Henry Wallace during the past four years as Vice-President, for eight years earlier while he was Secretary of Agriculture and well before that. I like him and I respect him and he is my personal friend. For these reasons I personally would vote for his nomination if I were a delegate to the convention."

The letter was a terrible blow to the Wallace camp, said the New York *Times*. Wallace was hastily summoned by his managers to hurry to Chicago. Was this the radiant endorsement about which Senator Guffey was so exultant? The convention at once took the letter as letting Wallace down. All the other candidates for Vice-President went to work with a will. But they all knew by this what Hannegan had been told—"to clear everything with Sidney." To Hillman's penthouse headquarters tramped the long line of candidates and their managers. When approached about Byrnes, Hillman turned thumbs down. He said "no" with final emphasis. Then the President got word to Byrnes to withdraw. He did so, saying he was withdrawing at the President's request. That left Barkley in a powerful position. Then Hannegan sprang the Truman letter. That left Barkley out. Barkley was slated to make the speech nominating Roosevelt that afternoon. He was in a room with O. Max Gardner of North Carolina and Jim Farley when he saw a copy of the Truman letter. Barkley knew that settled his hash and that Truman was the man of destiny, because the Douglas endorsement was meaningless. He was indignant. In a burst of righteous wrath he denounced Roosevelt and was about to tear up the nominating speech when Farley and Gardner restrained him. Later in the day he delivered that speech, glowing with an eloquent tribute to the man who, only a few hours before, he believed had double-crossed him. Deep and strong and terrible are the chains of party loyalty. But Barkley had gotten the party all mixed up with Roosevelt so that he could not disentangle them.

Roosevelt, of course, was nominated promptly that day. He had earlier written a letter to Chairman Hannegan saying he did not wish to run, "but if the people command me to continue in this office I have as little right to withdraw as the soldier has to leave his place in the line." He pointed to himself as the commander-in-chief who could not leave his place at the head of his armies unless removed by the people. Roosevelt, of course, had taken no chances on not being "commanded" to continue. The political machine of which he was the master had sent delegates to the convention instructed to issue the necessary "command."

After Roosevelt's nomination was voted, it began to look as if Wallace might break through after all. New York could not get a vote in its delegation for support of Truman. Neither could California or Illinois. To prevent Illinois from breaking away, Ed Kelly, the boss, nominated Senator Scott Lucas of Illinois as a favorite son. Meantime delegation after delegation had been shifting to Wallace. Every hour news came of additions to his supporters. The reports when the convention opened were that he had 300 votes. The number had risen to 400. Delegates were getting irked at the apparent weakness of all other candidates. The opposition to Wallace could not unite. The leaders, giving some excuse, adjourned the convention in an uproar to prevent a vote.

By next day, however, the support of Truman was being consolidated. On the first ballot Wallace led with 429½ votes, Truman 319½ and the rest scattered among 14 other candidates. But on the second ballot the steam-roller went into play, the switching started and Truman was nominated with 1100 votes to only 66 for Wallace. But not until Sidney Hillman had approved the change.

Roosevelt's stop in Chicago was merely a way station on his way to the Pacific coast. It was, like all his movements, clouded in ostentatious secrecy. While the convention was still in session he accepted the "command." It came over the air from an undisclosed Pacific coast Marine base. He said: " I am now at this naval base performing my duties under the Constitution. The war waits for no elections. Decisions must be made, plans must be laid, strategy must be carried out." This was part of the build-up for the commander-in-chief theme which was to be used to stir the patriotic sentiments of the voters. Roosevelt by this time had lost all sense of nice and delicate discrimination in his poses. After carefully managing his nomination through the Democratic leaders he could put on an act about running reluctantly, comparing himself to the soldier in the line who could not refuse the call of duty. The more subtle deceptions of his earlier years now gave way to a much cruder hypocrisy. He was on his way to Hawaii, with a six-day trip across the continent in a private luxury train and then a long and glorious sea trip to Hawaii and some other islands. The decisions, of course, could wait on these pleasant tours. He had been away from his duties, save for a few weeks, for the first half of the year. What essential part in the war was served by reviewing the troops and visiting the hospitals in Hawaii and other islands and entertaining the Pacific commanders with reminiscences of his exploits in World War I? Actually, the trip to the Pacific combined three very useful objectives—the spectacle of the Commander-in-Chief moving about running the war, a grand rest on the ocean voyage and a good chance to make campaign appearances amongst the shipyard workers on the coast and the soldier boys in the islands who would vote in the election. It took him 30 days away from the White House where decisions, if any were necessary, were really made.

However, he made one slip. He was photographed delivering his acceptance speech in a small, severely plain room at some Marine base. He sat at a table with his daughter Anna and his son Jimmy in the foreground. This picture ruined all his elaborate comedy in two particulars. The picture shocked the nation, revealing as it did his emaciated face and body. In addition, the original news photo showed a part of the white uniform of a naval officer. Walter Trohan, Washington correspondent of the Chicago *Tribune*, one of those newspapermen who are born and not made wondered who he was and why he was there. Trohan went to the Associated Press photo service to see the original. It contained the entire figure of the officer, which had been cut out of the published picture as nonessential. This curious newspaperman took the picture to the Navy Department to identify the officer. He was a Commander Bruenn—a naval doctor. A little more investigation revealed that he was Dr. Howard Bruenn, a heart specialist of Boston who had been inducted into the Navy for the express purpose of remaining constantly on duty to watch the heart of the man who, as Dr. McIntire proclaimed, was in perfect health. He had been with him since his Christmas illness and remained constantly at his side until he died.

Roosevelt at first planned to make no formal campaign. He changed his mind because it did not seem wise to expose himself to the frequent attacks upon his record which his Republican opponent, Thomas E. Dewey, was making. His first speech was not made until September 24 to a dinner given by the International Teamsters' Union dominated by Daniel Tobin—an AFL union. Its purpose was to put some emphasis on the support of the AFL in view of the bitter feeling among AFL leaders because of the dominant role Sidney Hillman's CIO was playing in Roosevelt's councils and particularly in its favored position before Roosevelt's Labor Board. In October he made a speech before the Foreign Policy Association in New York and drove around the city in a rain storm to exhibit his robust health. Then he went on to Boston, making two or three short talks on the way. There is no point here in describing the course of that campaign. He interrupted it for an occasion of far more importance to our story. In September he went to another one of those international conferences, this time at Quebec.

Chapter 11: How Germany's Fate Was Settled

On September 11, ten months after Teheran and in the midst of the campaign, Roosevelt and Churchill met at Quebec. The invasion of France was launched. Allied armies approached the Rhine. The Russians had crossed the Vistula and were diving toward the Baltic and soon the race would be on between the Allies and the Russians for Berlin. Roosevelt and Churchill met to discuss the fate of Germany, Lend-Lease to Britain after the war and minor points. They made a decision at Quebec which has up to this moment paralyzed utterly the making of a stable peace in Europe and is pregnant with consequences so terrible for the future that the mind draws away from them in consternation. That decision produced what Secretary Stimson describes as "the most violent single inter-departmental struggle of his career" and what Secretary Hull says "angered me as much as anything that had happened during my career as Secretary."[98]

Secretary Stimson says he returned from Normandy in July, 1944, to find the administration belatedly constructing plans for the occupation of Germany—with no decisions made and the occupation imminent. He lunched with President Roosevelt and urged him to appoint a Cabinet Committee to prepare such plans, and Roosevelt named Hull, Stimson and Morgenthau with Hull as chairman. Later he added Hopkins. This Cabinet Committee met soon after, on September 5, in Secretary Hull's office. Hull produced a program prepared in the State Department, whereupon Secretary Morgenthau presented that savage document that has come to be known as the Morgenthau Plan. The story behind this enterprise and the ultimate result is one very difficult for the normal American to believe. But it has since been fully documented.

Most Americans are aware that the American Communist Party is the absolute servant of the Kremlin. But what many Americans still do not understand, even at this late day, is the malignance of another batch of dedicated Communists who do not belong to the Party at all—who, in fact, keep carefully away from it. They work independently of the open Communist Party and deal directly with certain secret agents of Soviet Russia in the United States.

These people operate in what are known as underground cells. They have been, at various times, fairly numerous, but each cell in itself is small. They often have no connection with each other and may not be aware of the others' existence. There were several of these secret Communist cells operating in Washington in 1943 and 1944—and later. One of these became known as the Silvermaster group. Nathan Gregory Silvermaster had been with the Agricultural Department but became head of the Near East Division of the Board of Economic Welfare. At a certain point the FBI and the Intelligence Sections of both War and Navy reported that he was a dangerous Communist. But, as was the case with many of these underground operators, he had powerful friends in the right places. Lauchlin Currie, a presidential assistant, and Harry Dexter White, Assistant to the Secretary of the Treasury and later Assistant Secretary, vouched for him. He was permitted to resign quietly and return to his old job in Agriculture.

The Silvermaster group consisted of seven people, in addition to Silvermaster. They all held positions of importance inside various government bureaus. One of them was Harry Dexter White, a member of what is called the Little Cabinet. He was, in fact, Secretary of the Treasury, Morgenthau himself being a person of very limited abilities and still less capacity for leadership.

White's access to the most secret information was almost unlimited. He not only had at hand the Secret Service, which is a Treasury agency, but had at his call the most secret documents from other government agencies. His secretary, Sonia Gold, was a Communist supplied to him by the Silvermasters.

In the Spring of 1944 the Silvermaster group in Washington received instructions from a Kremlin agent outlining Russia's plans for Germany. They were simple enough—to wipe out her capacity as an industrial nation, to reduce her to the condition of a mere agricultural country. Where possible, her industrial equipment was to be removed, preferably to Russia. And she was to be dismembered.

These instructions from Moscow were passed on to Harry Dexter White by Silvermaster and he was pressed to discharge the commission with dispatch. He was selected, of course, because of his confidential relationship to Morgenthau. White went to work assiduously on his job.

By the end of September, 1944, Hull and Morgenthau were ready with their plans. On September 2, Hopkins called a meeting in his office of the men delegated by the Secretaries to prepare their statements. Harry Dexter White was there for Morgenthau. He revealed his plan—the plan that later became known as the Morgenthau Plan, but was actually the Stalin Plan for Germany. It was a plan literally to wipe Germany off the map save as a frail, hungry, broken people for generations. Part of Germany was to be handed over to Russia, parts to other countries. What remained was to be dismembered into a North and a South Germany. What industrial equipment could be removed was to be taken away. The rest was to be demolished. The mines were to be destroyed by flooding them. The Ruhr was to be taken from Germany and its products made available to France, Poland and others but not to Germany.

Then on September 5 came the meeting in Hull's office. Hull says that when he heard the Morgenthau-White Plan he believed it was a plan for "blind vengeance" and that the plan to flood the mines would be a crime against all Europe. Secretary Stimson was so outraged that he sent a strongly worded protest to the President.

The Cabinet committee, of course, could not agree. They met with Roosevelt four days later and Hull informed him of their inability to reach an agreement. Stimson sent a long communication to Roosevelt pressing vigorously for a rational occupation policy. There the matter rested for the moment. On September 11, Roosevelt went to Quebec to meet Churchill.

Neither Hull nor Stimson heard any more of the Morgenthau-White Plan during the Quebec Conference. But Roosevelt planned to deal with it there, and it was therefore necessary that neither Hull nor Stimson should be present. Roosevelt told Hull that only military matters would be discussed. What he told Stimson we do not know, since if military matters were the theme, certainly the Secretary of War should have been present. However, he did invite Morgenthau to Quebec, without informing Hull or Stimson. And there, without the knowledge of the Secretary of State or the Secretary of War, Morgenthau presented the infamous White Plan to Churchill and Roosevelt.

Churchill was angry and indignant. When his Foreign Minister, Anthony Eden, arrived at Quebec, he also vigorously protested against the plan. *But he found that Churchill had agreed to it.* Why? Churchill, seeing the approach of the war's end, was deeply troubled about England's financial position and was anxious to get from Roosevelt a huge grant of more Lend-Lease billions for post-war use. As long as Churchill objected to the Morgenthau-White Plan, Roosevelt held out against any more aid to Britain. Finally Churchill said: "What do you want me to do? Sit up on my hind legs and beg like Fala?"[99] Morgenthau, in a talk with Churchill, proposed credits to Britain after the war of $6,500,000,000. Churchill withdrew his objections and the Morgenthau-White Plan was approved.

What is not generally known about this agreement is that its last paragraph provided that the United States should take its soldiers out of Germany as soon as possible after the surrender, leaving Germany to be policed by the Soviet Army with the aid of Russia's neighbors—Poland, Czechoslovakia, Yugoslavia, Greece, Belgium and France. Had this finally been adopted, all Germany would be to-day a Russian satellite behind the Iron Curtain.

When Roosevelt returned to Washington he made no announcement of the agreement. He told neither Stimson nor Hull. It was not until three days later when the papers came through in a routine manner that Hull saw with amazement that the Morgenthau Plan had been adopted. And he saw also that Churchill was to get $6,500,000,000. "This," wrote Hull, "might suggest to some the *quid pro quo* with which the Secretary of the Treasury was able to get Mr. Churchill's adherence to his cataclysmic plan." Hull said he considered "it a tragedy for all concerned."

Stimson, who said he could not have kept his self-respect otherwise, wrote Roosevelt in protest. Hull went to the President personally and protested. As for Roosevelt, Stimson later reported that he seemed to have made no study whatever of the subject. In reply to Hull's protest, he first denied the agreement, then seemed "frankly staggered" when Hull read him the phrases "to reduce Germany to a country primarily agricultural and pastoral" and then insisted "he had no idea how he could have initialed the memorandum and that *he had evidently done so without much thought.*"

Most incredible of all is the picture of Roosevelt and Churchill at Quebec being presented with a so-called American plan to destroy Germany prepared by a man who was Assistant to the Secretary of the U. S. Treasury Department but actually a secret agent of Stalin. In the end the President was persuaded to get out of portions of this appalling agreement. But Stimson declared "the same attitude remained" and the whole world now knows of the wreckage that was carried on in Germany and the blow to the economy of all Europe that was delivered in the name of an "American" plan cooked up in Moscow.

Chapter 12: The Atlantic Charter Is Scrapped

Roosevelt was reelected. The results justified, from a political consideration, the wisdom of his alliance with Hillman and Browder. During the campaign, Roosevelt had denied vehemently that he had sought the support of Communists. Actually his name appeared as the candidate of the American Labor Party dominated by Browder and Hillman entirely. And he had accepted its nomination. He had also accepted nomination at the hands of the American Liberal Party, the pink fringe dangling somewhere between the fascist planned society and Stalin's proletarian dictatorship. In the election, Thomas E. Dewey actually got over 500,000 more votes on the Republican ticket than Roosevelt got on the Democratic ticket in New York State. It was Roosevelt's 490,000 votes from Browder and Hillman's American Labor Party and the 339,000 votes from the Pinkos that gave him his majority. While Dewey carried only 12 states in the North, the Roosevelt majority in many of those he carried was thin and would have been wiped out if the Browder-Hillman votes had not been given to Roosevelt. The administration was now the hopeless prisoner of these demanding and ruthless radical labor leaders, who had shown their ability to elect or defeat the Democratic party, who had filled all the departments and bureaus with their agents and who had insinuated their experts into the CIO labor unions and their propagandists into the radio, the movies and all the great instruments of communication and opinion—a fact which Mr. Roosevelt's successors would have to face when the war ended.

In the meantime, the war engrossed the attention of the people. And very soon after the election, stories about the conference at Teheran, details of which had been guarded very carefully, began to appear. It was being said that all the little liberated countries to which Roosevelt had made such definite promises and whose nationals in this country had been so solicitously courted during the campaign had been betrayed at Teheran. The dominant note in these criticisms was that at Teheran Roosevelt had scrapped the Atlantic Charter. That bold document had asserted that the high contracting parties "desire to see no territorial changes that do not accord with the freely expressed desires of the peoples concerned, that they respect the right of all peoples to choose the form of government under which they will live and they wish to see sovereign rights and self-government restored to those who have been forcibly deprived of them." The Teheran agreement violated every phrase and syllable of this pledge.

What had become of the Atlantic Charter? On December 20, 1944, the President at a press conference was asked about the Charter which he and Churchill had signed. His reply literally bowled over the correspondents. There was not and never had been a complete Atlantic Charter signed by him and Churchill, he replied. Then where is the Charter now, he was asked. He replied: "There wasn't any copy of the Atlantic Charter so far as I know." It was just a press release. It was scribbled on a piece of paper by him and Churchill and Sumner Welles and Sir Alexander Cadogan. It was just handed to the radio operator aboard the British and American warships to put on the air as a news release. Further inquiry revealed that Stephen Early had handed it out on his own with the signatures of Churchill and Roosevelt attached. And over on the wall of the National Museum in Washington, beautifully framed and illuminated after the manner of an ancient document—like Magna Carta or the Declaration of Independence—was the great Atlantic Charter itself, with the signatures of Roosevelt and Churchill. Daily visitors stood before it as before some great historic document. John O'Donnell, of the New York *Daily News*, asked the curator where he got it. He answered that it came from the Office of War Information. They had "loaned" the precious document to the National Museum. By inquiry at the OWI—that prolific fountain of phony news—O'Donnell learned that OWI had gotten it up and affixed the names of Roosevelt and Churchill. They had printed 240,000 copies of it. O'Donnell went back to the Museum with this information. And lo! the great Charter was gone. An attendant told him it had been ordered off the wall twenty minutes before. Thus ended the story of this wretched fraud. The fake document which was never signed and was nothing more than a publicity stunt to conceal the real purposes of the Atlantic meeting had been slain by its chief sponsor and, of course, all its high-sounding professions, after Teheran, had become as sounding brass or a tinkling cymbal.

Not long after this Cordell Hull resigned as Secretary of State and Edward Stettinius was named to succeed him. Hull was notoriously a sick man. He had been bypassed, even ignored, on numerous important issues and frequently kept in the dark. Sumner Welles, who was personally close to both Roosevelt and Mrs. Roosevelt, who had a far more active mind and a wider knowledge of foreign affairs than Hull, gradually elbowed him aside until a bitter feud grew up between the two men. As early as 1939, when Roosevelt was maneuvering for his third-term nomination, James A. Farley confided to Hull his own troubles. Hull exploded: "God, Jim! You don't know what troubles are. Roosevelt is going over my head to Welles and Berle. I was never even consulted on the Welles' trip to Europe. Then he's going over my head to ambassadors. He is in communication constantly with British leaders and others. He doesn't consult with me or confide in me and I have to feel my way in the dark. I have the devil's own time keeping him from issuing statements that would be most detrimental. He only discusses matters with me when he feels obliged to do so because of their importance."[100]

CHAPTER 13: THE FINAL BETRAYAL

On January 20, 1945, Roosevelt was sworn in as President of the United States for a fourth term. Three days later he left Norfolk on the heavy cruiser *Quincy* for what was to be his last act in the hapless drama of peace.

By this time Hitler's hard-pressed armies had been driven from all the territories they had seized in the east, save Czechoslovakia, Austria and part of Hungary. Practically all their hard-won aggressive prizes were lost. Cordell Hull had resigned and Edward Stettinius was Secretary of State.

Roosevelt had named former Justice James F. Byrnes as Director of Economic Stabilization in May. He took Byrnes along to Yalta as his adviser. The trip to this rendezvous throws a revealing light on the methods which characterized Roosevelt's costly improvisations in foreign affairs. He asked Byrnes to accompany him some time before Christmas. He did not mention the subject again until the night before his departure, when he repeated his insistent invitation that Byrnes go with him. Secretary Stettinius was to join them in Malta. Hopkins, who was ill in London, would also meet the party at Malta. On the journey over Roosevelt was ill. He kept to his room all the way save for lunch and dinner and a moving picture at night. He did not discuss the conference problems with Byrnes before leaving and on the way over his other advisers were not along and he avoided discussion with Byrnes. The Department of State had prepared an elaborate study of all the problems likely to arise, extensively documented. Byrnes did not learn of its existence until he arrived at Malta.[101] It is difficult to believe that a responsible statesman, unattended by his advisers and handicapped by a grave physical disability, could go to so momentous a meeting with two such astute colleagues as Stalin and Churchill without preparation.

The conference was held at the Livadia Palace, a former summer home of the Czars in the Crimea. It opened February 4, 1945. The chief questions were (1) the adoption of the Dumbarton Oaks plan for the United Nations, (2) the conditions of the approaching German surrender, (3) the treatment of Poland and the other liberated countries.

The United Nations plan, which had been agreed to in principle by Russia long before, was no longer an issue. There was the question of voting to be settled and this was done without any difficulty according to the usual prescription, by agreeing in full to Russia's desires, and a conference was announced to be held soon at San Francisco to prepare the charter. The governments of France and China were to be invited to join in sponsoring the invitations to the world for that event.

The Polish question was "settled." The formal proposal to hand over eastern Poland—east of the Curzon line—*was made by Roosevelt himself*.[102] As to western Poland, Stalin already had a government there named by him and composed of Communists representing no one but Stalin himself. Stalin wanted to be certain to retain that government. He agreed, however, that this provisional government should be "reorganized" to include "democratic leaders from Poles abroad." It was to be called the Polish Provisional Government of National Unity. He agreed to hold an election, which he said "he could do in a month." Did Roosevelt believe Stalin would hold a free election anywhere? He could hardly have been so naive. Actually the election was not held for 23 months and Poland ended with nothing but Communists in the government of a country where they did not represent 10 per cent of the people, while the other elements fled Poland for their lives.

Then, to seemingly correct this wrong, they agreed upon another one. To compensate Poland for that half wrung from her by Russia it was agreed to give Poland a part of East Prussia—a totally German land. The terrible lesson learned in Alsace and Lorraine, in the Sudeten lands, in the Polish Corridor settlements made in other wars which sowed the seeds of inevitable new wars, was totally ignored.

The conference also decided upon the partition of Germany into three zones, each to be occupied provisionally by the Russian, British and American armies, and to be separately administered. A reparations commission was set up to study the amounts. Russia wanted the amount to be 20 billion dollars of which she would take half. It was agreed that labor might be taken as a possible source of reparations. This was just a diplomatic way of authorizing the seizure of human beings to work as slaves after the war ended and is the basis of that dreadful crime perpetrated after hostilities ceased to which the President of the United States agreed. On this he must have agreed with a guilty conscience, for it was kept from Mr. Byrnes who did not learn of it until later.[103]

On the question of the war in the Pacific, Stalin now agreed specifically that he would come in against the Japs three months after Germany's defeat, provided the United States assisted in building the necessary reserve supplies and provided the *political aspects of Russia's participation had been clarified*. Stalin later gave our military mission a list of what he wanted in the Far East—fuel, food, transport equipment and other supplies for 1,500,000 men, 3000 tanks, 5000 planes. Stalin outlined his plan of attack—"his main effort to be with a highly mobile force that would sweep down from the Lake Baikal area through Outer and Inner Mongolia. The purpose of this wide movement was to separate the Japanese forces in Manchuria from those in China."[104] Of course his purpose was also to turn Manchuria into a Russian puppet state, which was precisely what Chiang Kai-shek so bitterly and properly opposed.

As the conference ended, Roosevelt remained an extra day because Stalin wanted to talk with him. He did so alone. What he wanted settled was "the political aspects of Russia's participation" in the Pacific. This he was able to do very quickly and to his complete satisfaction. In return for Russian participation in the Pacific, Roosevelt agreed that the Kuriles Islands would be handed to Russia, who would also get Sakhalin Island, internationalization of the Port of Darien, the lease of Port Arthur as a naval base and joint operation with China of the Eastern and Southern Manchurian railroads. And

Roosevelt promised to use his influence with Chiang to force him to agree. This secret agreement, like the one supporting the use of slave labor, was not made public and was concealed even from Byrnes who was Roosevelt's adviser at Yalta. He did not hear of it until after Mr. Roosevelt's death. Then he saw a reference to it in a Russian dispatch. By that time he was Secretary of State. He asked President Truman to have the White House records searched for this and any other secret outstanding I.O.U.'s.[105]

Russia had another demand. Stalin wanted Russia to have four votes in the assembly of the United Nations against the United States' one. He wanted three Soviet states, Byelorussia, the Ukraine and Lithuania—the latter of which he had just stolen and put under a puppet government—to have votes along with Russia. Roosevelt made a feeble protest against this, but it was put over later without a protest after Stettinius had agreed to give Stalin three votes. Roosevelt, before he went to Yalta, had boasted that if Stalin tried to get more than one vote he would demand a vote for each of the 48 states. Of course he did nothing of the kind. He did suggest that to avoid criticism at home the United States be given three votes too. And Stalin agreed. When Byrnes got back to the United States he found a note from Roosevelt instructing him not to discuss this agreement even in private. Later Roosevelt decided not to ask for the three votes for the United States. Byrnes says he never discovered the reason.[106]

When this conference ended, Roosevelt went to Egypt where he boarded the *Quincy* again and sailed into the Mediterranean. He was a very weary man, worn and spent with disease. He was trying now to get a little rest and quiet in this soft, sunshiny sea. But he received aboard the *Quincy* three kings—Farouk of Egypt, Haile Selassie of Ethiopia and Ibn Saud of Saudi Arabia. King Ibn Saud, one of the most powerful personalities in the Near East and a man of the most direct methods, had one great problem on his mind—Palestine. At this visit, according to Roosevelt himself, the President assured him that "no decision would be taken with regard to the basic situation in that country (Palestine) without full consultation with both Arabs and Jews." He assured Ibn Saud that *"I would take no action in my capacity as Chief of the Executive branch of the government, which might prove hostile to the Arab people."* This did not become known until October, 1945, after Roosevelt's death.[107] At Yalta, Stalin had asked him if he would make any concessions to Ibn Saud, to which Roosevelt replied the only offer he might make was to give him the six million Jews in the U. S.

Roosevelt took a leisurely trip home, to Alexandria, to Algiers, Gibraltar and then to the open sea. Sam Rosenman joined him to prepare the speech he would deliver to Congress on his return, for he considered this the great crowning incident of policy for binding up the wounds of the war-torn world. On the way home General Watson, his military secretary, died suddenly of heart disease. Roosevelt reached Washington the end of February. On March 1 he appeared before a joint session of Congress. He told the Congress that "more than ever before the major allies are closely united," that "the ideal of lasting peace will become a reality." There was no hint that the surrender which was now formally announced with respect to eastern Poland was in fact a major defeat. The disappearance of the Baltic states and practically all the Balkans behind Stalin's iron curtain was not announced in any other terms than as a great forward step in the liberation of Europe. As for western Poland, there were heavy overtones of guilt and frustration unintentionally evident. After all, there was no such nation as Poland before the First World War, said the President; *after all* most of the inhabitants of eastern Poland were not really Poles; *after all* the Poles were getting a big chunk of East Prussia as compensation; *after all* "the political and economic policy of the liberated areas will be the joint responsibility of all three governments."

He told Congress "our objective was to create a strong, independent and prosperous nation (in Poland). That's the thing to remember, those words, agreed to by Russia, by Britian and by me, the objective of making Poland a strong, independent and prosperous nation with a government ultimately to be selected by the Polish people themselves."

He ended by assuring Congress that the Crimean conference "marked the end of the system of unilateral action and exclusive alliances and spheres of influence and balances of power and all the other expedients that have been tried for centuries and have always failed."

In two months Roosevelt was dead. Truman became President. Shortly after, in May, the German Army surrendered. The fighting was in the West was over.

It is worth observing how statesmen can control their emotions to suit their policies. Poland had been thrown to the wolves in the new era of appeasement. When the Polish Premier Mikolajczyk, alarmed at the rumors rife about the undisclosed agreements at Teheran, asked Churchill pointedly what guarantee there was that what remained of Poland would be respected, Churchill grew angry. He told Mikolajczyk he was crazy. And he declared bluntly that he was not going to wreck the peace of Europe because of a quarrel between Poles.[108] Of course it was not a quarrel between Poles, but between Poles and the tyrant who had succeeded Hitler in the role of aggressor. It was only a few years before that Churchill had heaped his scorn upon Neville Chamberlain who appeased Hitler at Munich. In his best House of Commons manner he intoned the requiem of Czechoslovakia. "All is over," he said. "Silent, mournful, broken Czechoslovakia recedes into the darkness. She has suffered in every respect by her association with the Western democracies." Chamberlain appeased Hitler and averted war. Churchill got for England both a war and appeasement.

It must be said in fairness that Churchill's problem was profoundly complicated in the end. He at least was thinking in terms of the interests of the country he had sworn to represent. Roosevelt seemed quite indifferent to the position in which his country would stand at the end of the war, fixing his gaze instead upon a goal which, however noble in purpose, was, in the circumstances, utterly futile because of the man he was dealing with. Also, in Churchill's case, he was confronted with the double difficulty of protecting his own country at the same time from the wiles of Stalin and the gullibility of Roosevelt.

While the next meeting—the Potsdam conference—was not held until after Roosevelt's death and Truman had become President, it is necessary, to complete this story of our foreign affairs, to include a brief account of it.

The end of the war against Germany came in May. On July 3, James F. Byrnes was named Secretary of State. And on July 15 he and

President Truman, with Stalin and Churchill, began the Potsdam conference at Berlin.

Potsdam became a term of odium among the critics of the allied post-war agreements. At Potsdam the agreement reached covered most of the subjects that had been included in the earlier conferences. The humiliating failure of our whole post-war policy has been described as the fruit of Potsdam. Writing of this, William Henry Chamberlain sums up the verdict as follows:

> "Were the terms of the Potsdam agreement to be carried over any long term of years, they would lead to one of the greatest crimes or greatest follies in human history. Should they be rigorously enforced without giving Germany relief, a gigantic Buchanwald or Belsen would be created in the heart of Europe. Millions, perhaps tens of millions, of Germans would perish of malnutrition and associated diseases. It would literally be more human to select a quarter or a third of the German population and extinguish their lives quickly by means of firing squads or gas chamber."[109]

He quotes Sir William Beveridge as saying it was done "in a black moment of anger and confusion." And he adds that if common humanity should rebel at the spectacle our alternative would be to pour in hundreds of millions of dollars a year to escape the consequences of our own vengeance.

All this is true. But it is, I think, a complete mistake to lay these crimes at the door of the men who went to Potsdam for us. All the major decisions which make up the incredible record of surrender, blunder and savagery had already been made long before President Truman and Secretary Byrnes went to Potsdam. What Truman and Byrnes could have done at Potsdam other than they did is difficult to discover. The war was over. Europe lay in ruins. Roosevelt had conceded everything to Stalin. The only things he got on his own demand were the United Nations, which he got as Stalin wished it, and the Morgenthau plan. It would be well for us if we could lay the latter, too, at the door of Stalin, with whose ruthless philosophy it is as perfectly in accord as it is repugnant to ours.

It is the simple truth to say that Stalin had out-generaled Roosevelt at every point. Or perhaps it would be nearer the truth to say that Roosevelt had out-generaled himself. Stalin had merely to sit tight, to make known his wishes and Roosevelt laid them in his lap with eager compliance in the notion that he could thus soften Stalin. It is all the more incredible when we remember that the things he was laying in Stalin's lap were the existence of little nations and the rights of little peoples we had sworn to defend. And when Truman and Byrnes went to Potsdam what confronted them was an appalling mess.

On the other hand, they must bear their share of responsibility for the power that was put into Roosevelt's hands. But here again it is but just to say that Messrs. Truman and Byrnes knew little of what had happened at the preceding conferences. Roosevelt not only made agreements secret from the people but secret from his closest advisers in the government. He made agreements with Stalin hostile to the objectives of Churchill and kept secret from Churchill. He made secret agreements with Chiang Kai-shek, secret from both Churchill and Stalin, and secret agreements in derogation of Chiang Kai-shek's interests without his knowledge. And he made many secret agreements which no one in our State Department knew about until his death and then learned about them the hard way, by having them flung in their faces at embarrassing moments by Molotov.

The actual agreements at Potsdam may be summed up as follows: A blueprint for the control of Germany was made, based on the Morgenthau plan, which had already been agreed to, but relieved in some small degree of its original horrible severity. A council of foreign ministers was formed, including France, China, Russia, Britain and the United States, to draw up peace treaties. And the carrying out of all the agreements was to be supervised by the Council of Foreign Ministers.

The net result of all these various conferences and agreements was that our government put into Stalin's hands the means of seizing a great slab of the continent of Europe, then stood aside while he took it and finally acquiesced in his conquests. We gave him the planes, tanks, motor transport, guns, oil and other supplies to the extent of over 11 billion dollars without which he would have been helpless. We withheld our attack on Fortress Europe against the advice of all our military leaders until the prize was almost in Stalin's grasp. Then in a series of conferences with him we yielded it all in return for his promise to come into the United Nations on terms which enabled him to wreck that as an instrument of settling any serious international dispute.

It will not do to say that all we yielded was eastern Poland, Latvia, Lithuania, Estonia and parts of Rumania; that as to Yugoslavia, Rumania, Bulgaria, Czechoslovakia and Hungary, Stalin took these over by violating the agreement he made with us to hold free elections. Did Roosevelt really think Stalin would hold free elections when he agreed to let the Russian dictator conduct the elections—Stalin who had been exhibiting for years his ideas of "free elections" in Russia?

At the end of all this, Russia held in her hands a vast belt of land running from the Baltic sea in the north to the Black Sea in the south, comprising eleven nations with a population of 100 million people. These she held, not as parts of the Soviet Union, but as puppet states, presided over by Red Quislings of Stalin's own selection who represented him and not the people they governed, any more than Quisling represented the people of Norway.

CHAPTER 14: THE PRESIDENT'S DEATH

The story of any man's decline into disease and death naturally excites the sympathy of the human heart. The illness which caused Roosevelt's death was a personal misfortune. It was, in another sense, a misfortune for those who held power by virtue of his position. But it was an act of immeasurable gravity to involve the nation and, perhaps, the world, in that misfortune. The million young men in our armed forces who were killed or who were crippled, blinded or ruined for life in the war were no less the victims of misfortune and their plight, too, touches deeply the sympathies of the human heart. Did the nation not owe to them too, something, at least to the extent of not throwing away the fruits of their sufferings in order to gratify the ambitions of one man, even though he might be sick and dying?

It is, of course, easy to say that Roosevelt, broken on the wheel of service, was with tremendous courage giving the last ounce of his waning strength in the service of his country. But after all, his country in that critical moment of history was entitled to something more in a leader than the *last ineffectual ounces of his strength.* Throughout the war momentous decisions had to be made on military matters. But there were military leaders capable of making them. Once made, they had to be carried out on the field by fighting men. But the moment was close at hand when the decisions to be made were in the field of diplomacy and they would have to be made by Roosevelt himself; and when made would have to be carried out by him in conference with, and to some extent against, our allies. As I write a judge who is blind is being subjected to proceedings for his removal because, though he may be a good man, he is incapable of discharging his functions. A president, too ill to do more than a few hours work a day, whose hands trembled, whose energies were feeble, whose mind was weary and who, at times, was only partially conscious of his surroundings, was not the kind of representative America needed to confront the far more experienced and subtle Churchill and Stalin in the disposition of the affairs of the world. A chief of staff in Roosevelt's condition would have been summarily removed if he did not have the decency to resign. A department head in peacetime as feeble as Roosevelt would have been promptly relieved. Yet this America, so powerful in her economic energies, so tremendous upon the seas, in the air, upon the battlefield, whose might astonished the world, now, in the crucial moment of victory when she would capture or lose the fruits of the victory, put her fortunes into the hands of a drooping, jaded and haggard man, a mere shell, drifting wearily to the grave. But America did not know this.

The people of the United States are generous. We were at war and the President was the leader. A generous and patriotic disposition of the people is to submerge their critical feelings and to give the leader unquestioning loyalty. It was a sin of the first order to take advantage of this generous attitude to deceive the people There were, to sensitive eyes, obvious evidences of Roosevelt's illness during the campaign for the presidency in 1944, despite all the devices to conceal them. But when the people were told that he was well and strong and active, that "he was in top-top condition," that he was enjoying "excellent health for a man of his age," that he was a bit tired, to be sure, under the galling burdens of the war—as who would not be—the people believed these untruths. And when these guarantees of his health came from an admiral in the Navy delegated to watch over the President's health, they resented the suggestions of those who told them the truth. They did not suspect that the admiral was, if telling the truth, doing so, as Merriman Smith, United Press correspondent, says in the admiral's defense, in such as way as to be "misleading."

The truth is that Roosevelt was a dying man when he was elected, that many of those around him knew it, that the most elaborate care was exercised to conceal the fact from the people and that the misgivings of those who observed it were justified by events, since he died less than three months after his fourth inauguration. The progress of that illness and the means employed to deceive the people must be examined.

So much speculation followed Roosevelt's death and so much criticism was leveled against his official family that Rear Admiral Ross T. McIntire, his official physician, felt called upon to put in a book his formal apologia. The volume offers a connected account of Roosevelt's illness and pretends to be the candid statement of a man of science. During the campaign of 1944, Admiral McIntire made three public statements that the President was in perfect health.[110] He was severely criticized for this. He was a naval officer employed by the people to watch over the President's health and these statements had the effect of deceiving the employers of the President and of the Admiral—namely the people. Fairness to McIntire calls for some scrutiny of this charge. He was the President's physician employed by the government in that role. But he was not the President's personal physician in the sense in which one understands that relationship in private life. He was the President's physician but not the President's employee. However, it must be conceded that he could not discharge his functions as physician unless he enjoyed completely the President's confidence about his health. He could not hope to have this and discharge his functions intelligently if he issued statements disclosing the diseases and infirmities from which the President suffered. He would be within his rights, therefore, if, when queried about the President's health, he refused to make any disclosures. However, if it was proper for him to remain silent about the President's ailments, it was equally his duty to his employers—the people—not to issue statements in order to influence the course of a political campaign and advance the political ambitions of the President. Mr. Merriman Smith, the correspondent who covered the White House for the United Press, says in defense of McIntire that: "To his credit, McIntire never lied about Roosevelt's condition. He told the truth *but in language that could easily be misleading.*"[111] The object of an artfully devised statement that contained technically the truth but which was designed to mislead becomes a grave matter when we reflect that the persons to be misled were the Admiral's employers, the people.

As far as we know, Roosevelt's descent into that condition which took his life began after he returned from the Teheran conference in December, 1943. He went to Hyde Park for the Christmas holidays. There, according to Dr. McIntire, he suffered a brief attack of influenza followed by a bronchial infection. Whatever laid him low that Christmas week, the fact remains that from that time on he spent, until the day he died, less than half his time in the White House. During the year 1944 he was absent from the White House 175 days. Thirty of these were on a trip to the Pacific. There were perhaps two weeks consumed by the campaign. There was less than a week at the Quebec conference. The balance—much over 100 days—were spent at Hobcaw Barony in South Carolina recuperating or at Hyde Park or at a hide-out the President had in Maryland.

We have seen how, following the illness at Hyde Park in Christmas week, 1943, Roosevelt was indisposed continuously until finally doctors called into consultation advised that he go into the sun of the South and he went to Baruch's estate on the ocean in South Carolina, where he spent a full month in an effort to recuperate. And we have seen how, before he returned to the White House, Dr. McIntire put him on a daily schedule which limited him to four hours' work a day, ten hours of sleep at night, an hour and a half for meals in his private room and the balance of the time lying down, getting treatments or resting. This, we must recall, was the essential condition not until he recovered his health, but for the rest of his life if he wished to live—a program suited only to a man in semi-retirement at most. But Dr. McIntire never disclosed this until after Roosevelt's death, and for some strange reason did not even then realize that no man could discharge the grave responsibilities of the war on such a schedule and that the very necessity of such a schedule rendered him incapable of continuing in his high office.

What disease Roosevelt suffered from at Hyde Park and later, that produced such grave consequences, we do not know save upon the statements of Dr. McIntire. Many other doctors were called in to examine the patient, but none of these men has ever made any statements. However, while the illness seemingly began at Hyde Park after the return from Teheran, there is at least some evidence that he was far from sound before that time. Three men have written about the trip to Cairo and Teheran—Dr. McIntire, Mike Reilly, chief of the President's Secret Service guard, and Elliott Roosevelt. The President went to Cairo by sea. But he wanted to fly from there to Teheran. Reilly tells us that Admiral McIntire "did not want to submit some of the members of the party to the rigors of high altitude flight" but that "the President was not one of these members."[112] And McIntire volunteers the information that Roosevelt suffered no discomfort on high altitude flights and had shown no signs of anoxemia when flying at altitudes of 10,000 to 12,000 feet.[113] You might suppose from this Roosevelt was quite a flier. Yet he had never been in a plane since he flew to Chicago for his first acceptance speech 11 years before until he made the trip to Casablanca—his only flight while President before Teheran. However, Elliott Roosevelt in his book defeats these yarns. He tells how McIntire was worried about Father's projected flight. "I'm serious, Elliott," says McIntire. "I think he could fly only as far as Basra and then go on by train." Elliott wanted to know what height his father might fly, to which McIntire replied: "Nothing over 7500 feet—*and that's tops.*"[114]

Elliott talked to the President's proposed pilot, Major Otis Bryan who, with Mike Reilly, made an inspection flight from Teheran to Basra and back and reported that the trip could be made without going higher than 7000 feet, which, says Elliott, "pleased Father very much."[115] Thus McIntire and Reilly are both caught red-handed misleading their readers. This was before Teheran.

Whatever malady struck Roosevelt down at Hyde Park in December and kept him pretty much out of circulation until nearly the middle of May, 1944, we know that McIntire at that time caused a heart specialist from Boston to be inducted into the service to remain continuously at Roosevelt's side and that this heart specialist, Dr.

Howard Bruenn, said a year later at Warm Springs that he "never let Roosevelt get out of his sight," which is a most unusual performance in the case of a patient whose "stout heart never failed him," as Dr. McIntire puts it.

A great mystery surrounded this illness. Secretary Frances Perkins says that all "the cabinet knew about it was that it was not an ordinary cold." As cabinet meetings were skipped "they became concerned." When he did return it was understood that he had had a cold, "perhaps a touch of pneumonia, although one was not told and did not ask."[116] Why this secrecy even with the cabinet? He spent little time in the White House but that fact was not revealed. All during March he practically disappeared from the news, save once on March 17 when he emerged to call upon the Finns to quit fighting our noble ally Russia. On April 7, he appeared at his office and next day left for Hobcaw Barony for a month's rest. He was examined by two specialists before going there. McIntire says they found "a moderate degree of arteriosclerosis and some changes in the cardiac tracings."[117] Since McIntire brought in a heart specialist as Roosevelt's constant attendant and since it was arteriosclerosis which turned him into an old man who looked ten years older than the 69-year-old Churchill and which killed him a year later, we have a right to assume that the admiral-doctor was not dealing fairly with the American people in the rosy statements he issued about the President's health.

As a matter of fact, Dr. McIntire admits that while he was issuing these misleading statements to the American people, he was talking very differently to Roosevelt in private. He told the President, according to his book: "You may feel fine but you don't look it. Your neck is scrawny and your face is gulled by a lot of lines that have aged you ten years."[118] What did McIntire think had made Roosevelt's neck so scrawny, his face so thin and had imprinted on it those lines that "aged him ten years"? It was certainly not attributable to that "tip-top" condition, that "excellent health" which he was reporting to the public. He had Roosevelt examined by five specialists before he permitted him to leave the Hobcaw Barony retreat and, to be certain, he called in two more. When Roosevelt did go back to Washington on his four-hour day he spent little time at the White House. He wanted a retreat close by Washington and caused to be built a settlement for himself in the Catoctin Mountains in Maryland. There was a large cabin for him, one for the Secret Service guards, a guest cabin, a cottage for the secretaries and staff, a mess hall for the hired help, and a pool. The existence and location of this retreat were never made known. Roosevelt referred to it among the correspondents as Shangri-La. And it was to this isolated hideaway he went to escape the pressing duties of the presidency. It was here, perhaps, unknown to the public, he spent much of his time. This was the condition of the invalided President who was now preparing for a fourth try at the presidency on the theory that he was the only man in America capable of representing us in the peace negotiations and of standing up to the iron man in the Kremlin.

We must recall how, as the Democratic Convention was assembling in Chicago in July, Roosevelt started on his trip to the Pacific, stopping at Chicago to confer with Hannegan and at San Diego to make his acceptance speech. It was the picture taken of him as he spoke in San Diego that shocked the people. McIntire blamed this revealing photograph upon the photographers, as if they had committed some offense in not touching it up to suppress the truth. We are asked to believe that Roosevelt exposed himself to the "rigors" of this trip as part of his duty as Commander-in-chief. An executive who had been forced to remain away from his desk so long, now absented himself for another month just to inspect troops, hospitals and island bases, far from the only place where, as executive, he could make decisions—namely in Washington where all the military, naval and diplomatic services were centered. His conference with MacArthur and Nimitz lasted only a few hours. This whole trip was a long vacation for Roosevelt, aside from the purely theatrical and incidental emphasis upon the Commander-in-chief out in the thick of the battle-torn Pacific. However, on this trip his appalling physical condition was revealed to the commanders in Honolulu. They were shocked at his appearance, despite the long, restful sea trip. Here for the first time we hear of his conversation falling into intervals of irrelevance. Here at a dinner he sat reading a short speech. Suddenly he faltered and paused, his eyes became glassy, consciousness drifted from him. The man at his side nudged him, shook him a little, pointed to the place in the manuscript at which he broke off and said: "Here, Mr. President, is your place." With an effort he resumed.[119] As he was wheeled from his quarters, officers noticed his head drooping forward, his jaw hanging loosely. He returned to Washington on August 18. It was a long, restful interlude. Yet, though he was mentally refreshed, Merriman Smith, the UP correspondent, said "he was physically tired." But all this was concealed from the voters.

Roosevelt planned to take little part in the campaign because he was unequal to it, but he decided to make a few speeches at Washington, New York, Boston and Chicago and a few short ones at way stations. The speeches at Washington and New York convinced some of the doctors with whom I talked that he was approaching the end of his life. The brain is the control room of the body. From some compartment in that extraordinary instrument-room every part of the body is controlled. The face is one of the most complex muscular organisms in the body. It is capable of performing a great number of complex muscular operations simultaneously—sneering, smiling, wrinkling the brows, moving the eyes, and with the aid of the lips and the tongue, forming our entire vocabulary. And all these several functions are directed from various separate sections of the brain. A specialist looking at such a face in the movies and hearing its speech there or over the air can detect the difficulty or failure with which the brain obeys the commands of the will, the mumbled syllables, and uncompleted words, the flaccid and unresponding facial muscles, all of which signify to the expert that there is a cerebral disturbance of some kind. Physicians, and particularly neurologists, who saw these pictures of Roosevelt or heard his voice over the air predicted he would be dead within a year. But Dr. McIntire seemed to be blind to these warnings. Certainly Sidney Hillman and Henry Wallace knew it. And thus we saw that cabal to seize the Presidency of the United States for Wallace by way of his renomination for Vice-President—a scheme which, with Roosevelt's aid, came very near to success.

Everything that was done in the campaign was designed, while taxing Roosevelt's brain and heart the least, to create the impression that he was well and strong. The speech at the Teamsters' dinner was prepared by Robert Sherwood and was a dramatist's maneuver to cast Roosevelt in the role of a happy, merry, carefree jokester. The trip to New York around the streets was to exhibit him as a rugged campaigner. The rain which drenched it was not planned, but it added to the effect. Of course he sat the entire time in a large limousine, wrapped in heavy furs, with an electric heater under the seat and another at his feet. Whether the rain did him any good or not we cannot say. But it was quite successful in lulling the populace into supposing that the President was hale and hearty. On election night he was, as usual, at Hyde Park. Merriman Smith writes that as he came onto the porch after the returns indicated the result "he looked older than I had ever seen him and he made an irrelevant speech." At the Nelson House in Poughkeepsie that night the reporters sat around talking politics. Smith says they were "arguing entirely about the chances of his living out his fourth term. Those who believed he would were in the decided minority."[120]

After the election, Roosevelt dropped out of the news for some time. A story is told that shortly before election he had had another of those lapses of complete unconsciousness much the same as happened to him at Honolulu. He remained at Hyde Park until November 10 and then dropped out of the news until November 28. That day he went to Warm Springs for another rest until December 23 and then to Hyde Park for the Christmas holidays. Dr. McIntire attempts to convince us that all the trouble stemmed from his refusal to adhere to the semi-retirement schedule worked out for him. From election day to January 1, he was in almost complete retirement. He was not even up to the meager routine prescribed by McIntire.

As the fourth inauguration approached, one or two cabinet meetings were omitted. Secretary Perkins says it was understood the President was very much occupied. As he was about to absent himself for the conference at Yalta, it was assumed he was putting in much time preparing himself. Dr. McIntire remonstrated with him, but he says Roosevelt would not listen. Dr. McIntire kept in mind the advice that if his patient wanted to live he could work only four hours a day. It did not occur to him, apparently, that if he wanted to be President he could not do that. The day before the inauguration a cabinet meeting was held. Secretary Perkins says Roosevelt didn't look well. His clothes seemed too big for him, his face was thin, his color gray, his eyes dull. Everyone in the room sensed it and felt they must not tire him. After the cabinet meeting, Miss Perkins asked to see him. She had told him she intended to retire and had packed her papers for departure. She wanted a farewell talk. As she entered his room "he looked awful." He had the "pallor, the deep gray color of a man who had been long ill." He sat in an office chair with his hands to his head as if to hold it up. The two-hour cabinet meeting had wrecked him. His hands shook. He begged her piteously not to leave the cabinet yet. As she left she whispered to an attendant to bring his chair and to make him lie down. She tells how she went to her office frightened. She called her secretary to her office and closed the door. She said: "Don't tell a soul … I can't stand it. The President looks horrible. I am afraid he is ill." And some days later Henry Wallace's wife told Frances Perkins that she too was frightened. They agreed to keep quiet about it.[121] The spectacle of this dying man was naturally enough to crush a woman who was among his oldest friends, who had had great honors at his hands and who was devoted to him. It was enough to frighten her. But this man was about to be sworn in, within 24 hours, as President of the United States for another four years. It was this gray and fading ghost of a man who was about to be re-endowed with the authority and duty of going, within 48 hours, to meet the grim and resolute dictator of the Russians to rearrange the affairs of the world.

He left for Yalta the day after the inauguration. On the way over he was confined to his room. He was, as we have seen, unable to have any conferences with Mr. Byrnes, who was going as his adviser. He emerged from his room only for meals or a movie to which he was wheeled. Yet McIntire says he "reached Yalta in fine fettle." Pictures taken there and published shocked the nation. It was all the fault of the photographers, says McIntire. But why didn't the same pictures reveal Churchill, seven years older, and Stalin, two years older than Roosevelt, as gray, wan and ill? When the conference ended, Roosevelt started home. McIntire said: "Vital was the word for Roosevelt."[122] He described the President on the way home as spending most of the day with Sam Rosenman in the "drudging business" of preparing his speech to Congress. But the UP reporter Smith said he spent much of the day sitting on the deck in the sun, playing solitaire and reading detective stories.

McIntire admits that while delivering the Yalta speech, Roosevelt exhibited signs of fatigue. When it was over he went to Warm Springs to rest. But he was planning more trips—more gruelling trips, as McIntire thought of them when he was interested in explaining Roosevelt's rugged life. He planned to go to San Francisco for the inaugural meeting of the United Nations and then on to the

Pacific and into China. Obviously there was no important duty of the presidency that required him to go to the Pacific or to travel in China. His duties were at home. But these trips, despite the ballyhoo, were planned as escape voyages, expedients to avoid the drudgery of the Presidency which he was utterly incapable of facing, long restful days on shipboard in rest, idleness and sleep.

Roosevelt got to Warm Springs on March 30. On April 12 he was dead. But his doctors never flagged in their determination to exhibit him as a well man. McIntire says that by April 5 he "was feeling fine." Yet on that very day the correspondents, admitted to his cottage when he was receiving President Osmena of the Philippines in a purely formal call, described him as being in a sad way. His hands shook "more than ever," which implies that they habitually trembled but this day worse than before. He could hardly get a cigarette out of the package because of this trembling. Smith writes that in the last six months his hearing had become gravely affected and that his voice, once so strong that it could shake the windows, was now so thin that he could not always be understood. Yet when he died and the reporters reached his cottage, Dr. Bruenn's first words were: "He'd been feeling fine. He was awfully tired when he first came down here. But you saw him the other day (April 5)—*wasn't he in fine spirits?*" Smith answered: "Yes, he was in fine spirits. But he didn't look healthy."[123] Only his doctors seemingly were blind to that fact.

Admiral McIntire in his book bears down heavily on the terrible ordeal of travel to which Roosevelt was subjected. After describing the trips and shrewdly exaggerating their rigors, he says: "I submit that a sick and failing man could not have withstood these journeys, calling for mental and physical effort."

The doctor plays upon the average reader's conception of travel as he does it himself—rushing for trains, standing in line for tickets, jostling depot crowds. The President didn't travel that way. Without a thought about arrangements, his limousine took him to a specially constructed private station, then into his wheel-chair and onto an elevator built into the private car fitted with a large staff and every luxury. The car was specially built for him and presented by the railroads whose managers he loved to castigate as economic royalists. Then to a great war vessel specially outfitted with ramps and elevators for him at the cost of a hundred thousand dollars or more and with a numerous staff to answer his every call. These trips, involving long days on the ocean and only a few days at the destinations, afforded him time for complete rest and sleep in his cabin and on the deck in the sun. No sick man could ask for a more delightful form of rest—ten days across the Pacific and as many back, doctors watching over him, masseurs to give him exercise without any effort on his part, every whim anticipated and satisfied. The chief purpose of the long trips was rest. He might have flown, as he did to Casablanca, but the long ocean voyages were chosen as restoratives and not as harrying drafts upon his energies.

One of the rumors about Roosevelt that had wide currency was that he had had a heart attack or a stroke. McIntire writes: "The President never had a stroke, never had a serious heart condition and never underwent other operations than the removal of a wen and the extraction of an infected tooth."[124] Similarly Mike Reilly, head of his Secret Service detail, writes: "I will swear on everything I love or believe that the Boss never had a heart attack and that he was never seriously ill in the ten years that I worked for him until the day he died."[125]

Let us scrutinize these statements. I think it is true that Roosevelt never had a heart attack. As to having a stroke, that is another matter. The word "stroke" has a technical meaning. It may be used to describe an extensive cerebral thrombosis or clot in one of the important vessels of the brain, or a hemorrhage by rupture of a vessel—and cause death or paralysis in some part of the body. However, a man in Roosevelt's condition could suffer a condition that would be less serious—a blood vessel spasm which produces a sudden and transient semi-unconsciousness, such as Roosevelt had at the dinner in Honolulu and which only those very close to him perceived. He had a similar condition in the White House in the presence of an eminent visitor only a few days before the New York campaign trip. This would be called, not a stroke, but a cerebral vascular spasm. In the case of a cerebral hemorrhage a rupture of a blood vessel in the brain occurs, flooding the adjacent tissues and putting out of business the sections thus affected and hence paralyzing the functions of those areas of the body served by the flooded portions. If sufficiently severe or continuous it will produce death. An intermittent claudification or cerebral occlusion is the result not of a rupture but of the narrowing of the blood vessels in the brain—usually with lime deposits—diminishing the flow of blood or shutting it off entirely to a section of the brain for a moment or two or even a few minutes and producing an interval of mental vagueness or semi-consciousness or full unconsciousness until the spasm ceases and the blood resumes its course. It is similar to what is known as angina pectoris in which the vessels supplying the heart are shut off or occluded. But the heart cannot go without blood for more than two minutes without death and such attacks as Roosevelt suffered in the brain from cerebral occlusion would have been fatal in the heart.

Roosevelt may not have had a stroke, but he certainly suffered more than once a cerebral occlusion as distinguished from a hemorrhage. He may not have had an anginal attack but he did have something that threatened his heart, that produced a rapid physical deterioration and that led Dr. McIntire to put him for more than a year under the constant surveillance of a heart specialist.

Admiral McIntire puts much faith in a series of check-ups, some of which he publishes in his book and which, he assures us, revealed Roosevelt in a generally sound organic condition. But of what value were these check-ups when before his eyes his patient was gradually withering away, losing weight, growing pallid, drifting occasionally into irrelevance in his talk, becoming ever more listless and glassy-eyed? Everybody who came near Roosevelt saw this. Reporters commented on it. Miss Perkins was horrified at his inauguration. Ed Flynn, his campaign manager, writes that he had noticed Roosevelt's mental deterioration before his election for a third term, his delayed reactions for instance. Merriman Smith noticed his trembling hands, his halting speech, his irrelevant talks, his weak voice.

There is in fact no escape for the men immediately around Roosevelt. He was utterly unfit for his high office long before the election. He was dying slowly at first, rapidly later. And at his side as his chief adviser was another dying man—Harry Hopkins. Hopkins had had a portion of his stomach removed for ulcers and what was known as a gastro-enterotomy performed. After this his liver troubled him and the gall bladder failed to supply satisfactorily the essential bile necessary to digestion. He depended on tablets to supply bile by mouth. A second operation was performed and an attempt made to remedy the condition. Cancer of the plyorus was the most likely diagnosis, but it was never found, and the final opinion was that he actually died of sprue. At any rate, after the second operation he was slowly starving to death and sitting at times in a condition when he was only half conscious of his environment. These two dying men, floating slowly out of life, were deliberately put into power through a fourth-term election by a carefully arranged deception practiced upon the American people and upon some, at least, of the party leaders. Here was a crime committed against a great nation which had made tremendous sacrifices and against the peace and security of the world in a moment of the gravest danger. History will pronounce its verdict upon all who were guilty.

After Roosevelt's death a whole train of rumors began to circulate about the causes. And these rumors still persist. He was stricken at 1:15 P.M. and died at 4:35 P.M. Dr. McIntire was immediately notified of the stroke in Washington and he, Mrs. Roosevelt and Steve Early left at once by plane for Warm Springs, arriving there at 11 P.M. They immediately decided to have no autopsy. The body was consigned to its coffin and orders issued not to open it. It was taken from Warm Springs next morning at 9 o'clock. It reached Washington next day—the 14th—and after lying for a few hours without ever being opened was taken that night to Hyde Park for interment next day. It has been the custom in the past for the remains of deceased Presidents to lie in state in the Capitol. This was not done. Present in the cottage when the President was stricken were the artist, Mrs. Shoumatoff, who was painting his portrait, his two cousins, his valet, the lady for whom the protrait was intended and several others. The lady and Mrs. Shoumatoff took their departure immediatly. As Mrs. Shoumatoff was Russian-born weird stories that the President had been shot were built upon this circumstance. Other tales are to the effect that he shot himself, that he took poison or was poisoned and still another that he drove to the top of a nearby cliff and off to his death and that the body was reclaimed and brought back into the house, that the undertaker when he arrived found a bloody bandage on his head, and so on.

There is, of course, no truth in these stories. There were three persons in the room when the President suffered the final cerebral hemorrhage. His Negro valet saw him immediately after and carried him to his room. Later Dr. Howard Bruenn, Dr. James Paullin and

Major George Fox, his masseur were at his bedside and at one time Mike Reilly was there. There were three in the room when the President died. There is no reason whatever to suppose that the circumstances and cause of his death were not precisely as they have been officially described. He died of a cerebral hemorrhage caused by arteriosclerosis which had been slowly progressing during the preceding year and a half. The stroke was merely the final episode of an illness which had manifested every usual symptom and which was concealed from the American people.

Admiral McIntire is not the first physician to get himself into a stew about his distinguished patient and find it necessary to write a book in his own defense. At St. Helena the British government provided its illustrious prisoner, Napoleon I, with a physician. He was Dr. Francesco Antomarchi, a Corsican, who however, did not seem particularly fond of his fallen countryman and who failed signally to win Napoleon's confidence. Dr. Antomarchi persisted to the end in the belief that his royal patient was not seriously ill. Napoleon convinced himself that his physician did not know what he was doing and that the medicines he was prescribing were actually injuring him. Napoleon watched his chance and when the doctor's back was turned, handed the mixture just prepared for him to an aide who swallowed it and was immediately taken with a violent internal disturbance. The Emperor denounced Antomarchi as an assassin. Dr. MacLaurin,[126] who has written interestingly of this case, observes that from the symptoms now known to be present and even in the then state of medical knowledge at that period, the veriest blockhead would have known that the Emperor was seriously ill. Napoleon died shortly after the incident described above of cancer of the stomach. In this case, instead of passing up the autopsy, Antomarchi performed one himself in order to prove that there were no symptoms present to inform him of the presence of cancer and he wrote a book upon the subject.

Roosevelt died of a massive cerebral hemorrhage resulting from a progressive arteriosclerosis which Dr. McIntire says he did not observe and he insists that medical knowledge has not advanced to the point where an impending cerebral hemorrhage can be forecast. He tells us he discussed the matter with many excellent pathologists and that he has yet to find one willing to say "that one can tell *when* a man will have a cerebral hemorrhage or *when he will not.*[127] (Italics added.) A careful analysis of this statement makes it very clear that the doctor is depending upon the hurried reading which the casual person will give his words. Of course few doctors will say they can tell "when" a man will have a cerebral hemorrhage and "when" he will not. That is not the point. Few doctors can tell how long the blood vessels will hold out against the strain put upon them in cases of arteriosclerosis. They cannot forecast *the time* when a hemorrhage will occur. But they can tell that a man will have such an attack at some unpredictable time, and they can make a reasonable estimate of the so-called prognosis. They cannot, as the doctor artfully infers, say that it will not happen tomorrow or next week or next month. But they can say that the conditions making for such a disaster at some undetermined time are present. Even in January, 1944, the doctors found what McIntire called a "moderate degree" of arteriosclerosis. And it is certain that this was the disease which produced the stroke of April 12, 1945. And it is certain that there were obvious, even to casual observers, evidences of great deterioration both physically and mentally—the trembling hands, the loss of weight and the shocking emaciation, the terrible fatigue, the lack of ability to coordinate the muscles of the face, the intervals of irrelevance in the talk, and more than one instance of cerebral occlusion. Certainly there was something critically wrong with this patient and certainly he died from the very disease and cause which doctors who merely saw Roosevelt occasionally or in the pictures or heard him over the air predicted he would. McIntire, like Antomarchi, wrote a book about his patient and his death, but unlike Antomarchi he did not perform an autopsy. An autopsy might have disclosed other prior attacks.

It is not merely a question as to the disease that ended Roosevelt's life. Roosevelt's death is not the serious point. After all, when a president dies there is a vice-president to succeed him. The serious offense lay in palming off upon the country a hopeless invalid, by McIntire's own account incapable of discharging the duties of the presidency in a great and terrible national emergency.[128]

CHAPTER 15: THE ROOSEVELT MYTH

When the war drums rolled a great golden veil came down upon the American scene through which its actors would be viewed. Behind it they postured—statesmen and generals and admirals—in the role of heroes. And lifted above them all, posing in the full glory of the stage lights, decorated by propaganda with the virtues of a national god, was the figure of the Leader. When the battlefield is so far away, war is the greatest of all shows. It is the greatest of all booms. The money flows in rushing streams and for millions it becomes and remains the dizziest and most abundant memory of their lives. The lights have been going out, the bands have ceased playing, the propaganda machines are being slowly silenced and little by little life, scenery and actors are assuming their normal dimensions. Despite all this, many good people in America still cherish the illusion that Roosevelt performed some amazing feat of regeneration for this country. They believe he took our economic system when it was in utter disrepair and restored it again to vitality; that he took over our political system when it was at its lowest estate and restored it again to its full strength. He put himself on the side of the underprivileged masses. He transferred power from the great corporate barons to the simple working people of America. He curbed the adventurers of Wall Street, and gave security to the humble men and women of the country. And above all he led us through a great war for democracy and freedom and saved the civilization of Europe.

But not one of these claims can be sustained. He did not restore our economic system to vitality. He changed it. The system he blundered us into is more like the managed and bureaucratized, state-supported system of Germany before World War I than our own traditional order. Before his regime we lived in a system which depended for its expansion upon private investment in private enterprise. Today we live in a system which depends for its expansion and vitality upon the government. This is a pre-war European importation—imported at the moment when it had fallen into complete disintegration in Europe. In America today every fourth person depends for his livelihood upon employment either directly by the government or indirectly in some industry supported by government funds. In this substituted system the government confiscates by taxes or borrowings the savings of all the citizens and invests them in non-wealth-producing enterprises in order to create work. Behold the picture of American economy today: taxes which confiscate the savings of every citizen, a public debt of 250 billion dollars as against a pre-Roosevelt debt of 19 billions, a government budget of 40 billions instead of four before Roosevelt, inflation doubling the prices and reducing the lower-bracket employed workers to a state of pauperism as bad as that of the unemployed in the depression, more people on various kinds of government relief than when we had 11 million unemployed, Americans trapped in the economic disasters and the political quarrels of every nation on earth and a system of permanent militarism closely resembling that we beheld with horror in Europe for decades, bureaucrats swarming over every field of life and the President calling for more power, more price-fixing, more regulation and more billions. Does this look like the traditional American scene? Or does it not look rather like the system built by Bismarck in Germany in the last century and imitated by all the lesser Bismarcks in Europe?

No, Roosevelt did not restore our economic system. He did not construct a new one. He substituted an old one which lives upon permanent crises and an armament economy. And he did this not by a process of orderly architecture and building, but by a succession of blunders, moving one step at a time, in flight from one problem to another, until we are now arrived at that kind of state-supported economic system that will continue to devour a little at a time the private system until it disappears altogether.

He did not restore our political system to its full strength. One may like the shape into which he battered it, but it cannot be called a repair job. He changed our political system with two weapons—blank-check congressional appropriations and blank-check congressional legislation. In 1933, Congress abdicated much of its power when it put billions into his hands by a blanket appropriation to be spent at his sweet will and when it passed general laws, leaving it to him, through great government bureaus of his appointment, to fill in the details of legislation.

These two baleful mistakes gave him a power which he used ruthlessly. He used it to break down the power of the states and to move that power to Washington and to break down the power of Congress and concentrate it in the hands of the executive. The end of these two betrayals—the smashing of our economic system and the twisting of our political system—can only be the Planned Economic State, which, either in the form of Communism or Fascism, dominates the entire continent of Europe today. The capitalist system cannot live under these conditions. Free representative government cannot survive a Planned Economy. Such an economy can be managed only by a dictatorial government capable of enforcing the directives it issues. The only result of our present system—unless we reverse the drift—must be the gradual extension of the fascist sector and the gradual disappearance of the system of free enterprise under a free representative government.

There are men who honestly defend this transformation. They at least are honest. They believe in the Planned Economy. They believe in the highly centralized government operated by a powerful executive. They do not say Roosevelt saved our system. They say he has given us a new one. That is logical. But no one can praise Roosevelt for doing this and then insist that he restored our traditional political and economic systems to their former vitality.

The most tragic illusion about this man is that built up by the ceaseless repetition of the false statement that he gave us a system of security.

Security for whom? For the aged? An old-age security bill was passed during his first administration which provides for workers who reached the age of 65 a pension of $8 a week. Even this had to be pushed through against a strange inertness on Roosevelt's part—he only consented to the bill after severe prodding by the Republicans during the 1934 congressional campaign. Then the plan was sold to the people by Mr. Roosevelt as an "insurance" scheme, which it is not. Like many good ideas that went into his mind, it came out badly twisted. It contains a plan for building a huge reserve fund that amounts to nothing more than a scheme to extract billions from the workers' payrolls without any adequate return. In 20 years of operation, the government has taken from workers and their employers nearly 25 billion dollars which it has spent on everything under the sun except social security. Then it taxes the same workers and employers *again* to pay benefits. And while the benefits themselves have increased over the years, under the pressures of the Roosevelt inflation, so have the taxes, and the inequalities and injustices in the whole fake "insurance" scheme cry aloud for complete revision and correction.

But what of the millions of people who through long years of thrift and saving have been providing their own security? What of the millions who have been scratching for years to pay for their life insurance and annuities, putting money in savings banks, commercial banks, buying government and corporation bonds to protect themselves in their old age? What of the millions of teachers, police, firemen, civil employees of states and cities and the government, of the armed services and the army of men and women entitled to retirement funds from private corporations—railroads, industrial and commercial? These thrifty people have seen one-half of their retirement benefits wiped out by the Roosevelt inflation that has cut the purchasing power of the dollar in two. Roosevelt struck the most terrible blow at the security of the masses of the people while posing as the generous donor of "security for all." During the war boom and in the post-war boom created by spending 40 billion dollars a year the illusion of security is sustained. The full measure of Roosevelt's hopeless misunderstanding of this subject will come when security will be most needed—and most absent.

To say that Roosevelt roused in the people a social consciousness is absurd. There has always been a social consciousness in our people. And when Roosevelt as governor in New York took his first steps in this field, he was merely following in the footsteps of Al Smith, who made him governor. Of course when the depression arrived, its grave necessities stirred the minds of our people to social measures upon a greater scale. Roosevelt had never given the subject a thought until he was elected governor. However, has anyone ever bothered to consult those fruitful studies in social problems which Herbert Hoover caused to be made while he was Secretary of Commerce and President before the onset of the crisis brought this subject to everyone's mind?

As for the great war for freedom and democracy, it would be well to get that clear in our minds. In one breath we are told that

Roosevelt did not take us into that war—that we were dragged in by the dastardly attack by the Japanese at Pearl Harbor, while Roosevelt was trying to keep out. In the next breath we are told he took us into that war for freedom and democracy. But how has it advanced the cause of democracy? We liberated Europe from Hitler and turned it over to the mercies of a far more terrible tyrant and actually tried to sell him to the people as a savior of civilization. Behold Europe! Does one refer to the wreckage there as liberation and salvation? Is anyone so naive as to suppose that democracy and free capitalism have been restored in Europe? Fascism has departed from Germany, but a hybrid system of socialism and capitalism in chains has come to England, which is called social democracy but is on its way to Fascism with all the controls without which such a system cannot exist. And in America the price of the war is that fatal deformity of our own economic and political system which Roosevelt effected under the impact of the war necessities.

Roosevelt's star was waning sadly in 1938 when he had 11 million unemployed and when Hitler made his first war moves in Europe. All his promises had been defaulted on. The cities were filling with idle workers. Taxes were rising. The debt was soaring. The war rescued him and he seized upon it like a drowning man. By leading his country into the fringes of the war at first and then deep into its center all over the world he was able to do the only things that could save him—spend incomprehensible billions, whip up spending in the hot flames of war hysteria, put every man and his wife and grandparents into the war mills, while under the pressure of patriotic inhibitions, he could silence criticism and work up the illusion of the war leader. Of course the war against Germany was won—America with her 140 million people, Russia with her 180 million, France, England and the Commonwealth with another 100 million, with practically all the naval power and with the choice of the earth's resources, against 70 million of the enemy—of course we won. But at what price to our institutions? And then, while the war was still raging and as victory appeared, Roosevelt disappeared from the scene. The staggering debts, the larcenous inflation, the insoluble division amongst the victors, the appalling consequences of his fantastic surrenders to Moscow—all this is left in the hands of his successors, after the ballyhoo is spent, the fireworks extinguished, the martial music silenced and the money nearly gone, leaving only the great spectacle of a disordered, divided and bankrupt world.

On the moral side, let me say that I have barely touched that subject. It will all yet be told. But go back through the years, read the speeches and platforms and judgments he made and consider them in the light of what he did. Look up the promises of thrift in public office, of balanced budgets and lower taxes, of disbanded bureaucrats, of honesty in government and of security for all. Read again the warnings he uttered to his own people against those wicked men who would seize upon a war in Europe to entangle them upon specious visions of false war abundance. Read the speeches he made never, never again to send our sons to fight in foreign wars. Look up the promises he made, not to our own people, but to the Chinese, to Poland, to Czechoslovakia, to the Baltic peoples in Lithuania and Latvia and Estonia, to the Jews out of one side of his mouth and to the Arabs out of the other side. He broke every promise. He betrayed all who trusted him. If any escaped it was the British and the Russians because they were represented by two strong men who, in dealing with Roosevelt, were inflexible realists who knew what they were about, who played the game with him upon the basis of solid realism, as they should, who remembered their own countries and held him with iron resolution to his incredible pledges.

The figure of Roosevelt exhibited before the eyes of our people is a fiction. There was no such being as that noble, selfless, hard-headed, wise and farseeing combination of philosopher, philanthropist and warrior which has been fabricated out of pure propaganda and which a small collection of dangerous cliques in this country are using to advance their own evil ends.

POSTSCRIPT

As I write these lines it is 11 years since Franklin D. Roosevelt passed from the American scene. He died in the last moments of a cruel war, as military victory was descending on the allied armies. The conjuncture of victory and death conferred on him a kind of sainthood. Moreover, in these circumstances a well understood principle of Christian charity invaded the public mind and suspended criticism. Thus the myth of the Great Chieftain has been permitted to persist—a phenomenon widely exploited by his political heirs. And this influence was still in full vigor three years after his death when the first edition of this volume came from the press.

Another eight years have rolled over our heads since then, with the inevitable result that a spirit of rational criticism has appeared.

This chapter, offered as a postscript, is designed to take a brief backward glance over the events and characters described in this volume. It now becomes possible to answer more clearly a group of questions that must plague the minds of many Americans. Did we win the war? What has happened to our "noble allies"? What has happened to so many of those "little peoples" we were supposed to save? What has been the effect upon our own political and social system? What must be the definitive verdict of history upon this strange man? It is now appropriate to suggest some rational answers to these questions.

I.

A curious illusion that has captured the minds of the present generation is one in which Franklin D. Roosevelt is portrayed as the savior who took over from Herbert Hoover at the lowest point of the depression, and in which his first great achievement was the conquest of that disorder. It is certain that the depression created the atmosphere and the national temper that made his election possible. It is also true that he assumed his great office as the nation sank down into the lowest level of the depression. And it must be conceded that, amid the dramatic scenes which accompanied his assumption of office, there was something in his manner and particularly in that extraordinary and eloquent inaugural address, with its bold and confident summons to action, that produced for the moment at least the feeling that now a great and competent captain, in the darkest hour of the storm, had taken the bridge.

The younger citizens of our time, I am sure, will receive with astonishment the statement that Roosevelt never made any headway against the depression. It is certain that he had no clear understanding of the causes which produced it. The seeds of that disaster were first sown in New York State, of which Roosevelt was governor. The boom that exploded into the depression originated in his own state. The grave abuses of the corporation and the holding company, the orgy of speculation in Wall Street, the prostitution of the banks and their funds by the gamblers in stocks and the rushing cataract of freshly printed stocks and bonds succeeded each other to feed the flood in Wall Street.

The reader will fail to grasp the full meaning of these events unless he understands the origin of the depression. It was not in any sense a failure of the free enterprise system—generally referred to as Capitalism. It resulted from a group of grave abuses which afflicted that system. A giddy school of economics of that day fell into the illusion that the secret of permanent prosperity had been discovered. It was called the New Era. At its root were two outworn, yet still dangerous theories of social dynamics. One of these was that permanent prosperity could be created by a dynamic use of the banking system. Banks of deposit, they declared, could create all the money needed by the economic system. The bank could credit its customers with "deposits" without receiving any deposits. The bank could lend a depositor $10,000 by just writing in his passbook that he had a deposit of $10,000, although he had made no deposit. The bank took his promissory note and *loaned him a deposit*. In 1929 the banks had deposits of 59 billion dollars. There was only something over eight billion dollars of real money in existence in and out of the banks. I know this system of banking sounds a little crazy, but it is not in reality when used with reason. It can become dangerous when it is carried too far. In the boom years preceding 1929 it was not only carried too far, but it was subjected to an additional hazard because such a shocking amount of this "deposit" money had been syphoned off into the hands of the brokers and speculators on the stock exchanges. This was nothing new either. Used with caution, this too is a valuable device for providing the business world with liquid funds. But carried to excess and employed to create fantastic bales of newly printed securities rushing into a surging stream through the gambling posts of the stock exchanges, it became an obvious and serious abuse.

Stocks—evidence of ownership in corporation property—were dumped on the markets and became mere chips in a vast gamblers' paradise. By clever manipulation they were boosted in price and unloaded on the public on credit supplied by the banks. And a notion got around that a new heaven of endless profits and prosperity had dawned.

The focal point of this disease was in the banks. To illustrate, the banks in 1920 had something over 40 billion dollars in deposits. By 1929 they had nearly 60 billion. These were *deposit dollars* based on bank loans. This was inflation—inflation gone mad. And in October, 1929, like an overblown balloon, it burst with a resounding crash. It crippled the banks, which held as security for the loans great numbers of stocks that had become worthless. It destroyed the confidence of people in business. It of course ended the Great Boom and set in motion a series of crippling repercussions which brought on the Great Depression. This in turn culminated in the final disaster—the collapse of 1933 as Franklin D. Roosevelt was taking office as President.

These facts are recalled and emphasized to make clear that the crash of 1929 and the depression that followed it were due, not to inherent defects in the free system, but to a series of abuses that were imposed on it by elements in the business world itself. The Capitalist system can operate at its highest efficiency when it is managed in accordance with those economic laws suited to its special character. The period following the First World War was one in which business leadership lost its head and in which political leadership on the whole did nothing to keep business safely within its appropriate grooves. Almost every conceivable abuse that could afflict business was loosed upon it—and by men who supposedly had the greatest interest in keeping business in a state of health.

The Capitalist system is a free system. The citizen is at liberty to use his energy, his skill and his resources to plan, to build and manage. Out of this free society there arose in America an aggregation of producing, manufacturing, building, merchandising and financial institutions that created a state of national well-being which was the admiration of the world. But it cannot be expected to flow along day after day and year after year without experiencing certain jerks and stoppages. Some enterprisers will be injudicious or perhaps too bold in their experiments; some less so. This is not a system in which the decisions are made at the center by an infallible economic pontiff.

Against the system's frailties must be set off the great and decisive boon of freedom. It is the only system in which men can live in freedom. The great central frailty of the Socialist society and the Communist society is that the agencies of production and distribution and finance will be in the hands of something called the State. But the State is, after all, a concentration of power which inevitably must be in the hands of politicians. The politician who makes all the decisions is an individual whose training and talents belong to the field of political action, rather than the field of producing and distributing goods, and whose decisions about action will always be made in terms of political rather than in terms of economic well-being and efficiency.

The American Capitalist system had been producing goods and services on an unprecedented scale up to 1929. This was the fruit of private management and initiative. The depression and its ultimate crisis was the product of a collection of outrageous abuses of the system imposed on it by excessively acquisitive men, who had suddenly learned how to manipulate the corporate system, the banking system and the speculative markets to pile up swift and fantastic gains.

It must be remembered too that the depression here was not a mere American phenomenon. Actually the disorder first appeared in Europe, and found its roots in purely European conditions. The First World War had left its mark on the economic life of that unhappy continent. And it is a fact that the dislocations in Europe had begun to produce observable effects here which, while they did not cause the depression, helped to spark it and did add to its virulence. The crash came here in 1929, but the signs of approaching recession had appeared from 18 months to two years before and they were easily recognized. It must be said for Mr. Hoover, then President, that he was among the first to perceive these disturbing signs long before the crash. He actually issued a cautious warning on the dangerous situation in this country revealed in what he called "the fever of speculation" here and the rising difficulties abroad. While he was still Secretary of Commerce he wrote a member of the Federal Reserve Board cautioning that its easy money policy "might lead to dangerous inflation and perhaps a collapse." He warned against the dangerous use of brokers' loans—those 24-hour loans made by banks to brokers and which they in turn used to finance the speculative adventures of their clients. He warned that all this might lead to a disaster which "would bring the greatest calamities on farmers, workers and legitimate business."

It is a fact that the boom in commodity prices began to disappear in the wholesale and retail markets two years before the stock market crash. In other words, the rise in the prices of commodities did not keep pace with the rise in the price of stocks.

There is a serious hazard in the problem of governing society. The men in any free nation who come to power are the men who understand the art of attaining power. And this art belongs in the tool kit of the politician. But the problems the politicians must face and solve may well belong in a field of action which they understand only dimly. This was the case in 1932 when the American people were called upon to choose a President. The depression, crashing in the midst of Mr. Hoover's administration, inevitably dismissed him from the public mind for further leadership. How far he understood the challenging problems before him did not matter to the electorate. There he stood—the captain who was on the bridge when the hurricane struck. He was marked as the villain in the piece—the man who had led us into the storm. Whether this was true or not was irrelevant. Then, as a product of the irrational electorate in a moment of bewilderment, its choice fell on a leader who had marked talents as a politician. Whether he had any understanding whatever of the roots of the depression did not matter to the voters. Yet this was the only question that did matter. In two other surpassing crises in our history—the Revolution and the Civil War—two great and humble men appeared as leaders who were capable of seeing with clarity the nature of the problems that faced them.

I have always had a feeling that Providence had one eye closed when Woodrow Wilson was elected. He was not a wicked man. Unlike Roosevelt, he was a man profoundly read in the history and the art of government. But there was a heavy ingredient of airy philosophy in his make up. And to this was added his deep implication in the fortunes of his beloved British Empire. This got us into his war. When that struggle ended in victory he permitted his industrious mind to take in too much territory. The plaudits of the victorious allies encouraged him to spread the pinions of his mind and to move some distance off the ground. In this flight he tried to lead us into the League of Nations. Even though it foundered and died it created here a large and influential school of One-World philosophers devoted to the cult of internationalism.

Having turned away after a while from these gaudy ideas, America, leaving the war far behind, fumed its attention to the heady if banal excitement of the gamblers in all the big and little Wall Streets in the country. This wild route took us to the edge of the precipice in 1929 and over it into the depression. This was a disaster of obvious malignance. But a further evil followed on its heels when Franklin D. Roosevelt was elected President of the United States. At that moment America's luck ran out.

2.

The problem before Roosevelt as he took office in 1933 was simple in its statement. It was, of course, immensely difficult in execution. It may be stated thus: It consisted primarily in getting the American system of private enterprise back on the tracks and running again at a safe speed. This embraced several clearly defined objectives. One was the closing of the banks to end the wild withdrawals, and reopening them relieved of their grave disabilities.

Already something had been done in that direction as early as 1931, before Roosevelt was nominated, when the Senate Banking and Currency Committee began its investigation of the national banking system and the Federal Reserve System. In March, 1932, eight months before Roosevelt's election, the same committee, under Senator Peter Norbeck, Republican, began an investigation of the stock exchanges which continued over into Roosevelt's administration. As early as January, 1932, the Senate had ordered the investigation of the Reserve System. Also in 1932, Congress adopted a bill creating the Reconstruction Finance Corporation with an appropriation of two billion dollars to buttress the credit of banks in trouble. Throughout 1932, President Hoover appealed over and over for various measures. But, alas, 1932 was an election year. The Democratic politicians had been out of power for 12 years. The crash, bearing a Republican label, came to the Democrats as a gift from heaven—or perhaps from some other ethereal abode. But actually a beginning had been made, and it was these instrumentalities which in the end became the means of partially repairing the badly battered economic system.

All this called for a temporary increase in taxation to provide aid for the needy, some increase in government debt to provide funds for needed approvable and useful public works. But Roosevelt's mind was not geared to the task of reconstruction. He was in no sense a builder or rebuilder. He was in no sense a constructive statesman. He had practically no understanding of the natural laws which provide the energy for private enterprise. His knowledge of economics was a total blank. He was essentially a politician. He had a weakness for the dramatic and the vision of the storm with himself at its center riding the whirlwind infatuated him. It was this peculiarity—this mental and spiritual aberration—which became the inspiration for that incredible succession of alphabetical agencies which excited his imagination and filled the front pages of the newspapers during his first two terms.

The important fact about all this is that in his first two full terms of eight years, President Roosevelt never produced any recovery whatever. When he was elected there were 11,586,000 persons unemployed. In 1939—seven years later—when the war struck in Europe, there were still 11,369,000 persons unemployed. These figures are supplied by the American Federation of Labor. In 1932 when he was elected there were 4,155,000 households with 16,620,000 persons on relief. In 1939, seven years later, there were 4,227,000 households with 19,648,000 persons on relief. In the presence of these undisputed facts how can any sober-minded citizen suppose that Mr. Roosevelt brought recovery to the United States? Mr. Roosevelt and his advisers were well aware of this, though they did not admit it publicly. In November, 1937, several of his cabinet members told him plainly that they had got nowhere against the depression and that the country was heading for another crisis. The suggestion became a subject of heated discussion at a cabinet meeting. Roosevelt grew angry and, in an unguarded instant, confirmed these disagreeable complaints. He said: "I am sick and tired of being told by Henry (Morgenthau) and everybody else what's the matter with the country while nobody suggests what I should do." This, it would seem, settles for history the fact that after seven years in the White House,

Roosevelt had made no impression on the depression, that he had merely provided the unemployed with doles—a poor and meagre substitute for jobs—and now in the presence of the seemingly ineradicable shadow of depression, he blamed his advisers.

When he had appealed for election in 1932, he proclaimed his proposals for recovery:

> "We advocate an immediate and drastic reduction of governmental expenditures by abolishing useless commissions and offices."
> "Maintenance of the national debt by a budget annually balanced."
> "Stop borrowing and meet current deficits."
> "We are determined to reduce the expenses of government ... determined to achieve a balanced budget."

Roosevelt's first budget was $3,863,000,000. Since that year the government's budget has been unbalanced every year for 23 years with only three exceptions.

The sum of all this, of course, is that Roosevelt's first task—his greatest—as he assumed the presidency was to *make an end of the depression by creating an atmosphere in which the American system of private enterprise could function prosperously and soundly.*

The President did not restore prosperity until he took us into war. His task was not merely to produce prosperity, but to restore the system of private enterprise to health—first to rid it of those evils which had been grafted on it and then by every rational means to set it in motion under the stimuli appropriate to its special nature. This Roosevelt never did—and his successors have failed in that pressing task to this year 1956. Roosevelt had discovered—and his successors, Truman and Eisenhower, have adopted—the oldest of gimmicks for producing a boom—militarism and debt. We were at war in the world for four years, from 1941 to 1945, and again in Korea for three years—seven in all. Yet here is the record of government deficits—government by red ink—from 1933 to 1956:

1933	-	$2,245,542,000
1934	-	$3,255,393,000
1935	-	$3,782,966,000
1936	-	$4,952,928,000
1937	-	$2,777,421,000
1938	-	$1,176,617,000

1939	-	$3,862,158,000
1940	-	$3,918,019,000
1941	-	$6,159,272,000
1942	-	$21,490,243,000
1943	-	$57,420,430,000
1944	-	$51,423,393,000
1945	-	$53,940,916,000
1946	-	$20,676,171,000
1947	+	$783,788,000
1948	+	$8,419,470,000
1949	-	$1,811,440,000
1950	-	$3,122,102,000
1951	+	$3,509,783,000
1952	-	$4,016,640,000
1953	-	$9,449,213,000
1954	-	$3,166,966,000
1955	-	$4,192,000,000

This is the disgraceful history of a regime that came into power denouncing the government's small deficit and which has carried the nation along for 23 years on a succession of deficits that have produced for us a national debt of over *280 billion dollars*. As each offering of this debt comes due it must be renewed at higher interest rates. The interest alone on the public debt is now over twice the total cost of government when Roosevelt denounced Hoover for extravagance.

This staggering obligation of 280 billion dollars is a problem that has to be faced. All the prosperity which the nation has "enjoyed"—created by the mountainous sums paid for war, militarism and foreign and domestic handouts—remains unpaid for. Does anyone suppose that it will ever be paid? It consists of a numerous collection of separate bond issues. These continue to fall due. When each one falls due it must be paid. And some person or interest must be found willing to advance the money to pay it and accept a new bond. It was possible to force these bonds on the investing public during the war and under the influence of the unending succession of "crises." But this obviously cannot last forever. The day will come when this staggering load of debt must be faced.

In appraising the career of this shallow but bold man, it must be kept in mind that all the gaudy performances, all the handouts to the unemployed, all the billions paid to farmers to destroy food or to store it, all the extravaganza of "saving the free world," have yet to be paid for. And the nation draws closer and closer to that inevitable "pay-day." After all the heroics are silenced and all the captains and orators are retired or dead, a generation will appear that must face the bills—bills to be paid by the innocent victims of this costly and tragic circus. The depression which Mr. Roosevelt was to conquer has been hiding behind the immense curtain of the war and its gaudy post-war boom on the cuff. It will one day come peeping over the horizon for a return engagement. This was his first complete failure—his utter ignorance of the nature and the genius of the system of private enterprise.

3.

It would be just to say that when Roosevelt entered the White House, among most Americans, including professional politicians, the subject of Communist strategy and techniques was little understood. The old Socialists had a party. They called themselves Socialists. They were proud to be known as such. They functioned as a political party, not a conspiracy. That is one reason why the Socialists under Norman Thomas made so little headway. When the Communists moved into the picture in a large way they operated on a wholly different plan. There was, of course, the open Communist Party, headed by Earl Browder. But there was another branch of the movement—the conspiratorial branch. This department of the Communist drive was formed into numerous fronts and secret cells. For the most part their members denied they were Communists. They insisted they were economic reformers. And these numerous fronts were designed to appeal to every conceivable group in America that might have some pet grievance against society. The secret cells were engaged not only in espionage but in influencing American policy on the side of Soviet aims and domestic Communist objectives wherever possible. As a result of the depression, the numbers in the fronts and the cells became fairly numerous.

The work of these radical spirits, so far as government was concerned, was made somewhat easy by a curious phenomenon which appeared. The New Deal began in a carnival of rushing activity when Roosevelt took office. Wherever some group or state or industry or county or economic element appeared with a grievance, a bureau was formed. They were called agencies, commissions, councils or administrations or authorities or boards. I counted and identified iii of these administrative bureaus. The whole immense national and global task which the New Deal undertook became too vast for Congress to control. Congress therefore adopted the policy of creating these administrative bureaus and contented itself with a few simple directives and a handsome appropriation—and the bureau set off on its own hook. The policing of this incredible collection of bureaus, armed with dangerous powers and ample funds, became impossible. These bureaus had to have boards and executive personnel to plot and manage them. And all this became a wondrous gift to the Reds, who proceeded to infiltrate them on an amazing scale. Then from the bureaus came directives and regulations and rules, so that they actually became the legislative and appropriating instrumentalities of a large area of government.

It is, of course, impossible to follow the maze of adventures which covered the nation under the direction of these Red and Pink revolutionaries and their dupes. It is sufficient to say that for the most part these groups became task forces to cripple the American system and substitute the techniques of socialism.

The ease with which this adventure was carried out is best illustrated by the manner in which these Pink and Red ideological warriors moved even into the White House itself. Apparently they guessed shrewdly when they latched on to the apron strings of Mrs. Eleanor Roosevelt, the mistress of the White House. There was an organization known as the American Youth Congress which is discussed briefly in an earlier chapter. It had been branded by the FBI as a Communist front. It was headed by a gent named William Wheeler Hinckley. He was a frequent visitor to the White House and after four years of leadership in the Youth Congress he was promoted by the White House to a job in the U. S. Office of Education, then the Railroad Retirement Board and finally the Treasury Department. The House Committee on Un-American Activities eventually got around to investigating this group. Hinckley, Joe Lash, Joe Cadden and others, summoned as witnesses, were delivered to the congressional committee room in a White House automobile chaperoned by Mrs. Roosevelt. During the hearings, at one point one of these precious lads, tiring of the ordeal, went to sleep on Mrs. Roosevelt's shoulder. The whole gang were entertained at the White House and Franklin D. Roosevelt sent his personal greetings to this American Youth Congress when it met.

In 1938 the President began what came to be known as a purge of congressmen and senators who were *persona non grata* in the White House. At the time Earl Browder, who had the run of the White House, directed that purge and he personally telephoned from the White House to various places instructions for carrying out the purge. This is difficult to believe, but it is a fact. When Mrs. Browder attempted to enter the United States illegally by way of Canada, instructions to make her way easy and quick were telephoned to United States consular officials. The official who handled her case has testified that he was not to ask her any embarrassing questions. J. B. Matthews, who has the greatest abundance of reports, files and information on this subject, has written that a committee of five nationally known Communists called at the White House and presented the President with a portrait of himself. As they left the White House they were photographed with White House Secretary Marvin McIntyre in the group—a precious testimonial to show Moscow how well they were doing.

On one occasion Mrs. Roosevelt invited forty senators to the White House to meet her petted group of officials of the American Youth Congress. Roosevelt himself was constantly sending "greetings" to various Red organizations, such as the American Committee for the Protection of the Foreign Born, the Workers Alliance, the National Negro Congress, while Mrs. Roosevelt permitted the use of her name as sponsor or officer and sometimes as a speaker for more than 30 Communist fronts, leagues, councils and associations.

All these activities are cited merely to reveal the extent to which Roosevelt not only permitted but actually encouraged the activities of the Communist conspiracy in the United States. The gentlest comment one can make on this is that the man simply did not know what he was doing—a curious defense for one who was being hailed as a master mind. But the malignance of these performances cannot be exaggerated. There is, of course, much more to the story. The extent and seriousness of it can be understood only when we realize that it was this blindness of the White House which opened the way for the Red conspirators into almost every important function of political, economic and educational life. The movies swarmed with them. So did the stage, the American journals of opinion, and every other organ of information and opinion. It was this which enabled the Alger Hisses and the Harry Dexter Whites and the Owen Lattimores to penetrate into the most decisive agencies of policy in the government.

When Roosevelt faced Stalin at Yalta, Alger Hiss—Stalin's man —was at Roosevelt's side as his adviser.

When Roosevelt faced the problem of post-war Germany at Quebec, Harry Dexter White was there to shape Roosevelt's decisions.

When the question of China arose—who should control it, the Free Chinese or the Chinese Reds—there was the Institute of Pacific Relations, swarming with Reds, and its leading light Owen Lattimore, with an arm in the State Department. The result—the betrayal and abandonment of Free China.

Why was it possible for these enemies of America to obtain so powerful a hold on the mind and imagination of Roosevelt? The explanation is quite simple. Roosevelt was not a statesman. He was not a student of government. He knew practically nothing of economics. This is not to say he was without ability. But his ability was wholly in the field of politics—in the art of getting votes. But as he came to power the government was confronted with a collection of problems in the fields of economics—a subject of which Roosevelt was totally ignorant. What is more, he had no curiosity about the subject. America was faced with a group of problems in economic and social revolution to which he had never given a thought. It is not possible to explain the goings-on in the White House on any other theory than that he had not the faintest notion of the malignance of the social disease that was spreading around America.

The case of Mrs. Roosevelt is perhaps a little different. A homely and ambitious woman, greedy for notice, utterly ignorant of the dangerous game into which she had wandered, she was reduced to complete compliance by the task force of young Reds who fawned on her and, for the first time in her life, gave her a sense of importance.

Various other suggestions have been offered, but this one would seem to cover the case sufficiently.

The consequences of these performances of Roosevelt are difficult to believe. Yet the most important project in America today is for Americans to confront the stark realities of these last 20 years. While the activities of the American Reds seem to be directed toward promoting a Communist dictatorship here, this was by no means their immediate purpose. That purpose was twofold. One was to soften Roosevelt in order to reduce him to an easy compliance with Stalin in that grim and pragmatic gentleman's plans for Europe and Asia. The other was gradually, one piece at a time, to break down the Capitalist system by subjecting it to a collection of strains which would ensure its ultimate collapse.

The leaders of this movement in America saw possibilities in the war for a powerful blow against the integrity of the system of private enterprise. It had been almost fatally damaged by excessive private debt. The Communist leaders in America had a twofold purpose—of aiding Russia in her European and Asiatic exploits while at the same time weakening the system of private enterprise here by public debt. That they have been incredibly successful in both objectives is beyond quibble.

Up to the moment I write these lines, the immense boom created by government borrowings continues, but something has happened. The project of borrowing any further has filled the minds of the politicians with a deep-seated fear. They may not be Reds or Pinks or economic experts of any school, but they know there is a limit to government debt—despite the teachings of certain socialist crack-brains who came up in 1937 with the theory that government debt is meaningless because it is a debt owed by the people to themselves. Gentle, lily-fingered socialist pinks may swallow that, but the tough, pragmatic Communist theoretician knows that continuing debt can wreck the Capitalist society.

Yet no sweeter morsel was ever fed to the American politician than this theory, proclaimed with imposing Harvard authority in 1937, that FDR was on a rational course when he stepped up the policy of federal borrowings to buy endless minorities. But in the process of launching this new gospel it was necessary to tear the American Constitution to pieces and to deliver a mortal wound to the system of private enterprise. The reckless spending and borrowing to fight a war was continued when the war ended to buy a peace-time prosperity. But Reason, after its long sleep, begins to mutter disturbing warnings in the politician's ear. Leaders in both political parties have begun to talk about balancing the budget. But there is also a gnawing suspicion that this racket called the New Deal, which has been adopted by both parties, cannot be operated on a cash basis. Roosevelt and his successors pushed that policy as far as it can go. Thus practical men among the leaders are beginning to catch a glimpse of the terrifying truth. And thus another of Roosevelt's dangerous experiments—something which might be called "socialized capitalism"—moves toward its end.

4.

In the light of events and the part Roosevelt played upon the broad stage of the depression and the war, we may again ask — what manner of man was he? Beginning with that first inaugural address, as the nation sank down into almost total collapse, Roosevelt by some alchemy was suddenly transformed into a sort of demi-god —one of the great statesmen of all time. The backdrop of this performance was a scene of disorder and dislocation, the banks closed, business at a standstill, the people aghast at the enormity of the disaster. And then, as if by magic, Roosevelt strode upon the stage as if he carried with him a magician's wand. He was a superb actor. He had in his pocket a speech written for him by a master. His voice rang out over the frightened nation like the clarion call of a great prophet and marshal rolled into one. The magical effect of this single performance remained fixed in millions of minds for many years.

Roosevelt cultivated assiduously the impression that he was a great lover of the common man. And he at times liked to play the role of the good fellow, which he did with some histrionic talent. But Roosevelt was a good deal of a snob as he started life. He was the spoiled only child of middle-aged parents. His mother was a total snob. She never got over a sense of personal injury at what seemed to her the rowdy invasion of her home in Hyde Park by politicians and the press when Roosevelt became a candidate for governor and later a candidate for the presidency. The invasion of her home by a lot of newspaper men she looked on as a violation of its calm and dignity.

Roosevelt's early snobbery as a youth may have been due to the attitude of his parents and to the manner in which he was shielded from the common world. At Groton, his preparatory school, he was not "one of the boys." This was true at Harvard also, though in a lesser degree. He made the football team, but he had not yet learned the gentle art of fraternization. Later when he entered the New York State Legislature, he kept to himself for a long time. A newspaper correspondent of that period has described how she could see him walking around the chamber pretty much to himself. But after a time he got very much over this stiffness.

It cannot be said that Roosevelt lacked brains. But he was never a student. He is supposed to have been a reader of political literature and of military history. But he was a student only of naval history and collected a large library on that subject. He came to power in a grave moment when political ideas and economic theories were agitating the minds of all thoughtful and studious men. But his interest in political ideas can be very much misunderstood. Roosevelt was interested in political action. He was not grounded in those fundamental principles of human relationships and economic theories which thoughtful statesmen have debated for centuries. His talents were in the field of what may be called "party politics"—the struggle for votes, for power, for honor and office—rather than in the study of the great human elements and social forces that must be understood and controlled in the good society. He was utterly devoid of any interest in what might be called the philosophy of government. In the field of economics, as I have said, his mind was a blank.

When he entered the White House in March, 1933, the one and consuming problem that challenged his mind was the depression. No one can say with reason that the problem was simple. It called for a clear knowledge of the structure of business and the institution of banking as part of a logical economic system. It was precisely in this field that Roosevelt found himself in a wilderness. His blood was stirred by the immensely dramatic effect of his inauguration and the speech he had delivered. But he was then confronted with a call for action—practical measures to check the crisis and more practical methods to set our historic system in motion again. And at this point the man was shockingly helpless and hopeless.

A benevolent fortune had always seemed to hover over this favored land, but when Roosevelt walked into the White House, that good fortune walked out. Out of the chaos and bewilderment a kind of moral miasma seemed to ooze. And this malignant disorder set fire to the blood of whole troops of angry spirits, social and world architects and evangelists—such cocksure fellows as Harry Hopkins who was to become for Roosevelt his evil genius. He was one of those maladjusted and surly creatures whose code was churned up out of his angry soul. He was a thoroughly bad character who would have been at home in an earlier manifestation in the court of Louis XV. What Roosevelt needed was some rational and healthy advice on how to bring the nation out of the chaos into which it had fallen. Instead he found himself under the influence of a collection of revolutionary spirits who were aflame with the hope not of bringing a recovery of the free system but of completing its ruin and building on the wreckage some form of socialist heaven. Some of these wild spirits who swarmed into the Capital were mere screw-balls, but there was a more intelligent and malignant crew who were agog with the suddenly rising opportunity to lay the foundations of the new socialist society on the wreck of American Capitalism.

I repeat again that Roosevelt was not a student of ideas. He liked politics and he had a flair for it. But this crisis called for talents of a wholly different nature. He had also a certain dynamic personal quality—the kind one finds in romantic actors. And there is no doubt that in this moment of crisis, he became infused with the spirit of the great drama. He saw himself strutting the boards to almost continuous applause. As we have noted he loved politics and was a talented politician. But he was now called on to deal with grave social and economic values which he understood hardly at all. Of all the gaudy and cracked schemes he fathered and promoted, it must be said that he neither invented nor discovered any of them. Befuddled and bewildered by the immensity of the disorder, he was a shining mark for every crackpot who appeared with some new project for producing recovery and abundance.

He *was* a politician, however, and in the end the most dangerous group were the politicians. America, like all countries, is governed by politicians. And in the final analysis, it was this gentry which perceived the amazing weapon that had been forged for their use. While the Reds and Pinks and assorted bands of revolutionaries and crack-pots were promoting their several nostrums not for recovery but for the coming new heaven, another and far more indigenous group was beginning to see some wondrous and purely political values in all this. These were the politicians. They know that the great instrument of power in government is money. The politicians began to realize what was happening in Washington to the government money supplies—the indispensable munition of the officeholders. When Roosevelt took office in 1933, the federal government spent $3,800,000,000. In 1934, Roosevelt spent six billion. In 1935 he spent over seven billion, and eight and a half billion in 1936. The political power in these billions was something the politicos could understand far more clearly than the heady mixture of socialistic and fascistic philosophy which the New Dealers peddled.

By 1937 the struggle between the Republican and Democratic politicians had become a contest for the possession of this alluring boodle. Now, in the year 1956, when we are not at war anywhere, the Republican politicians who at first denounced so roundly the extravagance of the New Dealers, have taken from the American people the neat sum of *sixty-four billion dollars*. American politics today is nothing more—save for a few devoted souls—than a contest to determine which party will spend this great sum to buy the votes of a number of hungry minorities in order to keep themselves in power.

The central meaning of this, aside from its fiscal folly, is that the American politician, without troubling his pragmatic mind with the meaning of words, has discovered socialism—and embraced it—not as a great system of social organization, but as a wondrous machine for the purpose of buying votes—buying immense pressure groups with favors, laws and, above all, vast appropriations. Here are some samples: In 1927 the federal government spent $155,000,000 on Agriculture. In 1953 it spent over *three billion*.

In 1927 it spent $30,383,000 on the Commerce Department. In 1953 it spent *over a billion*.

In 1927 it spent roughly ten million dollars on the Labor Department. In 1953 it spent 300 *million*.

In 1927 it spent 19 million on health, education and welfare. In 1953 it spent a little short of *two billion*.

At the same time the power of the presidency has been shockingly expanded. In 1928 all the expenses of the President's office amounted to $585,000. In 1953 they amounted to nearly *six billion dollars*.

These vast sums are spent ostensibly by something called government. But in fact they come into the hands of and are spent by the politicians who operate government. Thus they can be used to purchase the support of large minorities. A clear and present case which has now been carried to the point of embarrassment and folly is the introduction into America as a permanent institution of the baleful system of militarism. The term "militarism" must not be confused with the subject of national defense. It is here—as it became in Europe—a social and economic institution and has evils in it altogether aside from the purely financial burdens. A European student of the system has offered an illuminating portrait of it. He wrote that: "It presents a vast array of customs, interest, prestige, actions and thought associated with armies and wars, yet transcending purely military purpose."

Militarism was responsible for driving millions of its victims away from Germany and Italy and other European countries to America. This system, of course, began under the sponsorship of those who love military power and who see in it the visible expression of national might. But once established it becomes the most cherished economic institution of the politicians. Out of a budget of 65 billion dollars in 1955, the costs of military, naval and related activities were over 40 billion dollars. This is a wonderful weapon for the officials in power. The enormous expenditure takes some three million men out of the labor supply and puts them in the armed services. At the same time it makes business for what may be called the military industry. Last year one large corporation alone got a billion and a half dollars in contracts from the federal government—although we are not at war anywhere.

It might well be that Roosevelt's fascination with the institution of militarism took its rise from his love of war and warships, of soldiering and weapons and uniforms, rather than in the mere political value of militarism as a maker of jobs. But it provided him with the gaudiest and most productive and, of course, the most dangerous boondoggle to bring at last the prosperity which had evaded him for eight years in the White House. It remains the chief base of the boom which continues to float along as I write these lines. Militarism and debt—these are the magic weapons which every country in Europe in the last 100 years has tried—some of them twice and others three times—and always with the same tragic consequences.

There remains one humiliating blot—perhaps the blackest—on the Roosevelt record. This was his betrayal of Eastern Europe and nearly all of Asia into the hands of Stalin. The story of the great conferences, as well as some of the more secret and less advertised little talks, appears in the text of this volume. It remains merely to offer a picture of the immensity of the betrayal of the free world by Roosevelt to the Communist revolutionists.

I have always believed that Stalin, long before he had any direct dealings with Roosevelt, had him studied thoroughly—his mind, his bias, his appetites, his knowledge of affairs, his vanity and his growing delusions of grandeur. It is certain that in all their contacts, Stalin walked off with his objectives completely satisfied.

It is perhaps forgotten that as World War II opened, Stalin and Russia appeared on the stage as the ally of Hitler. That struggle began when Hitler sent his legions across the German border in an attack on Poland on September 1, 1939. Immediately Britain and France, honoring their treaty with Poland, declared war on Germany. The struggle in Poland was swift and short. Within two weeks Poland was prostrate. Shortly after Hitler's assault, within a month, Stalin notified the Polish Ambassador in Moscow that Russian troops were being sent across the Polish frontier to protect Soviet interests in that country. The Russian and German armies made contact at Brest-Litovsk on September 18, without any serious fighting.

Once again Poland was dismembered. Germany took the western third of Poland and Russia the eastern two-thirds. Immediately Hitler sent his seasoned troops to the Western front along the famous Maginot Line. By this time the American people were clearly determined to stay out of the war. Joseph P. Kennedy, Roosevelt's Ambassador to Great Britain, issued a statement in which he said: "There is no place in the fighting for us ... As you love America don't let anything that comes out of our country in the world make you believe you can make the situation one whit better by getting into the war." This represented clearly the attitude of the American people.

But there is now no doubt that Franklin D. Roosevelt had made up his mind at an early date to put America into that war. How he actually accomplished it has been told in large part by a man of high authority who was at the center of the shocking episode (*The Final Secret of Pearl Harbor* by Rear Admiral Robert A. Theobald).

But however the project was managed, we must stand aghast at the manner in which the fruits of victory were delivered and to whom. You have but to look at the map to find the answer to the question—Who won the war? As the war in Europe began, with Hitler and Stalin as partners, the whole swarm of Reds and Pinks here—Roosevelt's numerous task forces in the United States who had embroiled him in so many pro-Communist schemes—were screaming at him to stay out of the war. Many of that abominable group of young Reds in the American Youth Congress could be found picketing the White House—the home of their blessed First Lady—against giving arms to Britain. But the moment came when Hitler, feeling he had the Western allies under control, decided to settle accounts with his erstwhile ally Stalin. When he struck, as if by magic all the Reds, organized and unorganized, from the colleges and the newspapers and the magazines and the radio, and even some pulpits, made a swift about-face and hurled themselves into the arms of their old friends, President and Mrs. Roosevelt.

From that moment the pro-Russian bloc in the United States inserted itself into the pro-war movement. Not only did they begin to play a controlling role in the push to get us into the war, but on a far more malignant scale they managed to control the mind of the slowly decaying Roosevelt. How that was done has been told in the pages of this volume. But it remains to describe very briefly the astounding success Stalin attained in running off with all the spoils of war. In a series of conferences which have been fully described, Roosevelt, and later Truman, surrendered into Stalin's hands a whole collection of peoples whose lands comprised, along with Russia, almost two-thirds of the entire land mass of Europe and Asia.

Here is a list of the countries which were surrendered by Roosevelt to the brutal tyranny of his "great friend" Stalin. Russia began the war with a population of 193,000,000. When the war ended, to these 193,000,000 were added the following countries and their populations:

Estonia	1,134,000
Latvia	1,994,000
Lithuania	2,879,000
East Germany	17,313,000
Czechoslovakia	12,340,000
N.E. Austria	1,700,000
Albania	1,175,000
Yugoslavia	17,004,000
Bulgaria	7,160,000
Hungary	9,600,000
Rumania	15,873,000
Poland	26,500,000
North Korea	9,000,000
Outer Mongolia	
Manchuria	} 601,912,000
China	
	725,584,000

Thus Stalin added to his empire some *725 million people*, which with the 193 million in Russia gave him dominion over *918 million human beings* in Russia and 16 other European and Asiatic countries.

As one looks back over these costly years of confusion and betrayal it is difficult to believe that one man—Roosevelt—in so short a time could inflict so much damage on a great system of social order that had endured for 145 years. The enormity of his offenses was lost behind the smoke and hurly-burly of the war. But now the facts are all before us.

If there were no other count against Roosevelt, the disgraceful behavior of his family in the White House stands out as the one black spot in the history of that ancient mansion. One of his sons was divorced three times, another twice, another once and the daughter once. Seven divorces in one family in the White House is a record which supplies its own commentary on their family life.

To this must be added the record of most of these young people and their mother in their frantic efforts to wring the last dollar of profit out of the Capitalist system which they were so busy destroying. The shameful account of this is described in this volume.

Any family in private life in a small city that provided such a spectacle of social and domestic conduct would have been subjected to a social boycott. When the performance was offered to the public with the White House as a stage and a President's family as the actors, the dark responsibility of Franklin Roosevelt and his wife can hardly be exaggerated.

Ushering this succession of brides and grooms into the White House was bad enough. But in terms of national interest, it was a minor episode compared with the shocking loan of the White House to a horde of Communist revolutionaries, including Earl Browder, the leader of the Communist Party, who used it as a base from which to promote Red objectives and thus gained a White House badge of approval on the gang itself.

But, in the end, there were two great crimes committed by Franklin D. Roosevelt against the nation which honored and trusted him. One was the delivery of all the gains of the Second World War to Stalin. Back of this historic offense, of course, was Roosevelt's slippery conspiracy to get us into the war by exposing our fleet and our soldiers in Hawaii and the Philippine Islands to an attack which he knowingly invited.

The second crime consisted in that series of performances and devices by which he twisted the very fundamental nature of our Republic and sanctified the crime by a historic assault on the Supreme Court—one of his most deadly accomplishments. By this means he deprived the Republic of the one great bulwark that could ensure its life within the limits of our Constitution. With this performance he had swept away the last rampart that stood in the way of the advancing socialization of America.

Finally, as the price in material values of his costly regime, he left America mired in a debt which rests as a crushing burden on a generation that had no hand in his hippodrome—a debt that can never be paid and which can be taken off our shoulders only by a great and devastating inflation.

To cap the record of his offenses and blunders, he managed before he died to entangle us in the quarrels, the revolutions, and the debts of every country in the world outside the Soviet orbit. Then to ensure the continuance of the applause that came to him from the wretched people and the hungry politicians who enjoyed the doles and the votes, he took care, well before his death, and at the expense of certain rich idolators and the American people, to build for himself a shrine which would assure his immortality.

REFERENCES

BOOK ONE: TRIAL—AND ERROR

1. Raymond Moley, "After Seven Years," (Harper, 1939), p. 152.

2. New York *Times*, May 14, 1933.

3. This incident is told in full in Moley "After Seven Years," pps. 138–161.

4. The material for what follows in this chapter was gathered partially from the following: Moley's "After Seven Years"; William Starr Myers and Walter H. Newton's "The Hoover Administration" (Scribner, 1936); Rixey Smith and Norman Beasley's "Carter Glass" (Longmans, 1939). Mr. Moley wrote from the point of view of Mr. Roosevelt, Messrs. Myers and Newton from the point of view of Mr. Hoover. However, I have had the opportunity of personally interviewing various persons intimately connected with these events and in some cases of examining notes made by them at the time.

5. All figures used throughout the text relating to government finances are based upon U. S. Treasury Reports.

6. Gaetano Salvemini and George LaPiana, "What To Do With Italy" (Duell, Sloan & Pearce, 1943). Mr. Salvemini has a choice collection of tributes to Mussolini from Americans.

7. Congressional Record, 69th Cong., 1st Sess., Jan. 14, 1926.

8. John T. Flynn, "The Code Chisel," *Collier's* Magazine, Nov. 3, 1934.

9. Charles Frederick Roos, "NRA—Economic Planning" (Principia Press, 1937), p. 59.

10. Hugh S. Johnson, "The Blue Eagle from Egg to Earth" (Doubleday, 1935).

11. Report of the National Recovery Review Board (Darrow Board), New York *Times*, May 21, 1934.

12. Frances Perkins, "The Roosevelt I Knew" (Viking, 1946).

13. Ernest K. Lindley, "Half Way with Roosevelt" (Viking, 1936), p. 151. For a full discussion of the origins of the NRA, see John T. Flynn's "Whose Child is the NRA?", *Harper's* Magazine, September, 1934.

14. Frances Perkins, "The Roosevelt I Knew," p. 252.

15. Raymond Moley, "After Seven Years," p. 159.

16. Emil Ludwig, "Roosevelt: A Study in Fortune and Power" (Viking, 1938).

17. The facts about this conference are drawn from Moley's "After Seven Years" and "Memoirs of Cordell Hull," New York *Times*, Jan. 26 to March 6, 1948.

18. "John N. Garner's Story," *Collier's* Magazine, Feb. 21 to Mar. 20, 1948.

19. Excerpts from "The Morgenthau Diaries," *Collier's* Magazine, Sept. 27 to Nov. 1, 1947.

20. Statement to me by Senator William E. Borah.

21. Excerpts from "The Morgenthau Diaries."

22. John T. Flynn, "The Social Security Reserve Swindle," *Harper's* Magazine, Feb., 1939.

23. "John N. Garner's Story."

24. Harnett Kane, "Louisiana Hayride" (Morrow, 1941).

25. Raymond Moley, "After Seven Years," p. 299.

26. George Creel, "Rebel At Large" (Putnam, 1947), pps. 280 to 287.

27. Frances Perkins, "The Roosevelt I Knew," p. 124.

28. The so-called "Wirt incident" was reported fully in the newspapers of the time.

29. Frances Perkins, "The Roosevelt I Knew," p. 330.

30. Benjamin Stolberg, "The Story of the CIO" (Viking, 1938). This volume contains an excellent and reliable account of the labor movement during the Roosevelt administrations up to 1938.

31. Martin Dies, "The Trojan Horse in America" (Dodd, Mead, 1940).

32. "Public Papers and Addresses of Franklin D. Roosevelt," Vol. 5, pps. 285–292 (Random House).

BOOK TWO: CONFUSION

1. Raymond Moley, "After Seven Years," pps. 369, 370.

2. "John N. Garner's Story."

3. Ibid.

4. My information comes from the United States Senator who took the warning to Roosevelt.

5. An extensive account of the Court-packing episode has been written by Joseph Alsop and Turner Catledge, "The 168 Days," *Saturday Evening Post*, Feb. 18, 1937. James A. Farley, "Jim Farley's Story" (Whittlesey House, 1948) has also given a rather full account. I have personally interviewed many of those engaged in that historic struggle.

6. There are several sets of statistics on unemployment for this period. I have adopted those of the National Industrial Conference Board as the most accurate as well as the most conservative. The estimates of unemployment by the American Federation of Labor's research bureau ran much higher.

7. The facts about these inner conferences were brought to light long after they took place by James A. Farley in "Jim Farley's Story" and by Henry Morgenthau, Jr., in excerpts from "The Morgenthau Diaries."

8. James A. Farley, "Jim Farley's Story."

9. The facts relating to the 1938 election activities of the WPA are taken from the official report of the U. S. Senate Committee on Campaign Expenditures.

10. Blair Bolles, in the *American Mercury*, Sept., 1936.

11. For a full discussion of the origins of National Socialism, Fascism and their relation to National Planning, see John T. Flynn's "As We Go Marching" (Doubleday, 1944).

12. *American Economic Review*, Supplement, Vol. XXII, No. 1, March, 1932.

13. George Soule, "The Planned Economy" (Macmillan, 1932), and Stuart Chase, "Autarchy," *Scribner's* Magazine, Sept., 1933.

14. Stuart Chase, "Autarchy," *Scribner's* Magazine, Sept., 1933.

15. Thorstein Veblen, "The Engineers and the Price System" (Viking, 1921), p. 81.

16. For a full discussion of these theories see "An Economic Program for American Democracy" by Seven Harvard and Tufts Professors (Vanguard, 1938); Alvin H. Hansen's "Fiscal Policy and Business Cycles" (Norton, 1941). For an analysis and answer to the Hansen theories see John T. Flynn's "The Post-War Federal Debt," *Harper's* Magazine, July, 1942.

17. Cordell Hull, "Memoirs," New York *Times*, Jan. 26 to March 6, 1948.

18. Ibid.

19. "Public Papers and Addresses of Franklin D. Roosevelt," 1937 Vol., 414 ff.

20. Edward J. Flynn, "You're the Boss" (Viking, 1947), p. 154.

21. Charles Michaelson, "The Ghost Talks" (Putnam, 1944), p. 147.

22. Frances Perkins, "The Roosevelt I Knew," pps. 125–128.

23. Ibid.

24. James A. Farley, "Jim Farley's Story," p. 152.

25. Ibid., pps. 151–173.

26. Ibid.

27. For a full account of the origins and performances of the Kelly-Nash machine of Chicago, see John T. Flynn's "These Our Rulers," *Collier's* Magazine, June 29 to July 20, 1941.

28. The facts concerning Sidney Hillman are taken from the reports of and testimony before the House Committee on Un-American Activities, "The Story of the CIO" by Benjamin Stolberg, numerous columns by Westbrook Pegler covering his investigations of the Rosen and Lepke cases, and from my own inquiries into the Lepke case.

29. James A. Farley, "Jim Farley's Story," p. 59.

30. Ibid., p. 257.

31. Frances Perkins, "The Roosevelt I Knew," p. 130.

32. Cordell Hull, "Memoirs."

33. Ibid.

34. Edward J. Flynn, "You're the Boss," pps. 156, 157.

35. Frances Perkins, "The Roosevelt I Knew," pps. 130–134.

36. James A. Farley, "Jim Farley's Story," p. 300.

37. Ross T. McIntire, "White House Physician" (Putnam, 1946), p. 125.

38. James A. Farley, "Jim Farley's Story," p. 233.

39. I have a letter from Governor Alfred Landon confirming these facts.

Book Three: Betrayal

1. New York *Times*, Dec. 24, 1943.

2. "Public Papers and Addresses of Franklin D. Roosevelt," Vol. I, p. 583.

3. Walter Davenport, "I'm Glad You Asked Me" (interview with James Roosevelt), *Collier's* Magazine, Aug. 20, 27, 1938.

4. Lists of James Roosevelt's insurance clients were published in many newspapers. The New York *Sun*, October 20, 1936, published the names given here. The number, of course, was greatly increased later, particularly during the war.

5. Congressional Record, Mar. 13, 1940, p. 4352. See also Washington *Post*, Feb. 23, 1940 and New York *World-Telegram*, Feb. 24, 1940.

6. Report of American Sugar Cane League, December, 1938, printed in part in Chicago *Tribune*, June 5, 1939. See also "I'm Glad You Asked Me" (*Collier's*, Aug.

27, 1938) in which James Roosevelt admits having this account.

7. Alva Johnston, "Jimmy's Got It," *Saturday Evening Post*, July 2, 1938. Also "I'm Glad You Asked Me," *Collier's*.

8. Arthur E. Mullen, "Western Democrat" (Wilford Funk, 1940), p. 321.

9. Westbrook Pegler in New York *Journal-American*, Aug. 29, 1945.

10. Congressional Record, Sept. 25, 1940. Also New York *Times*, Oct. 11, 1936 and Hearings before Special Senate Committee Investigating the Munitions Industry, Oct. 6, 1936.

11. Federal Communications Commission, Dockets Nos. 3964 and 3966, May 14, May 21, Aug. 13, 1936.

12. Hearings before Senate Committee Investigating the Rural Electrification Administration, May 22, 1944 (testimony of Lt. Clyde T. Ellis).

13. Hearings before Sub-Committee of Senate War Investigating Committee, August, 1947.

14. Westbrook Pegler in New York *Journal-American*, Nov. 6 and 9, 1945. I also investigated this subject personally.

15. Eleanor Roosevelt, "This Is My Story" (Garden City, 1939).

16. Mrs. Roosevelt's appearance on these programs is a matter of public record. Westbrook Pegler has investigated and printed in full the details of her coffee and candy programs.

17. In 1940, I made a complete investigation of Mrs. Roosevelt's earnings and obtained precise figures from agents and companies which employed her, including the sums she received from her lectures and radio performances. A complete list of her newspaper columns, her magazine and book publications, her lectures and radio programs revealed a minimum income in seven and one-half years of

$1,200,000. An examination of her activities since indicates that the total sum over the 15-year period is not less than $3,000,000.

18. "Public Papers and Addresses of Franklin D. Roosevelt," Vol. I, p. 583.

19. Hearings before House Committee on Un-American Activities, 1940–41.

20. Mrs. Roosevelt's acceptance of gifts, her flouting of rationing regulations during the war, etc., are matters of public record in the newspapers of the time.

21. Alden Hatch, "Franklin D. Roosevelt, an Informal Biography" (Holt, 1947).

22. Rita S. Halle-Kleeman, "Gracious Lady, life of Sara Delano Roosevelt," (Garden City, 1939).

23. Statement of Mrs. Barbour Walker, dean of William Smith-Hobart College at the time.

24. Frances Perkins, "The Roosevelt I Knew," p. 34.

25. Edward J. Flynn, "You're the Boss," p. 212.

26. Frances Perkins, "The Roosevelt I Knew," p. 12.

27. Edward J. Flynn, "You're the Boss," p. 67.

28. Statement by Alfred E. Smith to me.

29. Edward J. Flynn, "You're the Boss," p. 67.

30. Statement by Alfred E. Smith to me.

31. Compton Mackenzie, "Mr. Roosevelt" (Dutton, 1944), p. 143.

32. Edward J. Flynn, "You're the Boss," p. 68.

33. The facts about the payment of $250,000 to Roosevelt to run for gov-

ernor were given to me by John J. Raskob, then chairman of the Democratic National Committee, and corroborated by former Lt. Gov. William Bray of New York State who was present during these negotiations.

34. Reports of the Georgia Warm Springs Foundation.

35. The Elliott Roosevelt-Franklin Roosevelt-Hartford loan episode was first told by Westbrook Pegler. Public statements made by Hartford and Jesse Jones and printed in the newspapers at the time completely substantiated all of Pegler's statements. See also Hearings before House Committee on Ways and Means, September, 1945.

36. I am indebted for the correct statement of these facts to Mr. Philip H. Ward, a leading stamp authority and author of a column in *Mekeel's Weekly Stamp News*, who investigated this whole subject.

37. Congressional Record, 77th Cong., 1st Sess., Vol. 87, Part 7, p. 7902.

38. Hearings before the Joint Committee on the Investigation of the Pearl Harbor Attack, Part I.

39. Congressional Record, 77th Cong., 1st Sess., Vol. 87, Part 8, p. 8314 (Admiral Stark's report on the so-called *Greer* incident).

40. Hearings before the Joint Committee on the Investigation of the Pearl Harbor Attack, Part 15, Exhibits 49, 50 and 51.

41. Thomas A. Bailey, "The Man in the Street" (Macmillan, 1948).

42. New York *Times* Book Review, May 9, 1948.

43. Facts with relation to the Atlantic Charter meeting are taken from the testimony of Sumner Welles, Hearings before the Joint Committee on the Investigation of the Pearl Harbor Attack, Part II, pps. 479 *et seq.*, and Part XIV containing Exhibits 22A, 22B and 22C, pps. 1255 *et seq.*

44. Jan Ciechanowski, "Deafeat in Victory" (Doubleday, 1947), pps. 86, 87.

45. *New Republic*, Feb. 9, 1942.

46. Hearings before Joint Committee on Reduction of Non-Essential Federal Expenditures, June 1, 1943.

47. Facts about Bovingdon and Parmalee were first revealed by the House Committee on Un-American Activities.

48. Lawrence Sullivan, "Bureaucracy Runs Amuck" (Bobbs, Merrill, 1944). This volume contains an illuminating account of OPA and other wartime bureaus.

49. Henry L. Stimson, "On Active Service in Peace and War," with MacGeorge Bundy (Harper, 1948), p. 495.

50. Ibid., pps. 492 to 495.

51. Congressional Record, 78th Cong., 1st Sess., Vol. 89, Part 13, pps. 5999, 6000.

52. John O'Donnell in New York *Daily News*, May 21, 1945.

53. Ibid., Apr. 12, 1944.

54. Walter Davenport, in *Collier's* Magazine, June 3, 1944.

55. Phelps Adams in New York *Sun*, Apr. 17, 1944. See also editorial in New York *Daily News*, April 19, 1944.

56. New York *Herald-Tribune*, Nov. 7, 1942.

57. For an extensive account of the activities of the Federal Communications Commission, see Hearings before Select Committee (House) to Investigate the Federal Communications Commission, 1943.

58. Henry L. Stimson, "On Active Service in Peace and War," pps. 413 to 448.

59. Jan Ciechanowski, "Defeat in Victory," p. 80; New York *Times*, Sept. 25, 1941.

60. Jan Ciechanowski, "Defeat in Victory," pps. 96, 97.

61. Ibid., p. 100.

62. Demaree Bess, "What Does Russia Want?", *Saturday Evening Post*, March 20, 1943.

63. Forrest Davis "Roosevelt's World Blueprint," *Saturday Evening Post*, April 10, 1943.

64. Jan Ciechanowski, "Defeat in Victory," p. 231.

65. Elliott Roosevelt, "As He Saw It" (Duell, Sloan & Pearce, 1946).

66. A detailed account of the exchanges between Hull and the Polish Ambassador will be found in Jan Ciechanowski's "Defeat in Victory," pps. 138 to 221. Mr. Ciechanowski was Polish Ambassador to the U. S. See also Arthur Bliss Lane's "I Saw Poland Betrayed" (Bobbs, Merrill, 1948). Mr. Lane was American Ambassador to Poland.

67. John R. Deane, "Strange Alliance" (Viking, 1947), pps. 13 to 26.

68. Michael F. Reilly, "Reilly of the White House," with William J. Slocum (Simon & Schuster, 1947), p. 162.

69. Elliott Roosevelt, "As He Saw It," pps. 142, 143.

70. Edgar Snow, "60 Million Lost Allies," *Saturday Evening Post*, June 10, 1944.

71. Elliott Roosevelt, "As He Saw It," pps. 157 to 166.

72. Forrest Davis, "What Really Happened at Teheran" and "Roosevelt's World Blueprint," May 13, 20, 1944; April 10, 1943, *Saturday Evening Post*.

73. Elliott Roosevelt, "As He Saw It."

74. John R. Deane, "Strange Alliance," p. 43.

75. James F. Byrnes, "Speaking Frankly" (Harper, 1947), p. 71.

76. John R. Deane, "Strange Alliance," pps. 41-43.

77. Ibid., p. 90.

78. Ibid., pps. 39-45.

79. David Martin, "Ally Betrayed," (Prentice-Hall, 1946), pps. 224-231.

80. Louis Adamic, "Dinner at the White House" (Harper, 1946).

81. Elliott Roosevelt, "As He Saw It," p. 202.

82. Ibid., pps. 186-194.

83. Ibid., pps. 209, 210. See also Henry L. Stimson, "On Active Service in Peace and War."

84. Jan Ciechanowski, "Defeat in Victory," p. 232.

85. Ibid., pps. 330-331.

86. Ibid., pps. 330-331.

87. Ross T. McIntire, "White House Physician," p. 184.

88. "John N. Garner's Story."

89. James A. Farley, "Jim Farley's Story," pps. 108, 109.

90. Ibid.

91. Edward J. Flynn, "You're the Boss," p. 155.

92. James A. Farley, "Jim Farley's Story," p. 254.

93. Ross T. McIntire, "White House Physician," p. 175.

94. Ibid., p. 184.

95. Ibid., p. 186.

96. Ibid., pps. 187, 188.

97. C. MacLaurin, "Post Mortem" (Doran, 1922); "Mere Mortals" (Doran, 1925).

98. The facts outlined in this chapter are drawn from Cordell Hull's

"Memoirs," Henry L. Stimson's "On Active Service in Peace and War," and James F. Byrnes' "Speaking Frankly," all of whom tell in detail of the origins of the so-called Morgenthau Plan for Germany.

99. Excerpts from "The Morgenthau Diaries."

100. James A. Farley, "Jim Farley's Story," p. 233.

101. James F. Byrnes, "Speaking Frankly," p. 23.

102. Ibid., p. 29.

103. Ibid., p. 29.

104. John R. Deane, "Strange Alliance," p. 247.

105. James F. Byrnes, "Speaking Frankly," p. 43.

106. Ibid., p. 41.

107. New York Times, October 19, 1945.

108. New York Journal-American, Jan. 4 to Feb. 4, 1948 (a series of articles by the former Polish Premier Mikolajczyk).

109. William Henry Chamberlain, "The European Cockpit" (Macmillan, 1947), p. 144.

110. New York Times, Mar. 6, May 8, June 9, Sept. 26, Oct. 13, 1944.

111. Merriam Smith, "Thank You, Mr. President" (Harper, 1946).

112. Michael F. Reilly "Reilly of the White House," p. 171, 176.

113. Ross T. McIntire, "White House Physician," p. 24.

114. Elliott Roosevelt, "As He Saw It," pps. 146–147

115. Ibid.

116. Frances Perkins, "The Roosevelt I Knew," p. 389.

117. Ross T. McIntire, "White House Physician," p. 184.

118. Ibid., p. 194.

119. This was related to me by a high-ranking officer who sat only a few yards away from Roosevelt during the incident described and is corroborated by others present at the time.

120. Merriam Smith, "Thank You, Mr. President," p. 159.

121. Frances Perkins, "The Roosevelt I Knew," p. 391.

122. Ross T. McIntire, "White House Physician," p. 232.

123. Merriam Smith, "Thank You, Mr. President," p. 173.

124. Ross T. McIntire, "White House Physician," p. 15.

125. Michael F. Reilly, "Reilly of the White House," p. 196.

126. C. MacLaurin, "Post Mortem," p. 208.

127. Ross T. McIntire, "White House Physician," p. 239.

128. In examining the facts about Roosevelt's death I have had the guidance of eminent medical authorities.

BIBLIOGRAPHY

The following is a partial list of the volumes consulted in the preparation of this book. In addition, of course, is that vast reservoir of material contained in the daily newspapers, weekly and monthly magazines, reports and hearings of various committees of the House and Senate, and numerous other official documents of the government. Many of these are referred to in the footnotes. Also, several other works were appearing serially in magazines and newspapers when this volume was written. They were Winston Churchill's Memoirs (Vol. I), which ran serially in the New York *Times*; Robert S. Sherwood's "Secret Papers of Harry L. Hopkins," which ran serially in *Collier's* magazine and Harold L. Ickes' "My Twelve Years with F.D.R." which ran serially in the *Saturday Evening Post*.

Adamic, Louis: "Dinner at the White House" (Harper, 1946)

Beard, Charles A.: "American Foreign Policy in the Making, 1932–40" (Yale, 1946)

Beard, Charles A.: "President Roosevlet and the Coming of the War. 1941" (Yale, 1948)

Bingham, Alfred M. and Rodman, Selden; Editors: "Challenge to the New Deal" (Falcon, 1934)

Brown, Lewis H.: "Report on Germany" (Farrar, Straus, 1947)

Butcher, Harry C.: "My Three Years with Eisenhower" (Simon & Schuster, 1946)

Byrnes, James F.: "Speaking Frankly" (Harper, 1947)

Carmichael, Donald Scott; Editor: "FDR Columnist" (Pellegrini & Cudahy, 1947)

Chamberlain, William Henry: "The European Cockpit" (Macmillan, 1947)

Churchill, Winston: "Secret Session Speeches" (Simon & Schuster, 1946)

Ciechanowski, Jan: "Defeat in Victory" (Doubleday, 1947)

Collins, Frederick L.: "Uncle Sam's Billion Dollar Baby" (Putnam, 1945)

Commager, Henry Steele: "The Story of the Second World War" (Little, Brown, 1945)

Creel, George: "Rebel at Large" (Putnam, 1947)
Daniels, Jonathan: "Frontier on the Potomac" (Macmillan, 1946)
Deane, John R.: "The Strange Alliance" (Viking, 1947)
Dewey, Thomas E.: "The Case Against the New Deal" (Harper, 1940)
Dies, Martin: "The Trojan Horse in America" (Dodd, Mead, 1940)
Eisenhower, Dwight D.: "Eisenhower's Own Story of the War" (Arco Publ. Co., 1946)
Ezekiel, Mordecai: "$2500 a Year" (Harcourt, Brace, 1936)
Farley, James A.: "Jim Farley's Story" (Whittlesey House, 1948)
Flynn, Edward J.: "You're the Boss" (Viking, 1947)
Flynn, John T.: "As We Go Marching" (Doubleday, 1944)
Flynn, John T.: "Country Squire in the White House" (Doubleday, 1940)
Hallgren, Mauritz A.: "The Gay Reformer" (Knopf, 1935)
Hansen, Alvin H.: "Economic Policy and Full Employment" (Whittlesey, 1947)
Hansen, Alvin H.: "Fiscal Policy and Business Cycles" (Norton, 1941)
Hatch, Alden: "Franklin D. Roosevelt" (Holt, 1947)
Helm, William P.: "Harry Truman" (Duell, Sloane, 1947)
High, Stanley: "Roosevelt—and Then?" (Harper, 1937)
Hinton, Harold B.: "Cordell Hull" (Doubleday, 1942)
Hull, Cordell: "Memoirs of Cordell Hull" (Macmillan, 1948)
Huot, Louis: "Guns for Tito" (L. B. Fischer, 1945)
Ickes, Harold L.: "The Autobiography of a Curmudgeon" (Reynal & Hitchcock, 1943)
Johnson, Hugh S.: "The Blue Eagle from Egg to Earth" (Doubleday, 1935)
Kane, Harnett T.: "Louisiana Hayride" (Morrow, 1941)
Kennedy, Joseph P.: "I'm for Roosevelt" (Reynal & Hitchcock, 1936)
Kiplinger, W. M.: "Washington Is Like That" (Harper, 1942)
Kleeman, Rita S. Halle: "Gracious Lady" (Appleton-Century, 1935)
Lane, Arthur Bliss: "I Saw Poland Betrayed" (Bobbs, Merrill, 1948)

Lawrence, David: "Beyond the New Deal" (Wittlesey, 1934)
Lindley, Ernest K.: "Franklin D. Roosevelt" (Blue Ribbon, 1931, 1934)
Lindley, Ernest K.: "Half Way With Roosevelt" (Viking, 1936)
Lindley, Ernest K.: "The Roosevelt Revolution" (Viking, 1933)
Loeb, Harold and Associates: "The Chart of Plenty" (Viking, 1935)
Lord, Russell: "The Wallaces of Iowa" (Houghton, Mifflin, 1947)
Ludwig, Emil: "Roosevelt: A Study in Fortune and Power" (Viking, 1938)
Lund, Robert L., Coffin, Howard E., and Burkett, Charles W.: "The Truth About the New Deal" (Longmans, 1936)
Lyons, Eugene: "Our Unknown Ex-President" (Doubleday, 1948)
MacDonald, Dwight: "Henry Wallace" (Vanguard, 1947 & 1948)
Mackenzie, Compton: "Mr. Roosevelt" (Dutton, 1944)
MacLaurin, C.: "Mere Mortals" (Doran, 1925)
MacLaurin, C.: "Post Mortem" (Doran, 1922)
Marshall, George C., Arnold, H. H., and King, Ernest J.: "The War Reports" (Lippincott, 1947)
Martin, David: "Ally Betrayed" (Prentice-Hall, 1946)
McIntire, Ross T.: "White House Physician" (Putnam, 1946)
Michaelson, Charles: "The Ghost Talks" (Putnam, 1944)
Millis, Walter: "This is Pearl" (Morrow, 1947)
Milton, George Fort: "The Use of Presidential Power" (Little, Brown, 1944)
Mitchell, Ewing Young: "Kicked In and Kicked Out of the President's Little Cabinet" (Andrew Jackson Press, 1936)
Moley, Raymond: "After Seven Years" (Harper's, 1939)
Morgenstern, George: "Pearl Harbor" (Devin, Adair, 1947)
Mullen, Arthur F.: "Western Democrat" (Wilfred Funk, 1940)
Myers, William Starr and Newton, Walter H.: "The Hoover Administration" (Scribner, 1936)
Nelson, Donald M.: "Arsenal of Democracy" (Harcourt, Brace, 1946)
Nourse, Edwin G.; Davis, Joseph S.; and Black, John D.: "Three Years of the Agricultural Adjustment Administration" (Brookings, 1937)

Patton, George S., Jr.: "War As I Knew It" (Houghton, Mifflin, 1947)

Perkins, Frances: "The Roosevelt I Knew" (Viking, 1946)

Reddig, William W.: "Tom's Town" (Lippincott, 1947)

Reilly, Michael F.: "Reilly of the White House" (Simon & Schuster, 1947)

Robinson, Henry Morton: "Fantastic Interim" (Harcourt, Brace, 1943)

Roos, Charles Frederick: "NRA, Economic Planning" (Principia Press, 1937)

Roosevelt, Eleanor: "This Is My Story" (Garden City, 1939)

Roosevelt, Elliott: "As He Saw It" (Duell, Sloan & Pearce, 1946)

Roosevelt, Franklin D.: "Public Papers and Addresses, 1928–40" 8 vols., (Random House)

Roosevelt, Hall and McCoy, Samuel Duff: "Odyssey of an American Family" (Harper, 1939)

Trevor-Roper, H. R.: "The Last Days of Hitler" (Macmillan, 1947)

Tugwell, Rexford Guy: "The Battle for Democracy" (Col. Univ. Press, 1935)

Seven Harvard & Tufts Economists: "An Economic Program for American Democracy" (Vanguard, 1938)

Smith, Merriman: "Thank You, Mr. President" (Harper, 1946)

Soule, George: "A Planned Society" (Macmillan, 1932)

Starling, Edmund W. and Sugrue, Thomas: "Starling of the White House" (Simon & Schuster, 1946)

Stettinius, E. R., Jr.: "Lend-Lease" (Macmillan, 1944)

Stilwell, Joseph W.: "The Stilwell Papers" (Wm. Sloane, 1948)

Stimson, Henry L. and Bundy, McGeorge: "On Active Service in Peace and War" (Harper, 1947)

Stolberg, Benjamin and Vinton, Warren Jay: "The Economic Consequences of the New Deal" (Harcourt, Brace, 1935)

Stolberg, Benjamin: "The Story of the CIO" (Viking, 1938)

Sullivan, Lawrence: "Bureaucracy Runs Amuck" (Bobbs, Merrill, 1944)

Unofficial Observer: "The New Dealers" (Simon & Schuster, 1934)

Utley, Freda: "Last Chance in China" (Bobbs, Merrill, 1947)

Van Devander, Charles W.: "The Big Bosses" (Howell, Soskin, 1944)

Veblen, Thorstein: "The Engineers and the Price System" (B. W. Huebsch, 1921)

Wallace, Henry A.: "Democracy Reborn" (Reynal & Hitchcock, 1944)

INDEX

Fox & Wilkes

Charles James Fox (1749–1806) inherited wealth and guidance from his father, who tutored him in gambling and who advised, "Never do today what you can put off 'til tomorrow." In 1768, just nineteen, the roguish Charles Fox took his seat in Parliament and quickly earned the esteem of his colleagues, Edmund Burke among them. The two joined forces on many causes, including that of the American Revolution, until Burk'es horror over the French Revolution occasioned a permanent break. Fox fought for religious toleration, called for abolishing the slave trade, and advocated electoral reform. In defending his views he was a powerful orator, acknowledged as the ablest debater of his day. Neither party nor crown could dissuade him from following his own path. Above all things Fox hated oppression and intolerance, and in his passion for liberty transcended the conventional party politics of his day.

Like Fox, **John Wilkes** (1727–1797), too, could be extravagant in his passions. He married into his money and was an active member of the proudly blasphemous Hellfire Club. A few years after joining Parliament in 1757, he began a weekly journal, *The North Briton*, that became notorious for its wit and wickedness. In the famous issue #45 Wilkes assailed a speech given in the King's name; he was jailed for his temerity. His *Essay On Woman*, an obscene parody of Pope's *Essay On Man*, along with a reprinting of #45, led to further imprisonment and expulsion from Parliament. But the public rioted for his release and kept voting him back into office. Wilkes eventually won substantial damages and set important precedents regarding Parliamentary privilege and seizure of personal papers. After finally being allowed to rejoin Parliament in 1774 as Lord Mayor of London, he introduced libel legislation ensuring rights to jury trial, and continued to fight for religious tolerance and judicial and parliamentary reform. The monument on his grave aptly describes him as a friend of liberty.

Fox and Wilkes could be self-indulgent, even reckless in pursuit of their own liberty, but they never let personal foibles hinder them in championing the rights of the individual.